T0328320

THE GENESIS OF INDUSTRIAL CAPITAL

For William Hudson, Mary Annie Hudson
and Jennifer Hudson

THE GENESIS OF
INDUSTRIAL CAPITAL

A STUDY OF THE WEST RIDING
WOOL TEXTILE INDUSTRY *c.* 1750–1850

PAT HUDSON
Department of Economic History, University of Liverpool

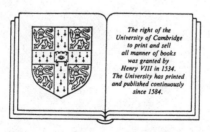

The right of the
University of Cambridge
to print and sell
all manner of books
was granted by
Henry VIII in 1534.
The University has printed
and published continuously
since 1584.

CAMBRIDGE UNIVERSITY PRESS
Cambridge
London   New York   New Rochelle
Melbourne   Sydney

Published by the Press Syndicate of the University of Cambridge
The Pitt Building, Trumpington Street, Cambridge CB2 1RP
32 East 57th Street, New York, NY 10022, USA
10 Stamford Road, Oakleigh, Melbourne 3166, Australia

First published 1986

Photoset and printed in Great Britain by
Redwood Burn Limited,
Trowbridge, Wiltshire

British Library cataloguing in publication data
Hudson, Pat
The genesis of industrial capital: a study of
the West Riding wool textile industry c.1750–1850.
1. Wool trade and industry – England – West
Yorkshire – History
I. Title
338.4'767731'094281   HD9901.7.W4

Library of Congress cataloguing in publication data
Hudson, Pat, 1948–
The genesis of industrial capital: a study of
the West Riding wool textile industry c.1750–1850.
Based on the author's thesis (Ph.D.) – University of
York, 1981.
Bibliography: p.
Includes index.
1. Wool trade and industry – England – West Riding of
Yorkshire – History.   2. Capitalism – England – West
Riding of Yorkshire – History.   I. Title.
HD9901.7.W47H83   1986   338.4'767731'094281   86–1007

ISBN 0 521 25671 2

CONTENTS

LISTS OF PLATES

LIST OF DIAGRAMS, GRAPHS AND MAPS

DIAGRAMS

GRAPHS

MAPS

TABLES

FOREWORD

For two or three decades, economic historians have responded eagerly to the calls of macro-economics and have thus greatly improved our knowledge and understanding of modern economic growth, especially of the industrial revolution. However, sometimes much effort and ingenuity has been devoted to goals which have proved somewhat elusive. Such has occurred in the field of capital and capital formation: in computing national investment proportions the essential spade-work of collecting and interpreting new data has been sometimes neglected.

It is therefore refreshing when a scholar of the new generation, like Dr Pat Hudson, brings back the debate to earth, to the workshops and mills spread among the bleak hills and the green valleys of the West Riding of Yorkshire, in a study which is solidly built upon a large quantity of archival material especially business records. The preparation of this work has involved an impressive labour input and it contains a great deal of original information.

On the other hand, this book is not the kind of myopic monograph, with a narrow outlook, which 'old economic history' has been charged with overproducing (not quite unfairly). Readers of Dr Hudson's book will soon realise that she has mastered the theoretical and semi-theoretical debates concerning 'the genesis of capital' during the industrial revolution and the vast literature which has accumulated around this theme. In her analysis, she has used skilfully, and with an open, undogmatic mind, various tools provided by earlier writers from Karl Marx to Franklin Mendels. At the same time she has avoided getting bogged down in semantic or scholastical controversies.

This combination of a theoretical and an empirical approach has been successful and Dr Hudson has made a remarkable contribution not only to the history of the wool textile industry in Yorkshire, but also to an understanding of the industrial revolution, in which the West Riding, as one of the first 'follower counties', played a key role. A major quality is the author's talent for questioning established orthodoxies. She stresses, for instance, that there is not much point in arguing about the proportion of fixed to circulating capital, because they were largely interdependent and interchangeable. This has wide implications, as new light is thrown upon the role of merchant capital. She suggests that the stress on the smallness of capital requirements at this time can be overplayed. She also disputes the overwhelming role which has been granted to ploughed-back profits, as well as the relationship between such reinvestment and 'frugality' among early industrialists. Possibly T. S. Ashton generalised too much from the cases of eighteenth-century Quaker ironmasters . . .

Dr Hudson has devoted a good deal of attention to the relationship between land and industry; between agrarian structures, the nature of pre-industrial-revolution units of production and different forms of transition to the factory system. She has made clear that such a relationship existed and how it worked. She has also shown once more how the transition to the factory followed many different channels, and it is fascinating to observe so much complexity and diversity in this respect, within a region which was, after all, quite small.

The heart of the book is the study of 'the web of credit' in Part 3. However a Foreword is not intended as an abstract of the book which it presents and I shall just stress that full justice is done to this crucial problem. Several of its aspects which have previously been neglected are thoroughly investigated by Dr Hudson (for instance the role of wool staplers), and new light is thrown upon such familiar topics as the connection between banks and industry which appears to have been underestimated by many earlier studies. The imperfection of the capital market and its very local and highly personal nature is once more demonstrated.

In every chapter, Dr Hudson marshals a mass of original data with acumen, lucidity and skill. The present writer was extremely interested to read her doctoral dissertation in typescript and is delighted to see it in book form, after revision. There is no doubt that historians of the industrial revolution will find the reading of this volume most rewarding.

François Crouzet

PREFACE

Since the rapid expansion of social science in the 1960s, interest in some of the traditional questions concerning economic historians has waned. 'Good Old Economic History'[1] gave way to the simultaneous claims of econometric history on the one hand and the new social history on the other. Valuable though these developments may have been, particularly the latter, it has meant that *economic* history, beyond quantitative and neo-classical analyses, has languished. The edifice of valuable empirical building blocks emerging from social and cultural history has not been matched by economic history studies. We have progressed some way in establishing the advantages and limitations of various theoretical constructs but, particularly in the field of industrial history, we have little more data to fill these theoretical boxes than we had in Clapham's day.[2] Since the classic works of Heaton, Wadsworth and Mann, Court, Clapham himself and the generation from the 1930s to 1950s (who were my staple diet as an undergraduate), the numbers of sectoral or regional studies of British industry have been few. The time is ripe for rehabilitation and renewal of this empirical tradition.

New studies will not, however, mark significant progress in the discipline if they replicate the traditional empirical approach ignoring the ways in which new interdisciplinary orientations have entered our perception of traditional questions. Economic history is nothing if it neglects the institutional, social and cultural dimensions of change. The economy is an embedded process impossible to extract from the plethora of 'non-economic' relationships, ideals, tradition, customs, beliefs and emotions. In a modest way and with some regard to these wider social and cultural issues the present work offers a study of a regional industrial

---

[1] Term used by Hartwell during the debate regarding the advent of quantitative and econometric studies: R. M. Hartwell, 'Good Old Economic History', *J.E.H.*, XXXI, 1, 1973, p. 37.
[2] J. H. Clapham, 'Of Empty Economic Boxes', *E.J.*, XXXII, 1922.

sector during a period of marked change. The focus is on finance: the accumulation and polarisation of wealth, a vital process in the growth of centralised, mechanised production.

Although the study has its empirical focus in the development and finance of factory industry in Yorkshire it provides insights into the emergence of industrial capitalism across a much broader front. There are parallels particularly with the growth and finance of other consumer goods industries which were dispersed in rural domestic units during the pre-factory period. The preoccupation of historians with the cotton sector during England's industrialisation has obscured the fact that in terms of both exports and production levels, wool textiles were more important than cotton until into the nineteenth century. Moreover, the wool sector exhibited a pace of technical and organisational change which was more representative of industry as a whole than was cotton. The wool textile sector, with Yorkshire increasingly at its centre, is thus one of the best windows through which to view the 'first industrial revolution' as a whole.

ACKNOWLEDGEMENTS

This book is a refinement and extension of my D.Phil. thesis which was presented at the University of York in 1981. My research started in 1973 but in 1975 I was appointed to a lectureship, work was shelved and my project scarcely saw the light of day for the next four years. Few pieces of research are spread over such a long time-span or accumulate such indebtedness to colleagues and friends.

I must especially thank Eric Sigsworth for a tour of the Halifax and Heptonstall area on a November afternoon in 1971. Unknown to him, this marked the start of my enthusiasm for the West Riding and its industrial history. Many other colleagues have contributed to the maturing of my project over the years and have encouraged me to persevere with it: the late Ken Ponting and the late Arthur John, Donald Coleman, Leslie Pressnell, Roy Church, Mike Collins, Stanley Chapman, Michael Dickenson, Michael Miles, Maxine Berg, Mike Sonenscher and John Styles.

The archive staffs of many London and Yorkshire repositories have been of great assistance, particularly Dr A. Betteridge at Halifax, Mr J. M. Collinson and his successor Mr W. J. Connor at Leeds, Mr J. Goodchild at Wakefield and Mr M. Morrish at Leeds University. I owe thanks also to the helpful archivists of Barclays, Midland and Lloyds Banks and of the Bank of England.

I am in debt to David Jenkins who endured the pains of prolonged supervision with patience and good humour and who transferred to me so much of his knowledge and interest in Yorkshire mills and manufacturers. My D.Phil. examiner, François Crouzet, gave me the confidence and encouragement to look for a publisher and made many helpful suggestions for which I am grateful.

The S.S.R.C. financed my research studentship, 1973–4, and the Twenty-Seven Foundation provided a grant to investigate material for Chapters 3 and 4. *History Workshop Journal* gave permission to reproduce a section of Chapter 3 which appeared in issue XII, 1981, and *Business History Review* allowed me to draw heavily on my article 'The Role of Banks in the Finance of the West Riding Textile Industry', in vol LV, 3, 1981.

Finally, as most of the work and writing of both thesis and book have had to be fitted into life outside the University, I must thank Tony for making it all possible.

University of Liverpool   P.H.
March 1985

PART 1
INTRODUCTION

1
THE STUDY OF
CAPITAL ACCUMULATION

There has been a tendency for economic theory of the last 100 years to ignore capital accumulation altogether and to be preoccupied with analysis of the detailed relationship between the output and price of commodities. To do this, the dynamics of economic growth in the long run are ruled out by simplifying assumptions. Capital accumulation together with population growth, technological change and socio-political variables are 'held constant' whilst micro- and macro-models are constructed, based on prices, incomes and the concept of market-clearing equilibrium. With few exceptions this rules out discussion of most of the questions of fundamental interest to the economic historian. To a large extent, and of necessity econometric history has adapted this neo-classical paradigm and economic development has taken a back seat.

The overall growth of economies was the key preoccupation of Classical political economy from Smith and Ricardo to Marx. But from the late nineteenth century the marginalist revolution directed attention away from development issues. Only since the mid-1950s has economic growth re-emerged as a focus of study and then only in the work of a minority of economists and historians. Responding partly to the tenacity of Third World underdevelopment, despite capital injections, people like Robinson and Kuznets turned their attention to the role of finance in economic growth.[1] At the same time a sequence of economic historians have attempted quantification and analysis of capital accumulation during Britain's industrialisation: Rostow, Deane, Pollard and, most recently, Feinstein.[2]

Revival of interest in Classical questions has brought some renewed interest in Classical theory, particularly Marxian analysis of economic development. This has produced a further set of relevant publications relating to issues such as consumption and investment ratios, 'primitive accumulation', the 'development of underdevelopment', the mainsprings of profitablity and reinvestment and the role of merchant capital in economic change.[3]

As a prelude to the present study it is worth surveying some of the literature of what one might call the minority traditions of economic history in recent years. Published theoretical work is, however, almost exclusively concerned with the functioning of the national economy as a whole. Thus, although it provides some useful theoretical insights, its main value here is in highlighting questions which can only properly be tackled at sectoral or regional level.

Capital accumulation during industrialisation

Work done in the last three decades on capital investment proportions during Britain's industrialisation has brought to the fore many questions vital to the present study. Was increasing industrial investment made at the expense of wage levels, consumption and living standards? How closely influenced was it by the distribution of landed wealth and the financial or industrial activities of landholders? What relationship did industrial finance have to mercantile investment, stockholding and credit? What role did banks and other financial institutions play? Full answers to these and other questions raised in the historiography can only be attempted by rebuilding the aggregate picture out of regional empirical studies.

The first major steps in analysing capital investment proportions were taken by Lewis and Rostow. Although based purely on *a priori* judgement, Rostow was quite precise with his postulate. He maintained that the 'take off' period in Britain witnessed a raising of the ratio of net investment to net national product from about 5% to over 10%.[4] Rostow's hypothesis prompted a number of empirical examinations in the 1950s and 1960s, most noticeably by Deane and Habakkuk who maintained that capital was not a strategic factor in the 'take off' period, as defined by Rostow, and that only the railway age saw capital proportions reaching around the 10% level for any sustained period.[5] Deane's findings were supported by other empirical work on the development of industrialised countries during the last century, noticeably the research of Kuznets, Solow and Cairncross.[6] By the mid-1960s, the accepted thinking on this topic was that changes in capital investment proportions in an economy during industrialisation were gradual. Improvements in productivity arose mainly from more efficient use of existing capital stock and from the centralisation and disciplining of a growing supply of wage labour. The industrial revolution in Britain got well into its stride with average net investment of under 10% per annum.[7] The view that growth does not invariably, or even largely, depend on a high level of capital formation gained strength from stressing the negligible results of extensive economic aid to the Third World countries since the Second World War. Political and cultural dimensions of development theory were gaining prominence at this time.

However, the debate with respect to the British case had by no means closed. Kuznets, along with Pollard, rejuvenated the whole discussion in the late 1960s by emphasising a factor of considerable relevance to the present study. This is the important distinction between net capital formation and gross capital proportions which include current maintenance and replacement resulting from premature obsolescence of machinery and equipment.[8] If gross figures are considered, the complexion of the debate is altered. Kuznets found 11.7% a 'not unreasonable' figure for the gross investment proportion in the early eighteenth century.[9] This mainly resulted from the short physical life of capital goods and the larger amounts of finance spent on repairs and maintenance at a time when technological advance was relatively slow. Gross investment proportions are obviously also the most relevant figures in a period of industrial and technical change when obsolescence and replacement costs might be high.

Using such figures Pollard has concluded that the proportions of British national income which were invested in the late eighteenth and early nineteenth centuries were much higher than Deane and Cole had suggested and much closer to those postulated in the theoretical schemes of both Rostow and Lewis.[10] Feinstein's more recent estimates have still further closed the gap between empirical findings and the Lewis/Rostow hypotheses.[11] He concluded that fixed capital formation in Britan increased at a rate more than double that previously suggested by Pollard for the period 1770–1830. For *c.*1830–5 Feinstein's calculations are close to those of Pollard. The differences between them regarding capital growth rates over the whole period are largely the result of Feinstein's much lower base year estimates for *c.* 1770 and his higher figures for the trade and manufacturing sectors particularly in the period *c.* 1790–1815.[12] It may well be that capital formation especially in the industrial sector has been seriously underemphasised in estimates prior to those of Feinstein. The changing rates of growth of the stock of capital as estimated by Feinstein are indicated in Table 1.1

Table 1.2 shows Feinstein's estimates of gross domestic fixed capital formation as a proportion of G.D.P. for each decade. The figures from the two tables taken together indicate that the 1830s and 1840s witnessed rapid rates of growth of the domestic fixed and reproducible capital stock. Growth rates per annum averaged more than twice that achieved in earlier decades largely because of the expansion of the capital goods industries including railways. However, gross domestic fixed capital as a proportion of G.D.P. had already risen over 10% by 1800 and then stabilised around 10–11% until after the 1850s. If overseas investments and stockbuilding are included, the trend of (total) capital formation as a proportion of G.D.P. remains the same: it rises to 1800, drops back during the unstable years of the late Napoleonic Wars and then increases once again in the 1810s stabilising around 14% until the mid-century despite a

Table 1.1 *Levels and rates of growth of the stock of capital,*
Great Britain, 1760–1860

	Fixed capital	Domestic reproducible capital[a]
A. *End-year levels (£m at 1851–60 prices)*		
1760	490	670
1800	730	990
1830	1,180	1,510
1860	2,310	2,760
B. *Growth rates (% p.a.)*		
1761–1800	1.0	1.0
1801–30	1.6	1.4
1831–60	2.3	2.0
1761–1860	1.6	1.4

[a] Fixed capital plus total circulating capital.
Source: Feinstein, in *Cambridge Economic History of Europe,* p. 83.

threefold rise in the annual G.D.P. at factor cost between the 1810s and 1850s.[13] These findings have important implications for the possible chronology of capital formation in the textile sector and, more importantly, for assessing the effects on manufacturers of competing investment demands in the rest of the economy.[14]

The implication which these estimates of capital investment proportions have for the classic debate about the social as well as the economic

Table 1.2 *Fixed capital investment proportions, 1761–1860*

Decade	Gross domestic fixed capital as a proportion of G.D.P. (%)	Total investment as a proportion of G.D.P.[a] (%)
1761–70	7	8
1771–80	7	10
1781–90	10	13
1791–1800	11	14
1801–10	10	10
1811–20	10	14
1821–30	10	14
1831–40	11	13
1841–50	11	14
1851–60	10	14

[a] Includes overseas investment and stockbuilding.
Source: Feinstein, in *Cambridge Economic History of Europe,* p. 91.

costs of industrialisation is not directly addressed by Feinstein. He does, however, calculate that total factor productivity only started to rise after 1800 and even then rather slowly.[15] Whilst the growth of output was largely accounted for by growing inputs, wages could only rise at the expense of profits.[16]

Overall estimates of income and income shares are not possible before the late nineteenth century but it is beyond dispute that the relative share of national income accruing to labour fell during the period 1750–1850 and working-class consumption remained, at best, static.[17] According to Perkin, between 6 and 14% of the national income may have been transferred from labour to capital between 1790 and 1850.[18] To a large extent this issue can best be addressed at local or sectoral level. As Hobsbawm argued some time ago, immiserising growth may well have occurred even where national aggregate indices suggest the contrary.[19] Imperfections and rigidities in the capital market could induce this. The largest potential savers and investors were merchants and landowners who generally invested their money outside of industrial developments in government bonds and stocks or else they spent it in unproductive ways. Thus the majority of manufacturers had little access to big money. To raise finance they were forced to press harshly on labour costs which, as the West Riding experience illustrates, were the most flexible of input costs. This flexibility was facilitated by the plentiful supply of cheap labour in many industrial areas, particularly of women, children and immigrants who were so important a part of the workforce of early factory establishments and of the putting-out system.

Shapiro has suggested that the mechanics of this 'exploitation' can only be understood by examining the significance of such things as the 'long-pay', payment by tokens, the involvement of entrepreneurs in retailing and the acceptance by retailers, and other members of the local community, of the manufacturer's notes for discount. Through quasi-banking, industrial employers could succeed in gaining credit not just from their immediate workforce but from the lower classes of the locality more generally.[20]

Feinstein's estimates highlight the rapid growth of domestic reproducible capital in the 1830s and 1840s. At the same time labour historians have rightly focussed on these decades which were characterised by intense and widespread protest. With respect to the textile trades, Foster has suggested the existence of near-revolution sparked by economic crisis: a result of technological innovation and falling unit prices of finished goods.[21] The extent to which labour costs were under pressure in the textile areas in particular requires further study at regional level.

Studies at regional level are essential if the working of the markets for both capital and labour are to be fully understood for any period before the late nineteenth century. The possibilities of raising industrial finance from external sources at local level conditioned the extent to which internal finance from profits was crucial. This is important in view of the fact that virtually every model of economic growth includes the need (in theory and at macro-level) to keep down wage rates in order to leave high profits for further investment. Lewis stressed that, in the British case, there was a fortunate situation of excess underemployed and unemployed labour in the agricultural sector such that industry could absorb workers without affecting the level of wages.[22] Kindleberger agrees that this type of 'dual economy' operated in Britain in the first half of the nineteenth century.[23] Only the sectoral and regional picture can illuminate this hypothesis as the labour market was far from nationally integrated or efficient. Much depended on the precise relationship between industry and agriculture within the industrial region itself as well as its links with outside areas of labour surplus, particularly Ireland.

Before leaving the debate about capital investment proportions during the industrial revolution, the question of circulating capital should be mentioned. Feinstein's calculations indicate that for British industry and commerce taken together the ratio of fixed to circulating capital invested changed from less than 1 to 1 (c. 1760) to more than 3 to 1 (c. 1860).[24] In the economy as a whole, capital sunk in stockholding and work in progress declined from an average of about 20% of domestic fixed investment (1761–1800) to just under half this level (9%) in 1860.[25] With the more rapid turnover of capital made possible by technological change and improvements in communications, industrial and commercial organisation, the mass of circulating capital almost certainly fell per unit of goods and services produced in the economy or by the individual firm. However, there is no doubt that there was a massive absolute increase in the short-term capital employed in production and trade. Furthermore, circulating capital remained much more important than fixed investment for the vast majority of textile and other manufacturing concerns before 1850. In the wool textile sector the proportion of circulating to total capital invested in business varied from 90% down to 50% (1750–1850) depending on the type of firm and the years under consideration.[26] This accords well with Edwards' findings for the cotton industry and with Weatherill's research on the eighteenth-century pottery industry. Of the five firms which Edwards studied during the period 1794–1805, none had a fixed capital proportion higher than 21% of the total capital invested.[27] For pottery producers circulating capital was overwhelmingly more important than fixed with most manufacturers tying up a large proportion of their assets in credit extension.[28]

These indications of the overriding importance of circulating capital are very relevant for the present study because the sources of long- and short-term capital were often quite separate and distinct. Thus the changing ratio of fixed and circulating capital required for competitive industrial enterprise has important implications for the raising of finance and its social and economic costs. Only by studying the experience of manufacturers in different sectors and regions can one understand how the decline in circulating capital proportions at macro-level made itself felt in the liquidity position and financial flexiblity of producers.

But precise proportions of fixed and circulating capital invested in industry may not be as relevant to the study of capital sources as they have appeared in the past. A new approach is required involving a much less rigid distinction between the two. Fixed and circulating capital were often interdependent and, to some extent, interchangeable. If the elaborate credit network which evolved in the different trades eased the manufacturers' need to tie up large sums of money in stocks, this obviously released funds for productive investment. If the domestic outworking system was gradually usurped by more centralised forms of production, partly because of the travel time and delays involved, the saving in circulating capital could be used to finance increased plant and equipment outlays. If bill-discount and short-term accommodation by banks expedited the purchase and sale of commodities, so the manufacturer could divert finance from circulation to production. If circulating capital and the influences which acted on requirements for this purpose were, in turn, major determinants of the finance available for investment in the expansion of plant and equipment, then fixed and circulating capital sources must be studied not separately, as in the past, but as an integral relationship both in the long term and through cyclical fluctuations.

The relationship between capital accumulation, economic growth and cheap labour has been a major preoccupation of historians studying the agricultural sector, the enclosure movement and the spread of rural by-employments in manufacturing. Debates concerning the inter-relatedness of agrarian and industrial history have been influenced a great deal by Marxist analyses of the importance of agrarian class structure and the dispossession of agricultural labour.[29] Obviously, the emergence of a large mass of 'free' labour in the countryside was of prime importance in the development of industrial capitalism. It has been stressed by historians of all ideological persuasions and has received particular attention in recent work on the demographic characteristics of regions of rural manufacturing and the links between expanding domestic industries and proletarianisation.[30] But the precise mechanism whereby labour transfers to manufacturing production, either as a by-employment or more completely, awaits further study. Recent work has indicated the complexity of local variations in the organisational structure of domestic industry and its relationship to patterns of landholding and agrarian labour.[31] This has suggested a need for further studies of the influence of land ownership and use on both pre-factory and post-factory industry at the regional level.

The concomitant development of the emergence of free labour was the concentration of property and wealth into fewer hands. The landed and mercantile groups are regarded as being the chief recipients during the eighteenth century, their incomes inflated further by the proceeds of commercial farming and expanding overseas trade. Feinstein's estimates of changes in the national wealth by sector indicate that the proportion of national capital invested in agriculture was falling whilst it rose in all other sectors, particularly industry and commerce.[32] But is this indicative of a real flow of wealth from land to industry and trade?

Concentrations of wealth in the hands of both landowners and merchants were not necessarily converted into capital for industrial development. The degree of separation between 'pre-industrial' and 'industrial' capital has been another focus of Marxist debate since the publication of Dobb's *Studies in the Development of Capitalism* in 1946. Dobb rightly pointed out that the mere piling up of wealth in seventeenth- and eighteenth-century Europe did not necessarily help the growth of capitalist production and could even have hindered the creation of wealth for productive investment by diverting consumption and investment into less productive channels.[33] This interpretation is to some extent supported by the evidence that new manufacturing techniques were often pioneered by small concerns and by individuals with comparatively little capital of their own. If, as evidence suggests, there was considerable enrichment of the landowning and mercantile groups, particularly in the eighteenth century, a study at sectoral level of the direct and indirect financial links between these groups and industrial enterprise would illuminate the 'dialectical relationship', posited but then neglected by Saville, between 'primitive accumulation' and the growth of capitalist industrial enterprise.[34]

Since the 1950s debate on the transition to capitalism many historians have stressed the importance of merchant capital and the extent to which it underpinned the whole financial basis of the period when handicraft and domestic manufacture dominated the industrial sector. The interesting question concerning the role of merchant capital is whether its immense growth in the period prior to the industrial revolution in Britain can be regarded as part of the 'process' of industrialisation or whether its predominance was symptomatic of, and tending to preserve, the older order.

The growth of a class of industrial capitalists from the ranks of the manufacturers themselves was seen by Marx to be a necessary precondition of any revolutionary transformation of production:

The transition from the feudal mode of production is two-fold. The producer becomes merchant and capitalist, in contrast to the natural agricultural economy and the guild-bound handicrafts of the medieval urban industries. This is the really revolutionary path. Or else the merchant establishes direct sway over production. However much this serves historically as a stepping stone – witness the English 17th century clothier, who brings the weavers, independent as they are, under his control by selling their wool to them and buying their cloth – it cannot by itself contribute to the overthrow of the old mode of production, but tends rather to preserve and retain it as its precondition.[35]

Some historians follow Marx closely in sustaining this interpretation of the inherently conservative nature of merchant capital.[36] The Genoveses in a recent contribution to the debate have stressed the boundaries within which economic and political progress occurred in the Old South and in eighteenth-century France: merchant capital bore fruit but the proceeds were not a source of dynamism in the progression to industrial capitalism. They endorsed the existence of societies whose social, political and ideological framework were far removed from that found in England during the same period.[37]

A regional study is a useful way of testing various theses concerning the nature of merchant capital. What influence did the merchant sector have on the development of the production process in the wool textile industry? Was merchant capital conservative? Did merchants find it difficult to shift their horizons from high to lower liquidity ventures? If so were there ways in which merchant capital was involved in centralising and mechanising industry aside and apart from direct participation or investment? Obviously, any sectoral study must address itself to these questions. Economic choices in this area as elsewhere were steeped in well-established cultural and social attitudes and traditions. The local and hence also the national economy is impossible to analyse as a process divorced from the social and institutional environment of decision-making; an environment most clearly perceived at regional level.[38]

Another topic regarding industrial finance which has been a focus of interest among historians of Britain's industrialisation is the mechanics and determinants of ploughed-back profit or reinvestment. Here, cultural values and norms – the motivations, personalities and religious beliefs of the early entrepreneurs – have assumed a central place in analyses.[39] However, Marx and more recently Sweezy have stressed that capital accumulation and reinvestment on the part of industrialists is essentially defensive.[40] This idea removes emphasis from the entrepreneur and his psychological or religious motivation. Instead the typical innovator and reinvestor is seen as the tool of the social relations (based on individualism and competition) in which he is enmeshed and which force him to innovate on pain of elimination. This approach implies a view of profits and accumulation which contrasts with the classic analyses of the Schumpeterian risk-taker who is *the* dynamic catalyst of the growth process.[41] Much established thinking regarding industrialisation and after sees profits as resulting from the innovating process: hence accumulation is a derivative phenomenon associated with the quality of entrepreneurship. The Marxian view maintains that profits exist in a society with a capitalist class structure even in the absence of innovation. The form of the profit-making process itself produces the pressure to accumulate, and accumulation generates innovation as a means of preserving the profit-making mechanism and the social structure on which it rests. These theses provide a set of propositions which it is useful to bear in mind when studying capital accumulation in domestic industry and the role, motivation and timing of plough-back during the transition to centralised and mechanised production.

Recent publications concerning themselves with the concept of proto-industrialisation have focussed on a range of issues identical to those raised in earlier theoretical schemes of Marxist and non-Marxist historians. The proto-industrial literature also has its own terms of reference and specific theses which provide insights useful for the present study.[42] The theory of proto-industrialisation concerns itself with the nature of industrial production and profits and the mechanics of change in the pre-factory period. Although its various exponents differ markedly in their conceptions, they have in common the view that industrialisation proper was preceded by a phase of dynamic change lasting two centuries or more. This 'proto-industrial phase' was dominated by the spread of rural domestic industry mass-producing various consumer goods for long-distance trade. The major distinguishing feature of the proto-industrial period was the inter-relationship between merchant capital and the family economy. The spread of putting-out industry in areas of peasant agrarian production is seen by Mendels and others as sufficiently pervasive and dynamic in its demographic, financial and socio-cultural implications as to impel the economy of Western Europe as a whole in the direction of full-blown industrialisation. Medick, Kriedte and Schlumbohm regard proto-industrialisation as a distinct 'mode of production' aiding conceptualisation of the 'transition period' between 'feudalism' and 'capitalism'.[43]

None of the proponents of the proto-industrialisation thesis insist that the passage from proto-industry to the factory was inevitable or automatic for all regions of rural household production. There are many examples of regions where the transition to centralised and mechanised production was slow or incomplete or where deindustrialisation occurred. The West Riding textile area can, however, be regarded as a good example of 'successful' proto-industrialisation where the inherent dynamics and limitations of proto-industrial production may well have promoted the development of more advanced industrial forms. Study of the industrialisation process in the West Riding thus provides a good opportunity to test aspects of the proto-industry thesis in detail. How important in the establishment of factory industry were the accumulation of capital and skills in the part of proto-industrial employers and workers? How inherently dynamic a force was proto-industry and how important was the social, agrarian and institutional environment within which rural industry emerged and functioned?

Both Mendels and Medick have rightly emphasised the fact that the division of labour time between agriculture and industry with priority for agriculture, whose work was regulated by the weather and the seasons, would necessarily limit the productive capacity of each cottage in a domestic system of production.[44] Furthermore, under a merchant capitalist organisation, expansion involved the increasing dispersion of workers and a growing distance from the employer which brought attendant disadvantages of increased time and cost of travel, lack of supervision, affecting quality control, and embezzlement by workers of raw materials. Thus it is argued that, by the mid-eighteenth century in England, merchant capitalists in many sectors were feeling the pressure of mounting marginal costs which eventually necessitated radical changes in methods of organisation and production. At the same time, proto-industrialisation had in theory created an accumulation of capital, wage labour and skills which facilitated the adoption of machine industry.

In reality, this process of transition from proto-industry to the factory was conditioned by a number of variables which differed from one industrial region to another. One was the differential nature of organisational structures involved in domestic systems of production. In some sectors the structure of merchant capitalist and wage-dependent domestic labour was not characteristic. Instead, the main element of production was the independent artisan owning his own means of production, working up his own raw materials and turning over his own capital at, within limits, his own pace. Such a structure was characteristic of many sectors in England including the woollen branch of the Yorkshire textile industry which presents a marked contrast to the worsted sector. Obviously the pressures, the ability and the desire to transfer to more capital-intensive forms of production varied according to the nature of the domestic structure involved. The degree of development of a wage-dependent proletariat, the extent of agricultural involvement on the part of workers, the nature of the competitive response, the power and influence of merchant and landowning capital were all variables dependent on the form of the domestic manufacturing structure. These variables governed possibilities of 'progress' from the proto-industrial phase to the development of factory production and require the attention of any regional study: 'The extent of capital accumulation as well as the political and social terrain in which it took place and the personnel in whose hands it fell determined very much the course of future industrialisation.'[45]

The political and social terrain of proto- and early-factory industry is a preoccupation of the present study. The emergence and development of rural domestic industry appears everywhere to have been conditioned by socio-political and cultural factors as was the accumulation and use of capital to finance the transition to the factory. Whether funds were

amassed by manufacturers, by landowners, by merchants or by financial
intermediaries such as banks, the extent to which this finance was directed into industrial use remained, as we shall see, a close function of pre-
existing institutional arrangements and of the customs, traditions and
social relationships of the older agrarian and mercantile order.

Sources of capital for industry

The sources of finance available to Britain's first generation of industrialists has been the subject of some research and debate. We are now aware
of the vast variety of possible sources but there is little consensus about
their relative importance and a great deal of scope for additional investigation.[46]

An article by Postan written in 1935 set the scene for much subsequent
analysis of capital sources. He raised a number of important questions
which have still to be answered, most importantly: was the supply of
investable funds sufficient for Britain's industrialisation or were shortages experienced which put a brake on development? Postan emphasised that Britain in the eighteenth century had wealth far beyond the
relatively modest requirements of accelerated industrialisation. Localised and specific shortages could occur, however, because the social and
geographical distribution of wealth did not match that of industry and the
development of conduits for the flow of savings into productive investment was slow. Thus he concluded: 'on the whole the insufficiency of
capital was local rather than general and social rather than material'.[47]
This interpretation placed stress upon the formal and informal channels
whereby capital from a variety of sources found its way into manufacturing. These channels together with the 'local' and 'social' supply of funds
can obviously be best understood by study and analysis at regional level.

But as Heaton emphasised two years later: 'Before seeking the source
of capital, it is worth asking "How much was needed by those who built
up enterprises with the new machines and power generators housed in
mills or factories?"'[48] It is common knowledge that in many branches of
industry before the mid-nineteenth century (and beyond), outlays on
fixed capital for the prospective entrepreneur were relatively small. The
textile industry in particular was 'the land of opportunity for the ener-
getic and ambitious man with little capital'.[49] Early textile machinery was
relatively cheap and could be easily acquired second-hand from sales of
bankrupts' stock.[50] Large items of plant and equipment could be bought
by instalments, as was the case with Boulton & Watt steam engines.[51]
Industrial premises varying in size from one room to an entire mill were
available for rent and factories with multiple tenancies of 'room and
power' were common. Purpose-built factories were the exception rather
than the rule before the mid-nineteenth century. Most commonly, buildings were converted from other purposes like corn milling, warehousing

or fulling, thus saving the capital cost of a new structure. Furthermore, in the textile sector, processes like fulling, scribbling, dyeing and finishing were undertaken on a commission basis so that the costs of stockholding and fixed capital often fell on shoulders other than the manufacturers'. These capital-economising features were not unique to the textile sector: they were common in metalware production and engineering, as well as in the broad spectrum of consumer goods manufacture from pottery to leatherwares. The immensely varied products of the textile and other industries and the specialisation which this induced enabled small concerns with limited investment to operate efficiently in many sectors throughout the nineteenth century.[52]

However, the stress on minimum capital requirements for early industrialisation can be overplayed. Even Heaton admitted that 'they were frequently large enough to harass and perplex those who needed funds for building or equipping plant of their own'.[53] Whilst devices such as renting, hire purchase and commission working indicate the ways in which capital costs could be economised on the part of individual business concerns, they do not in themselves explain very much about the sources of industrial capital. Who provided factories for renting? Who shouldered the burden of stockholding for commission workers? Why were second-hand equipment and premises commonly available for entrepreneurs? And how do the answers to these questions change over time, both cyclically and in the long term?

Although there remains a paucity of empirical work on both fixed and circulating capital sources for industry in the period *c.* 1750–1850, some works since the mid-1960s have indicated valuable guidelines and directives for more detailed study of the subject. Admittedly, eminent historians have also suggested that the question of capital sources is insoluble and that the only conclusion possible will be that the capital which financed the industrial revolution came from all sectors of the economy. However, the different sources are by no means of equal importance and it would be valuable if a hierarchy were to emerge from empirical study,[54] particularly if such a hierarchy took account of changes over time and through the life-cycles of firms.

A major consideration in studying the relative importance of different capital sources is the need to analyse two possibly quite separate types of finance: first, the source of the initial outlay which allowed new firms to build factories or existing small concerns to enter large-scale manufacturing and, secondly, the finance required for the later expansion of enterprises. These are significantly different aspects of the question of capital formation in the period. For both, the extent to which capital came from sources internal to the industry or from other sectors of the economy must be considered.

Previous analyses of the sources of 'initial outlays' for the establishment of centralised concerns particularly in the textile industry have emphasised several features: the *gradual* change from outwork to centralised production; the small size of many of the early factory concerns; the cheapness of machinery; the conversion of premises and other capital-economising devices such as renting and commission working.

These factors would lead one to conclude that the initial outlay involved in setting up a viable factory was relatively modest at the end of the eighteenth century. Thus one might expect that profits from production at the artisan level may account for a sizeable proportion of capital investment in early centralised concerns. This fact is well documented in a number of works but there has been little attempt to relate the incidence of artisanal backgrounds among factory entrepreneurs to the specific nature of domestic production in particular sectors. Clearly, artisan capital was more important in the growth of factory production in some trades than in others. In the Yorkshire textile industry, as we shall see, significant variations in the potential for artisan accumulation existed. It is necessary to ask which artisans were capable of accumulation and upward economic mobility and in which trades. It is also important to question the chronology of this upward mobility on the part of the artisan. His possibilities were clearly limited by the threshold of entry into centralised or mechanised production which varied not only between sectors of industry but also, very largely, over time.

The role of merchant capital has been discussed at some length in previous works but, again, there are several important questions which remain unresolved. In discussing 'initial outlays' one must consider the extent to which dispersed forms of production were conducted on a commercial-capitalist basis. Where the eighteenth-century putting-out system was dominated by powerful merchant-manufacturers one might expect them to play the major role in the transfer to mechanised production. Several factors conditioned the extent and timing of this role: the rates of profit earned from the putting-out structure, the demand for the product, the movement of marginal costs, the need to control quantity and quality of supply, the desire to prevent embezzlement and to increase labour productivity. The expected profitability of centralisation and mechanisation compared with the problems of retaining old structures in a competitive environment was also important.

Empirical study of the Lancashire cotton industry suggests that a number of merchant-manufacturers invested in the building of mechanised spinning mills in the last two decades of the eighteenth century. Samuel Oldknow, for example, built up a large putting-out business in the manufacture of muslins and went on to build a steam mill in Stockport and a large water mill at Mellor. Similar examples can be cited in the Midlands hosiery area – Richard Arkwright and J. Strutt both built mills from finance obtained in domestic hosiery production.[55] The early Scottish cotton spinning industry was to some extent underpinned by merchant capital and Chapman has also emphasised the importance of mercantile backgrounds amongst early cotton factory masters.[56] Perhaps the most spectacular examples of mercantile investment in industry are those of the London and Bristol iron merchants who played a decisive role in establishing the South Wales iron industry and the London coal merchants who invested in the Northumberland and Durham coalfields.[57] The current consensus is that merchants were active but mainly invested in industries producing the goods which they sold in order to ensure control of supply or quality.

Some studies of the wool textile industry have placed stress on the role of merchant capital. These studies, however, are confined largely to the financial origins of large and successful nineteenth-century textile firms such as Benjamin Gott & Sons and John Foster & Son whose archives have survived. Richard Wilson's more general analysis of Leeds merchants in the eighteenth century has shown that only very rarely were they prepared to risk their liquidity position in fixed capital outlays.[58] It is easy to gain an unrepresentative picture of the role of mercantile wealth in the initial outlays for factory production by considering only particular firms, particular branches of manufacture or particular time periods.

In considering the contribution of merchant capital in industrial development, it is much more important to emphasise its role in the provision of credit and circulating capital than in fixed investment for manufacture. Very little work has been done on this aspect and generalisations are in any case difficult as each branch of industry evolved its own marketing structures and credit networks. There is a general tendency to underestimate the extent of 'industrial finance' by merchants in this way because capital appearing in manufacturers' ledgers as 'bills' or 'creditors' is less clearly identified as an 'investment' than a loan, a shareholding or a bank overdraft. But firms which supplied industry with a large part of its circulating capital played a decisive role in fixed investment by releasing manufacturers' own resources for this purpose. The present study seeks to examine the chronology and importance of this role taking up Pollard's recommendation that the 'web of credit' should assume a central place in any exposition of industrial capital accumulation.[59]

Through the extension of mercantile credit, the inter-regional flow of capital was possible. Chapman has recently indicated that this flow also occurred on an international scale via the activities of foreign export merchants resident in the industrial areas.[60] But there is a need to examine the importance of this much more closely at a regional level. Analysis on a sectoral basis will also provide a case study which may throw light on more universal developments concerning the role of mercantile and manufacturers' trade credit and its relationship to the trade and investment cycles. The relationship between the extension of credit by manufacturers and their suppliers, the level of economic activity and the potential for expansion of productive capacity is inevitably complex and thus little researched. It is particularly complicated by the contrasting credit requirements of firms of different size. As Pollard has suggested: the larger the firm the more need there was to 'Prime the pumps of their customers and to pour untold thousands into a seemingly bottomless pit of stocks, consignments and credits granted without receiving credits on the other side of the ledger in anything like the same proportions.'[61] This would tend to confirm the picture painted by Heaton and Chapman of intense liquidity problems experienced by large firms at various points of the trade cycle.[62] Trade credit through boom and slump and for firms of different sizes and types is the subject of Chapters 5–8. Together they indicate that some branches of the wool textile sector at particular points of trade cycles and of commercial development were heavily dependent on their net-credit position.

The historiography of the role of 'landed' capital is as unsatisfactory as that regarding credit. In summarising the analyses available in 1965 Crouzet was moved to remark: '["landed" capital] seems to have played an altogether minor part in financing the industrial revolution with the exception of coal mining . . . As for the textile industries, investment by landowners seems to have been almost nil, although one or two instances are recorded in Scotland.'[63] Chapman agrees: 'The landed interest played a minor role in textile enterprise of the Midlands in this period.'[64] Some writers, however, have pointed out that many eighteenth-century industrialists came from rural families and had combined farming with industry over many years which had important implications for industrial finance.

Crouzet has noted that the ownership of a small rural holding facilitated the entry of some entrepreneurs into industry and supplied them with capital or perhaps gave them the means of obtaining more by mortgage. He argued that this agricultural finance was much less important in later expansion or in the founding of large industrial enterprises.[65] However, in the Scottish brewing industry and to a significant but lesser extent in the English brewing trade the finance and enterprise of yeomen farmers appears to have been important in firms of all sizes.[66] Evidence for the West Riding indicates that the artisan landholding was of much more importance than has previously been suggested.

The relationship between patterns of landholding, the evolution of artisan structures and the supersession of domestic production by the factory awaits precise study. It has been noted in recent work on 'proto-industrialisation' that subsistence agricultural holdings or access to the commonland on the part of domestic workers reduced the cost to the employer of labour reproduction and hence allowed the payment of industrial wages below subsistence level.[67] This in turn stimulated profit rates and the accumulation of capital on the part of the putting-out merchant or artisan family. Thus capital from land and industry were intimately linked in the functioning of rural domestic concerns.

Historically, the role of farming and landowning in the development of wool textile production had been significant. In both the woollen and worsted sectors of the eighteenth century, clothiers were almost invariably involved in farming too. In the woollen sector, in particular, by-employment in agriculture and the possession of at least a subsistence plot remained a common feature until well into the nineteenth century. The capitals of the dual enterprise tended to be inextricably merged – as is evident from the surviving books of account. Furthermore, the fulling process was generally undertaken in mills which had a manorial monopoly and had been originally owned and financed by the lord of the manor. In the late eighteenth century many of the fulling mills were still owned or built by local landowners. Landowners were also known to provide mills and other industrial premises for renting and to encourage domestic clothiers to settle on their estates by providing cottages and agricultural plots.[68]

A further aspect of the role of landed wealth in the industrialisation process and one seldom addressed by historians concerns the nature of landholding and inheritance practices among rural artisans and manufacturers, and the functioning of the land market at local level. This is likely to have been important at a time when such a large proportion of total wealth comprised land and agricultural buildings. Landholding and land transactions necessarily underpinned other forms of financial relationships and exchanges. Land was the major security upon which loans could be raised and upon which financial status, respectability and credibility often rested. Ownership of land as an indication of credit-worthiness may have been important in raising loans both short term and long, particularly before the advent of limited liability.

In analysing the extent to which industrial capital originated in other sectors of the economy it is important to study the nature of the provincial capital market and, in particular, the financial intermediaries who provided the more formal channels through which investment funds passed. Much of the work to date has stressed the social and personal character of the regional capital markets in this period as well as their highly localised nature. The bulk of short- and long-term loan finance seems to have taken place within a narrow geographical area and mainly comprised transactions between people related to each other personally, by religion or through business involvement.

The work of Anderson and Holderness has done much to illuminate our understanding of the important role played by the eighteenth-century attorney in negotiating loans for clients in his locality.[69] Anderson found that there was little tendency for investment funds to flow out of South Lancashire into Government securities. The bulk of local savings tended to be invested in the region in local ventures and was directed there by the attorney who was the most trusted financial intermediary of the community. The attorney's legal role in estate

agency and trusteeship placed him in a good position to influence the
flow of savings in a locality. He generally had a clientele for his legal services who provided a circle of potential investors from whom he could
raise loan capital. However, work on the provincial attorney, his precise
role and the implications of his activities for the size, source and direction of flow of capital particularly in the industrial areas, is at an early
stage.

The traditional view of the minimal relationship between banks and
the medium- and longer-term finance of industry in the eighteenth and
early nineteenth centuries is now in process of revision. Work by Pressnell and, later, Cameron and Mathias has modified previously accepted
opinion.[70] It remains the consensus that English bankers dealt primarily
in short-term credit but their role in financing the expansion of productive capacity is now also being recognised.

Even in their short-term and credit dealings banking activities released the manufacturers' own capital for fixed investment. By discounting bills, granting overdrafts and short-term loans, banks financed the
movement of goods and they also financed the production of commodities. The willingness of banks to discount bills of exchange created currency and thus helped them to play a large part in the eighteenth-century
economy. As in Lancashire, the Yorkshire textile entrepreneurs in their
relationship with local banks can be said to have constituted a mutual
credit source each endorsing the activities of the other. The rise of the
London discount market at the beginning of the nineteenth century
enabled banks in industrial areas to have bills discounted in London
through the agency of bill brokers which gave a considerable boost to the
credit facilities available to their manufacturing clients.

Aside from bill-discounting and temporary loans, recent work has
shown that banks were willing to finance longer term investment in
industry. A short-term loan could become an instrument of long-term
investment by being renewed either by agreement or unwillingly from
the bank's point of view when the borrower was unable to repay.
Examples in Yorkshire and elsewhere of the integration of finance capital and industrial capital, where bankers took on industrial enterprises or
where industrialists became bankers, prompt analysis of the incidence
and importance of such relationships. The role of overdrafts and loans
on mortgage of land or other collateral also requires further detailed investigation at sectoral level.[71]

A number of unanswered questions about the importance of miscellaneous sources of capital have been raised in previous studies. These
sources were largely derived from personal, family or religious links
between members of the industrial, mercantile and landholding communities. To test fully the various hypotheses concerning those links,
study is needed of the economic and social background of entrepreneurs
and of the personal foundations of financial inter-relationships in par-

ticular localities. Study of entrepreneurial origins and marriage patterns would also help to clarify the extent to which capital flowed directly from other industries connected socially rather than economically with textile manufacture. The present study throws up some clues concerning personal and familial relationships and their financial implications, but full analysis of this aspect of Yorkshire's industrial history requires separate, more specialised research.

To found a sizeable new undertaking diverse sources of capital were frequently used. Apart from mercantile credit, land mortgage, family, friends and the possibility of help from a bank, the formation of a partnership was an entrepreneur's natural expedient when in need of capital. It provided an opportunity to gain the support of richer individuals and, in this way, capital from other trades and from commerce could find its way into a particular sector of production. Early joint stock forms of organisation could also comprise a source of capital for the establishment of centralised production. The woollen industry provides an interesting example of the importance of communal effort and joint stock finance among small entrepreneurs. The loophole provided by the trust deed enabled groups of clothiers to evade the legal limitation on partnership size to form 'company mills'. Interestingly, such co-operative institutions appear to have been much rarer outside of Yorkshire. Only a detailed examination of the composition of partnerships and the ownership of industrial establishments can resolve the question of the relative importance of these miscellaneous sources of finance for the wool textile sector or for industry as a whole.

When one proceeds from examination of the sources of initial outlays for the founding of enterprises to studies of the financing of their expansion, bank credit, loans and partnership changes are again stressed in the historiography but one is struck by the emphasis placed on the predominance of self-finance: 'Enterprises increased their capital by ploughing back immediately, regularly and almost automatically, the greater part or even the whole of their profits.'[72] Surviving business ledgers do often show only minimal drawings made by partners particularly in the early years of a concern. For example, Heaton cites the case of the Brooke family of Huddersfield who for a period in the 1830s left 60–80% of profits in their woollen firm each year.[73] However, surviving books of account are neither representative nor easy to interpret and the evidence so far gathered has been insufficient to analyse ploughed-back profits in detail or to draw any firm conclusions about the extent, timing or motivation or reinvestment. How important was reinvestment in different phases of the life-cycle of firms? Can the motivation of plough-back be attributed to thrift and abstinence and associated with non-conformist ideology as many historians have suggested? The present study addresses itself to these questions.

In studying the role of ploughed-back profits it is essential to consider the source of such profits. Those variables which influenced profitability must be isolated as elements in the accumulation process. The most notable previous attempt to determine the mainspring of profitability in Britain's early industrialisation has now been largely discredited. Hamilton maintained that the price rise of the second half of the eighteenth century was sufficient to cause a profit inflation.[74] This occurred in two ways: through inventory appreciation and, more importantly, through a lag of wages behind prices. There are many criticisms of this thesis, not least of which is that it does not fit with the facts. Landes has pointed out that it is not proven that profit margins did increase in the eighteenth century.[75] Furthermore, industries making the most rapid technological advances were those where prices were falling. Windfall profits of the Napoleonic War period did not go to innovating industrialists as much as to farmers and merchants. Hamilton furthermore ignores the movement of prices of all factors of production apart from labour.[76]

For the Yorkshire textile sector, it is possible to analyse the returns on capital and the determinants of profit levels to a fuller extent than has previously been attempted. This enables the mechanics of industrial self-finance to be illuminated and makes possible some testing of hypotheses, particularly those of Pollard and Hobsbawm concerning the relationship between low wages and reinvestment.[77] Previous work, admittedly on firms which were larger than average and generally successful, indicates that net profits could be very high; in good years in excess of 15 or even 20%.[78] Some studies, particularly of the textile industries, stress that after the mid-1840s profits per unit of output were declining as a result of the secular fall in the prices of manufactured goods[79] but it is questionable whether the return on capital was noticeably affected. These findings are borne in mind when considering the experience of the wool textile industry.

One final aspect of capital accumulation which has been the subject of previous historical study relevant to the present work is that of the discontinuity of investment. The timing of investments can yield interesting clues about the sources of capital finance and the forces determining investment decisions. Gayer, Rostow and Schwartz, in Schumpeterian fashion, first emphasised that large-scale increases in productive capacity in the British economy of the industrial revolution and the later nineteenth century are concentrated in a small number of short periods which occur in the late phases of expansion of business cycles.[80] These cycles are the nine-year Juglar periods. Because of the fairly lengthy gestation time of investment projects in centralised industries, much of the clustering applies to investment *decisions* rather than their institution. Decisions taken in the optimistic climate of the later stages of a cyclical upswing often came to fruition after the peak, tending sometimes to mitigate the subsequent depression. These varying gestation periods complicate the study of the cyclical timing of capital accumulation and, hence, its implications for sources. Furthermore investment decisions could occur contracyclically, when firms expand or adopt some technological innovation to enable them to combat competition and depression more effectively. Study of the cyclical nature of accumulation is important, because the motivation of investment – whether projects are undertaken in a period of trade expansion and optimism or in the scissors movement formed by prices and costs in depression – affects both the urgency of demand for capital and the available sources of supply.

One debatable question remaining in considering the periodicity of investment trends is the effect of the Napoleonic War period and its aftermath. There was no general industrial investment boom at this time partly because the war induced a diversion of funds into foreign currency, agriculture and government stock.[81] The low accumulation of industrial capital was further aggravated because it was necessary for manufacturers to keep relatively more capital tied up in stocks owing to difficult conditions in foreign trade, particularly after 1806. This affected investment in fixed capital at a time when inflation had made its costs rise. The sources of wartime industrial investment were circumscribed and personal connections, together with plough-back, probably became all the more important.

The question of the effect of interest rates on industrial investment has also been a subject of debate. With reference to the war period, it has been suggested that industry suffered a shortage of capital because the legal maximum rate of interest imposed by the Usury Laws diverted savings into government stocks.[82] However, as will be demonstrated for the West Riding, the imperfections of the capital market, the role of land mortgage and the importance of internal self-finance may have effectively sheltered many firms and reduced their sensitivity to variation in the market interest rate through the eighteenth century as well as the first half of the nineteenth century.

Shapiro has emphasised some new aspects of the effect of differential interest rates even in the period when rates were pressing on the 5% level. The problem of enforcement of the Usury Laws in different sectors and over different monetary transactions may have worked to the benefit of the industrialist. For example, he could obtain high rates of interest on his book debts with no recourse to the authorities, and the limitation of yields on alternative investments may have encouraged the ploughing-back of industrial profits.[83] There are obvious problems in testing for a relationship between interest rates and gross capital formation and analysing the effect of legal loopholes which may have resulted in differential interest rates. But this is a contentious area demanding comment from any study whether national or sectoral.

In sum the historiography of capital accumulation and capital sources during Britain's industrialisation has highlighted a range of issues which provide an agenda for the present work. The mass of unanswered questions are focussed around three major priorities. First, the need to study the workings of the capital market at regional level. Only by so doing will it become apparent just what, if anything, the aggregate national estimates imply for those businessmen and workers whose lives were conditioned by the local rather than by the national environment. The relative importance of external and internal sources of fixed capital finance and the availability of the latter through local networks and institutions are the subject of Part 4.

Secondly, the interdependence between agriculture and industry, between landownership and finance and between inheritance and landlessness are all vital issues. They are addressed in Part 2.

Finally, perhaps the most under-researched of all areas is the role of trade and bankers' credit in financing production as well as trade. Circulating capital remained the major articulated concern of the manufacturers themselves; they had most of their funds invested in it and local gluts and famines were a feature of the times. Obviously, the credit matrix was a major determinant of the financial flexibility of manufacturers and of their capacity to extend and advance production. The complex web of relationships which underpinned trade credit, changes in practice over time and the importance of financial institutions, principally banks, are the subject of Chapters 5, 6, 7 and 8.

Although the three major sections of the work are diverse in the range of financial relationships which they address, these relationships have one feature overwhelmingly in common: all were underpinned by face to face contacts, by local knowledge and intelligence networks and by customs and traditions which were only slowly being broken on the rack of industrial progress.

2

AN INDUSTRY IN TRANSITION:
THE WEST RIDING WOOL TEXTILE
SECTOR, 1750–1850

It is not the place here to provide a detailed account of the development of the Yorkshire wool textile industry during the prolonged transition from domestic handicraft manufacture to factory-based production. Such has been tackled previously by a number of historians[1] but few have adequately stressed those aspects of industrial growth which are particularly relevant to the present study. The main concern of this chapter, therefore, is to throw light on the nature and chronology of industrial expansion and its implications for capital accumulation. The decades with which we are concerned saw an unprecedented increase in the degree of industrial concentration generated by technological and organisational change and a massive expansion in the amount of fixed and circulating capital employed. To what extent this increased mass of capital flowed into industrial production from other sectors anticipating a high return, or was generated from within industry itself, by what means businesses were established and expanded, by what means profits were accumulated and recycled are the major questions to be addressed later. With this in mind the emphasis here is on three important developments which are crucial to the study of capital accumulation. Firstly the changing nature of industrial ownership and the organisation of production will be documented. Secondly, attention will be drawn to the nature and chronology of technological change and its implications for capital finance. Finally, changes in raw materials, products, markets and merchanting, and in the nature and periodicity of cyclical trends affecting circulating capital requirements will be mentioned.

Before discussing these aspects of development, it is first necessary to consider the nature of the industry in question and, in particular, its lack of homogeneity. it is virtually impossible to speak of the Yorkshire wool textile industry as such. As early as the mid-eighteenth century such a diversity of cloths was being produced for a wide variety of different markets and using markedly different techniques of production, organisation and merchanting that it would perhaps be more justifiable to refer to a myriad of separate industries which had developed as distinct regional specialisms within the West riding textile area.

Some of the finest quality cloths were produced around Huddersfield, the weavers of Saddleworth being particularly famous for their skills. Broads and narrows of various descriptions were made there but particularly 'fancy' woollens, elastics, beaverettes, honleys and kerseymeres. The plainer undyed white cloth was chiefly manufactured at Alverthorpe, Osset, Kirkheaton, Dewsbury, Batley, Birstall, Hopton, Mirfield, Cleckheaton, Bowling and Shipley whereas 'mixed cloths' manufacturers resided mainly in the villages of Leeds Parish particularly west of Leeds in the vale of Aire but also further south to the west of Wakefield and in the vale of Calder. In the western section of the cloth area, particularly around Halifax but extending as far east as Leeds and Wakefield, lighter weight worsted cloths were being produced: shalloons, calimancoes, camblets and tammies. Halifax was the centre of shalloon manufacture whilst the Tammy Hall, established in 1776 at Wakefield, was testimony to the growing importance of tammy production in the town alongside its traditional product of heavier milled cloths.

Maps 1 and 2 illustrate the regional diversity of the industry within the West Riding over the period. The distribution of production of the various cloths can be seen to consist of several overlapping zones which became more complex but no less clearly defined by the mid-nineteenth century.

Abandonment of the generic term wool textiles has some justification but it would render impossible much convenient and relevant generalisation about Yorkshire's industrial development. One major distinction must, however, be repeatedly stressed as vital in understanding the varied nature of expansion within the industry: the contrast between woollen and worsted production. Writing in 1906, J. H. Clapham analysed various twentieth-century aspects of the woollen/worsted contrast emphasising that the ultimate distinction then, as earlier, was based upon the composition of the yarns: 'The worsted yarn is made of fibres, which, before being spun, are straightened out until they lie roughly parallel to one another. In the woollen yarn the fibres cross and intermingle in all possible directions.'[2] Woollen cloths are almost invariably fulled or milled (felted) after being woven whereas worsted fabrics are not, the warp and weft lines being therefore clearly visible in the latter. Upon these seemingly minor distinctions hang many fundamentally important contrasts between the history and development experience of the two branches of the industry within Yorkshire.

The old-established domestic woollen production in the Riding was traditionally in the hands of a multitude of independent clothiers who, working on a small scale, owned their own tools and the materials pass-

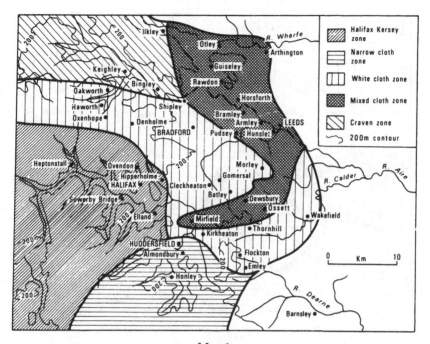

Map 1
The main woollen cloth producing zones of the West Riding,
early eighteenth century
Source: Based on Dickenson, 'The West Riding Woollen and Worsted
Industries', p. 63.

ing through their hands. By contrast, the worsted industry was unimportant in the Riding before the late seventeenth century and grew rapidly to compare with woollen production as a dominant industry of the region only with the expansion of stuff manufacture from the mid-eighteenth century. Almost from its inception, but particularly with the growth of the stuff trade, this branch was generally organised on a much more capitalistic basis with merchant clothiers of fairly substantial means putting out their materials for various processes to an army of wage-dependent domestic workers.[3]

This mid-eighteenth-century contrast has been partly attributed to the nature of worsted cloth in that the long-stapled wool necessary to form a durable weave without the strengthening process of fulling could only be procured from outside the region in Lincolnshire and the East Riding. The credit and connections for such a trade were necessarily the province of more substantial businessmen. There may be some truth in this as evidence suggests that established wool staplers of the early eighteenth century were dealing largely in shorter-stapled local wools for the woollen

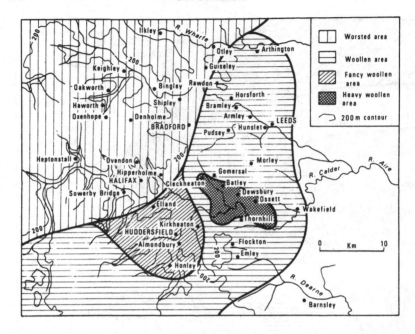

Map 2
The spatial distribution of the woollen and worsted producing areas of the West
Riding, early nineteenth century

trade whilst worsted manufacturers, by travelling or through agents,
generally managed the purchase of their own fleeces and bypassed the
stapler or middleman.[4]

This, however, no more than partly explains the fundamental contrast
between the domestic organisation of the two branches. The existence of
the merchant-capitalist in worsted production can be seen as a product
of the later growth of that branch in the Yorkshire textile area. The
traditional structure of the woollen industry had evolved slowly over
earlier centuries with the growth of broad and narrow cloth production
usually as an adjunct to farming in areas where soils provided a poor
return on the investment of capital and effort, where holdings were too
small to support population increase or where underemployment, both
chronic and seasonal, suggested a dual source of income. This slow evolution had been accompanied by the growth of marketing structures in the
towns, institutionalised, by the later eighteenth century, in the various
cloth halls built with the aid of clothiers' subscriptions. These developments were paralleled by the growth of an established niche in national
and international markets for the various woollen products manufactured in the Riding.

By contrast, worsted production, particularly the stuff trade, expanded rapidly from the mid-eighteenth century in direct competition with East Anglian manufacturers. In order to attack and win markets from their established rivals both in Britain and Europe, it is probable that a certain minimum of capital and size of operations was required. Bulk production of the cheaper worsted lines to compete in markets previously serviced by East Anglia, and to gain new markets in southern Europe and the colonies, could be achieved only by a large-scale concern with direct mercantile contacts and with capital sufficient to defray the initial costs of exploring new markets and overcoming the difficulties involved.[5]

The fact that worsted cloths must be made from longer-stapled wool had fundamental implications for the pace and nature of technological change in the two branches. The hand jenny was of limited use in worsted production but the two basic processes of spinning and weaving were adapted to powered mechanisation some two or three decades earlier in worsted than in woollen manufacture. This contrast was endorsed by the larger concentrations of capital generally available in the former deriving from the merchant-capitalist structure. Woollen yarns were eventually adapted to carding and spinning on the mule whereas worsted yarns were generally spun on the frame or throstle. The innovation of the power loom was much slower in the woollen branch. In coarse woollen production power weaving was used soon after its innovation in worsted production, but in most branches there was a delay of a decade or two. This was because the short-stapled fibres made the yarn weaker and more liable to break during handling. Great technological sophistication was thus required for powered spinning of woollens. The different chronology and nature of innovation in these processes and in those such as fulling, scribbling and dressing (unique to the woollen branch) and combing (unique to worsted production), radically affected the demand for fixed capital finance—both its absolute volume and the chronology of its growth.

Aside from the technological determinants of the need for capital finance in the two branches, the different markets which they faced and the timing of changes in the demand for the products both conditioned the pace of technological change and provided a separate variable governing the need for finance. If one adds consideration of the contrasting raw material requirements of the two branches, and their changes over time, a clearer picture of the woollen/worsted contrast and its corollaries for capital finance emerges. The chronology of capital expansion both fixed and circulating, and the likely sources of finance for much of this, were conditioned fundamentally by the contrasting nature of demand, raw material supply, technology and entrepreneurship in the two different branches of the industry.

Ownership and organisation: the woollen branch

The typical woollen clothier of the eighteenth century was either his own boss or had the prospect of attaining this status after a period as apprentice and journeyman. He generally undertook, alongside farming, most of the processes of manufacture from raw wool to semi-finished cloth. He employed his family and usually one or two journeymen and apprentices working either on his premises or in their own homes nearby. He owned the raw materials passing through his hands as he did the tools and equipment required for the majority of processes:

The manufacture is conducted by a multitude of master manufacturers, generally possessing a very small and scarcely ever any great extent of capital. They buy the wool off a dealer; and, in their own houses, assisted by their wives and children and from two or three to six or seven Journeymen, they dye it (when dyeing is necessary) and through all the different stages work it up into undressed cloth.[6]

The evidence which survives about the cost of hand looms, wheels and jennies, hand cards, tenters and other utensils owned by the typical woollen master suggests that his investment in these represented a relatively small outlay. Insurance valuations and probate inventories also indicate the relatively small capital requirements for fixed outlays on buildings for workshops and storage, additional to the domestic quarters. Comparison of fixed capital overheads with the value of raw wool on hand and in process of production indicate the much larger amount of capital tied up in stocks and variable funds.[7] However, even here investment was not generally large. It is likely that many manufacturers had to sell one cloth before they could buy materials to make another and thus lived 'from hand to mouth'.[8]

M. J. Dickenson's recent research, based on examination of over 700 probate inventories of the period 1689–1769, has indicated that woollen cloth manufacture was mainly in the hands of a multitude of small-scale clothiers with total movable assets (excluding debits) of £72 7s on average.[9] This figure certainly incorporates an upward bias as the smaller clothiers generally would not make a formal will. The average level of clothiers' assets varied greatly within the West riding textile region, being highest in the mixed cloth zone and lowest in the Halifax area. The development of an urban class of cloth makers, especially in Leeds Parish, was reflected in the relative unimportance of farming assets as a proportion of the total assets of clothiers in the mixed cloth zone. The percentage of woollen clothiers' total assets in textiles in the mixed cloth zone was twice that of the narrow and white cloth areas and more than four times the Halifax figure. Throughout the West Riding about 80–90% of investment in woollen textile production was in stocks of wool, yarn or cloth, only 3–6% in tools. Dickenson also indicates the low level of personal and household goods valued in probate inventories which suggests that the clothiers lived fairly frugal lives with only the bare essentials of furniture and household items.[10]

Thus the best evidence available suggests a multiplicity of units with small capitals, particularly small fixed capitals, at work in the woollen industry, the manufacture being generally undertaken as a by-employment alongside agriculture. The mixed cloth zone and in particular Leeds Parish, seems in the mid-eighteenth century to have been the heaviest capitalised, the most specialised and the most urbanised area of the manufacture.

Given these estimates of the low average level of fixed capital investment prevailing in the woollen branch, it is not surprising that one finds many examples of clothiers entering the industry with relative ease, their passage across the threshold being largely a question of ensuring a foothold in the complex network of credit operating in the trade in raw materials and finished cloths. In the latter context it was obviously an advantage to be well connected in the trade prior to setting up on one's own account. A period as an apprentice (either formal or informally in the parental home) was almost invariably a prerequisite of independent clothier status. A previous training in the trade was the *sine qua non* of the clothier's existence particularly as his own direct labours were the mainstay of the productive process. This fact is well illustrated in the evidence given before the 1806 Parliamentary Inquiry which, whilst stressing the decline of formal apprenticeship, does emphasise the extent to which clothiers appearing before the committee had undergone a long period of family-based training in different aspects of the production and trade.[11]

There are two exceptions to the general picture of the dispersal of capital and enterprise in the woollen branch before the late eighteenth century: the presence of centralised establishments for fulling the woven cloth and for the cloth finishing processes.

As is well known, water-powered fulling mills were first widely established in the thirteenth century from which time, as with corn mills, they were largely a manorial monopoly.[12] By the eighteenth century the landowner generally leased out a fulling mill to a fuller who inherited the local monopoly of supply of the service. As the trade expanded in the eighteenth century these traditional monopolies were unable to cope with the increased quantities of cloth requiring fulling. Long delays were experienced by clothiers bringing their cloth to full and long distances were commonly travelled where the local mill proved inadequate. This provoked the development of alternative facilities in private mills owned by local individuals and divorced from manorial ties. These mills were owned by a variety of persons, seldom the fuller himself. Dickenson cites seventeen wills in which fulling mills were bequeathed in the period

1703–65. The owners were indicated as gentlemen, grocers, tanners, victuallers and yeomen. Only one of the seventeen was owned by a fuller and the few surviving inventories of fullers support the view that the fullers themselves were relatively poor.[13]

Many of the new fulling mills of the later eighteenth century were set up by clothiers or groups of clothiers frustrated by the congestion experienced at the public mills. There is evidence to suggest that much of the capital injected into fulling came from within the industry itself, particularly where other powered processes were allied to fulling in the centralised mill.[14]

It is impossible to undertake a thorough survey of ownership of the fulling mills of the West Riding in the eighteenth century as surviving records are far from complete. There were over 100 fulling mills recorded by the 1770s, the majority of which, from their location on large estates, would appear to have been a legacy of the public mill provision.[15] By the early decades of the nineteenth century there were some 120 establishments where cloth was fulled and searched but by this period few mills concentrated solely on fulling, and less than half had developed out of the older fulling mills. There was thus a much greater diversity of location and ownership.[16]

The other process of woollen manufacture which induced a greater concentration of capital in the eighteenth century was finishing; both the dyeing and the dressing of cloths. Dyeing in the piece had developed as a separate and distinct trade by the 1690s. The size and nature of the utensils required for the process, and the desirability of a river site for water solvent and power to grind dyewares, dictated its divorce from domestic premises and the need for fairly large capital investment. The latter was endorsed by the cost of imported dyes and mordants. A sizeable proportion of a dyer's capital had to be tied up in stocks of these raw materials. Dyeing tended to be undertaken by drysalters whose main business was importing and dealing in dyes, cleansing materials and mordants, a trade which in itself required a fairly large capital.[17] Specialised dyers also existed; Dickenson's researches indicate that some dyers were small scale with £50 or less in movable assets in the mid-eighteenth century but the majority operated on a larger scale. Fixed capital invested in dyehouses and adjoining buildings seems commonly to have varied between £50 and £300. Most surviving dyers' inventories included more than £1,000 invested in fixed and circulating capital together, indicating that capitalisation in this branch could be a lot larger than was the case in the cloth manufacturing sector.[18]

Some of these dyers also undertook dressing processes – raising, shearing, tentering and pressing – although in the main these were done by specialised dressers in the three major mercantile centres of the region: Halifax, Wakefield and Leeds.[19] Of the 352 cloth finishers' inventories analysed by Dickenson for the period 1689–1769, 81% came from those three parishes. The mean value of their total assets was £149 12s compared with £72 7s for woollen clothiers. Many finishers had assets over £400; they had less capital in agriculture and were much more urban-based than the clothiers. About a third of their textile assets were invested in tools.[20]

Cloth dressers also generally invested more in stocks than woollen clothiers although a minority carried very few stocks, usually because they were directly dependent upon larger merchants or master cloth dressers for whom they were working on commission. The amount of stocks carried by the majority of dressing concerns through the eighteenth century indicates that dressers on the whole were not solely or even mainly acting on a commission basis. This casts doubt on R. G. Wilson's thesis that after the mid-eighteenth century merchants commonly took over the finishing stages of cloth production leaving master cloth dressers in the dependent position of works manager.[21] There is certainly some evidence of merchants owning dressing shops but it is likely that the capitalistically organised cloth finisher maintained his independent position through the period of the industrial revolution, aided by the close links which developed between particular dressers and the merchants for whom they did work or to whom they sold their cloths.[22] Concentration and specialisation in the cloth dressing branch arose partly from the cost of the tools involved but mainly from the need to tailor the supply of particular finishes to what could be very rapid changes in demand.

It would be a mistake to represent the ownership and organisational pattern of the woollen branch in the eighteenth century as a static picture. Two developments of the last decades of the century were of considerable importance in changing the pattern of ownership and capital concentration. First, the mechanisation of carding and scribbling occurred. This required water power and thus tended to be established alongside fulling in the mills. Secondly, there was a steady growth in the number of merchant-manufacturers.

The first water-powered scribbling mills probably appeared by the mid-1770s and by the 1790s they had taken shape of the lines they retained for many years. Experiments by clothiers to set up carding machinery and billys in their own cottages proved short-lived because of the superiority of water power sites and the large investment needed for this. Scribbling and carding were generally established alongside fulling in the existing mills which were frequently enlarged as a result. A large number of new combined scribbling, carding and fulling mills were also built in the last quarter of the eighteenth century. Allied to fulling, and working up the clothiers' wool into slubbings charging a piece rate, the mill established its place in the industry without dislocating its domestic organisation:

1
Cloth finishers
Source: G. Walker, *The Costume of Yorkshire* (1814).

Primarily the scribbling mill was a public mill performing a double function for its customers. It first carded the raw wool brought by the small manufacturers of the neighbourhood and slubbed the cardings, returning the material to its owners (or to their jenny spinners) in the form of slubbings wound on to cops. Later the cloth manufactured from this wool was brought back to the same mill to be scoured and fulled in the stocks. If, however, a scribbling mill was started merely to handle the wool of its owner instead of working for the trade, it assumed a new function and produced a very disturbing effect.[23]

This effect was a part of the threat posed to the domestic system by the growth of centralised forms of production out of the control of the traditional domestic clothiers. These developments were being felt, particularly in the Leeds area, by the time of the Parliamentary Commission of 1806.

The significant corollary of the development of scribbling mills serving the trade was that the woollen clothier now confined his domestic activities largely to spinning and weaving whilst the capital and enterprise in the preparatory processes as well as fulling fell to the lot of specialised concerns. Some of these grew out of the fulling mills, many seem to have been set up by individual clothiers anxious to keep full control over the regular supply of slubbings to their jenny spinners. A minority of scribbling and fulling mills were established in this period by persons with little or no previous connection with the woollen trade. But it was most common, from the 1780s, for groups of clothiers to combine together on a joint stock principle under a trust deed. They amalgamated their capitals and established mills to provide scribbling, carding and fulling services on a communal basis.[24] Unlike the wage-dependent domestic worker in the worsted trade the typical woollen clothier had the possibility of accumulating capital from the regular turnover of his own resources. Those who were most successful, who adapted their output to suit changes in demand or who were engaged in the production of those lines whose popularity was increasing in the later eighteenth century, were in a position to extend the scale of their enterprises to employ more workers on their premises, and perhaps to hold shares in a communal mill.

The tendency toward centralisation of capital was endorsed, particularly in the Huddersfield area, by two further developments of the late eighteenth century: the use of wool of finer quality and higher price from the west and south of England and from Spain and Saxony and the expansion and diversification of the fancy fashion branch of the industry. The former had a twofold influence. The control of embezzlement by outworkers became imperative and this could only be achieved by closer supervision of work.[25] Furthermore, more capital was necessarily sunk in stocks of raw wool which meant that the larger firms were better placed. The second development, the big expansion of the making of fancy cloths like kerseymeres, very different from the traditional broadcloths and narrow kerseys, necessitated a workshop or factory environment to ensure effective supervision of the spinning and weaving. These processes were all-important in achieving the quality required in fancy designs catering for the upper end of the domestic and foreign markets for fashion cloths.[26]

As early as 1806 the increasing financial and organisational control over manufacturing on the part of the mercantile group is clearly recorded. The *Leeds Guide* refers to clothiers as 'generally men of small capitals... [who] ...often annexe a small farm to their own business... [but] ...we regret to say that this state of the manufacture is likely to be impaired by the increasing habit of merchants concentrating in themselves the whole process of a manufactory'.[27] The developing importance of the merchant-manufacturer is also attested in the Parliamentary Report of the same year. The main grievance of James Ellis, master clothier of Harmley (*sic*) near Leeds was of merchants becoming cloth makers 'on this large system' with the result that 'Many who were masters are brought to be workmen.'[28]

It has been argued that the rise of the factory in woollen production was largely the result of decisions of merchants to turn to manufacturing in response to the rising demands of the markets and thus the desirability of gaining greater control over the supply and quality of goods. It was 'chiefly the merchants who, possessing the necessary capital, set up mills, allied industry to commerce, and provided the capitalist system of the 19th century'.[29] However, there is some dispute as to the origin of these merchant-manufacturers. Wilson has argued that few Leeds woollen merchants involved themselves directly in manufacturing apart from the finishing processes[30] and Crump and Ghorbal, the local historians of the Huddersfield area, have stated that it was 'mainly the merchant manufacturer *evolved from the clothier* [my italics] who created a new unit which soon became known as a factory'.[31] There is in fact evidence to suggest that the merchant-manufacturer, embodying the alliance of merchant and industrial capital, was evolving both from the mercantile and the manufacturing side simultaneously but mainly from the latter.

Apart from the increasing direct amalgamation of merchant and industrial capital, a further allied trend was a source of comment in the 1806 Report: 'A practice has also obtained of late years of a merchant giving out samples to some manufacturer whom they approve, which goods are brought to the merchant directly without coming into the Halls.'[32] John Hebblethwaite, a Leeds merchant, stated that the practice went on in his area 'to a very great extent'.[33]

Crump and Ghorbal explain that it was particularly the substantial clothier/merchants and merchant-manufacturers who sealed the doom of the cloth hall system. They increasingly preferred to give orders for what they wanted or, particularly in the fancy trade where novelty and design were of paramount importance, found it an advantage to show their cloth to customers in a private warehouse.[34] The decline of the cloth hall was, however, a slow process as the numbers of small domestic clothiers making plain cloths remained undiminished until the advent of power weaving began to make its mark from the 1840s.

Thus there were four basic organisational units in the woollen industry by the first quarter of the nineteenth century, all with different capital requirements.

1. The fulling and scribbling mill often owned by groups of small clothiers in shares.
2. The small domestic clothier, working on domestic premises or in a small workshop, making largely plain, undressed pieces and selling them in the local cloth hall.
3. The merchant-manufacturer evolved from both the woollen merchant and the more substantial clothiers, undertaking dressing and, increasingly, also the scribbling, carding, fulling, spinning and weaving processes in factory establishments.
4. The independent master cloth dresser working either on the commission

for a merchant, or buying cloths from clothiers to finish and then sell to merchants.

One of the most noticeable features of the organisation of the woollen industry in the succeeding quarter century was the persistence of the domestic clothier as an important figure in the trade. In 1833 John Brooke thought that the 'extent of domestic manufacture in Yorkshire has rather increased'.[35] The number of hand looms in the region in the 1830s is some indication of the vitality of the older system of organisation. William Stables testified that there were 12,000 weavers of woollens and fancy goods in the Huddersfield district alone in 1833[36] and Chapman counted 10,029 hand looms in the Leeds clothing district in 1840.[37]

A further feature of the organisational development of the woollen industry in the second quarter of the nineteenth century was closely tied to mechanical innovation. This was the increasing momentum of growth of the factory system which occurred particularly with the transfer of powered spinning to the mill. There was also a marked growth in the collectivisation of hand work to ensure effective supervision and reliability of supply. This was occurring among the merchant-manufacturers and the larger clothiers, particularly in the fancy trades; the continuation of a trend initiated in the last decades of the eighteenth century. A final organisational change of note, occurring in the 1830s and 1840s, was the increase in the numbers of company mills,[38] bolstering the artisanal units of the domestic structure and providing an alternative model of change to the capitalist factory proper.

Ownership and organisation: the worsted branch

The worsted branch of wool textile production presents significantly different organisational features and a contrasting pattern of change to that of the woollen branch. Shalloons and serges were the main cloths made at the beginning of the eighteenth century. There is evidence that some of the capital and enterprise in these manufactures came from East Anglia taking advantage, in particular, of the cheaper labour available in the West Riding, but the links between the two areas as far as capital and entrepreneurship are concerned tended to decline in importance as Yorkshire developed its own characteristic coarser cloths and as more native West Riding entrepreneurs emerged to conduct the industry.

In the first half of the eighteenth century worsted entrepreneurs varied greatly in the size of their undertakings, their capital assets and their backgrounds. Some were small, similar in size to the larger woollen clothiers and also involved in agriculture.[39] Overall, however, one can discern an important contrast in the typical size as well as the nature of undertakings in the worsted as compared with the woollen branch of the industry. There were a notable number of particularly large-scale and specialised concerns in evidence, some of which have left records sufficient for detailed historical study: Samuel Hill of Soyland, John Firth of Halifax, Jonathan Akroyd of Ovenden, Robert Heaton of Ponden Hall and William Greenwood of Oxenhope.[40] The kind of entrepreneurial figure which emerged in the eighteenth century, and particularly after mid-century, was typically an organiser of production – not engaging in the actual production process himself. In this way he differed from the master clothier in the woollen industry who commonly spun or wove himself. This distinction obviously gave access to the industry to people from other backgrounds and other trades who brought outside capital with them.

The nature and scale of operations of this group of businessmen was endorsed by the development around mid-century of the production of various worsted stuffs of middle quality like camblets, calimancoes, tammies, russells, prunellas and sagathays. The depression of the trade in some of Yorkshire's traditional woollen cloths in the 1750s, owing to the stagnation of South European markets and French competition, encouraged some of the larger woollen manufacturers (who had the necessary resources) to switch to stuff production particularly in the Leeds and Wakefield areas. It seems almost certain that stuff production in this period needed the resources of an enterprise of some size and capital. Apart from having to compete, particularly in overseas markets, with the established East Anglian manufacturers, the stuff business was one catering for an increasingly fashion conscious market. Those enterprises which were most successful therefore tended to be those which had sufficient capital resources to hold stocks of the various kinds of stuffs to anticipate rapid changes in demand. Alternatively, they had to be able to change their product quickly by having a large stock of tools and equipment on hand and a large amount of domestic labour on their payroll.[41] Furthermore, as Sigsworth has pointed out, the eighteenth-century worsted manufacturer had to finance production through the long period between the purchase of wool and the sale of cloth.[42] During this time all the journeying to and from his warehouse took place: the distribution of the raw materials and the collection of the finished product. Worsted production also comprised a larger number of processes than woollen production and the common eighteenth-century practice of oiling the fleece and leaving it for about twelve months, together with the limited use made of the jenny, further ensured that the turnover time of capital in the worsted branch was considerably longer than that in the woollen branch. The former thus required a more capitalistic form of organisation.

Dickenson's research on the surviving worsted inventories of the period shows that, on average, worsted masters had a good deal more capital invested in movable assets than did woollen clothiers. Analysis of 151 surviving worsted clothiers' inventories covering the period 1720–60 indicated a mean level of wealth in movable assets of £141 6s: twice that invested on average by woollen clothiers. Worsted entrepreneurs were also typically much less involved in farming than their counterparts in the woollen sector and they appear to have invested much more capital in tools and stock.[43] Where the scale of manufacturing grew sufficiently large, partnerships were formed often apparently on the basis of one partner owning all or part of the buildings and both jointly subscribing the circulating capital.

In sum, the eighteenth-century worsted industry in Yorkshire was one where the organisation of production was on a putting-out basis, where the typical worsted businessman was a person of some means and capital with no necessary prior connection with the trade. Market conditions over the long term were highly favourable and it is likely that the rewards for ingenuity and industry were such that businesses could be fairly rapidly expanded in scale. By the early nineteenth century there is evidence that many worsted concerns of considerable size existed particularly in the Halifax/Bradford area employing large amounts of scattered domestic labour.[44]

The volatile trade conditions of the Napoleonic War years appear to have arrested any rapid growth of the industry.[45] By the mid-1820s, however, rising marginal costs of the larger-scale putting-out organisations, the favourable climate of demand, the existence of entrepreneurs of sufficient means to experiment with new techniques and the relative ease with which worsted yarn proved adaptable to machine spinning, resulted in the start of a period of cumulative expansion based on technological advances which wrought immense changes in capital requirements and capital accumulation.

Because worsted spinning proved suitable for the Arkwright technique of mechanical roller spinning this branch of the industry benefited greatly from the developed technology of the cotton industry, in fact many of the early worsted spinning mills were converted from cotton production especially in the Keighley area in the first decade of the nineteenth century.[46] This represented a significant transfer, not just of technology but also of capital from cotton production into worsteds.

Evidence suggests that many of the key figures in initiating or converting the buildings of the first factories in the worsted branch were capitalists who had some experience in running putting-out concerns. Other significant sources of capital and enterprise were persons involved in merchanting, in wool stapling and in the cotton business. Many early worsted entrepreneurs also had family connections with landowners and farmers, which were a useful source of capital.[47]

By the 1840s the domestic worsted spinner or weaver was becoming a rare phenomenon. The proto-industrial unit in the worsted sector did not remain competitive with factory production for such a lengthy period as it did in the woollen branch where the domestic artisan structure proved more resilient and where technological change was also slower.

Finally, when considering the organisational structure of the worsted industry in the nineteenth century, a word must be said about the size of mill concerns and their tendency to vertical disintegration, both of which had important implications for capital accumulation. Most historians of the industry have stressed the fact that typical worsted mills were larger than their counterparts in the woollen branch. This feature seems to have become particularly apparent in terms of labour employed from the 1830s and 1840s when the extension of Arkwright-type mills proceeded apace. Tables 2.1 and 2.2 give an indication of this contrast in average mill size.

Table 2.1 *Average horse power and number of workers in Yorkshire woollen and worsted mills, 1838 and 1850*

	Woollen	Worsted
1838		
Average h.p.	16	16
Average no. of workers	45	76
1850		
Average h.p.	14	22
Average no. of workers	46	170

Source: Factory Returns, P.P. 1839 (41) (135) XLII, 1850 (745) XLII.

The larger average size of worsted mills was conditioned by a number of factors including the resources of the first generation of factory builders and the fact that spinning, the first process to be mechanised in this branch, had adopted a technology which imposed a minimum size on mill buildings. The tendency to vertical disintegration which speeded up the turnover time of capital in production probably also released considerable funds for fixed capital investment and expansion.

Vertical disintegration occurred more in the worsted branch than was the case in woollens as is indicated in Table 2.3. This was a result of the fairly rapid mechanisation of spinning and the lack of precedents in mill finance, construction and siting to equal the fulling, scribbling and carding mill of the woollen branch. These factors together encouraged a movement into the industry of entrepreneurs and finance from different sectors outside. This development, with the demand for worsted yarn from other areas of the country and from abroad, resulted in worsted spinning becoming an important separate industry in itself in the 1820s, trading a product far outside the confines of Yorkshire. Once this pattern of vertical disintegration had been set, it tended to persist. As weaving,

Table 2.2 *Number of persons employed in manufacturing establishments for which 'masters' sent in returns to 1851 census: Yorkshire*

Number employed	Woollen cloth manufacture	Worsted and stuff manufacture
1–9	52.3% (304)	28.5% (39)
10–49	38.6% (224)	37.2% (51)
50–199	6.9% (40)	23.4% (32)
200+	2.2%[a] (13)	10.9%[b] (15)
No. of employers	581	137

[a] Includes 3 employers of 350, 420 and 421 and 2 employers of 500 each.
[b] Includes 9 employers with 350–550, 1 employer with 1,000 and 1 employer with 3,000.
Source: P.P., Census Abstract, 1851, Division IX: Employers: Yorkshire.

Table 2.3 *Specialisation of function in wool textile mills, 1834*

Function of mill	No. of Woollen Mills	No. of Worsted Mills
Scribbling, carding, slubbing and fulling	65	—
Spinning[a]	14	72
Weaving	2	3
Integrated	46	10

[a] Includes some mills spinning and preparatory processing.
— = not applicable.
Source: Reports of Factory Commissioners, P.P. 1833 (450) XX, 1833 (519) XXI, 1834 (167) XIX, XX.

and later combing, were mechanised, these too often remained the province of specialised concerns.

Technical change

Acting on the foundation of contrasting structures of domestic production, the differing nature and chronology of technological change in the two branches presents a further element in analysis of the centralisation of production and its finance. In the woollen branch there were some early technological improvements which evaded the worsted sector either because of practical problems or because they were inapplicable. However, over the whole period to the 1850s the most striking feature is the greater adaptability of worsted fibre to fundamental technological changes in the major processes.

It seems that the fly shuttle was introduced in the Yorkshire woollen industry *c.* 1763–4 and was in fairly general use in weavers' homesteads by the 1770s. This obviously put pressure upon the supplies of spun woollen yarn and by the 1770s the jenny was also increasingly used in the West Riding. It needed little adjustment to serve the woollen industry and soon displaced the one-thread machine with an average of about forty spindles.[48] The jenny had the advantage of being small enough to fit into the homes of spinsters and did not therefore usurp the traditional and entrenched organisational structure of the industry. So well suited technologically and organisationally to woollen production was the jenny that at the time when Arkwright's water-powered frame or throstle was successfully innovated first in cotton and then worsted production, followed by the mule in the cotton industry, the domestic jenny continued as virtually the sole means of spinning woollen yarn until well into the nineteenth century.[49]

By contrast, in the worsted branch, the use of the fly shuttle generally followed the introduction of powered spinning. It seems that it was difficult to use the fly shuttle with wheel-spun yarn in the worsted sector and there was no innovation of the jenny in worsted spinning parallel to its development in the cotton and woollen trades. There is no record of the jenny being adapted to worsted production with any success almost certainly because the stronger worsted fibre imposed too great a strain on the early jenny. However, it was found that worsted fibre did lend itself, in a way that woollen fibres did not, to the process of spinning worked out by Arkwright using the water-powered frame or throstle. After the expiration of Arkwright's patents in 1781 it was possible for experiments with the technology of worsted spinning to switch from the jenny to roller spinning and this opened the way to the utilisation of water power in that branch.

Those branches of woollen production which were mechanised early tended to be those which resulted in least disruption of the eighteenth-century organisational structure. Machines carding on rollers with continuous processing facilitated by crank and comb doffing were used in Yorkshire before 1780. At first small hand- or horse-powered machines were used but the greater efficiency of water and then steam power promoted the use of carding technology alongside fulling in the local mill. In constructing these mills there were generally four types of machinery installed in addition to the fulling stocks: the willy or teazer, the scribbler, the carder and the slubbing billy. The latter in particular was a fairly complex machine derived from the jenny and having thirty to forty spindles which drew out the fibres giving them a slight twist and winding them on to bobbins or cops to make the slubbings easily transportable. From the research of D. T. Jenkins using insurance valuations it seems likely that these mills (the buildings and their fixed capital contents) represented an average capital investment of £1,000. In the early decades of the nineteenth century the use of steam, either as the sole source of power or to supplement the vagaries of water power, increased the average investment in this type of mill to around £2,000.[50]

At the same time mechanised finishing was becoming more wide-spread in the woollen sector with the innovation of the water-powered gig mill and shear frame. Records of their early use are scarce but the 1806 Inquiry suggests that they were fairly widespread particularly in Halifax Parish by the late eighteenth century. Other evidence indicates their widespread use in the area to the south of Huddersfield also.[51] Contemporary estimates may, however, be exaggerated because of the threat which they posed to the domestic system. Jenkins points out that there is no mention of the machines in inventories of the large manufactories around the turn of the century and a variety of sources indicate that they were virtually unknown in Leeds, the main centre of Yorkshire woollen cloth finishing.[52] Labour opposition severely limited their innovation in the West Riding.[53] In Leeds where finishing was geographically concentrated it was easy for workers to institute a complete ban on the use of this machinery. In the Huddersfield and Halifax areas where finishing shops were more dispersed it was difficult successfully to sustain an orthodox trade union approach and labour opposition there culminated in the Luddism of 1811–12. In both areas opposition reflected the stresses imposed by mechanical innovation on the traditional domestic structure, on the customary way of life and on old hierarchies of labour.

Although worsted yarn proved relatively adaptable to roller spinning by water power one must be careful not to exaggerate the speed of transition to the factory spinning even in this sector. The first factory was built in 1787 at Addingham on the Wharfe, but there were less than a dozen by 1800. Two major factors retarded development. First, the relative oversupply of underemployed labour, particularly female labour, in local agriculture meant that domestic spinners were available at a low wage. Secondly, at the same time as the first mills were opened in the West Riding the hand-operated spinning mule or throstle came into common use. It had the same principle as a modern worsted machine but contained only eighteen to twenty-four spindles and thus could be integrated into the domestic structure avoiding the need for costly outlays on specialised building. The general and widespread use of the hand throstle in the West Riding initiated a more gradual transition to factory spinning than that in the Midlands hosiery area.[54] It is likely that this contrast was endorsed by the coarser nature of hosiery and knitting yarns which were more easily adapted to fully mechanised spinning. However, by the 1820s hand spinning of worsted yarn in the West Riding was rare.

This had been achieved by constant improvements in the technology of powered spinning, including the invention of the false reed or slay, which enabled a better quality yarn to be produced, made weaving easier and enabled the more widespread use of the fly shuttle. From 1818 high wool prices stimulated further improvements in drawing and spinning, the introduction of the slubbing machine and roller and modifications which enabled a finer, stronger yarn to be spun from cheaper shorter-stapled wool. Continuous innovation in worsted spinning with consequent rapid obsolescence or near obsolescence of machinery continued through the rest of the first half of the nineteenth century with massive increases in the numbers of spindles per frame and in the amount of yarn spun per spindle. The long-established tendency for the spinning branch of the industry to produce a much larger quantity of yarn than the weaving sector could absorb was strengthened. From the 1820s increasing quantities of Yorkshire yarn were supplying other textile regions of Britain and Europe.[55] Many firms grew or were established to specialise in spinning for these separate markets. The fully integrated worsted cloth producing concerns which remained tended to be those which had advantages of specialisation at the high quality end of the market.

By contrast, the woollen sector was untouched by mechanised spinning before the early 1830s when the power mule was found to be suitable for woollen fibre. The growth of mule spinning in the woollen branch after this date dictated that the average spinning department was smaller than the Arkwright roller spinning mills which characterised worsted production. The latter offered much greater economies of scale. The pull of water-powered sites and the greater capital associated with the fulling and scribbling establishments meant that mechanised spinning in the woollen branch was almost invariably introduced alongside the already existing powered processes. It was mainly in the hands of merchant-manufacturers or company mill clothiers. Much woollen yarn continued to be spun on the jenny by the weavers and their families until the mid-century and in some cases even later.

In the mechanisation of weaving the worsted sector again progressed well in advance of the woollen branch although change was less rapid than with the mechanisation of spinning. The earliest recorded attempts to use a power loom for worsted weaving were by Cartwright at Doncaster in the 1780s and then, after a long lag, by Swarbrick of Shipley in 1822. But it was not until the 1840s that the power loom fully usurped the hand loom weaver. At this time power looms were increasing their speed, efficiency and competence. The Jaquard loom, with the addition of the multiple box, was particularly important because of the range of patterns it could produce. By 1860 there were few hand looms left in the worsted production of the West Riding. In the woollen sector at this time the power loom had only begun to leave its mark following a period of substantial experimentation in the 1850s. Weaving continued to be very

2
Domestic spinning
Source: G. Walker, *The Costume of Yorkshire* (1814).

much a hand process, the province of small domestic clothiers, in central-ised workshops of the larger clothiers or, particularly in the fancy trades, it sometimes became a part of the integrated factory whilst still retaining the hand technology.

The combing of worsted fibres was the last major wool textile process to be mechanised. Hand combers, employed by worsted manufacturers on a putting-out basis, were an aristocracy of labour in the early nine-teenth century despite the arduous nature of their tasks. The transfer of many former hand loom weavers to this occupation after the 1830s had already begun to undermine the status and earning power of the comber long before the evolution of a practicable combing machine. The com-plex history of invention and innovation in the combing process is not the concern here, but the practical outcome – that not until the 1850s was machinery innovated in any widespread sense – does have considerable implications for the present study. Until the 1850s combing was generally undertaken by specialised hand combing concerns (or less fre-quently by hand combers working in integrated worsted factories or in spinning mills). The predominance of separate combing concerns persis-ted in the era of mechanical combing – a further impetus to the tendency of vertical distintegration which characterised the worsted industry in the nineteenth century.

Changes in both the organisation and technology of the industry reflected themselves in the evolution and development of mill architecture and associated changes in capital costs. These varied both chronologically and between the different branches of the industry and must be considered in any investigation of fixed capital accumulation. The changing nature of mill buildings, motive power systems and all the associated fixed capital costs involved in the erection and fitting of a textile mill have been the subject of detailed investigation by Jenkins and it would thus be redundant to reiterate his findings here in any depth.[56] As more processes were centralised in both branches of the industry mills grew in size horizontally and vertically and structural modifications such as the use of iron frames were necessary to accommodate the weight of machinery and motive power installations and to guard against fire risk.

The important aspect of these developments to note here is the impact which they had on the threshold of entry into the different branches of the industry at different points in time. As Lawson wrote of the woollen branch in the 1840s and 1850s, 'the woollen business like all others is becoming more centralised, so that it is more difficult for one to begin business with a small capital than formerly'.[57]

Table 2.4 *Average value of mills, 1800–35*

Date	No. of mills in sample studied	Sample as proportion of total mills (%)	Average value of mills (£)
1800	153	63	1,657
1810	64	23	2,510
1820	36	11	2,870
1835	67	11	3,656

Source: Jenkins, *The West Riding Wool Textile Industry*, p. 154.

Some idea of this change in fixed capital entry thresholds can be gained by studying Jenkins' calculations of the average value of mills in different years. He adjusts these for additional site costs and for bias in the insurance valuations on which they are based (see Table 2.4). These figures, though interesting, are unsatisfactory as a firm guide to the changing capital costs of entry into factory industry, largely because Jenkins makes no distinction here between the two main branches of the industry let alone the varied typology within them. We have noted that, especially from the 1820s, the average size of worsted mills was considerably greater than that of mills in the woollen branch. Within the worsted sector it is likely that there were big differences in the threshold of entry between integrated firms and those which specialised in just one major process. Within the woollen branch, again one would expect size variations between the small-scale scribbling and fulling enterprises and the large-scale integrated mills of the merchant-manufacturers. Chapman has indicated that the average investment in an Arkwright-type spinning mill in the cotton industry in the 1800s was £3–5,000.[58] It is likely to have been similar in the worsted sector by the 1820s. If one separates out the average fixed capital investment in mill sites and building in the two branches it is clear that worsted mills commonly represented an investment which was 20–50% greater than in the woollen branch. This difference, although significant, is perhaps not as great as one would anticipate but it must be borne in mind that this considerably underestimates the divergence in the average size of manufacturing concern between the two branches. It was much more common in the woollen branch for manufacturers to share the same mill – in shares, by multiple tenancy or by the renting of room and power.

A second problem in using the Jenkins' figures as anything other than a tenuous guide to entry thresholds is the fact that they are expressed in current prices. The long-term price deflation of the 1820s and 1830s obviously affected the real costs of mill construction and the extent to which manufacturers could enter factory production or expand their concerns. In 1833, John Marshall suggested that the cost of mill construction had fallen about 25% since the war.[59] John Brooke and George Snull, giving evidence at the same time, confirm the fact that building costs had declined in these years.[60] Finally the Jenkins' figures can, of course, only give an idea about fixed capital entry thresholds and ignore circulating capital requirements which were equally, if not more, important in the establishment and functioning of concerns.

These same problems with the Jenkins' estimates (for our purposes) apply to the chronology which he gives to the build-up of capital in the industry. It is also a pity that the data is complete only to 1835 and that insurance records do not give gross figures (including renewals and replacements) which would more fully represent the capital costs of industry at this time. Nevertheless, Graph 2.1 is a useful indication of the timing of fixed capital expansion in the two branches of the industry. Significant phases of relatively rapid growth are identifiable, notably *c.* 1792–1803 (woollen branch), *c.* 1818–25 (worsted branch) and the period from the late 1820s to 1835. In the late 1830s and 1840s the indications are that fixed capital formation in the industry was volatile from year to year but continued to rise on trend in both branches.[61] This chronology, which highlights the volatility of capital formation, the different experiences of the two branches and the considerably higher trend levels from the 1820s, will be referred to in several of the later chapters when sources of finance are discussed. It is worth noting at this point that periods of expansion did not occur only or always after boom periods of trade.

Times of general trading difficulties such as the 1800s could be met

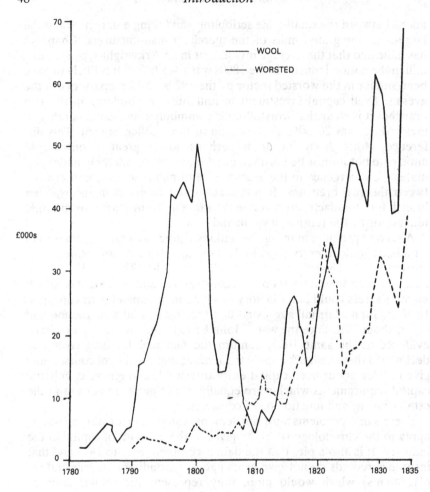

Graph 2.1
Three-year moving average of fixed capital formation in the Yorkshire wool
textile industry, 1780–1835
Source: Jenkins, *The West Riding Wool Textile Industry*, p. 176.

with continued expansion as was the case in the worsted sector in these
years. Similarly crises of the mid-1820s do not show up noticeably in the
expansion of capacity in the woollen branch.

Circulating capital

During the period 1750–1850 fundamental changes occurred in the structure of inputs into the industry, in the range and variety of products made

and in the markets served. Changes in all these and their associated credit practices radically affected the amount of circulating capital required to initiate and maintain a manufacturing enterprise. Input and market structures varied not just over time but between different branches of the industry and between different firms within the same branch, thus broad generalisations can be misleading. Most firms were atypical in some sense and this was increasingly the case in those branches where product specialisation was important.

On the supply side of the industry major changes occurred in wool purchase practices and in the sources of wool supply. Increasing use of foreign wool at first from Spain and Saxony and, by the 1840s, from Australia was accompanied by a secular trend in favour of shortening credit terms which made it more difficult for the potential manufacturer to insert himself into the credit chain. As Lawson wrote of the trade around the mid-century,

A man now would find it difficult after saving £20 to begin making woollen cloths, and make it pay as he once could, when he merely spent his money in wool, and readily got mungo, ware, oil, listing, scribbling warp and weft delivered at home all on credit till he was able to sell the cloth and pay for all out of it; or it might be, buy more wool with the money making a still larger lot before paying for the first.[62]

On the demand side of the industry any secular trend in credit practice appears to be difficult to discern. The common practice in the eighteenth century of selling for cash or short credit at the cloth halls or to local merchants seems to have rapidly given way, especially for the larger manufacturers, in the difficult years of the Napoleonic Wars. Long credit extension of eighteen months or more became common especially with those manufacturers involved in their own marketing.[63] The manufacturers' ability to extend longer credit was everywhere conditioned by developments in discounting and banking. English shippers who adopted the practice of advancing a quarter to a half of the value of cargoes on receipt also reduced the amount of credit effectively extended by the manufacturer. From the mid-1820s a long-term trend in favour of shorter book credit was initiated, two or three months credit becoming most common in the sales of cloth and yarn in both the domestic and the foreign markets. The reasons for this change are complex and are analysed in detail in Chapters 7 and 8.

Superimposed upon the trends outlined above were fluctuations caused by trade and price instability and by the cycles of productive activity which, again, are the subject of detailed discussion later. The important point to note here is that no clear relationship appears to emerge between the level of manufacturers' book credit and that of industrial activity. In an upturn of the trade cycle staplers and raw material suppliers would increase their credit to bolster the costs of manufacturers' purchases. Manufacturers would also tend to increase the level of credit extended to their purchasers. However, other forces worked simultaneously in the opposite direction. Increased prosperity and profit would tend to give added power to the seller to demand prompt payment whilst the buyer was better able to meet this demand.[64] In addition, and superimposed on the above contrary elements, was the effect of external credit (credit created by the financial sector via discounts and accommodation). This grew rapidly in importance, especially after the joint stock enabling legislation of 1826 which was followed by a mushrooming of banking facilities in the West Riding.[65]

In the downturn of a cycle external credit was rapidly withdrawn and in the atmosphere of pessimism there was a marked increase in liquidity preference which translated itself to some extent into a restriction of book debts. At the same time, however, declining prices and markets promoted a competitive struggle for survival in which credit was a valuable weapon. Those concerns who could afford to do so tended to lengthen their book credit to retain their business and, sometimes, to bolster the position of their customers, aiding them to weather the storm.

In assessing changes in circulating capital over time one also has the problem of accounting for variations in stockholding and inventories. Over the long term, one might expect a gradual decline in stockholding along with improvements in the efficiency and speed of transportation and communications. However, contrary forces were at work. As productivity and production increased and the practice of selling through the cloth halls declined, there may have been a tendency for finished goods to remain longer in the hands of manufacturers especially where unstable or distant markets were being served. It appears that this was to some extent obviated by working to order and by speculative dispatch. The trade cycle, with its radical effects on prices and demand, resulted in extensive stockholding at particular periods. Manufacturers who could afford to do so might hold finished goods back from the market if the price was too low or if they anticipated a future rise.

Wool also became a subject of extensive speculative activity as its price was subject to significant fluctuations, both seasonally and over the years. These increased with the growing use of specialised fibres and imports. Even without speculation, much could be gained in wool purchase by buying at 'quiet' times of the year and holding stocks until required. Hague, Cook & Wormald and Foster's both held large stocks of wool and other fibres in the 1830s and 1840s.[66] The extent of deliberate stockholding varied greatly depending on the ability of a concern to finance such activity or to call upon the credit to do so.

Assessment of circulating capital tied up by 'average' firms in the industry is difficult because few records of sufficient detail survive and those which do tend to be weighted in favour of the larger concerns who involved themselves heavily in merchanting and in stockholding. This wildly distorts the picture of the extent of circulating capital needed to enter and survive in manufacture alone. Some of the surviving figures of fixed and circulating capital ratios for different firms at different periods is given in Table 2.5

Table 2.5 *Fixed capital proportions for different firms in the wool textile industry, 1803–50*

Firm	Business	Years	Fixed capital as % of total capital	Average total capital (£)
Benjamin Gott & Company, Leeds	Merchant-manufacturers	1803–7	12	275,534
		1808–16	8	378,271
		1817–20	· 5	345,330
Clay & Earnshaw, Rastrick	Woollen manufacturers	1812–14	25	41,080
John Foster & Son, Queensbury	Worsted manufacturers	1834–47	32	52,255
		1848–56	25	135,651
B. & W. Marriner, Keighley	Worsted spinners	1843–50	43	19,419

Sources: Gott, item 20 (B.); Clay, item 10 (Ha.), item 1 (B.), item 2 (Tolson Memorial Museum, Huddersfield (Kirklees District Archives)); Foster, items 10–17 (B.); Marriner: Ingle, 'A History of R. V. Marriner Ltd.', p. 154.

Gott's were by far the largest firm in the West Riding and were heavily involved in merchanting cloth. Their figures are not much use as a general indication of fixed to circulating ratios in the industry but their movement over time may be more representative of general trends, particularly for those concerns heavily involved in merchanting. Foster's were also unrepresentatively large by the 1840s and again had considerable interests in direct selling.

Despite the unrepresentative nature of the surviving evidence, it would appear that fixed capital amounting to between a third and a half of total capital may have been common by the second quarter of the nineteenth century. It must, however, be noted that our evidence for this period is from the worsted sector where the substitution of capital for labour was greatest by the 1820s and 1830s and this is almost certainly an overestimate of fixed capital proportions in the industry as a whole. In the early years of the century fixed capital for those firms like Gott's who were doing their own and additional merchanting was probably under 20% of total capital.

If we compare the contemporary estimates of total capital in the industry in 1800 made by Christopher Rawden of Halifax, Gott, and Ratcliffe of Saddleworth[67] with Jenkins' estimate of gross fixed capital at that date, it appears that the fixed to circulating ratio for the industry as a whole was as low as a sixth. However, fixed to circulating capital ratios varied greatly between different types of concern as well as chronologically. It seems likely that putting-out concerns held about 95% of their investments in stocks and trade credits. Dickenson has shown this to have been the case for eighteenth-century worsted concerns. Analysis of 137 inventories, mainly dating from mid-century, indicated that worsted concerns had ten times more invested in stocks than in tools and equipment. The typical woollen artisan had a much higher proportion of his capital invested in fixed capital at this time. Dickenson's analysis of 305 inventories for the period 1750–69 shows that woollen clothiers had just over a quarter of their textile capital tied up in tools and other fixed equipment.[68]

In the commission fulling, carding and scribbling mills which formed more than half the total number of mills in the woollen sector as late as 1834, the low level of stocks carried could well have resulted in a larger proportion of capital being invested in the buildings and machinery. However, as we shall see, these concerns commonly extended long credits to their customers especially where the mills were held in shares. It is perhaps not unreasonable to suppose that fixed capital represented about a third of total capital in the fulling and scribbling mills.

It appears that variations in the composition of manufacturing capital occurred not just over the long term and between firms but also cyclically with the trade cycle. Gott's increased the proportion of their capital in trade during the volatile years 1807–20 and Foster's circulating capital shows a marked increase in the late 1840s.[69] That these moves were representative of wider practices becomes clear in the detailed study of credit, stockholding and the trade cycle undertaken in Chapter 8.

The most important thing to note at this point is that for virtually all firms circulating capital figured more importantly than fixed capital throughout our period. Before the second quarter of the nineteenth century circulating capital represented, for most firms, an investment two or three times as large as that sunk in plant and equipment. Thus if we are to study industrial capital in any meaningful way a large section of the analysis must be devoted to the sources of circulating capital and credit. Furthermore, as fixed and circulating capital were rarely distinguished in contemporary accounts and as the two were often interchangeable, a study of the sources of circulating capital can yield valuable clues to the dynamic of fixed capital formation and industrial advance.

PART 2
THE PRIMARY ACCUMULATION
OF CAPITAL

Do not all strive to enjoy the land? The Gentry strive for land,
the clergy strive for land, and buying and selling is an art,
whereby people endeavour to cheat one another of the land.

Gerrard Winstanley, *A New Years Gift
for Parliament and Army* (1650)

INTRODUCTION

The first chapter of this Part examines the nature and implications of the 'proto-industrial' phase of development of the Yorkshire wool textile industry. It is argued that the proto-industrialisation thesis can be misleading because it oversimplifies the way in which rural industry emerged (in its many forms) and the mechanism of its transition to centralised production. From study of the West Riding it appears that contrasting structures of organisation of domestic production can only be understood by placing them squarely in the agrarian context and by viewing their development in relationship to a long history of the differential decline of manorialism and the enclosure and consolidation of landholdings. The mechanism of transition to factory production is similarly more complex and varied than the proto-industry theorists suggest – related to commercial and technological imperatives as well as to the wider environment of 'primary accumulation'.

Because the nature and structure of landholding emerges as such an important contextual feature of the 'proto-industrial phase', the second chapter of this Part looks more closely at the financial relationship between landowning and industrial development before 1850. The contribution of landowners to the finance of industry, both direct participation and loans, is considered. Finally the unique sources for studying the land market in the West Riding are utilised to provide a case study of the extent to which industrial finance was derived from the mortgage and sale of land and property by both artisans and early factory masters.

The use of the term 'primary accumulation' in the title of this section is important. The term and its variant, 'primitive accumulation', have a long history since Marx first conceived of a period of 'capitalist' accumulation preceding the emergence of the capitalist mode of production proper.[1] What he had in mind was a period during which land and the means of production were concentrated in fewer hands and when the labour force emerged as 'free' both of feudal and coercive obligations and free of ownership ties to the land. Since Marx, the term primitive accumulation has been at times confined to the accumulation of capitals which were then channelled into industrial investment and provided the foundation for rapid and revolutionary changes. Landes uses the term frequently in this sense in *The Unbound Prometheus*.[2] Gerschenkron similarly adopts a one sided interpretation of the concept in his major work.[3]

The use of the concept here is intended primarily to reflect the accumulation of capital in the proto-industrial sector and the ways in which this was utilised or channelled into intensive industrial development. However, it is impossible to analyse these developments without stress being placed on the concomitant growth of the wage-dependent and landless population. Primary accumulation as a concept recognises the importance of the transformation of the pre-industrial social structure to the growth and transformation of industry. This occurred through changes in the distribution of property (mainly land) and incomes over a long period. The aim here is to show how this occurred; how proto-industry evolved, how capital was accumulated and how property, particularly land, was used to raise industrial finance for the growth and gradual transformation of industry.

3
PROTO-INDUSTRIALISATION

The concept

The theoretical construct of a proto-industrial phase of European development, preceding and paving the way for industrialisation proper, has opened up a new perspective on development in early modern Europe.[1] At its best the proto-industrialisation thesis represents an attempt to consider 'total' history: economic, socio-cultural and political development together.[2] The model focusses on the manifold implications of the spread of rural domestic industry. This is related to the expansion of extra-regional trade and associated with distinctive and dynamic social and demographic changes. By applying the model as much to the failure of some areas to develop from proto-industry to centralised production as to the success of others, stress is also placed on exogenous and endogenous socio-political and economic variables acting on and within a particular region to determine its possibilities of transition or retrogression.[3]

Intimately connected with the concept of proto-industry is the emphasis placed upon the 'region' as the most viable unit of analysis for the study of industrialisation.[4] The areas of Europe where the spread of rural commercial industrial production was most marked generally exhibited a juxtaposition of contrasting zones which maintained different ecological systems. Zones of small peasant farms producing food below subsistence requirements, but supplementing this with a money income earned from the sale of craft goods, emerged as the concomitant of the specialisation of adjacent areas in large-scale commercial farming. Some historians see proto-industrialisation as a regional process of economic specialisation dependent upon the gradual evolution of comparative advantage in the production of either craft or agricultural commodities.[5] The comparative advantage of proto-industrial areas in the production of tradeable craft goods was encouraged by the seasonality endemic to temperate peasant agriculture[6] and by the soaking up of seasonal labour surpluses so created, by different forms of the domestic system.

It is argued that the 'phase' of proto-industrialisation was quite distinct from earlier rural industrial developments. The economic and social symbiosis between agriculture and industry across the seasons and the pervasive inter-relationship between the family economy and merchant capital constituted a fundamental break with the past. A distinct and dynamic socio-economic system emerged[7] which in many regions and in West Europe as a whole prepared the ground for even greater changes later.

Many dynamic elements are ascribed to the proto-industrial phase. It is argued that the traditional Malthusian demographic balance between population levels and agricultural resources was broken by the ability of peasants to earn an extra-agricultural income and buy part or all of their subsistence requirements. Earlier marriage, greater subdivision of agricultural holdings and the gradual emergence of a 'free' rural proletariat ensued. Large families were encouraged as children became a more important asset to the family economy.[8]

Primary accumulation was enhanced, not just on the part of the entrepreneurs of the domestic system but also in the commercial agricultural sector and in the towns stimulated by the increase in inter-regional trade and ancillary industry. Entrepreneurial and productive skills were also built up and extended in the phase of proto-industry.

Thus proto-industry exhibited a particular dynamic – but this also bore the seeds of its own destruction. Domestic industry could only expand extensively and rapidly rising marginal costs were the inherent result of extending putting-out enterprises over wide geographical areas. As competition increased, production deadlines became both more important and more difficult to ensure in the absence of a regulated workforce, and the appropriation by the peasant producer of materials for his own use became a question not of traditional perquisite but of criminal embezzlement.[9]

The specific differential profit which the putting-out capitalist had been able to realise from the self-exploitation tendency of the peasant household economy[10] was nullified by the increasingly important problems of labour discipline. The backward sloping supply curve for labour came into play in exactly those situations of potential growth in which the capitalist could have obtained the maximum profits. This inherent limit of the proto-industrial system led either beyond itself to industrial capitalism or retreated, in the face of competition, from proto-industry to sweating or to deindustrialisation.

This theoretical framework, illuminating and satisfying in the abstract, poses problems when applied as an heuristic device to detailed empirical study. The traits of a distinct socio-economic 'system' are ascribed to the phase of proto-industry. This implies the prevalence of a particular level of development of the forces of production, and of the social relations of production, as well as a distinct and identifiable dynamic which impels the 'system' (*ceteris paribus*) towards the emergence of industrial capitalism. It is thus a fundamental problem that the proto-industrial model ignores the forms of centralised and partially centralised production so common by the early modern period.[11] Can the mining, metallurgical and building industries be incorporated within the model in some way or do they exhibit quite different economic, social and demographic characteristics, and different internal dynamics equally relevant to our understanding of the transition to industrial capitalism?

The problem of the proto-industry model is not confined to the lack of emphasis on centralised industries nor to the more serious neglect of the independent vitality and dynamism of towns and cities. It extends to the blanket nature of the model's conception of the emergence and dynamic of rural industry itself. Several recent works have emphasised the polymorphic nature of proto-industry in practice, and the immense variety of organisational and domestic structures found in rural manufacturing.[12] Within European proto-industry considerable differences of structure occurred between regions, between industries and between branches of the same industry. There were also marked changes in structures over time. This is largely associated with the concrete production processes of different industries.

At one extreme was a *Kaufsystem* of independent artisan producers using their own raw materials and tools and selling their finished products openly in the public market place for cash. At the other pole were *Verlags-systems* where domestic workers were employed as wage-dependent labourers and provided, at the cost of their independence, with everything from raw materials to tools and credit. In this latter case the worker's status was little different from that of an industrial proletarian labourer. Unlike the artisan of the *Kaufsystem*, his or her ownership ties to the land had become tenuous or non-existent and he or she depended entirely on the sale of his or her labour power. Between these two extremes existed a broad spectrum of organisational forms with their associated mix of agriculture and industry and their different household and property structures.

In some proto-industrial areas the family remained markedly the unit both of production and consumption. In others it was not the case that the numerous stages of a production process were performed co-operatively by household members. In 'advanced' forms of the putting-out system whole regions tended to specialise in the production of one particular component which was not a commodity in itself.[13] These household structures of production left little scope for ancillary juvenile tasks and may well have encouraged quite different familial and demographic changes to those found in 'co-operative' households where the work of children and women was crucially important.

The diversity of proto-industrial structures cannot be incorporated into the model simply by assuming that each represents a different stage

in some progressive and linear evolution towards modern factory production. This seems not to fit with the facts. So-called 'advanced' forms
of the putting-out system with well-developed regional specialisation of
labour, high degrees of wage dependency and increasing divorce of
labour from the land often proved to be a dead-end developmentally.
Deindustrialisation often followed, as in the case of Languedoc, or the
transition to factory production was slow and incomplete, as in the case
of Flanders and the West Country of England. One can also find
examples like the West Riding woollen industry where the transition to
factory production was not preceded by widespread rural proletarianisation caused by advances in the putting-out system. Unlike other woollen cloth areas of England, which Yorkshire surpassed in the eighteenth
century (and in the transition to factory production), proto-industry was
conducted largely by independent rural and semi-rural craft workers.
The diverse nature of proto-industrial structures leads one to question
generalised notions regarding their emergence and the particular dynamic embodied in them.

The West Riding with its contrasting structures of rural industry provides a potentially fruitful subject for research and testing some of the
premises and the generalisations of the proto-industry model. In particular and in the context of this study of the accumulation and concentration
of industrial capital two questions seem of particular relevance:

1. How does one explain variations in the organisation and development of
   proto-industry in the different branches of the trade?
2. Following on and related to the first question, how did these variations in
   the organisation of rural production affect the propensity for capital accumulation and hence the progressive revolutionising of the industry in the
   long term?

There are several well-rehearsed arguments which help to explain why
proto-industry, in its different forms, existed in Yorkshire by the eighteenth century. The general precondition for the spread of rural industry
in the area was twofold: the insufficiency of agriculture, through much of
the Riding, to provide the subsistence needs of a growing population and
a tradition of peasant skills in woollen cloth production for household
and local needs based on the use of local wools. This general environment was given further stimulus by the expansion of Britain's textile
trade with southern Europe and across the Atlantic, as well as by buoyant domestic demand conditions in the early eighteenth century.

We have noted that although in practice the divide was by no means
clear-cut two quite distinct domestic industry structures can be recognised within the wool textile industry by the mid-eighteenth century.
However, there was nothing in the nature of the production processes of
woollen textiles which dictated that they should be produced on a
Kaufsystem rather than on a putting-out basis. Indeed, in the West

Country the manufacture of woollen cloth was dominated by large-scale clothiers who put out wool to journeymen and their families to complete the various stages of production. The Gloucestershire trade was conducted by no more than 400 clothiers whereas in the West Riding there were at least 3,500 broadcloth manufacturers alone.[14]

The reason for the persistence in the West Riding of the traditional artisan structure, even in conditions of expanding commercial opportunity, is not easy to explain in simple terms. Miss J. de L. Mann has argued that the organisational contrast between Yorkshire and the West Country was determined by the type of cloth produced and that it would have been impossible to produce superfine cloth, with its expensive raw materials, on the Yorkshire system.[15] Yorkshire's rise to pre-eminence in the eighteenth century was certainly based on the production of cheap goods, 'cheap and nasty' as rivals in Norwich and the West Country maintained.[16] But finer cloths using high grade wool were by no means unknown especially in the Leeds and Huddersfield areas. Whilst not dismissing this argument, it clearly does not explain why extensive putting-out systems did not emerge in the Yorkshire case. After all, the worsted branch in Yorkshire was equally famed for its cheap goods. New and interesting light can be shed on this question by considering why the woollen/worsted organisational contrast manifested itself in a particular kind of spatial distribution. It was noted in Chapter 2 that even as early as the late seventeenth century different areas of the West Riding specialised in the production of different types of woollen cloths (see Map 1). By the late eighteenth century the worsted producing area had become clearly defined geographically, associated with the westerly areas of higher ground and sparser agricultural resources (See Map 2). Where worsted production had emerged in the eighteenth century outside of the western area, it tended not to develop an advanced putting-out structure and was relatively short-lived.[17]

What was it about the western region, particularly about Halifax Parish which determined that it would become the main seat of the worsted putting-out industry? To answer this question the agricultural environment and the social and political structure must be considered together with the distribution and characteristics of proto-industry as it obtained before the spread of large-scale worsted production.

The agrarian and institutional environment

A great many contemporary topographical descriptions of the West Riding survive for the late eighteenth century[18] providing a fairly detailed picture of the agricultural structure of the region from the early seventeenth century to the industrial revolution period.

It seems that there were three identifiable agricultural zones of the textile producing area. The first covered about a third of the West Riding as a whole extending from just west of Bradford to the western extremity of the county. This area was to become almost contiguous with the worsted region. It comprised upland and pasture where grass was the chief object and where little arable cultivation was possible. On the higher ground of this zone were immense tracts of waste generally held in common by the local inhabitants and pastured by them in cattle and sheep. Some were stinted, but the greater part were under no limitations and stock quality was very poor. The second zone comprised the lands adjoining the manufacturing towns where

the greatest part of the ground is occupied by persons who do not consider farming as a business but regard it only as a matter of convenience. The manufacturer has his enclosure where he keeps milk cows for supporting his family and horses for carrying his goods to market and bringing back raw materials.[19]

Bigland suggests that the common and optimum size of manufacturers' farms was 15–16 acres.[20] Some corn was grown in these more fertile areas. Thirdly, there existed a zone lying roughly east of a line drawn from Leeds through Wakefield where tillage was the main concern and grass only considered as a 'means of bringing corn husbandry to perfection'.[21] There was less wasteland in this zone but more land was farmed in common fields than was the case in the manufacturing area proper. At least one writer suggests that pressure from cloth manufacturers may have encouraged earlier enclosure and consolidation of farms in the mid-West Riding.[22] A compact plot with firm entitlement was not just more efficient for the manufacturer on the farming side of his activities, but was also a tangible property by which to be assessed and on which to raise trade credit and loans.[23]

Each of these agricultural zones had different social and economic characteristics. All contemporary accounts stress the prevalence of small proprietors throughout the manufacturing area: 'there are few parts of the Kingdom where this respectable class is more numerous'.[24] There were, however, considerable variations in the size of agricultural holdings between zones. In the arable easterly areas and in the river valleys there were few farms bigger than 400 acres and most were less than 50 acres.[25] Land was in even smaller allotments in the grazing areas. A farm of 100 acres would be considered large in the western grass zone.[26] Landholdings seem to have been particularly small in the upland areas such as those which formed the bulk of Halifax Parish. According to Defoe the hills around the town 'were spread with enclosures from 2 acres to 6 or 7 each, seldom more, and every three or four pieces of land had a house belonging to them'.[27] This area contrasted with those like the Aire valley which was the preserve of corn farms in larger holdings.

The extent of agricultural self-sufficiency, as well as the seasonality and regimes of farming in the different zones, made for different mixes of agriculture and industry. In the western zones, especially around Halifax, one finds the earliest evidence of the inability of agriculture to supply even the barest of subsistence needs and the spur to proto-industrial activity which this created. Ellis finds evidence of this as early as the fourteenth century[28] but it is in the preamble to the Halifax Act of 1555 that one gets a clear indication of the importance of rural industry in supporting the local population and allowing an increase in the number of households. It is important to note that this preamble also indicates that weaving and spinning were often carried out in separate households even at this early date.

Forasmuche as the Paryshe of Halyfaxe and other places theronto adjoyning, beyng planted in the grete waste and moores, where the Fertilite of Ground ys not apte to bryng forthe any Corne nor good Grasse, but in rare Places, and by exceedinge and greate industrye of the inhabitantes, and the same inhabitantes altogether doo lyve by cloth making, for the greate parte of them neyther getye the Corne nor ys hable to keep a Horse to carry Woolles, nor yet to by much woolle at once, but hathe ever used onelie to repayre to the Towne of Halyfaxe, and some other nye theronto, and ther to bye upon the Woolldryver, some a stone, some twoo, and some three or foure accordinge to theyre habilitee, and to carrye the same to theire houses, some iij, iiij, v, and vj myles of, upon their Heddes and Backes, and so to make and converte the same eyther into Yarn or Clothe, and to sell the same, and so to bye more Woolle..., by means of whiche Industrye the barreyn Gronde in those partes be nowe much inhabyted, and above fyve hindrethe householdes there newly increased within theis fourtye yeares past.[29]

One gets the impression from this quote that in the late sixteenth century landholdings were small and becoming smaller. Partible inheritance was much more widely practised in highland than in lowland Britain and was associated with pastoral regions not firmly held together by manorial discipline and where the family thus remained the most powerful agent of social control and discipline.[30] As we shall see, Halifax Parish was a classic example of this sort of environment. There as elsewhere partible inheritance may have been further encouraged by the ability to earn a living outside of the agricultural sector.

The inability of land in the Halifax area to support anything other than livestock grazing and the cultivation of a little oats, coupled with the small size of agricultural holdings, meant that it became the earliest site of extensive proto-industrial development in the West Riding. By the early eighteenth century it was dominated by the lower grade of independent clothiers who worked with their own family, seldom additional outworkers, and usually produced one piece of cloth weekly. Not surprisingly the kersey emerged as the staple product of the area. A document of 1588 indicates that six people were required to produce a kersey cloth in one week and Heaton has suggested that there was a distinct connection between the labour required to produce a kersey cloth and the normal size of clothiers' households in the area.[31] In addition to these households others devoted themselves to producing yarn or weaving cloth: a division of labour of which there is little evidence in other parts of the Riding at this time. Because of the prevalence of grazing and the small size of arable undertakings, labour demands in agriculture were fairly constant throughout the year leaving a permanent pool of unemployed or under-employed labour for commercial industrial production.[32] This may have tended towards greater reliance on industry and the growth of putting-out systems of production which required a greater constancy of labour throughout the year than was imperative to the artisan structure. By the eighteenth century the whole of the western region relied for much of its basic food requirements, particularly the staple diet of oats, on trade with the central and eastern parts of Yorkshire.[33]

The small clothiers of the Halifax area, living from hand to mouth with little agricultural resources and often on the brink of starvation, contrasted with the larger concerns found in the lowland areas especially around Leeds. Here, we have noted, agriculture was more varied and the land more fertile. Even as late as the end of the eighteenth century the mixed cloth area and the lower Calder and Aire valleys had a degree of self-sufficiency in basic foodstuffs.[34] The arable harvest of the area was such that seasonal variations in labour demands were considerable: 'In harvest the manufacturers generally leave their looms, and assist in reaping the crop.'[35]

There were small clothiers in this area but the characteristic proto-industrial unit was larger than that found in the west. Especially around Leeds, substantial clothiers employing several journeymen and apprentices were common. Not surprisingly one finds that the types of cloth produced in the Aire and Calder valleys included a large proportion of broad-cloths, which required considerable capital investment in looms and other equipment; and fine broads which required supervision, skill and attention to detail.

The narrow cloth zone was dominated, like much of the western area, by clothiers with little capital and land. Much of the area was contiguous with the highland farming zone, infertile and held in small plots. The area also contained fertile low land around Huddersfield and in the lower Colne valley. Here larger artisan clothiers were found supervising the workshop production of fine and fancy cloths.

The contrasts in size and nature of woollen clothiers' assets in the different agricultural zones is detailed in Tables 3.1, 3.2 and 3.3. The inventory figures used in these tables are from registered wills whose making and survival obviously exhibits a bias in favour of the larger clothiers. Thus the high proportion of clothiers in the Halifax zone with assets under £75 is almost certainly an underestimate of the number of very small concerns there.

It is also interesting to note at this point that the western zone and, particularly, Halifax Parish relied on export markets for about 90% of their

Table 3.1 *Zonal size distribution of clothiers' inventories, 1689–1769*

Zone	Average value of clothiers' net assets to nearest £	% of clothiers with assets	
		Over £400	Under £75
A	51	1.5	76
B	60	1.0	71
C	64	2.0	73
D	74	3.0	68

Note: A = Halifax kersey zone; B = narrow cloth zone; C = white cloth zone; D = mixed cloth zone. See Map 1.
Source: Based on data from Dickenson, 'The West Riding Woollen and Worsted Industries'.

Table 3.2 *Proportions of clothiers' total assets invested in agriculture and textiles, 1689–1769[a]*

Zone	% in agriculture	% in textiles
A	27	15
B	29	17
C	29	19
D	19	38

[a] Excludes household and personal assets and credits.
Note: For zone code see Table 3.1.
Source: Based on data from Dickenson, 'The West Riding Woollen and Worsted Industries'.

cloth sales by the 1770s, whereas other parts of the Riding had a sizeable proportion of their output (20–50%) destined for home consumption. The home market was generally less vulnerable to extreme fluctuations than was foreign demand. Some indication of the nature of markets for the different types of Yorkshire goods in the second half of the eighteenth century is given in Table 3.4.

Having said something about the agrarian environment of the various proto-industrial sub-regions of the West Riding, their institutional and social structure must be briefly considered.[36] The different ecological zones with their different farm sizes naturally gave rise to different income distributions and different social structures. Independent political factors also played a role in determining the socio-economic matrix of each area.

The most notable feature of landholding throughout the West Riding as early as the seventeenth century was the ubiquity of freehold as

Table 3.3 *Investment in agriculture by woollen clothiers, 1689–1769*

Zone	% arable	% livestock	% tools and implements	Total average investment in agriculture (£.s)
A	20.4	74.7	4.9	18.04
B	26.9	64.2	8.9	20.13
C	36.8	56.3	6.9	21.12
D	40.5	50.4	9.1	16.19

Note: For zone code see Table 3.1.
Source: Based on data from Dickenson, 'The West Riding Woollen and Worsted Industries'.

Table 3.4 *Proportions of various West Riding textile goods exported and for home consumption, 1772*

	Zone	% export	% home consumption
Broad cloth	C/D	90	10
Narrow cloth	A/B	20	80
Blankets	C/D	67	33
Bays and Rochdale goods	A	80	20
Kerseys and half thicks	A	90	10
Long wool manufactures (largely worsteds)	A/C	80	20

Note: For zone code see Table 3.1.
Source: Estimate of Thomas Wolrich, Leeds merchant, 1772, quoted in Bischoff, *A Comprehensive History*, vol. 1, pp. 187–9.

opposed to copyhold tenure. The contemporary literature gives the impression that perhaps as much as half to three-quarters of the farming land of the Riding was held in this way by the mid-eighteenth century. Nowhere was this more the case than in the Parish of Halifax, where copyhold land was rare by the early eighteenth century.

The great period of enfranchisement in Halifax Parish had occurred in the late sixteenth and early seventeenth centuries accompanied by sizeable enclosures of waste for sheep rearing. This had several consequences. First, manorial control was weakened. By the 1670s new civil township authorities dominated by substantial freeholders were running parochial affairs and by the 1760s with the emergence of new municipal bodies most manifestations of manorialism had entirely disappeared.[37] This created an environment in which partible inheritance would almost certainly be encouraged.

Enfranchisement and enclosure together also resulted, as one might expect, in a tendency towards social polarisation. On the one hand emerged sizeable freeholders and leaseholders, and on the other hand a class of cottagers and the landless. It is no accident that the late seventeenth and early eighteenth centuries saw the relative decline in numbers of independent clothiers in the township of Halifax and in the out-townships. They were gradually replaced by more specialised occupations: weavers (often putting-out work on spinning and other processes), spinners and combers.[38] Early enfranchisement and enclosure encouraged the accumulation of capital in the hands of some and a greater wage dependency on the part of others by the mid-eighteenth century. In retrospect this can be seen to have paved the way for the growth of putting-out systems of worsted production. It seems that these developments in the sub-manor of Halifax were unusual in their scale when compared to the West Riding as a whole.

Thus, to recapitulate, the putting-out structure of the worsted branch developed apace in the western area of the Riding from the mid-eighteenth century. It found a propitious environment in an area of infertile upland and pasture where land was held in small farms and plots and where pools of labour were underemployed throughout the year. This area had previously supported kersey manufacture by domestic households often living on the brink of subsistence, and increasingly relying on their textile earnings to provide basic foodstuffs. At the same time the independence and viability of these households was threatened by the subdivision of holdings and by the rise of larger textile freeholders and leaseholders who developed putting-out systems, employing spinners and weavers on piece rates. The viability of these small domestic concerns was further undermined by their heavy reliance on the fluctuating fortunes of foreign markets. It is not surprising that the biggest shift into worsted production on a piece rate basis came with the drying up of the markets for 'northern dozens' (kerseys) in the 1750s.

It appears that the more fertile agricultural holdings of the white and mixed cloth zones imparted a greater resilience to the independent artisan structure. These areas, apart from the city of Leeds, were also historically more dominated by traditional manorial controls, had more copyhold land and were later enclosed. These factors, together, may have retarded the emergence in the countryside of a sizeable cottager and landless class. This seems to have been particularly true of the Manor of Wakefield outside the sub-manor of Halifax.[39]

The degree of reliance on foreign markets with their inherent instability was also less outside of the Halifax kersey zone. This may have been a further factor in the survival of the independent artisan structure. Narrow cloths were particularly geared to the domestic market which accounted for about 80% of sales by the mid-eighteenth century.[40] This may help to explain the persistence of the small clothier in the highland areas above Huddersfield long after his demise in the neighbouring Parish of Halifax, despite similarities in the agricultural environment, but it cannot be a completely satisfactory explanation when many areas of artisan production had a healthy existence, despite being geared to the export trade.

A more convincing reason for the persistence of the artisan structure in the Colne valley is found in its institutional history. The Manors of Huddersfield Almondbury, Marsden, Slaithwaite, Whitely and Saddleworth were tightly and traditionally administered until the late eighteenth century and beyond.[41] Sykes, the Huddersfield historian writing in 1898, noted that some of the Dartmouth estates in Slaithwaite were even then held in precarious tenancy[42] and, until the copyhold agitation and court cases of the mid-nineteenth century, the Ramsden manors around Huddersfield were controlled to such an extent that 'supposed transfers were altogether ineffectual'.[43] The annual Ramsden rent audit as late as 1846 had a feudal atmosphere[44] and it was not until 1920 that the town of Huddersfield finally bought itself free of the Ramsden possessions.[45] The Court Leet records of the Manor of Wakefield indicate just how communal the system of agriculture still was in the late seventeenth century and copyhold land remained ubiquitous in the Wapentake of Agbrigg (which covered the south of the West Riding) until the twentieth century.[46] The strength of manorialism and its implications for property rights, the market in land and the formation of a wage-dependent proletariat, may be the main explanation for the persistence of small concerns using family labour in these areas to the west and south of the textile region.

There are also examples of worsted production outside of the western zone which deserve attention because their experience highlights the importance of some of the environmental factors already stressed. By the 1770s, the production of tammies, wildbores and camblets had found a foothold in the mid-Calder and upper Dearne valleys, alongside the traditional broadcloth production. It seems that the industry was largely composed of independent artisans employing journeymen and assistants and some outworkers but not developed on a large-scale putting-out basis. Of these artisans, 140 subscribed to the building of the Tammy Hall in Wakefield in 1777.[47] As early as the 1790s, however, the trade of the hall was declining and the main seat of tammy production removed to the Bradford area where it was the province of much larger putting-out and factory enterprises. Contemporaries placed blame for the decline of worsted production in the Wakefield area squarely on the shoulders of the rigidities of the traditional artisan structure in coping with the rapid growth and nature of demand in that sector. Clarkson, the Wakefield historian of the late nineteenth century, attributed the demise of the Tammy Hall to the trustees' insistence that a seven-year apprenticeship be served by all offering goods for sale.[48] A local newspaper of 1850 blamed the clothiers for refusing to admit lighter cloths (for colonial and

3
Typical domestic spinning/weaving premises of the East Pennines, *c.* 1760
Source: Photograph taken in 1985 by the author.

4
Woollen clothier's 'farm', mid–late eighteenth century
Source: Photograph taken in 1985 by the author.

foreign use) for sale in their building until as late as 1811.[49] It may have been simply a question of the inability of the artisan structure to compete with the greater efficiency and division of labour in the putting-out system, particularly as the cheaper unglazed tammy for foreign markets was gaining greater popularity at the expense of the finer cloths made earlier by the artisans for home demand.

The precarious position of the cottager in the highland zone made him more receptive to the idea of working for an employer on a piece rate basis. Once worsted spinning or weaving had gained a foothold in this area, it grew free of the traditional barriers to entry and rules regarding standards. These were a feature of the older-established woollen manufacture in the artisan tradition throughout the eighteenth century.

From manor to mill

How did the different proto-industrial structures evolve to create the factory system which was coming to dominate most areas of the Yorkshire wool textile industry by the mid-nineteenth century? How was capital accumulated and the transition to centralised, mechanised production achieved? Who formed the first generation of factory employers and employees and what was their earlier proto-industrial role?

Insofar as the proto-industry model sheds light on these questions, one would expect the build-up of capital, skills and experience in the hands of the proto-industrial entrepreneurs, as well as the formation of a wage-dependent rural proletariat, to be of crucial importance in determining the speed and nature of the transition to centralised production. To the extent that this was the case, one would further expect the 'more advanced' proto-industrial structure of the worsted sector to be more fruitful in creating the preconditions for factory production than the artisan structure of the woollen branch.

It is difficult, however, to make a straightforward comparison between the woollen and worsted branches in this respect because factors exogenous to the dynamic created by proto-industrial expansion appear to have been of crucial importance. In particular, the different raw materials, products and processes of the industries resulted in very different organisational and technological possibilities and incentives. Where more expensive raw materials, such as Spanish wool, were being used, as in the Leeds area broadcloth trade and in Huddersfield fancy cloths in the late eighteenth century, or where uniformity of quality was important, the advantages of centralised production would appear considerable. Cost reduction was another spur to centralisation in trades where competition was particularly fierce or where the demand for products was highly price elastic. This was the case with much of worsted production and with the cheaper ranges of plain woollen goods such as blankets. Considerable economies in costs could be achieved purely by centralising production without technical change. In 1795 Aiken considered that Yorkshire manufacturers could gain as much as a third greater production from a centralised workforce.[50] This advantage was probably much greater in prosperous years when the backward sloping supply curve for domestic labour may have affected putting-out concerns. In periods of depression factory manufacturers were forced to work below capacity despite high fixed overhead costs. Not surprisingly many early factory entrepreneurs hedged their bets by having a putting-out interest in addition to their centralised units.[51]

Equally important in influencing the transition to factory production in the two branches of industry were the different processes involved, and their adaptability to mechanisation. We have seen in Chapter 2 that carding and scribbling, the preparatory processes of woollen production, were easily adapted to water power from the 1770s and later steam. In the worsted sector, by contrast, combing proved the most intractable problem for innovation and was the last major process to be mechanised. Apart from the preparatory processes, the longer-stapled worsted wools were much more suited to mechanical handling. The powered spinning of worsteds quickly followed that of cotton whereas woollen spinning followed two or three decades behind. Even mechanical weaving was more difficult for short-stapled fibres and for fancy patterns which delayed its adoption in most areas of the woollen branch by several decades.[52] By the 1860s the worsted industry was fully a factory business including many large, horizontally integrated mills. The woollen branch at this time still had a sizeable element of its production in the hands of domestic workers. According to Clapham: 'In 1866 the hand weavers managed about a quarter of the looms; they still had some importance twenty years later.'[53] Some of these hand weavers were working in factories but others could be found working in their own homes as late as the last quarter of the nineteenth century. Although some large mills existed in the woollen sector the typical centralised concern was much smaller than in the worsted sector throughout the nineteenth century and vertical integration rather than horizontal specialisation tended to prevail.

Obviously, technical influences were important in bringing about these contrasts but if we accept that much early factory development occurred in the first instance in order to achieve organisational economies and efficiency,[54] and not according to technological dictates, then there is much left to explain. If it is further acknowledged that prior concentrations of capital were an important prerequisite of large-scale factory growth, the transition to centralised production in the Yorkshire case can be directly related to the proto-industrial structures and their implications.

One important aspect of the growth of factory production in both branches of the industry seems to have been the role played by merchant capital; we noted in Chapter 1 that the significance of merchant capital and initiative in industrial change is much debated and this is particularly true in the case of the West Riding historiography.

In order to consider the extent to which merchants directly involved themselves in factory production and to consider in broader terms the accumulation of capital and its investment in mill construction, the picture may be clarified by separate discussion of the two branches of the industry as they began to evolve from proto-industry to centralised and mechanised production.

Growth in the woollen branch was associated, as we have seen, with two major developments: the use of water and later steam power in carding and scribbling which led to their development alongside fulling in the traditional mills and the emergence of the merchant-manufacturer who tended to bring many of the processes of production under one roof, creating the earliest proper 'factories' in this branch of the industry. Some of these merchant-manufacturers originated from the development of direct dealing by the merchant with the clothiers and the gradual absorption and subordination of the latter by the former. Other factory manufacturers developed where the larger clothiers themselves decided to bypass the halls and the mercantile group and do their own dressing and finishing and their own marketing. All the evidence suggests that the latter road was the more important, despite the existence of some important exceptions such as Benjamin Gott who was responsible for the building of by far the largest woollen mill in the West Riding in the period.

If direct mercantile involvement was important anywhere it was likely to be so in the towns. Table 3.5 indicates that only about one in six mills in Huddersfield and Leeds had been built and were being run by persons of mercantile origin. Even with these individuals it is difficult to be certain if their mercantile involvement pre-dated participation in manufacturing. What is particularly interesting here is the extent to which woollen manufacturers with little or no obvious mercantile involvement were occupying if not actually owning these early mills.

Further justification for holding the view that the majority of early woollen mills were occupied and run, if not entirely financed, by manufacturers previously involved in proto-industry rather than by wealthy mercantile concerns, lies in the fact that the size and cost of a competitive mill remained small in the woollen branch until well into the nineteenth century. A large number were converted from existing corn mills and a few from malt kilns and similar buildings. More importantly, tenancy and multiple tenancy of mills was common throughout the period. It was

Table 3.5 *Ownership and occupancy of woollen mills in Huddersfield and Leeds before 1835[a]*

Town	Owned and occupied by 'merchants' or 'merchant-manufacturers'	Owned and occupied by woollen manufacturers	Occupied or part-occupied by woollen manufacturers
Huddersfield	4	5	13
Leeds	5	8	22

[a] Excludes cloth finishing mills.
Sources: Insurance valuations, the bulk derived from working papers of D. T. Jenkins, University of York, West Riding directories and miscellaneous sources. Hereafter indicated as Card Index.

not unusual to find mills with ten or twelve occupancies.[55] A small woollen mill could be rented for £100 to £150 per annum in the early nineteenth century and room and power for as little as £10 to £20.[56] This, together with the slow progress of technology, the experience and participation of clothiers in centralised production in the scribbling mills and the relative ease of raising finance on mortgage of both freehold and copyhold land and property,[57] smoothed the passage of the larger woollen clothiers into factory production.

The household unit of production was still the most viable in most branches of woollen production before 1850 particularly when use was made of the public and company scribbling mills. Even in 1844, John Nussey, woollen manufacturer of Birstal commented:

The woollen manufacture of this district may still be termed domestic. Many of the small clothiers have shares in the mills and those who have no interest in the mills enjoy the advantages of them. Wool is generally bought sorted of the stapler and sent to the mill for scribbling and slubbing for which a small sum is paid per lb. weight. It is then returned to the clothier who spins and weaves and looks after the processes of manufacture at his own home. It is again sent to the mill to be fulled. The clothier then prepares it for market and it is sold in bulk in the cloth halls to the merchant who dyes and finishes it.[58]

It would seem that once the *Kaufsystem* had survived the eighteenth century it tended to remain fairly competitive with the factory until well into the nineteenth century. The volatility of the trade cycle, particularly as it affected the cheaper end of the market and export trades, was felt relatively harder by factory producers with their high overheads than it was by the traditional dual occupational structure of the artisans. The agricultural holding was still a valuable cushion against hard times and the self-exploitation mechanism of the proto-industrial family economy, compared with the greater rigidities of wage labour, were a matter of note by contemporaries such as Thomas Bischoff, manager of the Leeds branch of the Bank of England:

the domestic manufacturers have been able to make the low qualities of cloth and particularly the sorts suited to the American market, upon lower terms than the larger factories ... the shippers for America have therefore during the last year made their principle purchases from the manufacturers who bring their goods to the cloth halls for sale.[59]

Thirty years earlier the importance of the long hours worked by cloth manufacturing households had been stressed before Parliament: 'You mean people working in their own cottages work extra hours to get more for their families which advantage cannot be allowed in a factory? ... Undoubtedly ... in a factory you confine them to the hours the master pleases, in the cottage they work very often 15 or 16 hours.'[60]

The proto-industrial model stresses the differential profit accruing to the putting-out capitalist through his ability to pay his workers a wage below the subsistence level but the artisan structure had the same sort of inherent flexibility of labour costs as illustrated in the following quote from the diary of a factory manager faced with a strike in 1820. We here have some clues regarding the long-term survival of proto-industry in its sweating forms:

The men who have turned out for additional wages ... are supported in it by many of the lesser manufactuers whose interest is evidently consulted [sic] by such support to the men employed by the larger manufacturers: inasmuch as the high wages demanded by the workmen, if complied with, would be a kind of bounty on the goods of the small manufacturer, who will be satisfied to sell their wares at a much less rate than manufacturers can do who pay wages for work done.[61]

The gradual demise of the proto-industrial structure in woollen production was accelerated in the 1840s by the speed of factory mechanisation of spinning and weaving. The problem of competing gradually ceased to be solely a question of comparative costs but as mass production increased, markets became periodically overstocked and profit rates in the industry fell.[62] As contemporaries recognised, only large-scale production could compensate for the low rate of profit:

[Profit] ... is smaller than it ever has been before, but they [the factory manufacturers] consider the quantity makes up for the low rate of profit.[63]

People now produce a larger amount of wealth and get more for it, but do not get as large a proportion of what they produce as formerly.[64]

Except in a few very specialised trades of hand production, domestic weaving became a sweated trade by the 1860s and then gradually disappeared.

When one comes to consider the transition to factory production in the worsted sector a different pattern of development and a different relationship to the proto-industrial structure emerges. It is quite clear that the putting-out system was creating considerable inefficiencies and diseconomies in the increasingly competitive environment of the late eighteenth century. In particular, frauds committed by the workers became increasingly problematic. This was a difficulty not generally experienced in the woollen branch because there were fewer waged workers, and those there were tended to be closely supervised in small workshops. In the worsted branch, however, wool combers commonly embezzled their employers' wool and the spinners reeled 'false' or short yarn. Combinations of operatives were often successful in ensuring that these appropriations continued with impunity,[65] despite attempts by the Worsted Committee to stamp it out.[66]

The growth rate of the Yorkshire worsted industry in the late eighteenth century, particularly the expansion of overseas markets, was faster than that of the woollen trade. This put sudden intense strains on the putting-out system. As we have seen, worsted yarn proved suitable for the Arkwright technique of mechanical spinning and thus benefited greatly from the developed technology of the cotton industry.[67] The change to power spinning on the Arkwright system required the construction of a four- or five-storey mill to make use of the power of a water wheel or steam engine and so imposed a minimum upon the scale at which the process could be brought into the mill by a single firm.[68]

It is almost certain that the key figures in initiating the building of the first worsted factories were capitalists who already had experience of running putting-out concerns, and had accumulated capital in that sector. Surviving records of businesses such as J. T. Clay & Sons Ltd of Rastrick, John Foster & Son of Queensbury, Richard Lister of Keighley, B. & W. Marriner of Keighley, T. & M. Bairstow Ltd of Sutton in Craven and many others certainly bear this out.[69] Furthermore, both Hodgson and Cudworth, the nineteenth-century local historians of Keighley and Bradford respectively, cite many examples of putting-out capitalists becoming factory entrepreneurs.[70] The other really important source of enterprise in early worsted mills seems to have come from persons formerly involved in the cotton trade or in wool stapling.[71] The high threshold of entry into factory worsted production and the prior accumulation of capital in that sector in the hands of merchant-manufacturers of the domestic system meant that there was very little upward mobility into factory production on the part of small clothiers. There are few examples of small factory producers renting room and power in a mill in the worsted sector and the majority of all worsted mills traced in the West Riding before 1850 were owner-occupied.[72]

The vast majority of woollen mills (about 70% of those whose owners and occupiers are identifiable) appear to have been both owned and occupied by woollen manufacturers. Many of these were heavily mortgaged to merchants, bankers and others, however. About 10% were owned by landowners and the rest by a remarkably diverse group of merchants, millwrights, ironworks owners, wiredrawers, bankers, bookkeepers, dyers and brewers. In the worsted industry the main owners and builders of mills appear to have been merchant-manufacturers, including putting-out capitalists, wool staplers, merchants and entrepreneurs previously involved in cotton, flax and even silk spinning.

The company mill

The company mill is worthy of separate analysis, not only because it became an important element of the proto-industrial structure, supporting the continued viability of the small artisanal concerns who were its main shareholders and customers, but also because its history is linked in a direct way with the agrarian and institutional environment described earlier.

From the first introduction of machinery the clothiers united to build mills in shares. At first a few and on a small scale as experiments by the more enterprising, then more extensively as the success of their neighbours and the increase of trade naturally and gradually led to the extension of the system up to the present time. The numerous woollen mills scattered throughout the populous clothing villages of the West Riding are principally owned and occupied by clothiers in shares.[73]

Company mills were a widespread form of endeavour in the woollen branch in the 1780s and 1790s and through the first half of the nineteenth century.[74] In the 1780s the demand for fulling and scribbling services began seriously to outstrip the supply offered by the traditional 'public mills' resulting in much inconvenience and delay for the clothiers. In 1785, for example, the fulling mills of the Ossett district were reported to be insufficient for the increasing demands of the trade:

[which renders] the clothmaker liable to infinite Grievances and Oppression, by obliging him very often to sell his cloths unmilled at an under price, in order to get returns for the Employment and Support of his Family and frequently to disapt [sic] his merchant from whom he received orders unless to get his cloths milled in time he consent to give some extra-ordinary premium or reward . . .
. . . the Woollen cloth manufacturers in and about Wakefield and Ossett . . . especially in the Dry seasons, hath been several times of late years greatly hindered and almost totally stopped by the Insufficiency of the Fulling Mills already being there . . . it is essentially necessary to the due Encouragement of the said Trade to erect the new Fulling Mill.[75]

The mill referred to in the above quotation was possibly the first company mill in the country although there is evidence that by the first decade of the nineteenth century they were numerous in the Leeds and

Wakefield areas. How were these mills organised and financed and what sorts of clothiers participated in their establishment?

Goodchild has isolated three distinct types of company mill distinguished by their source of finance.[76] First, there were those financed and bought or erected by a partnership of merchants and clothiers. The Ossett Mill Company was one of these with thirty-five shares in 1786. A handful of the shareholders were Wakefield merchants and wool staplers and four of these were, in the following decade, involved in the finance of other mills in the area.[77] Secondly, some company mills were formed in order to rent a mill whose erection had been financed by others – often a landowner, a merchant or a successful clothier. Healey Mill Company at Ossett was organised for this purpose. There were eight clothier shareholders (less than was usual in those mills which financed the building of premises) and they leased the mill for £800 per year from 1791.[78] Finally, there were mills which were entirely financed by consortia of clothiers. Some of these in fact stipulated that individuals had to be clothiers in order to buy shares and some insisted that shareholders had to live and work within a certain radius of the mill.[79] It was also common for shareholders to have a certain amount of custom to offer in return for a share in the investment.[80] This form of finance – the restriction of shareholders to local clothiers – seems to have been most common in the nineteenth century.

It was this type of company mill which was being described by Baker, the Factory Inspector in the early 1840s:

The history of Joint Stock Company Woollen Mills exhibits a singular instance of energy amongst the smaller capitalists of the manufacturing districts ... the clothiers of certain country districts, such as Farsley, Idle, Eccleshill, Batley, Dewsbury etc., put their heads together and subsequently their purses ... by erecting mills at home to scribble their own wool and full their own cloth ... In the formation of a company mill a number of clothiers (for they must be clothiers to be partners) of small capital meet together and determine to become a company of so many partners, from 10 to 50, in shares generally of £25 each, each person taking as many shares as his capital will enable him ... With this subscribed capital deeds of partnership are drawn, land is bought, a mill erected and machinery put up ...[81]

A specific mill was described but not named by Baker. It was financed in 1825 jointly by ten clothiers who between them held forty shares and together subscribed a total of £7,000.[82]

The 1844 House of Lords Report on West Riding Joint Stock Mills discussed the financial arrangements in more detail:

Where the shareholders are more numerous – say 40 (they seldom exceed but often amount to that number) they will subscribe £50 per share in the first instance. They then buy the land and proceed with the building. They next borrow on mortgage the largest amount which they can gain credit for which will generally pay for the building and steam engine; the machinery is obtained on credit.[83]

The use of the mortgage to secure loans for mill construction was, as we shall see in Chapter 4, highly significant not just for company mills but for all types of expanding industrial concerns. The Ossett Mill Company trustees were empowered to borrow £3,000 on mortgage in 1786 and raised part of this sum – £1,200 – from the Leeds Cloth Hall.[84] When Kellett, Brown & Company were establishing their mill they raised two large loans on security of mortgage. They borrowed £5,000 at 4½% interest from 'widow Ibbetson' in 1835 and another £5,000 in 1839 from Christopher Smith & Company, Leeds merchants, this time at 4¾%.[85] It seems to have been easier for smaller clothiers to raise money from private individuals than from banks at this time. Banks were more discriminating about the nature of the security and often would not lend unless a customer had a large turnover on their account.[86] Kellett, Brown & Company were twice refused an advance of £5,000 by the Bradford Banking Company in the mid-1830s.[87]

Kellett, Brown & Company of Calverley near Leeds was a fairly typical company mill launched in the second quarter of the nineteenth century from which period the vast majority of such mills appear to date. Apart from the two loans detailed above, smaller amounts were borrowed from local woollen manufacturers.[88] The other major source of finance was of course the shareholders. There were forty-three when the company was launched in 1834 and these each held between two and eight shares at £25 per share. The average amount invested per shareholder in 1834 was £62. Each year from 1838 to 1843 an additional call of £10 per share was made. The majority of shareholders appear to have been local clothiers although a handful are identifiable as merchants and tradesmen from Leeds.[89]

The establishment of The Gill Royd Mill Company of Morley in 1835 involved similar borrowing from the local capital market.[90] In addition to making calls upon shares,[91] bank loans were requested from Leeds Banking Company and from Beckett Blayd & Company, both to be secured by mortgage of land and other properties. The agency of an attorney was also regularly employed in the 1830s.[92]

Many of the company mills launched in the 1830s and 1840s seem to have continued in existence until well into the second half of the nineteenth century. The Rawden Low Mill Company founded in 1844 is a typical example. Comparing a surviving Share Book for the 1860s with the initial record of the fifteen founder-subscribers shows a remarkable continuty of involvement of the local clothier families.[93]

Table 3.6 gives a list of the company mills traced to the early 1840s. This is by no means a complete record of the company mills in existence in the period as insurance data and other records often list ownership

Table 3.6 *Company mills identified in the West Riding, c. 1785–1840s*

Date of first mention	Name of company mill	Location
1785	Ossett Mill	Ossett
1790	Spring End Mill	Horbury
1791	Healey Mill	Ossett
1797	Bell Mill	Driffield
1797	Bramley Hough End	Bramley
1799	Whitly Mill	Thornhill
1802	Cooks Mill	Thongsbridge
1802	Lower Mill	Thongsbridge
1802	Batley Old Mill	Batley
1803	Ellis's Mill	Batley Carr
1802	Thorne's Mill	Wakefield
1803	Mill at Laisterdyke	Nr Bradford
1805	David Washington's Mill	Wakefield
1808	Low Mill	Stanningley
1813	Union Mill	Ossett
1822	Albion Mill	Pudsey
1826	Union Mill	Pudsey
1830	Allenbrig Mill	Pudsey
1830	Sunny Bank Mill	Farsley
1831	Crawshaw Mill	Pudsey
1833	Junction Mill	Laisterdyke
1833	Mill at Quick	Saddleworth
1833	Clover Greaves Mill	Calverley
1834	Gill Royd Mill	Morley
1835	Baildon Joint Stock Company	Baildon
1837	Healey Low Mill	Ossett
1837	Claughton Garth Mill	Far Town (Pudsey)
1837	Cliff Mill	Pudsey
1843	Rawden Mill	Rawden
1840s	Victoria Mill	Uppermill (Saddleworth)
1840s	Birks Mill	Almondbury

Source: Card Index.

under the names of the trustees without designating them as such and it is impossible to distinguish these from a partnership.

One of the most interesting features of company mill development is that their spatial distribution appears to relate closely to the agrarian and institutional environment described earlier. Though an incomplete record, we can assume that mills listed in Table 3.6 are a fairly random sample as far as their location is concerned and it is immediately apparent that they were concentrated in specific geographical areas. First there was a clustering to the south of the Aire valley between Leeds and Bradford and a second concentration existed in the Calder Valley to the west of Wakefield. It may be worth enquiring what these areas had in common, if anything, which made them fertile ground for the development of company mills.

Although any conclusions here must remain very tentative, it appears that the location of company mills was influenced by the agrarian conditions which promoted the existence of fairly substantial artisan clothiers. The middle Aire and Calder valleys were both areas where land was generally held in larger plots by both freeholders and copyholders. The river valleys were more fertile than the nearby highland zones and the two areas where company mills later grew had emerged in the eighteenth century as the main areas of the production of mixed cloths (see Map 1). Mixed cloth production was generally the province of the more substantial clothier with a reasonable sized farming plot and a fairly viable dual occupational structure which cushioned him against years of bad trade and supported the accumulation of capital. It was this type of clothier who was obviously most able to contemplate the joint finance of mill construction or renting and could afford to invest in two or three shares at £50 which appears to have been the average price.

Such clothiers were also in a position to offer land or other security for loans raised by the mills. By banding together under a trust deed groups of clothiers could command a significant volume of credit and loan finance as they jointly represented reasonable security to both the potential short- and long-term lender. Loans, based on property security, raised from the local financial community were of immense importance in launching these company mill ventures.[94]

Of equal importance in assessing the significance of the company mill is the way in which work done by the mill on commission was charged and paid for. It seems that shareholders were committed to send their work to their mill for processing; some mills even insisted that shareholders promised a certain amount of work per year.[95] Most clothiers involved in the finance of company mills were probably only too pleased to send their work there and for the majority the promise of rapid and efficient service was the main motivation for becoming a shareholder in the first place. One can reasonably expect that company mill shareholders benefited from the lower prices charged. The traditional public mills had often held a monopoly position which was reflected in their pricing and as company mills spread it appears that commission fulling and scribbling in all mills became more competitive to the benefit of the clothier in terms both of cost and of speed.[96] It was not unknown in periods of bad trade conditions for company mills to waive some of their charges for a while to enable their proprietors to weather the storms of commercial life. In December 1844, for example, the Rawden Low Mill Company resolved that 'there be nothing charged for scouring the next three months'.[97] Another particular advantage for the clothier deriving from the company mill was the generous credit allowed to customers, especially to shareholders.[98]

All company mills got round the legislation against joint stock companies by organising under a trust deed, but there were problems arising from this legal form. They could neither sue nor be sued and they did not have the power to proceed at law against a member of the partnership. Partners had 'no security on each other'[99] for the money which they advanced and no legal redress if, for example, a book-keeper or treasurer absconded with the cash in hand. They could not even compel the sale of a share if the shareholder's account was long overdue. Much of the success of these ventures thus depended on the mutual trust and co-operation of the clothier communities. Despite these problems, it appears that company mills became even more prevalent in the 1850s and 1860s, particularly in the heavy woollen areas where they were adapted to the use of shoddy and mungo and took on rag grinding.[100] Clearly, the collective and communitarian spirit of the clothier communities was still sufficient to support these co-operative ventures at a time which is more commonly associated with the efflorescence of Victorian individualism.

The sources of 'human capital'

Although this aspect can only be touched on here, it is worth considering the formation of the factory proletariat and its relationship to the body of proto-industrial workers; an aspect of development crucial to our understanding of 'primary accumulation'. If we take Leeds and Huddersfield as reasonably typical of areas of factory woollen production as a whole we find that by the mid-1830s about 75% of factory workers were men, almost three-fifths of whom were over the age of twenty-one (see Table 3.7). It is possible therefore that many had been previously engaged in the proto-industrial sector. Scattered evidence from Parliamentary Papers bears out the fact that early woollen factory hands had had prior experience in local rural domestic production.[101] For example, in 1828, Gervaise Walker of Horbury near Wakefield witnessed what appears to have been a common sight in the woollen areas: 'in our village we have between 400 or 500 houses, and there are 80 houses standing empty, the hands have removed to Leeds and Huddersfield to the merchant manufacturers'.[102]

Immigration statistics of Leeds and Huddersfield give further weight to the proposition that early factory labour came from the proto-industrial sector. Despite their rapid growth, both towns had only around 14% of their populations born outside Yorkshire at the time of the 1851 census and well over 80% had been born in the vicinity or in the towns themselves. The composition of factory labour and details of immigration in Leeds and Huddersfield as well as Bradford and Halifax are given in Tables 3.7 and 3.8.

Thus the major seats of woollen factory production in the first half of the nineteenth century were drawing their labour force largely from the local textile area and predominantly employed mature males.

Table 3.7 Employees in woollen and worsted mills, 1835

Township	No. of woollen mills	No. of worsted mills	Total employees	Under 21 (%)	Males (%)	Over 21 (%)	Under 21 (%)	Females (%)	Over 21 (%)
Bradford	—	25	4,166	1,344 (32.3)	(38.8)	270 (6.5)	1,705 (40.9)	(61.2)	847 (20.3)
Halifax	—	14	769	224 (29.1)	(39.6)	81 (10.5)	402 (52.3)	(60.4)	62 (8.1)
Huddersfield	17	—	1,801	569 (31.6)	(76.6)	811 (45.0)	309 (17.2)	(23.4)	112 (6.2)
Leeds	42	—	5,420	1,812 (33.4)	(74.9)	2,250 (41.5)	631 (11.6)	(25.1)	727 (13.4)

— = none recorded.

Source: Factory Returns, P.P. 1835 (342) XL.

Table 3.8 Some indication of immigration into West Riding towns by 1851

Borough or town	% age born in town or borough	% age born in Yorks. outside of the borough or town	% age born outside Yorks.	Total inhabitants	% age of the occupied population dependent upon the textile sector
Bradford borough	45.0	35.0	20.0	103,778	59
Halifax borough	53.5	28.8	17.7	33,582	35
Huddersfield town	52.8	33.9	13.3	30,880	34
Leeds borough	68.9	17.1	14.0	172,270	32

Source: P.P., Census Abstract, 1851.

If we look at the recruitment of factory labour in the worsted industry, some problems occur in any straightforward application of the proto-industry model. Table 3.7 indicates that by 1835 in the mills of Bradford and Halifax 60% of the labour force was composed of women of whom 70% were under the age of twenty-one. Even the male labour force in these mills was largely juvenile, some 82% being under the age of twenty-one. It is thus unlikely that this labour force was composed of individuals with any lengthy experience of wage dependency in the proto-industrial sector, although their proletarian conditioning within the proto-industrial family may have been important in the transition to factory work.

It seems likely, however, that a sizeable proportion of this new factory workforce did not originate in the proto-industrial sector at all. Using Table 3.8 to compare Bradford and Halifax with the two woollen towns of Huddersfield and Leeds at the time of the 1851 census, the striking fact is that a significantly larger proportion of their populations was born outside of Yorkshire. Bradford's growth rate was phenomenal in the period 1820 to 1850 which may invalidate the use of immigration statistics in this way but Halifax had the slowest growth rate of the four towns in the period yet still shows high immigration rates from outside the textile area. Clearly, although proto-industry may have led to reduction of ties with the land and greater wage dependency this did not automatically ensure a ready drift of these same individuals into the factories. It is possible that this occurred more readily in the woollen sector where smaller factories and slower mechanisation made it easier to ford the gulf between proto-industrial work and factory employment, but even here there is evidence that independent artisans fought and resented the transition to wage dependency and factory discipline.[103] These remarks are very much of a preliminary kind to draw attention to an aspect of the proto-industrial debate requiring considerable additional research.

The various sections of the foregoing chapter suggest that the emergence and dynamic of proto-industry is infinitely more complex than the bulk of literature on the subject suggests. There is an obvious problem in the West Riding, as in all cases, of isolating the existence of a 'proto-industrial dynamic' from the technological and market imperatives at work in a particular sector of industry over time. These may have had their own independent influence on both capital and labour requirements and their supply. They, together with important elements of the agrarian institutional and social environment, created strict parameters within which proto-industry emerged, functioned and developed.

4

LAND AND INDUSTRY

We have seen that the growth of textile production in the West Riding before and during the eighteenth century involved a symbiosis between landholding and agriculture on the one hand and industry on the other. This relationship had many important implications for industrial finance.

The structure and pattern of landed wealth in the West Riding was important in raising finance for production and trade, particularly so in the case of the older-established woollen branch of the industry. From the earliest fulling mills of the thirteenth and fourteenth centuries this process became a manorial monopoly and was undertaken in premises owned by the local landed magnate alongside the traditional monopolies of corn mill and oven. As the centuries progressed and the monopolies died out many mills remained the property of landowners and continued to full cloth for the locality on commission. It is thus not surprising that when scribbling and carding was centralised alongside fulling from the 1780s a proportion of the finance for the extension and erection of these larger mills was provided by landlords. Even some of the later more integrated mills were built by landowners who either ran them or, more often, hired them out. Sometimes old agricultural premises were let out for industrial purposes at low rents in return for rebuilding, modernisation and improvement and landowners also commonly leased smaller workshops and working dwellings with garden plots for use by domestic artisans.

The proto-industrial structure of the woollen industry impinged on finance in another way. The artisan household with a small farm or landholding and a farm house and other buildings, whether copyhold or freehold, had the possibility, as we have seen, of raising finance on the security of the land and buildings or of selling them for the same ends. The mortgage market developed rapidly in the eighteenth century through the activities of intermediaries such as attorneys, and much mortgaging and land transfer was occurring by the end of the century.[1]

The mortgage of land to raise industrial finance was, in fact, a continuing feature of both the woollen and worsted sectors through to the mid-nineteenth century and beyond.[2]

It has been noted that the worsted industry followed quite a different path of development and hence of capital accumulation but there were similarities in the close relationship between landed wealth and industrial finance. As in the woollen sector many worsted producers of the eighteenth-century rented premises from a local landlord or else owned farm premises which could be used to raise finance. Many of the larger-scale putting-out producers originated from a background of landowning and farming as did Foster and the Marriners, for example. Not only could agricultural property be used to raise finance but landholding connections were a useful source of loan capital. It appears that landowners and especially the spinsters and widows of landholding families were among the suppliers of loans to the industry in the late eighteenth and early nineteenth centuries.

The full implications of these various aspects of the relationship between landed capital and industrial finance are examined below under three heads: direct finance, investment via the capital market and the raising of funds through mortgage and sale of land.

Landowners and direct industrial finance

Throughout the eighteenth century one finds some evidence of landowners providing artisan clothiers' dwellings and small farms for hire in conjunction with commission fulling mills. Sir Walter Calverley at the beginning of the century induced many clothiers to come and reside on his estate by providing fulling mills and by making it possible for the farmer to be a clothier and the clothier to work as a farmer.[3] Several other Yorkshire proprietors attempted with success to foster the joint occupation of farming and weaving which was viewed as an avenue of estate improvement. This improvement aspect seems to have been a major motivation behind the participation of landowners in industrial finance until well into the nineteenth century, as we shall see.

A typical development occurred at the end of the eighteenth century when rising urban rents were forcing Leeds clothiers to remove to nearby rural areas. Several landlords took advantage of the exodus to induce clothiers to live on their land which was formerly used for farming at lower rents. They were able to do this easily because short leases prevailed in the West Riding often of one or two years or less for agricultural land.[4] Sir James Graham, giving evidence in 1806, described his own involvement in this movement.[5] When his agricultural leaseholds in the Aire valley terminated in 1796 he divided the farms into small allotments of 5–10 acres for clothiers. He also built three large mills in the area which alone were let for a total of £3,958 per annum by 1819. By the

1840s Graham owned four mill complexes in the Kirkstall area: St Anne's Mill, Savin's Mill, Abbey Mills and Burley Mills. Annual rental from these amounted to £2,320 and all had seen considerable extension and improvement in the early decades of the nineteenth century.[6]

So successful in revenue terms was Graham that other landowners followed in his footsteps and the subdivision and leasing of landholdings, especially around Leeds, proceeded apace enabling clothiers to rent a cottage and land of convenient size and geographical position. Graham was landlord of at least 160 clothiers' holdings in 1806 whilst Walter Spencer Stanhope was landlord of more than 60 such tenancies as well as several mills on his neighbouring estate at Horsforth.[7] So much were these two involved in the affairs of the woollen industry that they both served on the Parliamentary Committee of 1806, but in this level of commitment they may well have been unusual.

Rate valuations are useful in indicating more generally the extent to which landowners owned and leased out clothiers' premises and mills but only a few have survived for the eighteenth century and the coverage is little better for the early nineteenth century. Although a full survey is therefore out of the question, a sample of the surviving valuations gives a useful indication of the general position. Table 4.1 exhibits the results of isolating the textile industrial premises owned by landowners in five different townships of the Riding at different points in time.[8]

It appears from the table that landowners were participating in the provision of premises for the wool textile industry but as far as Ossett, Skircoat, Halifax, Warley, and Northowram were concerned this represented only a small proportion of industrial premises and under 3% of the total rateable value of the townships in all cases at the times when the valuations were made. The explanation for this relatively minor contribution of landed wealth in industrial finance must be sought in the structure of landholding which predominated in most parts of the Riding. The extent of small freehold and copyhold farm properties was ubiquitous and a matter of note for all contemporary topographical writers.[9] Coupled with this, many of the landed estates of the Riding were owned by absentee landlords.[10] Farmland, especially in the west of the area was poor and did not excite large numbers of resident improving landlords who, on the spot, may have had more interest in local industrial ventures. Examples, such as Graham, from the Aire valley may misrepresent the textile region as a whole as small freeholds and absentee landlords were less characteristic of the area around Leeds than they were elsewhere.

Much fuller information of the role of landowners in the direct sponsorship of industry can be gained by studying their estate records. The Savile Estate Papers provide an interesting example. This family which resided in Rufford, Nottinghamshire, by the late eighteenth century, was one of the largest landowners in Yorkshire with property in no fewer

Table 4.1 *Landowners and the ownership of textile industry premises in selected townships, 1782–1839*

Township	Date	Name of landowner	Industrial premises
Skircoat	1782	Lady Irvin, Marchioness of Hertford	Farrow Mill: RV £35
Skircoat	1839	Thomas Groves Edwards	Washer Lane Mill: RV £165
Halifax	1797	Lady Irvin	'mill': RV £90
Ossett-cum-Gawthorp	1807	Lionel Pilkington, Bart.	Park Mill: RV £30
Ossett-cum-Gawthorp	1819	Richard Walker, Esq.	Four clothiers' premises and workshops: RV £48 Mill, warehouse, etc.: RV £21. 10s.
Ossett-cum-Gawthorp	1819	Rev. William Wood	Workers' cottages Clothiers' premises
Ossett-cum-Gawthorp	1819	Earl of Cardigan	Tenter grounds
Ossett-cum-Gawthorp	1837	Earl of Cardigan	Gawthorp Mill, engine house, 5½ h.p.: RV £49
Ossett-cum-Gawthorp	1837	Earl of Cardigan	Clothiers' premises, shops, dryhouse: RV £166
Warley	1805	John Dearden, J.P.	Seven clothiers' premises and shops
Northowram	1837	Sir Geo. Beaumont	New Bank Mill: RV £113

Note: RV = rateable value.
Sources: Ossett Valuations (J. G. MSS), other valuations (Ha.).

than thirty-six townships of the West Riding. By the late eighteenth century they were certainly in possession of several fulling mills such as those at Lower Westwood which included scribbling and carding premises.[11] Full Survey and Valuation Books for the Savile's Yorkshire properties for 1809 give a clear indication that textile property owned by the family was limited given the extent of their landownership. Later, though less complete, valuations for 1839 and 1840 indicate a decrease in their ownership of textile premises rather than the reverse.[12] As absentees the Saviles were probably more representative of landowners in the West Riding as a whole than were Graham or Stanhope but the sheer extent of their landholdings does not make one entirely confident of their typicality.

A much greater risk of bias occurs in studying the Papers of Lord Dartmouth who made himself an important figure in the industrial history of the Colne valley. He was a rare example in the West Riding of a prominent, active, improving landlord but the Dartmouth Estate Terriers do provide a unique opportunity to study the motive and the precise mechanism of a landowner's relationship to industrial ventures.[13] By the

Table 4.2 *Survey and valuation of West Riding textile premises belonging to the Saviles of Rufford, Notts., 1809*

Township	Premises	Tenant	Annual valuation (£)
Denby	Marshall Mill, house, and lands	Isaac Wheetman Dickinson	40
Denby	House, dyehouse, and land	Benj. Robinson	11
Elland	House, shop, and stable with land	Godfrey Mann	35
Golcar	Mill, lands, and house	William Sykes	468
Golcar	Mills, house, dyehouse, and land	James Shaw	224
Ovenden	Mixenden Mill, house, and dwellings	John Sutcliffe	40
Hunsworth	Privilege of water to Binkinshaw Mill	John Ellinson	2
Rawtonstall	Hebden Bridge Mill	Thomas Sutcliffe	84
Rishworth	Mill and land	John Wheelright	110
Soothill	Mill and land .	Robert Wooller	276
Thornhill	Mill, dam, and lands	John Sykes' trustees	280

Source: Savile Estate Papers, Survey and Valuation Book 1809 (Hu.).

1820s the Dartmouth family held over 7,500 acres of land in the textile area and, as shown in Table 4.3 the extent of their textile involvement was very significant.

Apart from the mills and other premises mentioned here, Dartmouth owned and leased smaller clothiers' dwellings and farmsteads but in all townships where Dartmouth held property agricultural investment was much more important in rental terms than industrial premises. Even in Slaithwaite, which contained the largest number of Dartmouth's mills, industrial premises yielded only 10% of his total rental income from the township in 1828.[14]

The most interesting aspect of Dartmouth's Estate Survey of 1805 is the light which it throws on the way in which he and his tenants jointly financed the improvements of both farming and commercial premises. If tenants advanced money themselves for rebuilding, conversion or extension of premises, a lease was often granted for twenty-one or sometimes forty-two years at an artificially low 'reserved rent' calculated to act as an incentive for such improvements. Virtually all Dartmouth's Slaithwaite mills in 1805 were leased on reserved rentals which were nothing like the estimated real annual value as the last two columns of Table 4.3 indicate. Reserved rents were saving the tenants of eleven Slaithwaite mills alone over £1,000 per annum by 1805 which, in the short term, represented a significant subsidy to the industry. Dartmouth's steward explicitly recorded the reserved rent policy for agricultural improvements[15] and this

Table 4.3 *Textile premises owned and leased out by Lord Dartmouth, 1805*

Location	Premises	Rental (£.s)	Real annual value (£)[a]
Slaithwaite	Waterside Mill (C)	122.00	300
	Slaithwaite Mill, warehouses, etc.	160.00	250
	New Mill	30.00	400
	Shaw Carr Wood Mill	20.00	65
	Upper Clough House		40
	and Lower Heywood Mill	10.00	100
	Blackmoor Holme Mill	5.00	80
	Brinkshaw New Mill (C)	10.10	100
	Hold Head dyehouse	5.00	40
	Upper Holt Mill	50.00	—
	Lingarths Mill (C)	5.05	30
Farnley	Six groups of clothiers' premises	128.10	
Farsley and Rowley	Birks Mill	5.05	
	Fenay Mill	112.00	
	Rowley Mill	6.19	
	Farnley Mill	5.05	
Honley	Steps Mill	98.00	
	Meltham Mill	7.07	
	Wood Bottom Mill	5.05	
	Dyehouse	5.05	
	Honley Mill	110.00	
Kirkburton	Dogley Mill	72.10	
Almondbury	Mill Side tenement weavers' workshops	30.10	
Morley	Morley Mill	100.00	

Note: (C) = cotton mill.
[a] Available only for Slaithwaite mills.
Source: D.E.T., Register, Survey.

seems also to have been followed with regard to industrial premises.

In addition to reserved-rent leasing Dartmouth was also active in granting finance for mill building. There seems to have been two types of financial contribution which he was prepared to make, both determined by the expected increase in either rental revenues or estate value which mill building or improvement would imply. First, finance was sometimes extended at interest. In the early nineteenth century as much as £1,000 at a time was loaned in this way at interest rates as high as 8%.[16] The interest and repayment charges were incorporated in the annual rental payments and were obviously unaffected by the Usury Laws. A lease for a guaranteed number of years was included in the agreements.

In 1792 Dartmouth gave £1,250 for building Morley Mill for which he was to receive £100 per year for forty years.[17] In 1803 he advanced £600 at 8% to Varley and Eastwood towards the building of Waterside Mill.[18] This loan-type of finance was still a feature of the Dartmouth estate administration as late as the 1840s although, interestingly, by this time there had been a general decline in direct financial involvement.[19] Interest rates charged by Dartmouth throughout the period were often higher than for other sources of funds. For example, in 1842 the occupiers of Blackmoor Holme Mill were anxious to build a new reservoir. Dartmouth offered a loan of £6–700 but his interest charges in excess of 5% resulted in the loan being rejected.[20]

The other type of financial outlay practised by Lord Dartmouth was the outright grant of funds towards mill building or extension in the knowledge that this would bring higher rental income. Sometimes as much as £1,000 was involved in a single building but often it was less than this and the tenants paid a substantial proportion of the costs themselves. Where tenant finance was apparent, reserved rents were lower than was the case where Dartmouth had provided the bulk of funds. Where, as at Fenay Mill, Dartmouth had laid out a large sum (in this case more than £1,300) the twenty-one-year lease was agreed at a rental of £112 which was equivalent to the estimated annual value. Where buildings had been built or considerably improved by the tenants, perhaps with the aid of a loan from Dartmouth, reserved rents were only a small proportion of the 'real' value, often 10–20%. Of Dartmouth's nineteen textile mills in 1805 he had heavily invested in the finance of eight of them, laying out an average of £642 per mill.[21]

Having noted the enormous variation on the extent of direct landowner participation in textile finance, the very significant contributions of Graham and especially Dartmouth compared with the limited involvement of absentees, it is necessary to turn to insurance records, factory returns and other sources for more representative data on mill ownership.

In undertaking this survey one obvious problem which must be mentioned is the problem of defining 'landowner'. Merchants, bankers and industrialists themselves commonly invested their accumulated wealth in a landed estate but where it was possible to identify such individuals they were excluded from this survey and only families with a landowning history of at least two generations were counted. Small owner-occupiers were also excluded. Mill ownership details gained from insurance records and other data, whilst not complete, should at least reflect the relative importance of landed wealth. The surprising fact is that very few examples of ownership come to light apart from those already mentioned in this chapter. Sir Thomas Pilkington seems to have owned three mills; George Hathorne of Finsbury Square, London, one; Thomas Pownell of Bedford, one; John Lister Kay of Denby Grange, one; Joshua Crompton, Lord of the Manor of Esholt, two; John Spencer Stanhope of

5
Crank Mill, Morley, part-financed by Lord Dartmouth
Source: William Smith, *The History and Antiquities of Morley* (1876)

Horsforth, one; Robert Spencer of Sowerby, one; and the Earl of Scarborough, one.[22] The Ramsdens of Huddersfield are notably absent from this list. They may have owned mills which have not been recorded but it is unlikely that their involvement was at all significant despite their being a major resident landowning family.

The evidence suggests that landowners owned no more than fifty at most of the mills traced before 1850, representing less than 6%. It is, however, likely that they contributed a higher proportion of the total fixed capital invested in textile industrial premises for several reasons. First, the mills owned by landowners seem to have been slightly above average in size especially in the woollen industry and, secondly, this survey excludes those buildings not classified as mills, i.e. workshops, dyehouses, clothiers' premises. These smaller units of production were often let alongside agricultural premises and were particularly common in the woollen districts where the activities of landowners seem to have been most prominent.

Even allowing for these considerations it is unlikely that direct landed finance of fixed capital in the woollen and worsted industries accounted for much more than 10% of the total fixed capital formation in the period 1780–1850. Furthermore, it seems that a large proportion of this direct finance was concentrated in the woollen branch of the industry and in mills built before about 1815: a legacy of the close relationship between landowning and the provision of local fulling mills. Landed finance may thus have been of significance in the first boom of fixed capital formation in the woollen branch in the 1790s (see Graph 2.1) but was less important thereafter.

The ubiquity of freehold and copyhold tenures, the proliferation of absentee landlords and the preference of landowners for the direct finance of transport or mining projects rather than textiles must contribute to an explanation of this phenomenon. Where direct participation was in evidence a transfer of funds from land to industry is apparent although it must be recognised that high rentals and interest rates and the lapsing of reserved-rent leases all drew money back into the agricultural sector over succeeding years and was the price which industry paid for this finance.

Landowners and the capital market

Another aspect of industrial finance on the part of landowners was the provision of loan capital via the medium of the eighteenth- and early nineteenth-century capital market. In the eighteenth century, the capital market was strongly influenced by personal and social factors which may have acted as a barrier to the flow of landed wealth into industry where there was no direct personal connection. However, the increasing activities and the proliferation of financial intermediaries, in particular attorneys, was coming to influence both the size and direction of the flow of long-term funds between different sectors of the local economy.[23]

The business of attorneys in the eighteenth century was dominated by the collection of estate rents and by the administration of landed property, including that of absentee owners. As the discount of bills and the arranging of loans became an increasing part of the attorneys' business, it is not surprising that their landed clients were often those first approached to obtain funds for both short- and long-term investment. They had the bulk of the unemployed funds in the community and were willing to put this out through the medium of the attorney in return for interest or, often, for an annuity income. In order to ascertain some idea of the extent of landed finance being put out for loan in the textile areas the Cash Books and Day Books of John Howarth, an attorney practising at Ripponden near Halifax, were studied for the period 1780–96.[24] Howarth's business was probably fairly typical of that of other attorneys of the textile area.[25] His records indicate that the largest single source of

loan capital after that provided by Howarth himself was from landed
sources especially from female members. Table 4.4 sets out in summary
form details of the extent of landed sources of loan finance for sample
time periods. All loans were charged at 5% interest. Unfortunately, it is
difficult to trace the nature of all the borrowers and virtually impossible
to know what they did with the money. A few were themselves landowners, the majority identified were substantial merchants, such as
Joseph Priestly of White Windows, but only a handful are identifiable as
manufacturers. About 40% remain unidentified.

Table 4.4 *Details of loans raised by John Howarth, attorney, Halifax,
selected years 1789–96*

Date	Total loans documented No.	Total loans documented Amt	Approx. proportion (%) loaned by: J.H.	Approx. proportion (%) loaned by: Landed families	Percentage secured by: B	Percentage secured by: M
Feb.–Dec. 1789	18	£9,115	53	38	33	39
Jan.–Dec. 1790	22	£8,337	37	32	18	45
Feb.–Feb. 1793–4	14	£5,372	41	29	29	50
Feb.–July 1795–6	32	£8,271	56	31	34	44

Note: J.H. = John Howarth; B = bond; M = mortgage.
Source: John Howarth, Cash Books (Ha.).

Of the loan capital coming from landowners most was from a limited
number of individuals. By far the most important individual in the period
studied was a Mrs Brisco who had an estate in Wakefield. In each of the
chronological periods of Table 4.4 she lent £1,900 (two loans), £2,150
(five loans), £1,540 (two loans), and £2,840 (three loans) respectively.
Miss Elizabeth Metcalfe and Thomas Lambert of Elland Hall were two
other important landed 'financiers'.[26]

Occasionally there is some indication of the duration of these loans as
interest payments are recorded. With at least 5% of loans it is possible to
see that they were extended for terms exceeding five years, e.g. the loan
in October 1789 of £1,300 from Mrs Brisco to George Hargreaves a merchant of Midgeley and Manchester.[27] Two or three years seems to have
been the most common period although there is evidence that many borrowers were doing so to pay off a previous mortgage and, in effect, were
permanently indebted to one or another lender for substantial sums.[28]

One must turn to textile business records to see if these give any complementary evidence of the direction of flow of funds loaned by attor-

neys. In the period 1780–1811 the firm of Benjamin Gott & Company, and its predecessor, Wormald & Fountaine, borrowed some £89,625 on security of bonds, promissory notes and mortgages.[29] This was at a time when the concern was amassing funds to embark upon manufacturing and to build and later extend their mills. The loans were for periods varying from six months to twenty years but the vast majority (63%) were for twelve months or less. The most heavy borrowing tended to coincide with the years of most investment in mill construction and extension. Of the £89,625, £17,360 was borrowed from widows and spinsters, a large proportion of whom are identifiable as being from landed families, and a further £9,600 was loaned by 'gentlemen' and 'esquires' the majority of whom, one can assume, had some kind of landed estate. Excluding monies borrowed from those described as merchants or professional persons who may well have held land, about 15% of Gott's borrowing seems to have been derived from landowning sources, but this large and wealthy concern must be considered atypical. Gott and his partners, with their family connections, could call on landed sources of finance to a much larger extent than could the average firm.

The wider importance of landowners' lending to the textile industry can be indicated by examining the title deeds to industrial premises and land which survive among the business collections. These show the loans for which property mortgages were the security. It appears that the activities of attorneys continued to be important in the first half of the nineteenth century in arranging these loans within the local capital market and as long as this continued to be the case it is likely that landed capital played some part. By the 1820s and 1830s manufacturers were very clearly among the most important of the clients seeking finance and most manufacturers of any size had a regular attorney who would arrange for loan capital when required. For example, the Marriners paid Christopher Netherwood 'a tidy sum' in the 1820s for arranging a number of loans for them on security of property.[30]

When one comes to study the mortgage deeds which survive among business papers of firms the salient feature is that the mortgagees were more commonly wool staplers or merchants (and even professional people such as clergy or surgeons) than landowners. This seems to have been as true for the late eighteenth century as for the nineteenth. For example, when Benjamin Hallas, clothier, of Ossett was raising finance for the construction of Pildacre Mill in the 1790s, he borrowed £490 from William Thompson, a Leeds coalmaster on bond, £720 from a Wakefield hatmaker and his widowed sister on mortgage, unnamed sums from two Wakefield attorneys and only about £500 from the executors of the late Katherine Nevile of Chevet Hall, near Wakefield, again on mortgage.[31] Similarly, Gott raised over half of his finance in the period 1780–1811 from merchants and relatives who were not significant landowners.

Of some twenty-five mortgage deeds of textile premises, land and other property pledged by clothiers and manufacturers in the period 1780–1850 as security for loans only three involved landowners as mortgagees, whereas six involved staplers, two bankers, two attorneys, five merchants and the rest remain unidentified.[32] This evidence may not represent a significant contradiction of the Howarth material as his Cash Books indicated that landed loans were never much more than a third of total loan funds and these were going to all types and descriptions of borrowers: other landowners and merchants principally. It is quite probably the case that throughout our period bond and mortgage loans to manufacturers came principally from merchants and staplers who were in closer touch with the pulse of industry or may have known the borrower through a personal or commercial connection. This seems to have changed little and was even endorsed by the rise of private and joint stock banks as the major financial intermediaries of the region.

The mortgage and sale of land

The preamble from the statute of 1703, which established the West Riding Registry of Deeds, demonstrates the early importance for clothiers of raising money on the security of their freehold lands:

The West Riding of the county of York is the principal place in the north for the cloth manufacture and most of the traders therein are freeholders and have frequent occasions to borrow money upon their estates for managing their said trade, but for the want of a Register find it difficult to give security to the satisfaction of the money lender, (although the security they offer be really good) by means whereby the said trade is very much obstructed and many families ruined.[33]

Two decades earlier Andrew Yarranton had pointed out the advantages for the Dutch who had:

fitted themselves with a Publick Register for all their lands and houses by means of which such property was readily accepted by the banks as security for loans of Ready Moneys at all times without the charge of law or the necessity of a lawyer . . . a register will quicken trade, and the land registered will be equall as cash in a mans hands and the credit thereof will go and do in trade what Ready Moneys now doth.[34]

This was the other significant financial aspect of the symbiosis between land and industry in the West Riding: the ability of manufacturers to pledge their freehold and their copyhold land as security for loans to aid the running and the expansion of their business. Table 4.4 gave some indication of the large extent to which mortgages were used as loan security in the late eighteenth century. The Registry dealt almost entirely with freehold lands, copyhold and short leasehold being excluded. It does, however, appear, as we shall see, that copyhold lands were almost equally valuable as mortgaging assets. The device of conditional surrender of copyhold land (conditional on repayment of a loan) was used and recorded in the Manor Court Rolls. Where the Court Rolls were carefully kept and all surrenders detailed as in the Manor of Wakefield, the 'mortgage' was as effective as that of a freehold although any encumbrances by virtue of the copyhold lease obviously made the property less desirable as an asset, and hence as security, than an unencumbered freehold.

The fact that the West Riding Registry of Deeds was one of only five in the country in the eighteenth century emphasises the importance and ubiquity of freehold property owned by Yorkshire manufacturers.[35] It is possible that pressure for enfranchisement and enclosure in the eighteenth century was partly a function of the desire of domestic artisan clothiers to acquire fixed title to land and hence to a greater call on loan capital. Pressure from local populations dominated by clothiers for enclosure awards prompts speculation on this point. In Ossett, for example, in the years before the Enclosure Act of 1807 many clothiers seem to have been buying up land in order to secure a better deal from the award. Out of thirty-five freehold clothiers in Ossett in 1807, thirty benefited greatly from the enclosure award of 1813[36] and by 1819 clothiers owned 12% of the land (by rateable value) in the township.[37]

The Registry provides a unique source for the study of land transactions and especially mortgaging and sale to raise finance in the crucial period of transition to centralised production. The problem is that with 11,844 volumes and poor indexing, it is extremely difficult to use. Simple quantitative analysis from the index as has been undertaken for the early twentieth-century housing market[38] is impossible as there is no index by type of transfer before 1885. The only viable approach for this study was to trace the activities of clothiers and entrepreneurs in a sample region.

Ossett township was chosen for this exercise. An unusually comprehensive set of surviving rate valuations enable one to track down clothiers and other textile entrepreneurs in the area. Furthermore, being in the Manor of Wakefield meant that Ossett copyhold transfers could also be examined. There is no doubt that Ossett was unrepresentative of the West Riding as a whole – any township selected on such criteria would have been. Ossett was dominated by the production of different types of *woollen* cloth by the early nineteenth century, principally blankets. There were few significantly large manufacturing concerns and the township possessed considerable copyhold land – more so than freehold. The results of research on Ossett are presented here not as indicative of the practice of the West Riding as a whole but as merely suggestive of wider developments.

The Poll of the Knights of the Shire of 1807[39] indicates that there were thirty-five clothiers in Ossett township who were owners of freehold land. Of these, twenty-one are recorded as a party to one or more freehold land transaction in the period 1801–19. The period 1801–19 was chosen for examination because of the difficulty involved in study of a less circumscribed time. The problems and advantages in choosing this particular period are dealt with later. Several clothiers, particularly those from the main clothier families (Brook, Briggs, Dews, Hallas, Phillips, Mitchell, Scott and Wilby), were party to a significant number of land deals including mortgages, indentures and sales. A list of the clothiers traced with a summary of their landholdings and the transactions in which they were involved is given in Table 4.5. Mortgaging may have been a more extensive practice than the table suggests as indentures are not always indicated as feoffments and thus were very probably collateral agreements. Some are marked as such.

Where mortgages occurred the mortgagee was usually another clothier or a merchant.[40] The property mortgaged was not always land but included the commercial clothiers' premises and even more unusual items:

13th February 1807: Demise for 1000 years by way of a mortgage for securing £1,200 and interest, Benjamin and William Hallas and John Phillip[s] to Christopher and Joseph Emmett of Halifax, dealers in leather and co-partners ... various lands in Ossett including Pig Hills ... [and] ... 2 sittings in the North Gallery of the Chapel.[41]

This latter example gives one a clue as to the importance of social and particularly religious connections in finding loans.

From the purchase and sales activities it is possible to see some clothiers as active in building up their estates in the period and buying from local landowners to extend their influence (and hence their future call on loan capital): for example the Mitchell and Phillips families.[42] Others, like the Dews, were selling land. Perhaps these moves reflect the varying fortunes of the clothier families but sales of land were often made to finance industrial expansion. In the late 1790s Benjamin Hallas financed the construction of Pildacre Mill partly through sales of his freehold land.[43]

One interesting development which it is possible to trace is the use of land mortgaging and sale to finance company mill growth. Healey Mill Company was jointly financed and run by fourteen local clothiers including members of the Mitchell, Phillips and Dews families.[44] As well as owning two mills they jointly were in possession of 24 acres of land.[45] In the volatile years of trade in 1815–17 they made two major sales of property. The first was in 1815 when they sold land and a mill to three clothiers who were residents of Emley, Penistone and High Hoyland but who moved to Ossett to run the mill.[46] The second was in 1817 to Wentworth, Chaloner & Rishworth, the Wakefield bankers, to whom they sold a scribbling, carding and spinning mill with cottages and tenements.[47] This mill was almost certainly the one insured for more than

Table 4.5 *Summary of freehold land transactions of Ossett clothiers, 1801–19*

Name of clothier	Extent of landholding in township, to nearest acre and other property 1801	1819	Dates and details of transactions
John Brook	—	1 CP	1805 P 1815 S 1816 S
James Briggs	—	9 M D W H	1810 S 1816 I
David Dews	—	—	1807 S
Joseph Dews	—	—	1801 S
Joshua Dews	—	—	1817 S
Robert Dews	—	CP	—
Benjamin Hallas			1807 M £1,200
William Hallas	—	105 M DHs CPs	1810 P
George Hallas			1814 S
			1814 A
Mark Phillips	—		1807 M £1,200
John Phillips	—	Hs CP	1804 S
Randolph Phillips	6	3	1805 P
Phillips family	3	—	
			1809 S
David Mitchell	17	—	1801 P
James Mitchell	3 CPs H	7 CP	1804 I
Joseph Mitchell	—	—	1810 P
			1815 P
			1810 S
Other Mitchells	—	6 CP	1814 S
Scott family	4 CP Hs	9 CPs Hs	
			1801 I
David Wilby			1804 P
Wilby family	34 CPs Hs	27 Hs CPs	1805 S
			1805 I
			1814 M £1,000

Key:
- — = information not recorded.
- CP = clothier's premises, i.e. workshop, cottage, garden.
- CPs = several workshops with cottage and garden.
- M = mill.
- D = dyehouse.
- W = warehouse.
- H(s) = house(s).

- P = purchase (feoffment, lease and release).
- S = sale.
- I = indenture.
- M = mortgage £ amount secured.
- A = assignment.

Sources: W.R.R.D.; Ossett Valuations (J.G. MSS).

£4,000 with its contents in 1819.[48] It is possible that Wentworth & Company had been the firm's bankers and had insisted on purchase to cover an overdraft. In the same year the Healey Mill Company bought another mill 'newly erected' from Luke Robinson, a Wakefield wool stapler, and two Ossett clothiers, Benjamin Archer and John Brook.[49] By 1829 when Healey Mill burnt down it was again owned by Messrs Wilby & Company, a group of local clothiers.[50] The salient feature of the history of these transactions is the extent to which buying, selling and pledging were each used at different times in response to the vagaries of trade, and the state of the firm's liquidity. A similar story for Spring End Mill can be traced through the deeds.

Before turning to look at copyhold transactions there are two factors which may have considerably distorted the activity in the land market in these years from what was perhaps the norm and these must be acknowledged. First, the Napoleonic War period was accompanied by rapidly rising land values. Dartmouth's agricultural rents, for example, were raised by between a third and a half in 1799–1804 alone.[51] This may have led to a quickening of the land market for speculative gain. At the same time, interest rates were high and mortgages may have been more difficult to obtain. Secondly, and related to the first point, the Ossett Enclosure Act occurred in 1807 and the award was made in 1813. Before 1807 it is possible that the accumulation and consolidation of holdings occurred as a preliminary to enclosure. For example the Deed of Lease and Release of Lands from the Mitchells to Robert Saxon, a clothier, in January 1810 is specifically marked as 'in preparation for the Inclosure award'.[52] After the award it is possible that further 'abnormal' transactions occurred as the market settled down.

Partly in order to test the extent to which an unrepresentative period of land deals had been used in the study of freehold transactions, the copyhold changes of Ossett clothiers were traced for a longer period – from 1799 to the 1850s. Like the Registry of Deeds, the Wakefield Manor Court Rolls present a formidable source which dictated that the transactions of a sample of clothiers should be used. Those with surnames A–M were chosen to facilitate search of the vast number of index volumes. The result of the survey of Ossett clothiers' copyhold land deals is set out in summary in Table 4.6.

It seems certainly to have been the case that mortgaging as well as buying and selling of clothiers' copyhold land was just as common (if not more so) than deals of freehold and there seems to have been no significant change in activity in the land market in the second quarter of the nineteenth century. This indicates that the effects of the War period on the mortgage and sale of land may have been less important than some historians have suggested, especially in industrial as compared to agricultural areas. In about a third of the mortgage deals mentioned in Table 4.6 the clothier was acting as mortgagee, often for another clothier or manufacturer, so the flow of capital via the mortgage market was not just a one way process and can be seen to have been providing a source of mutual financial assistance within the clothier community.

Of course, as with the mortgaging and sales of freehold land, it is by no means clear why the sales and mortgages occurred or for what purpose the money was being raised. It seems not unjustified to regard the sale of clothiers' land and its mortgaging as making a significant contribution to the underpinning if not to the expansion of the industry. One is prompted, not unreasonably, to think that this was the case where sales and mortgaging seem to have been concentrated at times when clothiers were expanding their interests or, alternatively, fighting against poor trading conditions. For example, the Hallas family were very active in the land market throughout the first half of the nineteenth century. At first they were raising finance for the construction and expansion of their mill at Pildacre, and towards 1830 they were trying unsuccessfully to stave off bankruptcy. Thomas Collett's transactions in the 1820s could well be related to his entry into mill manufacture in partnership with Wheatley and Overend at this time and the Greaves family, similarly, commenced occupation of Union Mills at Ossett following transfers and mortgaging of their copyhold land in the 1830s.

Several important points have emerged in this analysis of the relationship between landed wealth and investment in the textile sector. Direct investment by landowners in ownership and finance of mills seems to have been less significant than some previous authorities of the Yorkshire industry, notably Heaton and Crump and Ghorbal, have suggested. Less than 6% of mills built before 1850 were owned by landed families although up to the 1820s their involvement had been somewhat greater especially in the woollen sector with its closer proto-industrial ties to the land. Even where landowners such as Lord Dartmouth were active in mill building and finance, substantial rentals and interest charges and the lapsing of reserved rent leases were the high price which industry paid for finance from this sector.

The flow of landed capital into industry may have been of some importance where it passed through the formal and informal channels of the capital market of the period. Whilst the attorney remained a central figure in local finance his work as estate agent and rent collector promoted a continuing involvement of landowners in lending within the community. However, landowners appear to have been a less important source of loans for manufacturers than money raised within the trade itself, particularly from merchants and staplers.

The final contribution of landed wealth to the underpinning and expansion of industry, and probably the most important aspect, was the sale and mortgage of farms and fields to raise industrial capital. The sale of land, together with the increasing use of the land mortgage, seems to

Table 4.6 *Summary of copyhold land transactions of Ossett clothiers, surnames A–M, 1799–1853*

Name of clothier	Extent of landholding in township to nearest acre and other property			Dates and number of transactions	Number of mortgages
	1801	1819	1837		
Abraham Archer / James Archer / Archer family	CP	M	2 CP	1813–30s (11)	—
Benjamin Baines	CP	5 CP	—	1824, 1825 (2)	1
James Brook		—	3 CPs	1831–9 (5)	1
John Brook		1 CP	1 M H	1801–32 (4)	1
Joseph Brook		Hs		1816–41 (11)	1
James Briggs		M D W H	CP D	1809–36 (3)	2
George Briggs			—	1825–62 (2)	2
Benjamin Bedford				1799–1838 (12)	1
James Burbery	10 CP H			1804–5 (2)	—
Thomas Butterfield		3 H		1799–1815 (4)	—
George Berry				1814 (3)	1
Thomas Collett			6 M	1823–35 (6)	1
David Dews				1799–1814 (6)	1
Thomas Dews		CP	CP	1834, 1853 (2)	—
John Ellis			9 CP	1821–45 (4)	—
Samuel Ellis			6 CP	1825, 1831 (2)	—
William Fearnley			—	1803–18 (3)	—
John Fozard			2 CPH	1825–39 (6)	1
Joseph Fozard		1 CP H	—	1824–37 (4)	2

Name				
John Gartside	—	—	1807–37 (7)	2
John Greaves	—	—	1799–1812 (7)	—
Thomas Greaves	—	12 M H	1827–30s (3)	—
William Gunson	—	2 CP H	1831–50 (8)	—
Benjamin Gunson	—	2 CP H	1822, 1836 (2)	—
Benjamin Hallas elder ⎫ Benjamin Hallas jnr ⎭	105 M D Hs CPs	23 M C Ps Hs	1799–1830s (39)	1
William Hallas	—	—	1799–1827 (5)	2
William Hanson	—	—		2
Benjamin Mitchell	—	6 CPs	1833 (2)	2
David Mitchell elder	17	—	1799–1812 (10)	1
Eli Mitchell	3 CPs Hs	9 CP	1831–54 (7)	2
James Mitchell	7 CP	7 CPs	1804–14 (2)	—
John Mitchell	—	—	1834–49 (11)	—
Joseph Mitchell	—	—	1804–13 (3)	—
Thomas Mitchell	7 CP	—	1821–47 (5)	—
Joshua Moss	—	CPs	1825–42 (3)	—

Key:

—	= information not recorded.
CP	= clothier's premises, i.e. workshop, cottage, garden.
CPs	= several workshops with cottage and garden.
M	= mill.
D	= dyehouse.
W	= warehouse.
H(s)	= house(s).

Source: Wakefield Manor Court Rolls (Y.A.S.).

have been a major source of investment funds for industry. The survival
of many mortgage deeds among business papers bears testimony to this
and examination of the West Riding Registry of Deeds and the Wakefield Manor Court Rolls confirm the existence of an active market in land
and property securities involving all types of manufacturers throughout
the first half of the nineteenth century and earlier. This appears to have
been particularly the case in the communities of the woollen area such as
Ossett.

Thus it is difficult to agree with Postan and others that 'Surprisingly
little of the wealth of rural England found its way into the new industrial
enterprises.'[53] Direct financial involvement of landowners in sectors
other than mining and transport may well have been limited but the complex relationship between landholding and the evolution of rural
industry had important financial consequences which are all too often
underplayed or ignored by historians.

PART 3
THE WEB OF CREDIT

In every commercial state, notwithstanding any pretension to equal rights, the exaltation of the few must depress the many.

Adam Ferguson,
An Essay on the History of Civil Society (1765)

INTRODUCTION

As Edward Law remarked before the House of Lords Committee on the Woollen Trade in May 1800, 'from the wool grower to the consumer a piece of broadcloth passes through an hundred different hands'.[1] At each change of hands the possibility of credit extension arose. The dynamic potential of the textile manufacturer, enmeshed in the centre of this credit web, was much conditioned by prevailing credit terms. To understand how the organisation of trade and credit practice changed over time is thus of fundamental importance in analysing the sources of finance for the growth and expansion of production.

Technological and organisational developments in wool textile manufacturing were accompanied by considerable change in the methods and organisation of trade in both the raw materials and the finished products of the industry. The geographical distance over which trade took place (associated with changing markets and sources of raw material supply); the activities of merchants, middlemen and factors; the development of speedier communications; changes in the turnover time of capital: all these affected the chain of credit, linking the various parts of trade to the whole. Superimposed upon the effects of these long-term factors, credit practices were further influenced by short-term economic instability and trade fluctuations.

The manufacturing concern would feel the effects of both short- and long-term factors via its ability to draw on credit from its sources of supply, and by the speed and nature of incoming payments for finished products. Drawing heavily on surviving West Riding business records,[2] supplemented primarily by bankruptcy data, bank records and evidence from Parliamentary Papers, Chapters 5–8 explore the nature and transformation of the credit matrix within which the manufacturer functioned.

As a preliminary it is useful to distinguish between two very different types of credit which had a contrasting impact on the position of the manufacturer and which were subject to different influences. 'Internal credit' or 'open credit' are terms applied to the book debts of a firm which were often subject to a discount if paid promptly. A firm giving this type of credit facility usually included an element of interest in its pricing and thus carried out a quasi-banking function. Before the 1830s the interest charged on book debts was often much higher than the 5% allowed by the Usury Laws. A yearly figure of 8% was quite common.[3] This made internal credit an attractive proposition for the supplier at a time when the law prevented such returns in practically all other spheres.

'External' trade credit refers to the taking of a bill of exchange or similar paper as payment for a debt. The seller of the goods could discount the bill with his bank or a London discount house, or pass it on at a discounted value to a client thus realising immediate funds. The credit created was usually the product of accommodation provided by the local and national discount market, principally the banking sector. In commercial transactions internal and external credit were commonly combined; a buyer being given a period of open credit following which payment was made in bills. Bill discount could significantly release a manufacturer's funds from the trade account into more productive use.

5

WOOL PURCHASE

The most important element on the supply side of the industry was raw wool. Throughout the period it remained by far the greatest prime cost for most firms not specialising in weaving or finishing only. Estimates from the 1850s indicate that wool accounted at that time for between a third and a half of total costs, and between a half and two-thirds of prime costs for worsted manufacturers.[1] The woollen branch must have been broadly similar. Thus wool trading practices particularly the extension of credit by suppliers, formed a major influence on the amount of variable capital needed by the manufacturer.

The bulk of wool consumed by the West Riding textile industry throughout this period was of domestic origin, bought either direct from the growers or, more usually, through factors. Even in 1850 it is variously estimated that as much as two-thirds of the raw wool absorbed by the British woollen industry as a whole came from the domestic clip.[2] However, from the late sixteenth century, changes in commercial agriculture, particularly the spread of enclosures and the cross breeding of sheep for mutton, resulted in the progressive deterioration of the English fleeces in most counties.[3] English wool grew longer and coarser which made it admirably suitable for combing and worsted production but much less suitable by the late eighteenth century for the woollen industry, especially the finer products. The industry responded by increasingly mixing the finer and softer Spanish and German wools with the domestic clip, and by the late 1820s many woollen manufacturers were using as much, if not more, of these imported fibres than the English wool.[4] The use of Australian wool was extended rapidly from the 1820s to become the largest single source of imports by the mid-1840s.[5] The worsted branch of the industry used a much smaller proportion of foreign wool before 1850 although by the 1830s and 1840s it became technically possible to use shorter wools like the Australian in worsted manufacture. The practice of using other fibres with wool resulted in the purchase of imported alpaca and mohair by some firms, and in the heavy woollen sector, particularly in the manufacture of blankets, the use of recycled wool was an important feature from the 1830s. The rag supply sprang partly from domestic sources but a large proportion was imported from the Continent.[6]

With these developments in mind it is necessary to consider the purchase of wool of a number of different kinds, from a variety of sources and through several channels. But this must be set against a backcloth of the movement of wool prices reflecting supply conditions which had influences on credit.

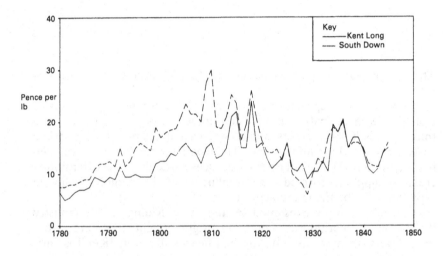

Graph 5.1
Movements of the average price of two types of English wool, 1780–1850
Sources: P.P. 1828 (515) VIII, p. 15; P.P. 1836 (465–II) XIII, pp. 543, 560; P.P. 1846 (109) XLIV, p. 109. See Mitchell and Deane, *Abstract of British Historical Statistics*, pp. 495–6.

Evidence of the movement of English wool prices is collected in Graph 5.1. Local indicators for the West Riding suggest similar trends.[7] From these figures, concentrating particularly on the Yorkshire evidence, it would seem that the 1770s to the early 1790s were decades when the wool market became easier. According to Bischoff the average price of English wool per lb in the 1760s was 9½d whereas in the 1770s it was only 8d.[8] Improved breeding and closer attention devoted to sheep rearing had increased the production of English wool, whilst importation from Ireland and other sources was becoming considerable. These factors, along with the slump caused by the American War, brought down the price of wool very quickly. By 1779, with an average price of around 6d per lb, English wool reached the lowest levels of the century. Wool growers were compelled to sell cheaply and yet they had considerable stocks remaining on their hands. John Hustler, the famous Bradford wool stapler, stated that there was a stock of wool on hand unsold in the wool counties amounting to two or three years' clip in the early 1780s.[9] Although prices were higher from the mid-1780s, Hustler estimated that six months' stock was still on hand in the wool counties by the mid-1790s.[10]

Under the influence of wartime dislocations, tariff changes and speculative buying, the wool supply situation changed markedly from the mid-1790s. European imports were curtailed whilst the demands of the industry were volatile. Thus, domestic short-stapled wool was at a premium, as illustrated by the differential movement of South Down and Kent Long prices. At the same time, high food prices stimulated a diversion of land and resources from wool into grain and meat production in some areas. The result was highly unstable wool prices. As early as 1800 manufacturers were complaining that they could not get enough wool to fill half their European orders.[11] Shortages seem to have been a recurring problem of the war period, aggravated by speculative forestalling on the part of the wool traders. From 1819 wool prices were falling again. Improved domestic supply was supplemented by increasing imports subject to only a nominal tariff after 1823.[12] The buoyant condition of wool textile manufacture in the period 1829–36 seems to have been largely responsible for the rising trend of wool prices at that time. The more depressed conditions of the late 1830s and early 1840s stemmed this rise. The influx of Australian wool, particularly from the 1840s, ensured much easier conditions of wool supply and generally lower prices for several decades.

After 1815 the increasing import of short-stapled wool competed with the domestic clip of the South Down type to depress its price relative to that of English long wools like the Kent. The more rapid expansion of the worsted branch of the industry in the first half of the nineteenth century further stimulated demand for long staples and boosted their price relative to short wools. However, by the 1840s, Australian imports which included longer staples and the use of shorter wools in some worsted production combined to bring the prices of various staples closer into line.

It is unfortunate that there is no reliable price series for imported wool but it would appear justifiable for the present purpose to use the English wool data as a general indication of the movement of wool prices, particularly as a strong relationship appears to exist between their trends and the changing level of imports indicating the substitution effect.

The structure of wool purchase

Against this backcloth of change in wool supply and prices, alterations also occurred in the practice of wool buying by manufacturers and these had important credit implications.

From the early eighteenth century the larger Yorkshire manufacturers were in the habit of buying a proportion of their wool direct from farmers and factors in the wool growing counties. Manufacturers themselves travelled to the wool growing areas in the weeks following the annual clip, or bought wool through the offices of travellers or agents. Samuel Hill of Soyland made such journeys each year through several counties in the 1730s.[13] John Sutcliffe of Ovenden a smaller, and perhaps more typical, worsted manufacturer bought wool from Lincolnshire through an agent.[14] In 1800, Christopher Rawden was in the habit of buying direct from growers for his worsted business and John Brooke, woollen cloth manufacturer of Honley, bought wool in Sussex, Norfolk and Suffolk in the early decades of the nineteenth century.[15] It is possible to find many such examples of direct buying as late as the mid-nineteenth century, especially in the worsted branch which remained more dependent on English wools.

Buying in this way eliminated the profit of the middleman or stapler, enabling the manufacturer to obtain wools at the most advantageous prices. It also ensured a more regular supply and avoided the effects of forestalling. However, these advantages were balanced by the fact that credit facilities were sometimes sacrificed. Unlike factors and staplers, growers usually demanded immediate payment in cash or short dated bills. Farmers in areas distant from the West Riding were suspicious of trade bills and drafts on West Riding banks. They had a marked preference for cash.[16] Only where a regular and trusted relationship was built up between grower and purchaser over many years is there much evidence of longer credits.[17]

The advantages of some direct purchasing seems to have outweighed the disadvantages for those manufacturers who could afford the time and money involved. The manufacturers' capital necessarily tied up in stocks from one clip to the next, as well as the cost of travel, was considerable. The smaller clothiers, typical of the woollen sector, had no choice but to purchase their wool locally as they required it from staplers at the markets. They usually bought two or three stones at a time (enough for one week's work for a family domestic concern), and relied on the measure of credit which their supplier allowed them.[18]

The general tendency from the late eighteenth century amongst all but the biggest manufacturers, especially in the woollen branch, was to buy more and more of their English wool through middlemen and staplers.[19] Specialisation of production enlarged the advantage of buying wool ready-sorted. Thus one could obtain only that part of the fleece which particular types of cloth required:[20] 'I used to buy in the counties, but lately, manufacturing a particular sort of wool only, it has suited my purpose better to buy from the staplers.'[21] By 1800, when John Ratcliffe a

Saddleworth manufacturer made this statement, it was possible to obtain English wool of up to nine different sorts: Royal Prime or Picklock, Prime, Choice, Super, Head, Downrights, Seconds, Abb, Livery and Britch.[22] Buying through staplers also reduced the need to stockpile, thus freeing the manufacturers' capital for more productive use.

By the second decade of the nineteenth century, it was only periods of very high wool prices and speculative activity that induced large numbers of manufacturers to descend on the wool counties with the aim of cutting out the margin of the staplers and dealers.[23] By 1815, when wool prices peaked, it was a matter of remark that in Newark, Lincs., '[the Yorkshire Manufacturers] are riding about the country as if they were mad'.[24] It was only in the worsted communities, such as Keighley, that the tradition of buying direct remained strong by the second quarter of the nineteenth century.[25]

A further factor encouraging the practice of dealing through staplers in the purchase of wool in the early nineteenth century was the extended use of imported wool, particularly in the woollen branch. Here, however, there was frequently a divergence of experience between the mass of small businesses and the handful of large concerns. For the multitude of small manufacturers, the wool stapler became the main source of foreign wool. Larger manufacturers were encouraged to deal direct with importers in London, Hull and Liverpool. In some cases they extended their trading interests to Europe, Russia and other parts.[26] The extension

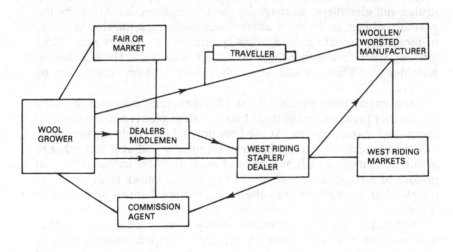

Trade links with direction of significant credit extension

Diagram 5.1
Credit relationships in the trade in English wool

of the auction system from the late 1830s, especially sales of Australian wool in Liverpool and London, encouraged firms with the necessary capital to bypass the local dealers and to buy in bulk at cut prices.[27]

Leaving aside the trade in foreign wool for the moment, it is evident that the purchase of English wool can be represented diagramatically in such a way as to highlight the credit relationships which require examination (see Diagram 5.1).

Growers and dealers

It is unfortunate that few records of the wool growers of the period have survived.[28] Any study of their trading practices must rely heavily on evidence from wool purchasers: the manufacturers themselves and their agents or the staplers. Staplers and those manufacturers who bought their English wool direct attempted to secure the most advantageous purchase terms by a combination of three different methods. First, there was much dealing direct in bulk with the growers, sometimes on credit. Often agreements were made to purchase the whole clip in advance. A second method involved buying through agents or dealers in the wool counties or in London. This trade was often financed either by the stapler or by the manufacturer who sent a large proportion of the purchase money to the agent in advance.[29] Finally, wool was bought for cash at the annual wool fairs at Guisborough, Beverley, Thetford, Boroughbridge and elsewhere, although by the late eighteenth century the importance of fairs in the wool counties was declining somewhat in favour of more direct dealing. By the last quarter of the century many large growers were forwarding their fleeces to Wakefield, Halifax, Leeds, Keighley and Huddersfield where they were sold on commission by dealers.[30]

Through the whole period *c.* 1750–1850 there is no indication that long credits ever prevailed in the trade between wool grower and the staplers, agents and manufacturers. At the fairs they sold for cash or short dated bills, and purchasers visiting the farms frequently vied with each other to obtain discounts for cash purchases of the bulk of the annual clips.[31] In periods of high prices, credit in this branch was known to dry up completely. For example in 1815 the Leicestershire farmers were said to 'want most of the money before the wool is weighed'.[32]

Even in periods of less feverish activity there is little evidence that wool growers advanced credit on any scale to expedite the disposal of their crop. Being storable, the clip was usually retained rather than sold below par. In 1821, for example, James Liptaft, grazier of Braunston, Rutland, consigned three years' growth to Wakefield for sale.[33] By 1828, following the lower wool prices of the mid-1820s, James Fison, a Thetford wool dealer, was of the opinion that the farmers had become 'the warehouse keepers or stock keepers for the dealers and manufacturers'.[34] It is perhaps not so surprising that one finds little evidence of variation in the growers' credit practices associated with the state of trade.

The records of three Yorkshire wool stapling concerns, who had extensive dealings with growers in a large number of the wool counties, survive to render a clear picture of the trading terms prevailing between the growers and their customers.[35] In the last quarter of the eighteenth century the indications are that some credit could be expected, especially between long-established trading connections.

David Spencer, a Keighley wool stapler buying from Boston and Sleaford in Lincs. in 1798, paid his suppliers through orders on their local banks usually due in three months although the 'time' varied from 'on demand' to five months. By dealing with a large number of regular suppliers (forty in all), and spreading his debts, Spencer was able to gain a total credit of £2,986 in November 1798, £3,974 in July 1799 at the height of the wool season, £4,256 in January 1800 and £4,500 in August 1812.[36] John Jowitt & Sons of Bradford bought largely from dealers rather than growers but several examples from their late eighteenth-century ledgers indicate a time allowance from their regular growers of two to four weeks, followed by payment in bills at two months.[37]

In the first quarter of the nineteenth century the incoming correspondence of Joseph Jackson, Wakefield wool stapler, covering the period 1809–21, indicates that growers who dealt with Jackson on a regular basis generally allowed six weeks' credit after which bills at either one or two months were acceptable. Payment within four weeks usually qualified for a discount.[38] Although it is difficult to discern any cyclical or secular trend in credit terms, a seasonal pattern is evident. Outside the wool season (i.e. June to August) and particularly by early spring, their liquidity position dictated that growers were more anxious to trade in cash.[39]

The trade which growers did by forwarding their wool to agents and staplers in the West Riding for sale on commission resulted in the extension of some credit by growers. It was usually agreed that if the wool remained unsold for a period exceeding about four weeks, growers would apply for an advance from their agent.[40] Despite this, Jackson who dealt with at least twenty growers in this way was frequently exhorted to sell at no more than two months' credit, or not to sell on credit at all.[41] Thus, even where growers had cut out the profit margin of the local dealer, they did not involve themselves in the extension of finance to the industry beyond a circumscribed period of two to three months at most.

By the late 1820s any credit dealings which were practised by growers in the earlier years appear to have been on the decline: 'Credit is curtailing,' stated Jowitt in 1828, 'and it [English wool purchase] is becoming more a business for money.'[42] To some extent Jowitt's remarks may have been coloured by his arguing the case for increased tariffs on imported wool. Evidence from his ledgers for the 1830s and 1840s supports the idea that credit terms were shortening, although by the late 1820s, Jowitts, like most other staplers, bought their English wool through dealers and factors rather than direct from the growers. It is possible that this reflects the easier credit terms to be gained by avoiding direct trade with the growers. Charles Bull, stapler of Lewes, Sussex, had generally obtained two months' credit from his growers in the early nineteenth century; by 1825 he expected only two or three days' credit:

I certainly from my long knowledge of the different farmers and I trust from the regularity of paying the farmers, very often have got two months credit from them; but many of them now want their money and it is difficult to obtain that credit which they would readily have granted in other times.[43]

It is necessary to look away from the growers to identify the more important sources of credit extension in the wool trade. As we have noted, except in periods of very high wool prices, Yorkshire staplers and manufacturers dealt more with middlemen and agents in the wool counties and in London than they did direct with the growers. Jowitt's, for example, dealt with about 300 suppliers in the period *c*. 1790–1830s, over half of whom are recognisable as dealers selling ready-sorted wool rather than fleeces.[44] Were it possible to distinguish the nature of all suppliers, it is likely that even more dealers would be identified. The credit terms of these middlemen were frequently more flexible than those of growers. Some allowed as much as three months' credit—or allowed half payments after six months if half was paid immediately in ready cash. A discount of 2½% was usually allowed on payment within the specified time and if 'time' was extended for any reason it was customary to charge 5% interest.[45] Odd examples from the records of other dealers show that the terms that Jowitt's faced were fairly typical. The six months' credit allowed by Joseph Wheatley, a Leicestershire supplier of wool and noyles to Benjamin Hallas, an Ossett clothier, in the early 1790s and again in 1801 seems unusual. Even Wheatley, a long-established correspondent of Hallas, allowed only four to six weeks' credit on the bulk of his sales in the period 1789–1800s.[46] Corroborating evidence for the 1830s is gained from the papers of William Haigh, clothier of Saddleworth, who was buying his English wool through a London dealer, George Davis. Davis' terms were two months' credit followed by bills at two months.[47] The credit terms which Jowitt's received from their dealers are detailed in Table 5.1. They indicate a slight secular increase in the first quarter of the nineteenth century, possibly coinciding with the increasing competition from imported wools and the decline in credit allowed by English wool growers. At no period is there evidence to suggest that the sustained credit extension of these English wool dealers and middlemen was large in early nineteenth-century terms. Four months seems to have been the norm by the 1820s.

Table 5.1 *Credit periods allowed by English wool suppliers[a] to J. Jowitt & Sons, 1775–c.1830*

Date	No. of suppliers studied	Most common credit period allowed without interest	Upper limit of credit period allowed without interest	Most common nature of payment
1775–7	2	2 weeks	—	Cash or bills at 2 months
c.1790–1815	146	4 weeks	3 months[b]	Bills at 2 months
c.1817–30	197	8 weeks	3 months	Bills at 2 months

[a] Excludes growers where identifiable.
[b] Six months' credit was found only in the case of Jas. Pinnack & Sons of Winchester, 1802–5, supplying high sorts.
— = information not recorded.
Source: Jowitt, items 1–4, 12 (B.).

The key figure in credit dealings in the wool trade throughout the period was the wool stapler. Yorkshire staplers were deeply involved in financing both the purchase of wool and its sale on credit to manufacturers. As the direct purchase of wool by the bulk of manufacturers declined in the first quarter of the nineteenth century, the pivotal nature of the stapler increased.

Even in the last quarter of the eighteenth century, staplers like the Emmets of Halifax and the Jowitts were extending massive amounts of finance in advance to their suppliers and agents who were scouring the wool counties buying for them. These agents were occasionally employees or travellers but more often they were independent concerns who charged a commission of ½–2½% for their services. The Emmets commonly advanced a half to three-quarters of the cost of purchase to their supplier Gillyat Sumner, a Beverley fellmonger, throughout the period 1785–1815. The rest was usually sent when the wool arrived which meant that they were often out of pocket for three to five months.[48]

Similarly, Jowitt's paid their commission agents, both in London and in the wool counties, in advance so that the latter were rarely called upon to use their own capital. George Overitt, commencing as commission purchaser for Jowitt's in Norfolk and Suffolk in 1802 was immediately advanced capital to cover much of the season's purchases and allowed a commission of 2½% 'as much as is generally given'.[49] His father-in-law John Syder buying fleeces for Jowitt's since the late eighteenth century charged 1% commission and was advanced up to £2,000 each wool season by 1808–13.[50]

Joseph Jackson, Wakefield wool stapler, bought an increasing amount of his English wool through commission agents in the period 1808–21.

His travelling partner, James Lupton, alone was furnished with more than £1,000 a week in the wool seasons, for buying wool at fairs, from growers and through dealers. Substantial commission agents such as R. & N. Burton of Allingate, Lincs., were sent large financial drafts in advance to use for purchasing from growers like the Duke of Rutland who gave substantial discounts for cash purchases.[51] Jackson was even known to extend accommodation at interest to independent dealers to enable them to purchase larger quantities of wool which he would then sell for them on commission.[52]

Assuming the representativeness of the records of Jowitt's, Jackson and Emmet's, it appears that a large proportion of Yorkshire purchases of English wool were financed by West Riding staplers.

Imported wool

Before considering the mechanism and practice whereby the staplers disposed of their wool to the Yorkshire manufacturers, something must be said of the organisation of the trade in foreign wool. Most staplers and several manufacturers were significantly involved in this by the first quarter of the nineteenth century as the importance of foreign wools in U.K. manufacture was becoming very significant (see Table 5.2). Manufacturers and staplers received their earliest supplies of imported wool from Spain, Portugal and Germany through importers and dealers mainly situated in London. This tended to strengthen the links between the Yorkshire wool market and London, even in English wool dealings.[53]

Table 5.2 *Estimates of the approximate proportion of foreign wool used in U.K. wool textile manufacture*

Date	% proportion of foreign wool used	Source of estimate
1790	3	Glover, 'Dewsbury Mills', p. 5
1820	10	Based on Luccock's estimate
1828	28	Based on Hubbard's estimate
1840	30	Glover, 'Dewsbury Mills', p. 5
1845	36	Based on Southey's estimate

Note: The proportions for 1820, 1828 and 1845 were calculated by converting Luccock's, Hubbard's and Southey's estimates (respectively) of English wool production from packs to lbs and comparing these, net of exports, with weights of imported wool, see Bischoff, *A Comprehensive History*, vol. 2, Appendix.

By 1810, when imported wool perhaps accounted for some 7–8% of total wool used by English manufacturers,[54] Jowitt's had more than half their suppliers situated in London and many were supplying them with foreign wools. They also had half a dozen suppliers of Spanish wool in

Bristol, which seems to have been important in the import of Iberian wool until at least the 1830s. Over half of Jowitt's foreign wool suppliers were working for a commission of between ½ and 1%, depending on the source and quality of the wool. Interestingly, it seems that, unlike commission buyers of English wool, those involved in imported wool tended to use their own capital and not to be significantly indebted in any long-term sense to their correspondents in the manufacturing areas, whether staplers or manufacturers.[55]

As early as 1796 Williams & Newland of Chichester, Sussex, made explicit their terms of trade on Spanish wool: six months' credit was allowed, followed by a bill at two months or, if a bill was sent at one month from invoice, a discount of 4% was allowed. Similar terms were applied by Brooke & Company, Spanish wool suppliers of London, with credit extending to eight months on some consignments without interest being charged. Unlike the Sussex firm, Brooke & Company were working for Jowitt's on commission.[56] Further evidence of credit allowed to Jowitt's on imported wool is detailed in Table 5.3, which exemplifies the contrast between these lengthier credits and those found in the trade in English wool. The table also indicates some change in credit practice over time, more credit tending to be the rule in periods of lower wool prices. Importers, unlike growers, were perhaps more prepared to extend credit to expedite the disposal of their stocks, especially if further shipments were on the way and would soon have to be paid for.

Table 5.3 *Credit periods allowed by imported wool dealers to J. Jowitt & Sons, c.1790s–1848*

Date	No. of suppliers studied	Possible maximum credit period allowed without interest	Most common period of credit taken	Most common nature of payment
1790s–1810s	3	8 months	4 weeks	Bills at 2 months
c.1814–19	3	6 months	—	Bills at 2 months
c.1819–21	3	2 months	—	Bills at 2 months
c.1821–30	1	4 months	2 months	Bills at 2 months
1830–48	9	6 months	4 weeks	Cash

— = information not recorded.
Source: Jowitt, Ledgers 1791–1848, items 2–4, 13 (B.).

Before the extension of the auction system in the 1830s, Yorkshire manufacturers purchased the bulk of imported wool through a local stapler. Larger concerns such as Clay's of Rastrick, Cooke's of Dewsbury, and Salt's of Bradford who had more direct trading links seem to have been exceptions to the general rule.[57] The trade in wool from Germany and Spain was partly financed by foreign exporting firms who sent wool to be sold by West Riding dealers on commission. Thus William Willans & Company Ltd of Huddersfield were selling wool for a number of German and Spanish concerns by the 1820s. Money was remitted to these concerns only after the wool was sold and commission deducted. Sometimes a long dated bill was sent which could be negotiated for cash at an earlier date.[58] At the same time a few Yorkshire dealers were also involved in financing the import trade themselves. Willans were buying wool from Germany through purchasers such as C. F. Nauk of Hamburg who charged 2–2½% commission but used their own capital.[59] Jowitt's similarly bought substantial amounts of German wool from Hamburg and Breslau in the 1830s and 1840s. Much of this trade was done in partnership with N. P. Simes of Leeds; they usually paid within eight weeks of the arrival of the wool.[60]

By 1830, imported wool, particularly from Germany, accounted for perhaps 30% of the raw wool used in the industry and the terms on which it was sold by the importers and dealers, credits of up to six months, were of increasing importance to the liquidity position of both staplers and manufacturers. The importance of staplers in the supply of imported wool to the Yorkshire industry changed quite markedly from the late 1830s as it was in this decade that wool auctions held in London and Liverpool began to play an important role.[61]

Australian Merino wools upon which the auction system focussed were cheaper than similar Saxony and Spanish types and found a market particularly among the Yorkshire woollen manufacturers. The worsted industry, however, stuck largely to longer-stapled English wools, even after combing improvements, mainly because they were necessary for the lustres and mixtures produced.

Table 5.4 *English and imported wool used in the woollen and worsted branches, 1857, 1858*

	Worsted branch 1857	Woollen branch 1858
Imported wool used (m lb)	15	76
English wool used (m lb)	80	80

Source: Barnard, *The Australian Wool Market*, p. 22.

By 1858, when Australia provided about half of British wool imports, the woollen branch was utilising 83% of the retained Australian wool imports. The West Riding industry always accounted for a larger than proportionate absorption of these Australian imports. They had been first used in Yorkshire and were of great importance to the fancy and cheaper quality goods in which the area specialised.

From the early 1840s there is much evidence of the woollen manufacturers involving themselves in direct purchase of wool at the auctions,[62] and this was an area where temporary advances by banks seem to have been forthcoming.[63] Barnard has suggested that the staplers were slow to get into the colonial wool trade and that manufacturers were 'forced to conduct their selection and purchasing themselves'.[64] This may be true, to some extent, of the woollen branch of the trade with its heavy and increasing reliance on imported wool but staplers appear to have played an important role also, as we shall see.

It is certainly the case that Yorkshire staplers were not heavily involved in financing the importation of colonial wool until the late nineteenth century when large firms like Jowitt's began to set up branches in Australia.[65] English staplers and dealers were reluctant to assume the risks of assembling supplies 12,000 miles away and colonial growers played a major role here, frequently extending credit for ten months or more. They were aided in this by drawing on the importing agent and discounting the bill.[66] The importing agents were also heavily reliant on London and Liverpool banks for short-term accommodation frequently secured by bills of lading.[67] By 1850 the links between specialised importers and banking and acceptance houses were often very close.

Bank credit seems to have been of importance in all branches of wool purchase. Manufacturers and staplers buying at auctions and from importers were particularly aided by bank credit. Primarily, this was granted by local West Riding banks[68] but London discount and acceptance houses often provided further financial assistance.

Auction room terms were generally cash within fourteen days so the extent to which auctioned wool reached the West Riding through staplers and agents rather than by direct purchase was important in allowing a margin of credit to the industry. A sizeable and important body of London dealers bought at the auctions for resale to manufacturers and staplers in the manufacturing areas. They were generally able to make large bulk purchases and thus secured better terms than the manufacturers who attended personally but whose requirements were smaller. These dealers usually allowed two or three months' credit to their purchasers followed by bills at two months. This seems to have been the standard practice throughout the 1830s and 1840s.[69]

The wool stapler

As early as the mid-1750s wool staplers were regarded by their contemporaries as men of great commercial status and importance.[70] There is no doubt that the 'Sheet Anchor of Great Britain'[71] played a pivotal role in the trade and finance of the textile localities. The majority of manufacturers relied on the substantial credit extended by the staplers throughout the critical time of centralisation, mechanisation and extension of productive capacity in the industry.

The Jowitt records give the clearest picture of the way in which one stapling concern organised its credit terms for the trade from the 1770s to the mid-nineteenth century. Their earliest surviving ledger covers sales accounts for the period 1775–7, and gives details of transactions with seventy-five different purchasers of wool.[72] The vast majority were small clothiers buying wool two or three times each month, a few stones at a time. This confirms the fact that small domestic manufacturers lived from hand to mouth as far as their raw material was concerned, and tied up little of their capital in stocks. The staplers were the stockholders for the bulk of the manufacturers in this period. The typical small clothiers such as William Brook and William Page of Morley were buying 12–13 stones of wool each month throughout the year in two or three purchases per month. Credit terms varied greatly between different purchasers and obviously depended on Jowitt's knowledge and assessment of their clients' credit-worthiness. In 1775 credit terms varied from four weeks to six months followed by bills at three months. The most common credit period was three or four months, followed by bills at three months. Regular purchasers, who were proven to pay promptly on the expiration of the credit period, were often allowed six months' credit without charge. Others, like William Medley of Churwell, who only made one purchase, was charged 5% interest on his credit. Several examples occur of payment by instalments: David Smith of High Burton buying packs of wool arranged to pay a third immediately, a third in six months and a third in nine months.

Over time, one can discern some change in credit practice with longer periods becoming more common in 1776–7. Purchasers like Samuel Horsfall of Drighlington had his regular credit allowance of four weeks in 1775 raised to six to eight months in 1776–7. Six to twelve months' credit became increasingly common, with examples of individuals such as Joshua Willans of Ossett being allowed more than twelve months' credit. Clothiers who paid within the 'time' were allowed an abatement but these were insufficient (and probably not intended) to encourage cash sales. There was no consistent abatement practice; abatements were small and usually represented a rounding down to the nearest whole figure.

By the 1780s and 1790s Jowitt's were dealing with over 400 purchasers.[73] Again, a marked feature of credit terms was their variation between customers; from one to nine months (three months being the most common) in 1790 after which further 'time' was charged at 5%. It was not unusual for purchasers to take twelve months or more to pay; for part of this facility they paid interest. Again the more important regular purchasers were allowed longer free credits; for example, Joseph Walker of Hunslet was allowed eight months in the period 1790–5 before interest was charged. William Langley and James Brown of Leeds were allowed six months. A 2% discount was allowed for payment in less than three months, and 5% for payment within two weeks, but few clothiers chose to pay in cash. By the turn of the century a 10% sample of Jowitt's purchasers (forty-four individuals and concerns) showed thirteen taking longer to pay than the agreed time (and paying interest for the additional credit), eleven paid before the expiration of the credit period they had been granted and became eligible for a discount and the remainder took advantage of their personal credit allowances.

By the late 1780s Jowitt's had a considerable trade in Spanish wool which they tended to sell on slightly longer credits than their English wool, perhaps because more credit was in turn available from their imported wool suppliers than from English wool traders. Thomas Clough of Bramley, a substantial and regular client, was allowed six months' credit on Spanish wool compared with only three months' on most of his English wool purchases in the late 1780s.

The 1790s and early 1800s saw little discernible change in Jowitt's credit terms although 1803 and 1804 seem to have been tighter years following the long period of commercial crises and instability of the 1790s. The Emmets of Halifax were at this time having great difficulty in securing payment for wools which they had sold. From March 1794 through the 1800s the Emmet Letters give evidence of the scarcity of bills and money and the corresponding way in which the staplers were forced to extend their credit periods or see their clients bankrupt: 'I cannot get money in that is 12 months old and some 18 months or more', wrote Emmet to Sumner in March 1797,[74] and by November 1799, in reply to Sumner's request for an extension of finance for wool purchase: 'you write for bills as if you thought we have them for picking up in the streets ... bills is not to be had here after six, twelve and eighteen months credit so wools are lowering very fast'.[75] By October 1803 the continued disruption of trade and associated bankruptcies were causing further unwilling prolongation of credit. There was a 'great risque [*sic*] in buying wool ... also in selling it; payments being very bad, also a vast many bankruptcies about us, we hardly know who to trust'.[76] Two months later: 'There is no wool here to be sold for money and if you sell for credit there is a great risque to run not knowing who to trust so that trade is very bad at present.'[77] By 1804 even extended credit terms had not ensured the sale of Emmet's stock and although conditions improved a little in the following year, 1806 saw a return to commercial circumstances which forced Emmet's to give favourable credit terms.[78]

During the second decade of the nineteenth century it appears that Jowitt's reacted similarly to the instability of wool prices and industrial activity of the period by extending, or being forced to extend, longer credits. The common credit period became ten months, with payment following in bills at three or four months. Less than 10% of purchasers went beyond ten months, although interest was charged only after twelve months on most accounts. The majority of purchasers took full advan-

tage of the credit periods allowed them and sometimes credit was prolonged further by paying with a promissory note at interest.

The deemed credit-worthiness of customers was the major determining factor in credit allowances. This is illustrated by the fact that Jowitt's
credit rating figures were pencilled in at the head of the accounts. In
determining these credit ratings the size of a concern does not appear
to have been such an important factor as the duration and stability of a
concern's commercial relationship with Jowitt's.

In the early 1820s the most common credit period fell to between six
and eight months but again there were enormous variations between different customers.[79] A gap in the accounts prevents one from comment on
credit practice in the mid-1820s but by 1829 and in the 1830s and 1840s, in
easier conditions of wool supply, credit terms extended by Jowitt's seem
to have stabilised at from three to six months' credit (depending on the
customer) followed by bills at two months. Time was charged after six
months. About one in eight customers settled within four weeks, gaining
a discount.[80] Thus, generally speaking, as far as the Jowitt evidence is
concerned, credit terms became more customary and more stable by the
1830s and 1840s, and were also, as a rule, markedly lower than they had
been in the difficult and volatile years of the wars and their aftermath.
Table 5.5 summarises the evidence of Jowitt's credit terms for the whole
period.

Turning from Jowitt's in search of complementary information, the
accounts of David Spencer, Keighley wool stapler, indicate that in the
mid-1790s he was allowing three months' credit to his regular customers.
He had some fifty to seventy customers towards the end of the decade,
most of whom were continuously indebted to him for amounts varying
from around £1 to over £1,000. The average debt was around £80. Spencer was continually advancing to the industry amounts varying from
£2,000 to over £8,000.[81] A large proportion of Spencer's assets (around
50%) were tied up in credits granted to (or just taken by) his clients.

Dawson, Humble & Son, wool suppliers of Bradford, were also allowing three months' credit on their wool sales in the 1790s[82] and in the following decade the evidence suggests that a period of three months
remained common. The correspondence of Jackson, the Wakefield
stapler, for 1809 indicates that a period of two to three months was general.[83] Credit allowances of three months or shorter in this period contrast sharply with the longer credits allowed by Jowitt's; however
Jackson's customers do include a very high proportion of dealers and
other staplers which may explain the difference.[84]

John Brigg & Company, worsted spinners and weavers of Keighley,
were buying wool from eighteen different staplers during the period
1822–35. Most allowed two months' credit followed by bills at two
months, again indicating that Jowitt's credit terms may have been a little
more generous on average than was usual before the 1830s.[85]

Table 5.5 Credit periods allowed by J. Jowitt & Sons to wool purchasers, 1775–1840s

Date	No. of purchasers studied	Most common credit period allowed without interest	Upper limit of credit period allowed without interest	Most common type of bills where specified
1775	75	3–4 months	6 months	At 3 months
1776–7	75	6–8 months	12 months	—
1790–1802	400	3 months	9 months	—
1803–4	206	2–3 months	9 months	—
1804–7	206	3–6 months	9 months	—
c.1810–15	212	10 months	12 months	At 3 and 4 months
1815–20s	638	6–8 months	12 months	—
c.1829–40s	509	3–6 months	6 months	At 2 months

— = information not recorded.
Source: Jowitt, Ledgers 1775–1854, items 1–5 (B.).

Data from the purchase books of various manufacturers most of whom bought wool from several different dealers confirm the Jowitt evidence that the 1830s and 1840s saw some tightening and stabilisation of credit in the industry although the variation between different suppliers and different customers remained notable.[86] Clough's of Keighley were allowed eight to twelve weeks followed by cash or bills from William Horsfall & Bros., Keighley, William Barff & Sons, Wakefield, and William & Samuel Johnson of Halifax, their staplers, in the 1830s.[87] In the same decade the terms of Bairstow's, Bradford and Leeds staplers, varied from one week to three months, although the most common agreement was four to eight weeks followed by cash or bills. Discount of 1–1½% was allowed for immediate cash and discount of ½% if cash was paid after the credit period. Some instalment payments were made over six or seven weeks for large purchases.[88] In the 1840s the Clough and Bairstow records both show that one and a half or two months' credit was most common with 2% discount for cash under two weeks and 1½% discount for cash payment after the expiration of the credit period.

B. & W. Marriner, worsted spinners of Keighley were buying their wool from East Riding and Lincolnshire growers and fairs as well as from West Riding staplers. Indebtedness to their three West Riding staplers 1818–41 accounted for a large proportion of their total debts throughout the period (averaging 59%). This increased markedly from about 1827 reaching peaks in 1828 (86%), 1830 (87%), 1833 (93%) and 1835 (93%).[89] The latter three years, especially 1833–5, were years of rapid expansion and boom conditions in the wool textile industry generally. Many new factories were built, machinery and industrial capacity extended, wool consumption increased and the population influx into the West Riding was unprecedented.[90]

Marriner's made substantial additions to their premises and equipment in 1821, 1831, 1834 and particularly in 1837 when a new steam engine, engine house and spinning mill were added. If one allows twelve months or more for the gestation of capital[91] (from projected expansion to the completion of new plant) it does not seem unreasonable to postulate a relationship between increases in indebtedness allowed on wool purchase and the ability to expand.

Similar evidence of indebtedness to staplers is available for Hague & Cook blanket manufacturers of Dewsbury.[92] In the case of Hague & Cook it seems that the financial and commercial crisis experienced in late 1825 was accompanied by markedly increased total credit from their wool suppliers. Unlike Marriner's, whose debts to suppliers declined markedly in 1825–6, Hague & Cook were a well-established and sound concern by the 1820s with fingers in banking and other economic pies. It may well be that assessed credit-worthiness was the most significant factor in determining the extent to which firms could hope to get support from their staplers in hard times.

Bankruptcy records give a final clue to the pervasive importance of indebtedness to staplers.[93] One very interesting and detailed set of surviving papers concern the bankruptcy in 1826 of Joseph Harrop of Grasscroft in Saddleworth, clothier, dealer and chapman. Harrop was a substantial manufacturer possessing two mills (Royal George and Throstle Nest), a house, warehouse, dyehouse, a barn and land. His total real estate was worth £37,203. An amount totalling £14,448 was owed to staplers which represented 25% of total debts.[94]

Other examples of manufacturers' bankruptcy papers give further weight to the importance of staplers in the finance of the trade.[95] A rich source of such information is the manuscript account of local bankruptcies kept by John Jowitt of the Bradford wool stapling concern during 1839–47.[96]

Table 5.6 indicates the extent of indebtedness to staplers of various types of wool textile manufacturers at the time of their bankruptcy. These are likely to represent minimum figures as Jowitt's account is probably incomplete. Nevertheless, the debts to staplers are substantial in the case of all types of concern from the smaller clothiers to the larger concerns of cloth manufacturers and worsted spinners. This, of course, says nothing about credit but provides further clues regarding its importance.

Table 5.6 *Average indebtedness of bankrupt wool textile manufacturers to staplers*

Year	Cloth manufacturers (£)	Merchant-manufacturers (£)	Clothiers (£)	Worsted spinners (£)	Fancy manufacturers (£)
1839	—	—	1,900(1)	26,000(1)	—
1840	4,891(5)	—	1,252(11)	1,963(3)	1,200(2)
1841	8,250(2)	9,100(2)	555(4)	—	—
1842	—	—	387(13)	1,000(1)	—
1843	1,963(3)	—	3,556(4)	—	—
1844	2,250(1)	2,665(2)	—	—	—
1845	2,400(1)	500(1)	3,400(3)	300(2)	—
1846	—	—	423(5)	—	—
1847	1,933(4)	—	1,507(3)	6,333(3)	—

Note: Numbers of bankruptcies studied are given in brackets.
— = information not recorded.
Source: Jowitt, item 62 (B.), see Hudson, 'The West Riding Wool Textile Industry', Appendix A.

Before concluding our account of the role of the wool stapler in the finance of the wool trade, and hence of the industry itself, it is worth considering the capital sources which enabled him to extend credit of the type detailed. From what is known of the growers' and importers' credit it seems certain that the staplers were extending credit to a much greater extent to their purchasers than they were able to receive from their suppliers. This was the case even in the 1830s and 1840s; although staplers' credit was curtailing and stabilising, so also was the credit of their suppliers, both growers and importers.

By the mid-eighteenth century wool staplers as a group were important figures in the financial, commercial and social life of the major West Riding communities especially Leeds, Wakefield and Halifax. Once established as important figures in this branch of business the staplers commonly became respected and trusted pillars of the community. This enabled them to call upon loan capital of various kinds and this seems to have been most important especially in the case of short-term loan capital from attorneys and banks. As we shall see in Chapter 9, staplers themselves were among the most important group in the establishment of private West Riding banks from the mid-eighteenth century to the 1820s and of joint stock banks in the later period.

The mix of banking and stapling obviously worked well; capital acquired in the short term on the banking side of the business could be employed in credit extension in the wool trade. Those staplers who could offer the facility of a secure and regular credit would ensure for themselves a regular set of customers bound to them by a continuous debt relationship.

Most staplers were heavily involved on the boards and in the shareholdings of the early joint stock banks in the area.[97] This enabled them to command a regular overdraft of considerable proportions. The eight staplers holding accounts with the Bradford Banking Company 1827–30 had chronic overdrafts averaging £1,629 in those years and five of them continued with similar balances 'in the red' throughout the 1830s and 1840s. All had a considerable shareholding in the company which ensured favourable treatment and most had securities permanently pledged.[98]

Similar evidence of staplers' indebtedness to banks could be quoted from the minute books and securities records of other banking companies throughout the 1830s and 1840s. The Huddersfield Banking Company, the Mirfield & Huddersfield District Banking Company and the Halifax Joint Stock Banking Company yield notable cases. For the Jowitt concern a fairly full set of bank overdraft figures are available for the period 1790–1860s enabling one to see clearly the existence of the chronic overdrafts so important to the stapler's own credit extension.[99]

An examination of wool staplers' bankruptcy accounts indicates a wide range of indebtedness. Banks figure very prominently but the next most important creditor is the local mercantile community. Local merchants, staplers and wool dealers as well as more distant trading connections were important sources of credit and loans in the 1830s and 1840s.

Often they held as much as a quarter of staplers' debts. Securing this finance seems sometimes to have been intimately connected not just with commercial and personal relationships but with religious affiliation; Henry Burgess and James Hubbard, staplers of London and Leeds, who became bankrupt in 1820, owed the bulk of their debts to persons specifically described as Quakers.[100]

Thus the trade in English wool was characterised by cash or short credit dealings with growers and at fairs, growers tending to curtail credit even with their regular customers by the late 1820s. Dealers and middlemen in the wool counties gave an added element of credit to the system but, in credit extension to manufacturers, the key figure, whether he bought direct from the grower or from dealers, appears to have been the wool stapler. The increased importation of European wools from the late eighteenth century strengthened the position of the stapler in the wool supply before the 1820s, after which large-scale auctioning of Australian wool at discount prices increased the temptation to manufacturers to bypass the profit margins of the middlemen. This development increased the disparity between those smaller manufacturers whose lack of resources dictated their exclusive reliance on local staplers and those large concerns, usually factory producers, who could afford the cash or command the bank credit to pay on the auctioneers' terms. This fact almost certainly encouraged the gradual demise of many small clothiers, who were forced to pay higher prices for their wool. The credit offered by staplers retarded this decline, as did the use of recycled wool, but, except in the high quality or specialised cloths, raw wool prices were such an important aspect of competitive struggle that the clothiers' fate was sealed.

The staplers' credit shows some interesting variations, particularly a notable tendency to increase in both high and low points of the trade cycle. Credit extension during periods of instability and liquidity problems in the industry was often forced on the staplers by the knowledge that many of their clients were on the brink of bankruptcy and hence foreclosure. Periods of buoyant demand and activity in the industry, accompanied by easy bank credit for established staplers, often led to credit extension to cover the increased costs of manufacturers' wool purchase. The notable feature of staplers' credit terms, in the 1830s and 1840s in particular, was their relative stability through peaks and troughs of the cycle. Stability of credit terms ensured that the level of credit extended to credit-worthy firms in boom years (when both purchases and the costs of wool rose) could be very considerable.

The implications of variation in staplers' credit terms over time and between different customers are discussed more fully in Chapter 8. It is worth noting at this point that this sort of credit pattern is likely to have encouraged rapid expansion at the peak of cycles, particularly for the staplers' regular and trusted customers (perhaps even encouraging greater instability and speculation than would otherwise have occurred), whilst also sheltering such well-connected firms from some of the worst effects of the depression years.

6

MATERIALS, PLANT, SERVICES
AND LABOUR

This chapter deals with credit practice in the supply of important inputs to wool textile production other than raw wool. The first two sections deal with raw materials and capital equipment respectively whilst the third section concerns itself with the supply of services such as fulling, scribbling, dyeing, dressing and carriage. The final section deals with that most important of production costs: labour, with the complex nature of 'wages' at this time, and with the devices used by manufacturers to create credit for themselves in this sphere.

Raw materials

At the end of the eighteenth century the use of fibres other than wool was insignificant in the woollen and worsted trades, but by the 1850s cotton warps accounted for about 6–7% of prime costs in the worsted branch and 1% in the woollen branch of the industry nationally.[1] In Yorkshire these proportions were higher as this was the first area to incorporate cotton warps on a large scale, from the 1830s, in the making of a wide range of cheap cloths.[2] Even in woollen production cotton warps were used extensively in Yorkshire by the 1840s especially in the heavy woollen areas where they were found to mix well with shoddy wefts.[3] Cotton warp purchases were thus of great importance to a large proportion of West Riding concerns, especially those making particular sorts of cheap cloths. For these firms, like Robert Clough of Keighley, cotton warps accounted for as much as a third of the cost of total fibres purchased by the 1840s.[4]

The earliest record of cotton warps purchased by a West Riding concern dates from 1800 when Clay & Earnshaw were buying them to make cords. They were allowed six months' credit by Daniel Lees of Oldham who supplied them with warps each month. Their other suppliers,

Taylor's of Lower Thorpe, allowed three months' credit.[5] Further evidence does not survive until the widespread use of cotton warps from the late 1830s by which time shorter credits seem to have been the rule. Robert Clough had four major cotton warp suppliers in the early 1840s. Their credit allowances were all under three months with ½–5% discounts allowed for immediate cash purchase.[6] One of these cotton warp dealers, John Dewhirst, was also amongst the suppliers of T. & M. Bairstow Ltd in the 1840s. Bairstow's had regular deliveries and paid every six weeks or so in cash. The cash payment gained them a 2½% discount.[7]

It thus seems that in the 1840s, when cotton warps had become such an important input in the industry, regular purchasers could gain a credit period of four to six weeks which could be followed by payment in bills at two or three months. Alternatively, cash payment after the credit period resulted in discounts up to 5%.

Worsted spinning was becoming a specialist occupation with its own final product traded far beyond the confines of the local industry. Of 387 worsted firms traced in 1850, 42% were spinning concerns, 20% were weaving and only 38% carried out both processes.[8] Even in the woollen sector, characteristically dominated by vertically integrated concerns in the nineteenth century, about 10% of firms were weaving specialists in 1850.[9] Obviously, where a firm was weaving and finishing rather than doing all processes, the credit extended by woollen yarn suppliers was of immense importance.

Detailed evidence of the credit terms of five major worsted yarn suppliers covering the 1830s and 1840s is available in the Purchase Ledgers of T. & M. Bairstow who were buying much of the yarn they used from outside concerns on a regular basis.[10] The most common credit allowance through the period seems to have been two months. In addition many bills were used in the transactions which effectively added another two months on to the credit period. As Bairstow's was a well-established concern by the 1830s, dealing with regular suppliers, they are likely to have obtained generous credit terms. Overall it is likely that yarn supply was similar in credit practice to that prevailing in the supply of cotton warps.

The increasing importance of recycled wool as raw material in the woollen industry, from the 1820s, prompts examination of credit practice in this trade. Before the perfection of the carbonisation process after mid-century the use of recycled wool was mainly confined to the making of heavy and coarse woollen products, yet its importance as a proportion of the total amount of woollen fibre used in the U.K. industry was very marked by the 1840s. Malin has recently shown that the importance of recycled wool has been underestimated by historians who relied on figures of total rather than clean-wool weights.[11] His more accurate estimates of recycled wool as a proportion of total clean wool used in the

U.K. are as follows:

$$
\begin{array}{ll}
1840\text{--}4 & 7.5\% \\
1845\text{--}9 & 14.2\% \\
1850\text{--}4 & 19.4\%[12]
\end{array}
$$

In the West Riding the proportion of rag wool used was much higher than this, for the area was by far the most important seat of the shoddy trade. In fact, very little waste wool was used in the U.K. outside of Yorkshire in this period and it is possible that the West Riding figure of recycled wool used as a proportion of total clean wool was as high as 25–30% by the late 1840s. Individual firms manufacturing particular sorts of heavy or coarse woollens, such as pilots, army cloths and blankets, relied very heavily on waste wool in their production as their surviving blend books of the 1840s and 1850s suggest. Thomas Taylor of Batley was using over 60% by weight of recycled wool in a large proportion of the cloths which his firm made in 1843–4.[13] By the 1850s the proportion had increased to over 70% in some cloths and Henry Day of Hanging Heaton used 77% waste wool in some of his manufactures.[14] As recycled wool was much cheaper than even the worst grades of raw wool, the proportion of recycled wool used on a cost basis was lower. The surviving blend books suggest that in the 1840s and early 1850s the cost of recycled wool accounted for between 26 and 41% of the total wool costs in certain sorts of cloths.[15]

As soon as its use became widespread, much of the rag wool needed in the West Riding was imported from the Continent, particularly from France and Germany. This trade was in the hands of merchant importers and rag grinding concerns who bought their rags through agents on the Continent. In the 1840s Germany imposed a duty on the export of rags which, according to Jubb, prompted many West Riding rag grinders to locate their concerns in Germany from where they exported shoddy.[16] At this time many German rag grinders and dealers settled in the heavy woollen area as is evidenced by the proliferation of German names in the commercial directories.[17] These forms of commercial organisation resulted in credit extension by foreign concerns as well as by the multiplicity of merchants, middlemen and dealers involved.

By the late 1840s there were regular rag wool auctions at the railway stations of heavy woollen towns. The terms of purchase here, as with most other auction systems in the period were 14 days cash but few manufacturers were involved with purchasing direct from the merchants in this way. Dealers and middlemen proliferated in the trade both at this point and in the trade between rag grinder and manufacturer.[18] Many dealers specialised in assembling particular sorts of shoddy for different types of manufacture and offered a variety of credit terms to the multitude of small concerns which characterised the heavy woollen areas.

All the evidence suggests that credit practice in the shoddy trade was generous, a period of four months or more being quite common in the 1840s, similar to the terms available in raw wool transactions. Henry Day, pilot manufacturer, was probably unusual in buying his rag wool for cash in this decade.[19] There are two complementary reasons why credits proliferated. First, this was a rapidly expanding trade in the 1840s with many new entrants competing for business.[20] Secondly, shoddy purchasers were typically small concerns who in the competitive climate of the times may have relied heavily on the best credit terms which they could obtain, and did not have the resources to buy for cash.

In 1858 the principal shoddy and rag wool merchants of the Dewsbury district met to 'take into account the present system of long credit and heavy discounts which of late has become so unsatisfactory'.[21] From the tone and substance of the 1858 Resolutions it would seem that there was general recognition that credit terms in the 1840s and 1850s had been extending to six months or more and attempts were then being made to induce purchasers to pay within four months.[22]

Alpaca and then mohair fibres were used from the 1830s by a handful of large manufacturers, and a few smaller ones making particular sorts of worsted lustres. Although prices and credit terms on these fibres affected only a few firms towards the end of the period under consideration, their high cost made them a very important element for these firms. Often over half the production cost of lustre cloths was accounted for by the cost of the alpaca or mohair input.[23]

The small amount of surviving evidence on trade practice in this branch indicates that no more than two or three weeks' credit was allowed by the importers who dominated the trade. Payment seems to have been made in cash or 2 or 3 months bills giving a total possible credit of some three to four months maximum.[24] English demand for alpaca and mohair was highly imperfect as was the supply before mid-century, and in the 1840s the common practice with the larger West Riding manufacturers was to buy up and hold stocks as they became available regardless of the credit terms. Foster's of Queensbury bought up large stocks for cash through their commission agents in London. At this time it was not unusual for Foster's to be holding stocks equal to between a third and a half of total annual U.K. imports of alpaca and a sixth of annual imports of mohair.[25] Foster's bought collusively with Salt's, from big importers such as Jack Bros. of London, which enabled them to keep their input costs low but meant that competing manufacturers had limited access to supplies.[26]

Dyewares were expensive and important elements in production costs. Whether dyeing was done by specialist concerns or by the manufacturers themselves credit allowed in supply of dyewares was of great significance. Mid-nineteenth-century estimates indicate that dyewares accounted for about 3–5% of the prime costs of production, in both the woollen and worsted sectors.[27] For dyers, of course, dyewares were by far the most important input cost. Waddington's of Leeds, for example, calculated that dyewares accounted for three-quarters or more of dyeing costs in the 1820s.[28] In addition it was always necessary for dyers to hold large stocks of different dyewares in order to cater, without delay, for different demands and changes in fashion. This meant that much capital was tied up in expensive stocks for lengthy periods. Credit obtained on the purchase of these goods was invaluable in aiding the finance of the necessary stockholding. Furthermore, credit extended to dyers enabled them, in turn, to grant credit to the manufacturers.

The most complete set of records relating to the late eighteenth-century trade in dyewares pertains to the firm of J. & J. Holroyd, dyers of Sheepscar, Leeds.[29] Holroyd's did an enormous trade with a turnover of more than £15,000 per annum, and had fingers in many speculative pies such as the shipping of cloth to South America. Doubts therefore arise as to the typicality of such a concern and caution must be used in making broad generalisations from their practice.

Holroyd's main supplier of dyewares by far was Stephen Todd of London to whom they were permanently indebted in large sums. Throughout the period 1783–98, year-end debts to Todd varied from £4,756 to £14,580 and in eight out of the thirteen years debts exceeded £10,000. Interest was charged at 5% on these book debts most of which were outstanding for two years or more. From 1798 Todd ceased to supply goods and the debt was slowly wound down but not until 1808 was repayment complete. At the same time as the book debts were accumulating, Todd was making other loans to Holroyd's, probably to help finance some of their speculative ventures. Although the debt relationship between Holroyd's and Todd is perhaps atypical in itself, and in its extent, it is symptomatic of a common feature of the trade in dyewares which was the close commercial and credit links established between dyers and drysalters and their London importers and suppliers.[30]

A more typical supplier of Holroyd's may have been Isaac Bradley, vitriol dealer of Hull. Here again, however, long credits were the rule – some twelve months elapsing before payment for vitriol consignments in the 1780s. In the early nineteenth century Rogerson of Bramley was dealing in dyewares as well as scribbling and fulling for local clothiers. As with his mill accounts, ware debts were supposed to be settled six-monthly but more often than not clothiers ran over their time.[31] No evidence survives of dyewares purchase practice in the 1820s and 1830s but in the 1840s Grace & Jepson, drysalters of Leeds, were selling argol, tartar, indigo and vitriol to several local dyers and manufacturers. Six months' credit was often allowed followed by cash or bills at two months. Occasionally, cash was paid within three weeks to gain 1% discount but four to six months was the most common delay before payment.[32] It thus seems that the trade in dyewares throughout the period was characterised by long credits of six months or more.

The late eighteenth-century practice in the supply of soap seems to have been to allow two to three months' credit with a 3% discount if cash or short bill payment followed.[33] By the 1830s and 1840s a range of different terms is evident, two weeks' to four months' credit being allowed followed by bills or cash and with an appropriate discount, usually 2½%, for immediate cash.[34] Most large manufacturers by the 1830s seem to have bought their soap direct from dealers in Hull and Liverpool who allowed the above terms. Smaller concerns probably relied more heavily on local dealers but it seems that these local merchants allowed similar fairly easy credit terms.[35]

There is evidence of longer credit in oil supply. Clay & Earnshaw of Brighouse were getting six months' credit from Michael Walter of Wakefield in 1799[36] and four months' credit seems to have been common practice with Willans' suppliers in the 1820s with 5% discount for cash.[37] By the 1830s and 1840s, however, the evidence suggests a tightening of credit as a period of two weeks followed by cash payment was the prevalent practice with purchases made by Keighley worsted concerns, such as Bairstow's, Clough's and Brigg's in these decades.[38] This, however, may merely reflect the fact that these three well-established firms were preferring discount prices to credit allowances.

Coal was used extensively throughout the period. Even before steam power was important, coal was required to provide heat in dyeing and scouring. In the 1780s and 1790s a big dyeing concern like Holroyd's would need to spend more than £100 on coal every four to six months. Their main supplier, Charles Bradling of Leeds, allowed debts to be paid off yearly each spring effectively giving up to twelve months' credit.[39] Rogerson's scribbling and fulling mill consumed coal worth 5% of total mill outgoings over the year in 1808; but no detail survives of the payments on his coal account.[40]

Coal mining was widespread in the textile area and coal needed by the industry was locally supplied: some manufacturers like John Foster even mined their own.[41] It seems that by the 1820s and 1830s, when steam power was becoming more widespread, and the demand for coal greater, fairly short credits on coal purchase were common. Kellett, Brown & Company were paying within two or three weeks of receiving their coal, 3% discount being allowed for cash payment in the 1830s.[42] There is no evidence of firms being heavily indebted to colliery owners in the period indicating that long credits were probably rare.

Premises, machinery and implements

Whether commercial premises were rented, built or bought by manufacturers, there were ways in which time could be gained in paying for them. The traditional practice with rented premises, as with agricultural land and property was to pay rent half yearly or more occasionally yearly in

arrears.[43] Some idea of the extent to which clothiers and early mill manufacturers could benefit from this is gained by studying the rate valuation
books which survive for a number of clothing townships from the late
eighteenth century. Rateable values were commonly calculated at one
eighth to one fifth below the annual value or potential rental.[44] A sample
study of the townships of Warley, Ossett and Farnley at different survey
dates from the 1790s to the late 1830s indicates that the vast majority of
clothiers' premises and textile mills were rented rather than owner-
occupied.[45] Rents for the former varied from £3 to £14, being typically
£11–12.[46] With mill premises the credit gains from renting could be substantial. In the first decade of the nineteenth century, mills of the fulling
and scribbling type seem to have been available for £55–60 on average,
but the range was extensive. In Ossett and Warley, estimated rentals
varied from £12 to £167.[47] By 1819 the range of estimated rentals for the
five mills in Ossett was from £50 for Emmerson's mill to £156 for the
Healey Mills complex. In the 1830s mill rentals in Ossett averaged
£300.[48]

Complementary information of commercial rentals in the first half of
the nineteenth century is available from the Dartmouth, Savile and
Graham Estate Surveys. Dartmouth possessed twenty wool textile mills
as well as five cotton mills through most of the period. The average
annual commercial rental of the woollen mills from the 1790s to 1830s
was £133.[49] On the Savile estates in 1809, eleven mills with their adjoining land and other premises were let for amounts varying from £30–300,
averaging £85.[50] On the Graham estates in Kirkstall by 1849 four large
mill complexes were let at rents from £300–975, averaging £560.[51] Scattered references in business records[52] indicate that the examples quoted
from the estates of Dartmouth, Savile and Graham and from Ossett and
Warley townships are fairly representative of the range of mill rentals as
a whole. Thus considerable credit must have accrued to firms and to the
industry overall, where mill rentals were paid in arrears.

As we have already noted, multiple tenancy of mills and the subletting
of room and power were common features.[53] Both multiple tenancies
and sublettings seem to have been undertaken on the basis of payment in
arrears, either half yearly or quarterly. Rental of room and power in the
first half of the nineteenth century could cost anything from a few pounds
to several hundred pounds a year. In 1838, for example, Thomas Water-
house rented the middle room of Marriner's New Mill with power for six
spinning frames of 576 spindles and thirty-two power looms. For this, he
paid 4s 6d per spindle and £3 10s per loom quarterly. This worked out at
£241 10s per quarter and payment was made quarterly in arrears.[54]

Although rental and leasing agreements were formally a question of
paying every quarter or half year, in most cases there was always pressure placed on the mill owner in bad years to allow some flexibility. It was
after all better for him to allow tenants to run into arrears than to have

the mill lying idle. In these circumstances either tenants were allowed to pay their rents late or rents were reduced to prevent tenants having to leave. The rental of Shaw Carr Wood Mill was reduced from £220 to £120 per annum in 1842 to enable the earlier tenants to regain it. Since the slump of the early 1840s the mill had stood empty and despite being advertised only one applicant had been forthcoming.[55]

From the available evidence it is not unreasonable to assume that perhaps as many as a half of clothiers' and mill premises were rented through most of the textile area.[56] It thus seems that credit on commercial rent payments was an important feature of the industry throughout the period and that it could be significant for both large and small manufacturers alike.

Where a manufacturer built rather than rented his premises some credit was available from the suppliers of materials and from the construction concerns. The available evidence suggests that this credit was not very significant, however. Cash terms for materials were common in the nineteenth century, perhaps because there were so many competing demands for construction goods from urban development and transport expansion. Settlement in two or three weeks, with a maximum credit of three months from masons and building contractors, seems to have been the common practice.[57] It is possible that slightly longer credits were common earlier in the century especially for substantial customers. Lupton's were allowed six months' credit from Martin Cawood & Sons, Leeds builders, in the early 1820s, and a period of six months seems to have been common in the case of the larger builders employed by Gott in the first decade of the nineteenth century.[58]

Insufficient detail has survived of credit allowed on the purchase of textile machinery to enable definitive statements about its nature or change over time. In the mid-eighteenth century it appears that many clothiers and outworkers made their own equipment, particularly looms and tenters. Sometimes they were assisted in this by local carpenters.[59] This is evidenced by the fact that many clothiers' wills include amounts of wood 'sufficient for a pair of looms or tenters'.[60] Even the larger concerns and early factory businesses commonly made much of the less complex machinery themselves, particularly before the spread of steam power when mills were often remote from specialist machinery suppliers.[61] Only from the 1820s when technology, especially in the spinning sector, became much more complex, did most larger manufacturers begin to buy the bulk of their machinery from specialised concerns.

For those factory manufacturers who did buy their machinery and equipment, it would appear that much of this was acquired second-hand. Numerous adverts in the Leeds and Bradford press of the late eighteenth and early nineteenth centuries offer textile machinery for sale. The following is typical: 'To be sold. About eighteen hundred spindles with the necessary preparing machinery, lately erected for the spinning of wool.

The above machinery is in good condition and the yarn spun on them has met with a good Reception in every market where it has been exposed for sale.'[62]

Terms of sale, where specified, were usually cash or 'at auction'.[63] As many of the sellers were bankrupts, a quick sale for cash was desirable. The high failure rate in manufacture coupled with the rapidity of technical improvement by the 1830s and 1840s meant that many manufacturers bought at least a part of their machinery second-hand. Marriner's purchase of £384 worth of spinning machinery when they took over Greengate Mill in 1818 was typical, as was their payment in cash.[64]

John Brigg & Company, worsted spinners and manufacturers of Keighley, settled periodically for small purchases of utensils and machinery, such as spindles and shuttles, in the 1830s. Some regular suppliers were paid after three months others were paid for purchases accumulated over the previous twelve months. More irregular suppliers usually gave only two months' credit. In the 1840s the two major 'machine makers' who attended to regular repairs and renewals were paid every six months or so for amounts up to £100.[65] Similarly, Lupton's paid for purchases of utensils and tools within three to six months in 1832.[66] This confirms the scattered evidence from the cotton industry where machinery manufacturers in the early nineteenth century gave up to six months' credit followed by 5% discount for payment in bills at three months.[67]

The one major exception to the practice of relatively short credit in machinery and utensil purchase is found in the acquisition of early steam engines and their associated installation and gearing costs. Jenkins and others who have examined the Boulton & Watt papers in detail have drawn attention to the credit arrangements on the sale of the early engines of the late eighteenth and early nineteenth centuries.[68] These credit deals often amounted to a 'hire purchase' arrangement. Manufacturers were allowed several years to pay in yearly or six-monthly instalments. John Wormald, for example, paid Boulton & Watt £200 yearly towards the 'erection of an engine and applying it to work' in the 1800s.[69]

These credit agreements, although best documented in the case of Boulton & Watt, were not confined to this concern. The fierce competition between the early steam engine manufacturers, particularly between Boulton & Watt, and Fenton Murray & Company of Leeds and, later, Sturges & Company of Bowling, dictated the use of credit incentives to promote sales.[70]

Evidence unearthed by Jenkins suggests that textile manufacturers frequently fell behind with their instalment payments on their steam engines:

almost all the Yorkshire textile manufacturers who purchased one of their [Boulton & Watt] engines were slow in settling their accounts. Thus in May 1797, the firm had to write to Joshua Foster at Horbury demanding payment and suggesting that interest should be charged. At the end of 1798 the account was still out-standing and interest was being paid. At about the same period, they were demanding payment from Messrs Blagborough and Holroyd, the Batesons of Wortley, John Wood of Bradford and Nevins and Gatcliffe of Hunslet.[71]

John and James Walker were purchasing their engine from Boulton & Watt on an instalment basis in the 1790s at the rate of £100 per annum. However, a great deal of correspondence was necessary, payments were frequently delayed for long periods and legal action was threatened.[72]

By the 1830s, credit on steam engine purchase may have been declining. In 1836 Foster's bill for £1,136 from John Sturges & Company of Bowling for installing 'Ingan, and shafting' was paid for within six months in four instalments over that period.[73] Unfortunately, other records have not come to light to confirm or deny the existence of a trend.

The prevalence of credit on steam engine purchase and associated costs, at least in the early decades of steam power, must have had an important impact on the ease of transition to mechanised production. Jenkins has stressed the relatively large proportion of mill investment which was taken up by the power plant and associated work. The average engine in the Yorkshire wool textile mills by 1835 cost about £850 excluding millwrights' costs.[74] With these additional costs included, investment in power plant accounted for up to 20% of the total fixed capital outlay of the factory manufacturers.[75] This proportion could well have been significantly higher in the worsted sector by the 1830s where engines were commonly powering the spinning process.

Thus, although credit allowed on machinery purchase may not have been of great importance to the manufacturer, steam engine credit almost certainly was, particularly before the 1830s.

Services

The biggest financial outlay for the woollen clothier after the purchase of his raw materials was the payment for fulling and the other processes done from the 1780s and 1790s at the local mill. The method of payment for these services was thus of crucial importance to the liquidity position of the manufacturer.

Dickenson's findings suggest that fullers in the eighteenth century were men of small means who generally rented their mill or were employed by the owners of mills.[76] Despite their small means, these fullers seem to have been important figures in the extension of credit to their customers. Clothiers' probate inventories of the eighteenth century abound with unpaid debts owed for fulling which is not too surprising when one notes that the prevailing practice was to complete the lengthy fulling and tentering processes before any payment was demanded.[77] In

6
Late eighteenth-century mill of the fulling/scribbling/spinning type,
water-powered
Source: Photograph taken in 1985 by the author.

addition a credit period was usually allowed: often as much as three to six months elapsed before payment became due.[78]

Given the small financial resources of eighteenth-century fullers it would seem that the fulling mill owners were the real sources of credit rather than the fullers themselves. Most commonly, fullers were employed on piece rates. For example in the 1780s Charles Chiswick was employed by the Ossett Mill Company at a salary of 7d a cloth for broads, 2d for narrows and the drawback on soap.[79] Thus it was the capital of the fulling mill owners which was extended to the clothiers in the form of credit. These owners came from several different backgrounds. Dickenson has traced the owners of seventeen fulling mills during the period 1703–65 from probate records. Of these only one was described as a fuller himself; the others were gentlemen, grocers, tanners, victuallers and yeomen.[80] Thus it seems that credit was extended from landowning and farming, retailing and the professions to clothiers in the supply of fulling services. From the 1770s and 1780s, with the incorporation of carding and scribbling alongside fulling in the mills, many new premises were built and old ones extended.[81] At this time it seems that more of the mills became the property of clothiers, groups of clothiers, staplers and commercially minded landowners who were responding to the opportunities presented by increasing demand.[82] These owners continued the practice of extending long credits to their customers or, where they rented out their mills rather than running them, the traditional practice of charging rents quarterly or half yearly in arrears was a factor in enabling the millers to grant credit in turn to the clothiers.

There is not a great deal of evidence of the precise periods of credit allowed on payment for fulling, carding and scribbling in the eighteenth century. Partly because of the shortage of small coin, clothiers' debts were usually allowed to accumulate for three to six months before a bill was rendered. Mill 'pay days' were often held quarterly or half yearly following the traditional practices for the rental of land and agricultural property. Lady Day (25 March) and Michaelmas (29 September) were the traditional agricultural rent days in Yorkshire and in many other parts of England in the eighteenth century.[83] Since the innovation of the fulling mill as a manorial monopoly in the thirteenth century, it had been closely linked with the running of the agricultural estate and with traditional agrarian practices. It is not surprising, therefore, to find this form of payment prevailing in the fulling mills. What is a little surprising is that throughout the first half of the nineteenth century fulling, and by this time carding, scribbling and slubbing also, continued to be paid for in lump sums periodically, on mill pay days, following the traditional practice.

Rogerson and Lord, scribbling and fulling millers of Bramley, held their mill pay days in the early nineteenth century as follows:

1808	2 March	1812	4 March
	2 November		4 November
1809	8 March	1813	3 March
	5 July		3 November
	9 November	1814	2 March
1811	6 March		
	6 November		

Except for the anomalous inclusion of a third pay day in 1809 Rogerson's pay days were held half-yearly near to Martinmas and Lady Day.[84] It is likely that this was typical practice.

During the week or fortnight before pay day, bills or 'notes' were made up and delivered by hand to customers in the neighbourhood. This could take the best part of two days, the catchment area in Rogerson's case being some 4 or 5 miles radius from the mill and including between 120 and 150 clothiers. Pay days were often held at the mill but sometimes also at different locations to reduce the travel time for the clothiers. As was the traditional practice on agricultural rent days, mill pay day attendance brought a free round of refreshment. Supper, ale, 'a glass' and tobacco were provided at a cost to the miller of around 18d per head.[85]

Despite these inducements, it seems that most mill pay days brought scant rewards and millers were forced to extend their credit for longer periods. 'Jno. Varley, Stanningley had pay Day for mill and had only two persons at it', wrote Rogerson in his diary in 1811.[86] In November 1808 he himself had fared little better: 'Our pay day . . . has been a very poor one we have received about one sixth of what we have owing.'[87] Most of Rogerson's diary entries on pay days are gloomy in tone; a yield of a third of debts owing was considered a reasonable expectation: clothiers proved 'devils to bleed'.[88] As half yearly pay days did not ensure regular payment of accounts, millers had to chase around the countryside from door to door collecting debts. When Rogerson's mill had been going a little over a year, £1,100 was owing to him. Eighteen months later £164 of this was still owing.[89] Rogerson, Lord and their foremen were constantly making tours of the clothiers' houses looking for their money: Pudsey clothiers were noted as particularly recalcitrant.[90] After a debt had remained unpaid for some time the millers could refuse to undertake work for the clothier concerned or to hold back his cloths or wool in lieu of payment. Sometimes customers left cloths as security for their debts: 'Received a cloth from Jno. Gaunt of Pudsey for some slubbing that we had stopped for the money he owed us – we have the liberty to sell it on the 1st of April next for the debt if he does not bring us our money on that day or before.'[91] On 4 February Gaunt delivered three more pieces of cloth to be sold the following April as security for his debt.

This incident illustrates the sort of credit periods permitted and under what terms. Gaunt owed money for some twelve months or more giving cloths as security for the last few months of non-payment. Sometimes the liquidity position of clothiers together with the shortage of coin in circulation resulted in the miller being forced to take cloths in payment but in times of really bad trade, as in autumn 1808, neither money nor cloths were to be had: 'On going into Pudsey among our customers we find there is neither money nor goods.'[92]

If Rogerson's can be regarded as a fairly typical fulling and scribbling concern, it would seem that credits granted in this branch of the trade were lengthy indeed in the early years of the century. Half yearly pay days gave a credit of up to six months in the first instance and this was prolonged in practice in the majority of cases until door to door debt collection or the next pay day yielded the cash. Occasionally as much as two years elapsed before debts were paid off. Slumps in trade seem to have corresponded with the greatest difficulties of payment and forced credit extension but in more buoyant conditions shortage of coin and the pressure placed on the clothier to produce more resulted in inability to pay the miller much more promptly. Thus in July 1809 Rogerson wrote that although trade was pretty good he had only had an indifferent pay day.[93]

Rogerson and Lord had between 120 and 150 regular customers and with debts outstanding often of over £1,000 this represented an average debt per customer of £8–10.[94] A chronic credit of this sort could be of great significance to the liquidity position of the small clothier in this generally difficult period of the Napoleonic Wars and their aftermath.

Complementary evidence of the credit and forced credit practices prevailing in the fulling and scribbling trade is provided by the case of Dewsbury Mills. These mills were taken over by Hague & Cook in 1811 who started cloth spinning and manufacturing in 1815.[95] After four years of running the commission services together with manufacturing it was found that, despite the size of its business, the commission side of the concern was earning less than 10% of profits.[96] Thomas Cook's diary entry of July 1819 indicates that the major problem concerned the difficulties of securing regular payment from the small clothiers: 'the best plan would be to let the fulling mills to the millers for the mill accounts are the last and worst paid'.[97]

From the late eighteenth century, particularly by the second quarter of the nineteenth century, the provision of fulling, carding and scribbling services became dominated in some areas of the West Riding by the establishment of company mills.[98] Insofar as these mills added significantly to milling capacity, breaking the monopoly position of the traditional establishments, they would obviously result in declining charges and, possibly, in easier credit.

Credit terms, which may have been influenced by the increased competition for business in the trade, were also affected by the fact that the company mills largely serviced their own shareholders.[99] An inducement to purchasing a share in one of these mills was the possibility of preferential treatment in charging for work done. There is little overt evidence of differential pricing with preference given to shareholders before the 1860s but it is likely that this did occur earlier.[100] The Gill Royd Mill Company gave a slight preference to their shareholders in their credit terms in the 1830s.[101]

If company mills were largely run as non-profit-making institutions for the benefit of shareholders one would expect pricing and credit terms to be favourable. However, it does seem that clothiers expected their investment to yield dividends. Shares were offered by some mills to individuals unconnected with the textile industry, and customers sometimes included a large proportion of non-shareholders.[102] Even if dividends were not the prime concern, clothier shareholders would feel some pressure not to allow large debit balances to accumulate as bankruptcy would result in the forfeiture of their investment. For these reasons, as the evidence suggests, company mill credit policies allowed for fairly generous terms but most mills early adopted strictly stated rules concerning this.

It seems to have been common by the 1820s for company mill accounts to be made up and rendered every four months.[103] Some had six-monthly settlement agreements as had been the earlier practice in the trade. In 1838, the regular customers of Kellett, Brown & Company of Clover

Greaves Mill, Calverley, were supposed to settle their scribbling accounts every six months, a 10% discount being allowed for cash payment or short bills at this time. Fulling accounts were similarly settled but as charges were lower in this department no discounts appear to have been given for cash. In practice some customers settled three times a year and practically all payments were made in cash.[104]

In the late 1830s and early 1840s, the Gill Royd Mill Company delivered their customers' accounts three times a year just prior to the mill feast days or pay days held in February, June and October. Customers with accounts over £5 were entitled to a free dinner but it seems that, like Rogerson twenty years earlier, this mill company had great difficulty in getting shareholders and other clients to adhere to the pay days.[105]

Problems increased during the first three years of the firm's existence so that by January 1838 it was decided to call a special meeting of shareholders to make rules for the better payment of accounts. The resolutions of this meeting indicate that up to four months' credit prior to the mill feast day was taken for granted, but that clothiers had commonly taken a year or more to pay. Under the new rules interest was only charged on overdue accounts after the expiration of between four and eight months.[106]

7

Gill Royd Mill, Morley

Source: William Smith, *Rambles about Morley, with Descriptive and Historical Sketches: Also an Account of the Rise and Progress of the Woollen Manufacture in This Place* (1866).

Rawden Low Mill Company had quarterly pay days in the mid-1840s but similar terms were again made explicit in the shareholders' minute book: 'Resolved . . . If they are not paid before the second pay day after the note is delivered he will be charged £5 per cent per annum until all is paid.'[107] As with Gill Royd, the Rawden Mill company attempted to ensure that easy credit terms would not prove too damaging in periods of liquidity crisis by offering generous discounts for payment on pay day or thereabouts.[108]

In the eighteenth century dyeing in the piece was a quite separate trade as it demanded more skill and capital than the clothier normally possessed. Even in the nineteenth century, most manufacturers had their dyeing done by specialised concerns working for them on a commission basis. The dyeing of wool was less costly and difficult and was often done by the clothier or manufacturer himself or sometimes by the scribbling or fulling miller. Rogerson, for example, was dyeing wool for his clients in the early nineteenth century.

The common practice of dyers and drysalters throughout the period was to charge after the completion of work which in itself, as with fulling and scribbling, was effectively an extension of credit to the manufacturers. Eighteenth-century dyers had significantly large book credits recorded in their probate inventories. For example, Robert Walton, dyer of Skircoat, was owed £346 at the time of his death in the 1770s. This represented more than a quarter of his total assets and was four times greater than his book debts.[109] Larger-scale clothiers generally dealt with several dyers and could thus in theory gain considerable credit by spreading their debts.

The Business Ledger of J. & J. Holroyd, dyers of Sheepscar, Leeds, which covers the period 1783 to 1825, indicates that dyeing done for small-scale but regular customers was usually paid for within four weeks of completion.[110] The range of credit periods taken, however, was large. Some clothiers paid immediately in cash, others paid after four months with bills at two or three months. Thus a maximum credit of six or seven months was possible although four weeks was the most common time taken by clothiers with small accounts.

The bulk of Holroyd's business was with large merchants and merchant-manufacturers. On these bigger accounts, such as that of Messrs Bischoff who were important Leeds merchants, longer credits seem to have been allowed or taken. Four to nine months commonly elapsed before payment for work done. It was not unknown for Bischoff's account to remain unpaid for twelve months or more and sometimes payment was in cloths rather than cash as Holroyd's were doing some trading of their own.[111] Other big clothiers and merchants were given twelve months or more to pay.[112]

Andrew Peterson, a Wakefield merchant was able to gain four to six months' credit on his dyeing account with Joseph Holdworth & Company and up to sixteen months from John Hoyle of Halifax. He also dealt with John Wood of Wakefield who was paid anything between four and sixteen months after the work was done throughout the period 1795 to the early 1810s. Occasionally Peterson paid within four weeks and qualified for a 7½% discount. By the second decade of the nineteenth century Peterson was regularly paying within four weeks and gaining a 10% discount.[113] Either credit had tightened or Peterson's circumstances were such that he could afford to succumb to the inducement of taking the discount instead of credit. Certainly, long credit from dyers was still in evidence. In the 1820s and 1830s William Haigh, a substantial clothier of Saddleworth, paid every twelve months for his dyeing which was done by two separate concerns, one of which was dyeing wool rather than pieces.[114]

Worsted manufacturers could also gain credit from their dyers.[115] The Ledgers of T. & M. Bairstow, of Sutton in Craven, show that credit taken on dyeing account was fairly circumscribed in the 1830s and 1840s. In the 1830s J. Mallinson & Company of Leeds asked for settlement every three months and often took cloths in exchange. A decade later most of Bairstow's regular dyers were paid every two months.[116]

Thus from the mixed and incomplete evidence available, it would seem that the clients who gained most from the credit extended by dyers throughout the period were established merchants and large-scale manufacturers. These often paid off their dyeing accounts only after 12 months or more of work had been done. Long credit of twelve to eighteen months seems to have been particularly prevalent before the 1820s. The bulk of small-scale clothiers sold their cloths undyed and unfinished to the merchants but those who did commission their own dyeing could expect a credit of one to six months.

As generous discounts of 7–10% were offered for earlier settlement by the 1830s, well-established firms, such as Bairstow's seem to have preferred cheapness to credit. It is also possible that the dyeing of worsted piece goods was a trade where less credit was allowed by the 1830s and 1840s. The widespread introduction of cotton warps in the late 1830s demanded great expertise in dyeing and it may well be that a seller's market obtained for a while. This enabled successful dyers of union cloths to demand prompter payment.

Cloth dressing was another trade done by separate firms well into the nineteenth century. In the eighteenth century the master cloth dressers were concentrated in Halifax, Wakefield and Leeds. They finished cloths on a commission basis for merchants and large-scale manufacturers and the bigger concerns bought cloths to finish for themselves. Analysis of the inventories of 352 cloth dressers in the period 1689–1769 showed that on average 39% of their total assets were held in the form of book credits. The more substantial dressers had on average as much as £420 owing to them which represented 57% of their total assets.[117] However, it is likely that much of this credit went to merchants who bought cloth in the balk at the halls and had it finished themselves. Andrew

Peterson of Wakefield was one such merchant. In the 1790s he was obtaining four to five months' credit from dressers such as J. & J. Holdsworth.[118]

From the 1820s, with the emergence of merchant-manufacturers undertaking their own marketing, credit from cloth dressers is likely to have become more important to manufacturing concerns, but no records have been traced for this period. As with dyeing, the practice was to charge only after work was completed but we have no specific idea of the extent of additional credit allowed after the 1790s. Many firms did both dyeing and dressing and it is therefore likely that credit terms for dressing were similar to those for dyeing.

In the eighteenth century the vast majority of clothiers undertook their own carriage of raw wool and cloth – usually on their heads or backs. Wealthier clothiers and putting-out merchants kept horses for the purpose. As the typical clothier bought his raw materials locally and sold his cloth at the nearest cloth hall it was not necessary to purchase additional transport services. For the putting-out capitalist the need to dispense raw materials and collect goods was to some extent obviated by the common practice of having taking-in warehouses at suitable locations for the domestic workers to attend, thereby shifting the burden of carriage on to workers who were not paid for this service. Thus the transport costs to the industry were felt mainly by those who bought their wool outside the stapler system and those who came to do their own marketing.

The practice by the late eighteenth century on the part of carriers, shippers and wharfingers involved in the wool trade between the South East wool counties and the West Riding was to ask for periodic settlement of accounts every quarter or half year. Jowitt's the staplers dealt with half a dozen such concerns in the 1790s.[119] Most raw wool was moved coastwise from ports like Yarmouth, Colchester, Lynn and Boston to Hull where it often had to be stored until conveyance to the West Riding became available. Wharfingers in Hull such as Widow F. Taylor, Taylor & Markham and John Tillotson, undertook this responsibility as well as arranging for forwarding of the wool.[120] Jowitt's paid their account with these concerns every six months. Their Yarmouth shippers were paid every three or six months.[121] Carriers were often employed in the wool counties at centres like Sleaford and Gainsborough. In the early nineteenth century Joseph Jackson employed G. & G. Capes of Gainsborough whose account was paid after delays of five to six months.[122]

In the late eighteenth century in reasonable spring weather when the roads were not too soft, overland carriage of wool from Warwick to Wakefield took eight to ten days. In bad weather it could take two to three weeks or more. Coastal trade from the South East ports to Hull took one or two days, and from Hull to the West Riding was a journey by water and road of some one to three weeks depending on location in the

West Riding. These times were gradually reduced by river, canal and road improvements until by the 1830s they were almost halved.[123] Added to this, however, unloading, storage and dispatch from Hull could delay wool for days or even weeks and the fear of wool getting damp and mouldy in transit was a perennial one for the manufacturer or stapler.[124] If, as seems likely, wool took some three to five weeks on average to reach the West Riding from wool counties like Suffolk and Lincolnshire, the credit granted by carriers was of considerable importance in aiding the finance of this period of transit.

The cost of wool transit from Hull to most textile centres of the West Riding added ½–1% on to its purchase price in the late eighteenth and early nineteenth centuries. From Lincolnshire to the West Riding added 2–4% on to the purchase price of wool on average.[125] This gives one some idea of the importance of the credit periods allowed on this margin of the cost price of wool.

Manufacturers, particularly those buying wool from outside Yorkshire, sometimes had occasion to employ the service of canal companies rather than dealing with carriers. Lupton's bills from the Aire & Calder Navigation Company in the period 1818–26 indicate credit of two to four months followed by payment in cash.[126] Road carriers transporting cloths to south Lancashire were similarly fairly tight in their credit allowances by the 1820s and 1830s.[127] Scattered evidence suggests that short periods of credit of one to three months remained common in payment for both canal and overland carrying services until the mid-nineteenth century and beyond.[128] Railways appear to have been used to only a small extent by Yorkshire textile manufacturers before the mid-century and even then only in the carriage of finished cloths. The most important lines for the Yorkshire trade, such as the Lancashire and Yorkshire, had yet to be built and railways, in any case, were not noted for giving credit above the nominal two to three months.[129]

Labour

From the late eighteenth to the mid-nineteenth centuries the labour involved in the West Riding wool textile industry became more and more dependent on money wages. With this came the increased importance of any credit gained by the manufacturer in the payment of his wage bill.

Wages accounted for as much as 62% of running costs in some of the commission scribbling and fulling mills in the early nineteenth century.[130] By the mid-century contemporary estimates indicate that wages accounted for between a quarter and a third of total prime costs for the industry as a whole.[131] A further more detailed idea of the importance of the wage bill to different branches of the woollen manufacture at different periods is given in Table 6.1, which is based on Von Tunzelmann's estimates.[132]

Table 6.1 *Percentage of labour costs of woollens in each process*

	1724	1781–96	1798	1796–1805	1820–7	1830
Spinning, etc.	44.4	41.2	41.8	21.4	20.6	22.0
Weaving, etc.	25.8	33.2	29.0	44.1	48.9	40.1
Finishing	29.7	20.7	29.2	25.1	26.8	31.3

Source: Von Tunzelmann, *Steam Power and British Industrialisation to 1860*, p. 244.

It is difficult to get direct evidence of the precise way in which wages were paid by clothiers to their journeymen and assistants. Although the practice was dying out in the eighteenth century, employees were sometimes engaged by yearly contract in accordance with a statute of 1563.[133] This placed an obligation on the clothier to keep his men on through thick and thin, but the commitment was two-way in that the employee could not quit even if his employer could find no wages for him. Clothiers could easily get away with paying their journeymen in cloths or in foodstuffs, and in considerable arrears. Apprentices, still fairly common in the late eighteenth century, were given only their board and keep.

Much of the contemporary literature on rural domestic industry and on early factory industry alludes to the importance of truck and delayed wage payments to the manufacturer. Most historians explain the prevalence of truck, token payments and delays by reference to the acute shortage of coins of small denominations especially before the 1820s.[134] Obviously these shortages could cause severe problems for manufacturers with sizeable pay rolls and the methods which they used to circumvent these difficulties such as payment in tokens, shop notes or promissory notes often brought other members of the local community as well as the employees themselves into the credit network. By paying the workforce in tokens or notes the manufacturer could gain a valuable period of credit. Like a note issuing banker, he had the short-term capital advantage of the margin between his issue and the reserve that he had to keep against the probable return of his issue for redemption. Shopkeepers, by accepting the manufacturer's tokens or notes, were according him the benefits of a banker as his promises to pay his debts had thereby become currency. Truck payments, likewise, as we shall see, involved an important credit element.

If, as has been variously estimated, labour costs were as much a quarter to a third of the prime costs of manufacture even at the end of the period, then any delay in payment especially if followed by payment in truck or tokens could make a big difference to the liquidity position of any concern. For this reason it seems likely that undue weight has been given to the shortage of coin in explaining delays and truck payments. The potential gains from these methods were so great that this was sufficient in itself to prompt their adoption. This was particularly true where employers were trying to compete with those who already paid their workers in arrears and in tokens or truck, as witnesses before Parliament in 1842 made clear.[135] As late as the 1840s, when wage costs as a proportion of total costs for the employer were declining in most branches of the wool textile trade, contemporaries estimated that a saving of 10 to 15% could be made on the wage bill by payment in truck.[136] Truck meant that the employer could take advantage of the credit granted to him in the purchase of the provisions for his workforce, as well as making a good profit on their sale because of his position as monopoly supplier.

By the 1830s coin shortages were less of a problem than earlier, yet truck payment throughout the country and particularly in the West Riding was on the increase.[137] This would indicate that the most important spur to truck and delays in wage payment was the ease with which wages could be squeezed as a means of cost competition especially during downturns of the trade cycle.

We have little direct evidence of credit in wage payment in the West Riding for the eighteenth century except that employees of putting-out systems were paid piece rates in arrears on completion and delivery of the work. At this time deductions for rental of equipment and premises, or for faulty workmanship, were made. Domestic weavers were often paid monthly in the early nineteenth century as was the case with Marriner's and Foster's employees.[138] Much payment seems to have taken the form of agricultural goods and foodstuffs: wheat, wool, wood and milk, the monetary wage being only a small part of remuneration.[139] When competition from factory production began to be felt first in spinning and later in weaving, the indications are that workers were forced to accept longer delays in wage payment and more payment in truck.[140]

An interesting picture of the methods used by one firm to pay their domestic workers is gained from a study of the early accounts of John Foster & Sons. Foster's employed well over 100 domestic handloom weavers by the late 1820s and the accounts of each of these have survived.[141] In the 1820s these workers were 'paid' monthly in arrears. However, this monthly transaction was only a notional one, a credit being assigned to the weaver's account. Foster's were selling goods to their workers regularly in the month before pay day. These goods included coal, candles, cloth, flour, malt, milk, sugar, treacle and cheese. The weavers were permanently indebted to the firm. In 1831 they were earning (notionally) between 9 and 15s a week but most of the workers, such as Joseph Shackleton and John Ingram, had chronic debts for groceries and provisions amounting to £6–8. No money changed hands: the workers' wages were merely regular deductions from their standing debts.

Foster's gained several advantages from this system. First, they got round any problems caused by the shortage of cash to pay wages.

Furthermore, the 'loyalty' of workers would be cemented by the continuous debt relationship and monopoly prices were charged for the provisions. In addition, although the weavers were permanently indebted to the firm the credit which Foster gained in buying many of the groceries meant that he himself was not out of pocket.[142] In fact he had, perhaps, a net credit gain in wage payments of a month or two. The financial gains from payment in kind could be substantial and this expedient seems to have been employed on a wide scale throughout the textile area and among both factory and domestic employers.[143]

In the scribbling and fulling mills wage payments were normally on a piece rate basis and paid in arrears. Fullers were allowed 3 or 4d per cloth milled in the 1780s but were only paid after each fortnight or sometimes after a longer delay.[144] In the early years of the working of Rogerson's mill at Bramley the workers were paid irregularly in arrears usually with delays exceeding two weeks. As the concern became more firmly established, Rogerson made it a practice to reckon and balance the wages every fortnight but whether his employees were paid every fortnight promptly is not recorded. Even a fortnight of arrears in his wage payment by 1812 yielded Rogerson a credit of £400 for up to fourteen days.[145]

The firm of Robert Clough of Keighley, worsted spinners and manufacturers, shows a similar pattern of delay in wage payment especially during the crucial early stages of establishment and expansion. Mill workers in the 1820s and 1830s were paid irregularly, often as much as three months in arrears.[146] Scattered evidence from a number of surviving business records of the first half of the nineteenth century indicates that the most common practice for mill workers was weekly or fortnightly wage payment.[147] Particularly in periods of bad trade and intense competition delays could be extended and compounded by the use of truck. Newspaper evidence for the 1820s indicates that truck payments were on the increase in the West Riding, especially in the bleak year of 1826 when many employers were hard-pressed to find cash.[148] Factory manufacturers were under pressure to continue to produce speculatively through periods of low demand in order to keep their fixed overheads functioning, which meant that they had to find wages at a time when sales were low or absent.[149] In April 1826 the woollen manufacturers of Saddleworth were reported to be giving shop notes to their employees instead of money wages,[150] and in the following month, Halifax worsted weavers were being paid in goods instead of money.[151] In 1829 one of the main grievances of the Leeds stuff weavers was that the employers in the town invariably paid in truck.[152]

Although the 1831 Truck Act made payment in goods illegal the practice seems to have continued unabated and even increased.[153] Difficulties of detection and the fear on the part of employees of victimisation combined to allow this. As competition in the industry increased, manufacturers were often faced with a choice between truck payments or bankruptcy.

Most of the Yorkshire witnesses before the 1842 Select Committee on the Payment of Wages allude to the rapid extension of the truck system from the early 1830s and especially its prevalence in the depression years of the 1830s and early 1840s. There is little mention of long delays in wage payment but truck and payment in shop tokens seem to have been endemic. Workers commonly laboured five or six weeks without receiving a penny in money; instead they received provisions of various kinds. As credit on grocery purchases could run to four months,[154] this gave the manufacturer who paid truck a total credit period on his wage bill of more than five months.

Mary Wright, a hand weaver, had worked for one Joseph Armitage for two years and in that time she had only received 1s in money; the rest had been paid in goods.[155] Armitage, like most of the manufacturers in the Shipley area, owned a truck shop but he also was in the habit of paying workers in cloths which was a way of getting rid of idle stocks and thus killed two birds with one stone. Often these cloths were worth more than the worker was owed and the latter was thus obliged to continue working in order to pay off the debt. The price of objecting to this situation could be high especially in periods of depression when lay-offs in the industry were rife. Miles Brearly, a Bingley clothier, stated that he had 'heard working men remark that they were not safe to retain employment unless they were in their masters' ribs'.[156]

Truck was often paid in rags or in unfinished cloth which was valued at two or three times its normal price and which could not easily be sold to realise cash without considerable expense or further processing. Where groceries or coals were given in lieu of wages they were usually charged at 5s in the £ above their real value.[157] Squire Auty was of the opinion that wages in the Bradford area since the mid-1830s were chiefly paid in 'shop goods, eatables, ... wearing apparel ... [and] ... sometimes in worsted stuffs'.[158] In the district of Windhill and Shipley he maintained that there were only two manufacturers who paid wages in anything but truck.[159]

Most of the Yorkshire witnesses agreed that truck payments were especially prevalent among smaller manufacturers outside of the big towns. These smaller rural employers could exert greater pressure on the local populace as they were often the sole source of employment. More importantly, the pressure of competition from larger manufacturers forced employers to adjust those of their costs which they could alter most easily. Inevitably these were labour costs. Jennings of Idle, although against the truck system in principle, maintained that it was impossible to compete in the market without it. He calculated that, on his wage bill of £90 per week, he would gain £4–500 yearly by paying in truck.[160]

The truck system seems to have been an important means of cost competition especially in periods of commercial depression. It is no accident that the Select Committee on the Payment of Wages was held in 1842. Contemporaries recognised only too well the economic circumstances which led to the extension and dominance of truck payments in the 1830s and 1840s: 'The truck system is bad of late because of the bad state of trade and high unemployment';[161] 'wages cannot be lower than they are now they are brought down to the lowest'.[162] Periods of depression not only put pressure upon manufacturers to pay in truck but the high unemployment in these years also put the workers in a weak position to resist.

Through good and bad years truck was particularly common in the payment of wages to those workers who were easy to replace. Hand weavers were particularly vulnerable in the 1830s and 1840s. Their position was under threat of mechanical innovation especially in the worsted branch and their skills could easily be replaced by the influx of cheaper immigrant labour into the West Riding in these decades. Hand combers were similarly affected by labour oversupply in the 1840s and 1850s. By the 1830s unskilled factory hands also found it difficult to fight against truck payments as there were always others willing to step into their shoes. As Auty stressed in 1842: even in prosperous times, the substitution of women for men in factory work resulted in constant fear of replacement on the part of male employees leaving them vulnerable to truck and other abuses.[163]

Thus it seems that throughout the period under consideration, and particularly in the second quarter of the nineteenth century when the climate became more intensely competitive, when depression periods were frequent and severe and when many workers were threatened by replacement, delays in wage payment, truck and other devices gave effective and important cost advantages and credit to manufacturers. This credit commonly extended to three or four months which was of great significance at a time when wage costs amounted to some 30% of the prime costs of wool textile manufacture.

7

THE TRADE IN WOOLLEN
AND WORSTED PRODUCTS

The liquidity position of the manufacturer depended not only on the credit which he could gain in purchasing his raw materials and other inputs, but also on the credit which he, in turn, was forced to extend to his customers. Credit practice in the sale of woollen and worsted cloths and yarn varied in accordance with changes in the nature and organisation of trade. This chapter will outline the chronology of change in the geographical distribution of trade, in the state of the home and foreign markets and the way in which the trade was initiated, organised and financed. Little research has been done on the finance of Britain's trade during this important period aside from N. S. Buck's early study of the North American market of the first half of the nineteenth century.[1] Chapman's more recent work has challenged Buck's notion that manufacturers began to dominate the merchanting of British goods after the Napoleonic War.[2] The time is thus ripe for re-examination of the changes occurring in finance and credit provision associated with the export of British manufacturers. How important was manufacturers' capital in this trade compared with funds provided by the mercantile and banking sectors? The answer to this question has, of course, important implications for the supply of finance to extend production.

The nature of change in the trade in wool textiles is best clarified by considering a number of sub-periods which exhibit specific organisational and geographical characteristics. Although, in practice, the observable features are not capable of being rigidly confined to a strict chronology, four time periods can usefully be discerned:

1. The mid-eighteenth century to the 1790s: merchants and cloth halls.
2. The 1790s–1815: years of mixed fortune.
3. 1815–1830s: the merchant-manufacturer and the 'Bradford Principle'.
4. 1830s–1850: bank credit and speculation.

The mid-eighteenth century to the 1790s: merchants and cloth halls

Thomas Wolrich, a Leeds merchant, writing in 1772, estimated that domestic consumption accounted for around 27% of the total output of the Yorkshire wool textile industry.[3] Ten years later Thomas Hill calculated that 73% of the Leeds trade was directed at foreign markets.[4] Cautious use of the Port Books confirms the impression that around two-thirds of Yorkshire's output went abroad in the third quarter of the eighteenth century.[5] With the exception of the narrow cloth area in the south and west, all the Yorkshire cloth zones were heavily dependent upon exports, often as much as 90% of production of broads, kerseys and worsteds found their way abroad at this time (see Table 3.4).

Much of the growth of the Yorkshire industry during the century after 1750 resulted from the cultivation and expansion of overseas markets. Particular success was achieved after the 1730s in exporting direct from the West Riding to the markets of southern Europe, and later to the Americas. Although some cloths continued to be channelled in the traditional manner through London merchants, especially the Blackwell Hall factors, by the late eighteenth century this method of organisation was very much of secondary importance, especially for the foreign trade. The Yorkshire textile trade had become dominated largely by the local mercantile community, particularly by the merchants of Leeds. This development had important implications for finance and credit provision.

Blackwell Hall factors essentially acted as agents charging a commission on sales to the buyers. By the end of the eighteenth century, Hanson & Mills, a fairly typical concern, were charging 8% on sales which was 'a constant rule of the trade'. No commission was charged to the clothiers although charges were made for warehousing and other overheads involved in the storage of cloths and the securing of sales.[6] Although the factors generally gained no commission from clothiers, they made profits in other ways, especially by the provision of credit. In many respects the factors undertook some of the business of banking: organising finance and lending at interest. Clothiers were seldom in a position to extend much credit to their clients. This was particularly the case with the woollen manufacturers of the West Riding who generally had less financial resources than their counterparts in the other English cloth areas. At the same time credit was essential in the trade in cloth. Domestic wholesalers and retailers commonly demanded six to twelve months' credit in the mid-eighteenth century. In the export trade, which had a slower capital turnover, more than twelve months' credit was common.[7] This was the opportunity for the factors who, drawing on the facilities of the London money market, were able to provide and organise credit and act as middlemen in money as well as in cloth.

Cloths sold by the factors at 'full credit' allowed the purchaser twelve months to pay during which time interest was charged. Clothiers who needed to realise cash during the period before the goods were sold were allowed to draw bills on the factors based on the value of the goods supplied. The formal custom of the trade during the eighteenth century was that bills could be drawn as soon as the transaction for sale was agreed but not earlier. In practice factors such as Hanson & Mills allowed clothiers to draw up to a prescribed limit on the security of the resting cloths but treated their bills as loans for which interest was charged. In addition, probably to get round the Usury Laws, different and lower prices were negotiated for such credit cloths.

The quasi-banking activities of Blackwell Hall factors could lead to instability and bankruptcy if stretched to their limits. John Pearce came to grief in 1810 after his system of fraudulent invoicing failed. He had been invoicing his suppliers for sums 100% higher than the sale price of the cloths involved and adding similar margins to invoices for wool which he was selling to clothiers such as John Simpson of Holbeck. Such invoicing allowed Simpson to draw bills to the sum of £600 on Pearce providing that enough cloths were sent in eighteen months to realise a profit of £600. When he and others failed to make such projected profits bankruptcy ensued.[8]

It seems to have been the case that many of the cloths purchased by London factors from Yorkshire were bought through West Riding middlemen and merchants rather than direct from the clothiers themselves. The factors informed the middlemen of the type of cloth required and they then undertook to buy them in the halls or direct from various clothiers. As they were allowed immediate payment on at least a proportion of these cloths sent to London before they were sold, the middlemen were usually in a position to pay fairly promptly or used some of their own capital to do so. At the cloth halls terms were fairly rigid: cash on the nail, or within fourteen days at the most.

Direct sale by clothiers to middlemen or factors did not lead to longer delays in payment in times of buoyant demand as the option was always open to clothiers to sell in the halls. In periods of poor trade, however, when clothiers became more desperate to shift their produce, they may well have been forced to grant credit. London factors certainly seem to have tightened their credit arrangements in bad years by calling in the loans made on security of cloths.[9] There is evidence, in such periods, of payment in bills, delaying payment until after cloths were dyed, and of straight delays in payment of up to four months. As long as the domestic system was dominant, however, there were limits to the extent to which credit could be forced from the limited means of the clothier classes: 'Even with direct orders the domestic system entirely relied on a quick settlement in cash and small bills of the clothiers' accounts.'[10]

William Lupton, a Leeds merchant who did some trade through London factors in the late eighteenth century allowed two months'

credit, followed by payment in bills at two or three months.[11] It seems
that the bulk of Lupton's cloth purchases were made in the halls on the
usual terms but there is some evidence to suggest that payment for direct
orders could be delayed for some time if necessary. Joshua Riley,
'Carsey maker', was forced to allow four months' credit to Lupton in the
1760s.[12]

In many cases the London factors and merchants were more than just
commission sales agents for the cloth manufacturing areas; they actively
financed the purchasing as well as the holding, storage and sale of the
cloth. As well as dealing through West Riding merchants, they often had
salaried employees in the clothing areas in charge of buying from the clothiers. Such a person was being sought in the following advert from the
Leeds Intelligencer of July 1782 which gave an address in Lombard St,
London:

To manufacturers and others. A person at this time wants to engage with an
agent who has a competent knowledge of the different articles manufactured at
or near Leeds to purchase goods on the best terms, whose character must be
unexceptionable as two or three thousand pounds will be in his hands for that
purpose.[13]

These agents paid the clothiers partly in ready cash and partly in bills,
some of which could be drawn on the London factor or his local financial
agent at a discount to realise immediate cash. Sometimes a combination
of bills made payable at two, four and six weeks after issue were used, in
effect rendering payment by instalment. There seems, however, to be
little evidence of clothiers being out of pocket to their purchasers for
longer than four to six weeks; about 90% of Yorkshire cloth was sold
through the halls before 1800 and cash within fourteen days remained
the prevalent practice. Finance of the delay between sale by the clothiers
and sale to the consumer, either in Britain or abroad, was being borne by
the Yorkshire middleman and by the London factors using the money
market of the Capital. The cost of such credit was paid by the merchant-
purchaser (and hence often by the final consumer) who paid the London
factor both commission and interest and who extended credit to the
wholesalers, retailers and merchants of the foreign and domestic markets.

From the mid-eighteenth century, as we have noted, an increasing
amount of the trade in Yorkshire cloths was being handled by local merchants. Once sufficient capital and prestige (hence calls on capital) had
been amassed, it was only a small step from being the agent of a London
or foreign merchant on commission to undertaking the trade on one's
own account.

Before the 1790s the main foreign markets for cloth still lay in Europe
and the turnover time of capital for the Yorkshire merchants, although
slow, was nevertheless speedier than for those involved either at that

time or later in the trade with the Levant, the Far East or the Americas. Wilson has suggested that the turnover of capital in the Leeds trade in the second half of the eighteenth century was around two and a half times the capital outlay in one year.[14] There was thus considerable need for credit to finance the delays in the chain of transactions and to ensure that the manufacturer was 'in funds' at an early date in order to reproduce the cycle of production.

Some idea of the direction of trade of the Yorkshire merchants in the period and of the credit practices involved can be gained by studying the surviving ledgers of William Lupton, who was a fairly typical middle-ranking merchant of the Leeds cloth trade at that time. By the 1760s Lupton had three major branches of trade: London; Germany, the Low Countries and Dunkirk; and southern Europe, especially Portugal and Spain. On all his European accounts, such as that with Damien Clossett of Liège, an average of six months' credit was allowed followed by bills at short date.[15] This had been the traditional practice of the firm since the 1740s.[16] Occasionally further credit was reluctantly extended particularly in periods of trade depression, although interest was charged after six months as a disincentive.

As the climate of trade became more competitive in the late eighteenth century and as more newcomers entered the field, there is evidence that credit periods were extended further and abatements allowed on invoices as a form of competition. The 'six months rule' in the European trade, which had guided merchants like Lupton and his contemporaries from the early eighteenth century, was being regularly broken – a trend hastened by the rapid development of more distant trades, like the American, with slower turnover.

It seems to have been common with some of Lupton's contemporaries by mid-century to allow six months' clear credit after which one third payment was expected with a further third at nine and the remainder at twelve months.[17] Interest was only charged on debts unpaid after the expiration of the agreed times. Thus, long before the big expansion of the American market from the late eighteenth century, it was quite common for Yorkshire merchants to become heavily involved with their foreign purchasers. William Denison in 1779, for example, had difficulties in extracting £6,200 from a Geneva import house, and when his brother died in 1785 debts of £61,259 were due to his estate from 143 foreign firms in amounts ranging up to £3,652. Three and a half years later the executors still had almost £10,000 outstanding from thirty-one firms including £1,917 from just one Lisbon concern.[18]

The role of West Riding merchants in credit extension to their clients was equally prevalent in the home trade. Defoe provides an excellent description of the inland trade in the 1720s, and in looking at the ledgers and correspondence of the Lupton concern and assuming it to be fairly typical, the practices described by Defoe seem to have changed little before the turn of the century except that more samples were transported by coach rather than packhorse.

> There are ... a set of travelling merchants in Leeds, who go all over England with droves of Pack horses, and to all the fairs and market towns over the whole island. I think I may say none excepted. Here they supply, not the common people by retail, which would denominate them pedlars indeed, but they supply the shops by wholesale or whole pieces, and not only so, but give large credit too, so that they are really travelling merchants, and as such they sell a very great quantity of goods, 'tis ordinary for one of these men to carry a thousand pounds value of cloth with them at a time.[19]

Lupton had an extensive trading network in Scotland, organised on such a system of travellers in the 1780s and 1790s. Most 'journey account' transactions were paid on six or twelve months' credit at this time although many trusted and long-established customers, such as Alex Goven of Glasgow, regularly ran over to fourteen months or more.[20]

Although credit was long and lengthening in the trade of the Yorkshire merchants by the 1780s, there seems to have been no major change in the treatment of their clothier clients. The bulk of cloths continued to be bought in the cloth halls and, even outside, most purchasing was a ready-money business or conducted in short dated bills. With a few notable exceptions the merchant-manufacturer was as yet a rare figure and the Yorkshire merchant was therefore the major agent in providing the credit involved in the realisation of manufacturers' funds.

The 1790s–1815: years of mixed fortune

The rapid expansion of exports especially after 1783 opened the flood gates to new entrants into the merchanting field. The eighteenth century until then had been characterised by the prevalence of old-established houses who took some care in knowing the reputation of their clients and were unwilling to jeopardise their regular returns by inordinate lengthening of credit. So long as the West Riding trade was controlled by men who operated on such principles, the expansion of exports was modest compared with later trends.

The three decades following the mid-1780s saw not only new entrants to the ranks of the mercantile group but also the emergence of the merchant-manufacturer. The larger manufacturers were beginning to try their own marketing, dispensing with the halls and the middlemen. To capture trade the newcomers had to compete with the larger resources of the London factors as well as with the local merchants. Credit extension, usually to twelve months or more played a major role in the competition for business.

Longer credit up to two years with interest charged after twelve months was especially prevalent in the American markets.[21] Together with the emergence of consignment business, this in no small measure contributed to the uneven returns and general instability which characterised the transatlantic trade. Even in the traditional European market, credit was lengthening in the 1790s. Older firms were being forced to respond to the competition from newcomers in order to maintain their business. Even Lupton's, who according to their Letter Books seem to have been more cautious than most, were more often than not giving ten or twelve months' credit in the European trade by the 1790s.[22]

In analysing the effects of increasing competition in the late eighteenth and early nineteenth centuries, one must bear in mind the implications of the political and economic instability of the Napoleonic War period and its immediate aftermath. Inflation of the war years together with the trade, blockade and tariff warfare wrought havoc with both the foreign and domestic markets and resulted in a fight for survival by the merchants.

Even in the domestic markets, the high prices of basic provisions severely curtailed the purchasing power of the mass of population. Wholesalers and retailers demanded longer credits or were unable to pay their suppliers after term. At the same time the Yorkshire merchants, who had to pay promptly for their cloth, could not afford to let their credit terms extend indefinitely. Lupton was under great pressure at this time to extend his credit allowances or to give larger abatements for prompt payments on his domestic accounts. Robert Johnstone & Company of Ayr were allowed four months' credit and an abatement of 5% but were demanding better terms in 1803 to which Lupton replied: 'were we to prolong payment ... it would surely derange our system ... As we must pay on the nail for every article, our work would surely stop and we could neither serve you so well nor so quick.'[23]

Although Lupton stood firm in the face of some of these demands, it was difficult to do so in years of really volatile trade which were such a characteristic of the early nineteenth century. By the second decade high wool prices and reduced credit in wool supply were having an effect on what little credit was available to the merchants from the manufacturers. Lupton wrote to Edith Tanner of Wexford in November 1814:

We shall be obliged to you for a remittance for the balance of goods sent on the 18th September last year. The demand for wool and consequent high prices has entirely put an end to any little credit we used to obtain with our purchases and puts it out of our power to extend to term to our correspondents.[24]

Lupton's demands for speedier remittances were a constant feature of the years 1814–16 when payments in the domestic and Irish trades were frequently outstanding nine or ten months or more.[25] If an account had a regular turnover it was regarded more leniently but where orders ceased

8
Clothiers off to market with their Galloways
Source: G. Walker, *The Costume of Yorkshire* (1814).

9
The Leeds Coloured Cloth Hall
Source: G. Walker, *The Costume of Yorkshire* (1814).

and debts remained 'dead', imminent bankruptcy was suspected and the need to get payment became more urgent.[26]

Lupton's Scottish accounts also gave trouble in these years and he was forced to allow debts to remain outstanding sixteen months or more in several cases and twelve months became fairly common in 1816.[27] Even purchasers as near at hand as Rochdale frequently bought at twelve months' credit in this period.[28] As early as 1800 twelve months' credit appears to have been common in the domestic trade. Jeremiah Naylor, a Wakefield cloth merchant, giving evidence on the home trade before Parliament in that year stated that 'our general credit is 12 months'.[29]

Competition between merchants and merchant-manufacturers in credit and abatement terms was even more prominent in trade with the Americas. This became particularly acute after the turn of the century when political and tariff problems led to vast oscillations of the market. By 1800 North America alone took 40% of British wool textile exports and an even higher proportion of the Yorkshire trade, probably well over half.[30] Whilst trade was expanding in this direction, as it did from the mid-1780s and into the 1790s, there was room for both adventurous and conservative mercantile groups alike. With the problems of the first decade of the nineteenth century, however, with so few markets freely open to Britain, those Yorkshire merchants with the best chance of survival were those who were most aggressive. It was necessary to send agents and partners to North America forcefully to conduct trade on the spot, to expand the risky consignment business and be prepared to try new outlets in Central and South America. The possibility of following these risky paths depended in no small measure on ability to provide the sort of credit and financial terms necessary.

As the trade with North America was not only the most important single outlet by far (despite major interruptions) during these years, and because it exhibits some of the wider features of trade and credit practice in this difficult period, it is worth considering this branch in some detail.[31]

The major characteristic of trade with North America in the period before 1815 was the dominance of English capital and entrepreneurship. The vast bulk of trade and the long credit necessary to finance the turnover time of capital, was undertaken by British merchant houses. This was also true of the trade with Central and South America. Although there is some evidence of Yorkshire manufacturers getting directly involved in the Atlantic trade from an early date, especially after 1806 when markets were being desperately sought,[32] this accounted for only a small proportion of the trade before the 1820s. American houses with their agents buying goods in England for shipment were also relatively unimportant in these years. As Thomas Martin, a Liverpool shipper, giving Parliamentary evidence in 1808 stated: the great mass of goods sent to America was sent on British account and the amount shipped on American account in consequence of orders given, or because of purchases by Americans in Great Britain, was insignificant.[33]

Good shipped by British merchants on their own account were consigned either to their agents or branch houses in America or to American commission houses. Whichever was the case, the business of selling cloths to their final consumer or to retailers in the interior was often a protracted one. Importing houses invariably found it necessary to extend credit to the dealers and wholesalers who were their customers in order to ensure sale. According to one contemporary, previous to 1812 the country dealers generally purchased goods from the city merchants on a nominal credit of six months. A common condition was that the country merchant should make payments from time to time as he was able, paying interest on that amount which remained unpaid at the end of six months, but he was considered liable for the whole debt at the expiration of the fixed time of credit. Thus credit was extended for much longer than six months – commonly for eight, twelve or more months.[34]

Since the importing merchants as well as wholesale merchants of the U.S. found it necessary to extend credit to their customers they in turn were forced to a large extent to rely on the credit facilities offered by the British houses. Buck suggests that long credits could thus have been forced upon British merchants but were the means by which they maintained their hold on the American trade before the build-up of indigenous capital and financial facilities.[35]

A clear picture of the long credits common to the American trade is given in the hearings before the Committee on the Orders in Council of March 1808.[36] George Wood, a partner of Thomas Phillips & Company of Manchester who were mainly in the American trade, stated that goods were exported to America on a nominal credit of twelve months but that remittances were seldom received in less than eighteen months, interest being charged for the additional period. Bills of exchange were usually sent, payable at sixty days after sight, which arrived fourteen to sixteen months after shipment of goods. Wood's firm had debts outstanding from America which were of three to five years standing and the majority were still considered good. Interest was charged on debts after twelve months and it was considered 'no great reflection on his [the importer's] character . . . if he is occasionally a few months in arrears'.[37] William Bell, another export merchant, allowed twelve months' credit on his American accounts but generally received payment only after eighteen months or more.[38] Thomas Martin and Shakespeare Phillips, both of Liverpool, confirmed that twelve to eighteen months was the usual credit found in the American trade.[39]

Further delays in the realisation of funds from the trade with the Americas occurred because much of the payments mechanism was tied up with the shipment of American produce to the continent of Europe. As an integral part of his American trade William Bell for example was involved in conveying American goods to Europe and conveying West Indian produce in American ships.[40] Several Leeds concerns similarly got involved in the import trade in order to secure the means of payment for their exports to the Americas.[41] Unfortunately hides, skins, tobacco and other goods took some time to sell but there were few alternative expedients.

Bell estimated that only about a third of exports to America were 'returned' in the form of goods or remittances sent direct to Britain, the rest was paid for through trade with the Continent.[42] Abraham Mann, another merchant involved in the American trade, was paid partly in consignments of produce and partly by remittances for the Continent.[43] With the South American and West Indies trades, outside the scope of imperial preference, the intricacies of the payment system were even more problematic and protracted: 'The greater parts of the Returns for manufactures which were exported to those parts of the world [West Indies and South America] came home in sugars and coffee, which not being entitled to sale in the home market, there were no immediate means of realising their value.'[44]

These delays in realisation from the distant trades were not financed solely by the British mercantile houses though they were the linchpin of the system before the 1820s. The British discount houses and banks were of key importance in shouldering the real burden of credit provision.

In extending credit, the merchants of Liverpool and Manchester drew on London bankers and brokers as well as local finance houses. Gurney's frequently discounted bills for the distant trades which had two or three years to run. Thomas Richardson of Richardson, Overend & Gurney, giving evidence in 1823, indicated that discounting the bills of brokers, given on security of goods deposited in their hands, had been particularly important in the years 1812–14 when trade had been seriously interrupted. Three other London brokers confirmed the importance of this activity.[45] A Liverpool merchant giving evidence in 1819 indicated the pervasive influence of the London discount market in the trade of Liverpool in particular:

The practice in Liverpool by which all goods are bought and sold is that at the expiration of a given credit of from 10 days to 3 months, as may be agreed, payments are made in bills of exchange on London and sometimes in the acceptances of the purchasers made payable there at dates from two to three months. These bills form the great circulating medium of Liverpool.[46]

Some Yorkshire manufacturers were beginning to play a greater role in credit provision by the second decade of the nineteenth century, but here again the discount market was of major importance. The amount of cloth sold through the halls was now declining: a trend associated partly with the extension of factory manufacture. The system of direct ordering was dominating by the 1820s, which gave greater scope for the merchant to extract credit from the manufacturers. This was particularly possible where the market situation placed the manufacturer in a weak bargaining position and where the local banking structure provided short-term credit and discount facilities to the manufacturing group. The manufacturers ostensibly extended credit to the merchants who gave definite orders for goods and shipped at their own risk but they often drew bills on the merchant on delivery and placed themselves in funds immediately. The credit function was thus shifted to the discount houses and the banks. In effect the merchants of London, Liverpool and the West Riding commonly extended credit back to the manufacturers from three to nine months. This occurred by allowing consigners of goods to draw bills upon them as soon as the goods were shipped. These bills, often drawn for amounts of 60 to 75% of the invoice value of the cargo, could then be placed with an acceptance house and liquid funds made available for investment in further production.[47]

The instability of foreign markets after 1806 gave further impetus to the larger manufacturers to contemplate undertaking the risks of trading direct. The merchants could curtail their commitments in bad years or switch to their home market contacts, but the manufacturers, especially those with high fixed overheads, could not close down their mills:

There is a considerable injury to the manufacturer in being obliged to stop his work, his machinery gets out of order, his workmen get dispersed through the country ... and when it is understood that his business is stopped he loses custom, and when he begins again, it is almost the same as beginning a new business; it is therefore extremely important that the manufacturer should go on though on a limited scale.[48]

The pressure was on the manufacturer to get rid of his produce at or even below prime cost in bad years which gave considerable boost to the business of speculative consignments. Lupton's who did some of their own manufacturing by this time were invoicing their consignments to Boston and New York at prime cost in the second decade of the nineteenth century.[49] In 1807, when the closure of the Portuguese market coincided with the beginning of problems in the trade with America, a number of Leeds manufacturers sent out representatives to Brazil in the wake of the fleeing Portuguese court.[50] Others sent consignments of cloth there in the hope of sale.[51]

Thus manufacturers, unable to close down their mills in a depression, were being forced into merchanting themselves, a trend which was to become even more prevalent in the 1820s. The painful slowness of returns from such ventures brought many manufacturers and merchants to the brink of bankruptcy. The example of the firm of Rhodes &

Glover, merchant-manufacturers involved in the Brazilian trade, illustrates some of the problems incurred. To make the venture pay Glover in Brazil was forced to get involved in shipping and commission services outside of cloth export and the returns to England invariably arrived in the form of commodities which were difficult to sell. When Rhodes, after waiting some eighteen months for substantial returns, received ten bales of deerskins from Glover in May 1809 he despondently remarked 'perhaps to cast them into the Thames will be the best end we can make of them'![52]

Only the more substantial manufacturing concerns could afford to involve themselves in such ventures where capital was tied up for so long. Judging by the Gover–Rhodes correspondence, credit of two or three years was not uncommonly needed in the Brazilian trade and calls upon bank capital in the form of medium-term loans, as well as discount facilities, were essential to such undertakings. Rhodes owed his bank £22,000 in August 1814.[53] Lupton's were in a similar position with their bank, Beckett, Blayde & Company of Leeds. In the period 1811 to 1821, ten of their twelve year-end balances were in debit, the average overdraft being £3,450.[54]

Thus, in summary, the period from the 1790s to 1815 saw increasing competition in the merchanting sphere in both the home and foreign trade and an associated lengthening of credit. The West Riding merchants played a major role in the provision of this credit, together with the mercantile groups in Liverpool and London. The discount and banking houses of Yorkshire, Liverpool and London were, however, of fundamental importance in underpinning the lengthening and increasingly complex credit network. The manufacturers, particularly the larger factory concerns in the unstable years before 1815, were sometimes forced to extend their mercantile role and hence their credit provision to ensure the sale of their goods. In so doing they too relied heavily on discount and credit facilities of the local and national money markets. Their credit rating with such concerns was of great importance in determining success.

1815–30s: The merchant-manufacturer and the 'Bradford Principle'

The peace of 1815 and the reopening of the American market ushered in a new period of rapid trade expansion which had its own special characteristics.

The expected full recovery of the European markets for British cloth failed to materialise as indigenous industries became more competitive. The decline of the older markets was, however, compensated for by the growing demands of the North American continent, and the volatile demands of the Far East. Exports expanded rapidly in volume but their value was slow to grow as the effects of the post-war deflation and the more permanent trend of declining prices for manufactured products set in. Three major factors combined to create the falling price trends for Yorkshire cloths in this period. First, wool prices, both domestic and foreign, began to decline in the 1820s from the high points reached in the war years (see Graph 5.1). Secondly, centralisation and the slow spread of mechanisation were beginning to result in increasing returns to scale, and a lowering of costs allowed lowering of prices. Finally, and perhaps most importantly, almost perfect competition, especially in the production of the more homogeneous, cheaper cloths, forced down the prices of the finished articles.

It was at this time that the 'Bradford Principle', so called in Yorkshire, first came overtly to prominence: the idea of expanding sales aggressively at low unit prices relying on a rapid and large turnover to ensure high overall profits.[55] From this time the dominant idea in most branches of the Yorkshire trade, especially in worsted yarn and cloth making, was 'rather [to] produce a large quantity at a small profit than a small quantity at a higher percentage'.[56] Such a principle rested on the possibility of mass sales to compensate for low unit profits and mass sales depended on the full exploitation of the export market.[57] The trend towards the mass export of cheap cloths was endorsed in the case of the American market by the tariff structure which applied tariffs pro rata and hence impinged much more heavily on expensive cloths.

These fundamentally important changes in the principles underlying trade for the majority of manufacturers placed great strain on the older organisational structures. Despite the stronghold which credit provision gave to the merchant houses, the larger British manufacturers found the system of sale to merchants too restricting in the face of the enlarging volume of production. Buck describes the situation well:

The manufacturer felt, in the lowered unit cost resulting from a greater volume of products, a constant pressure to increase his production and found that he could no longer rely on the British merchant to purchase his entire output. It was therefore necessary for him to become an active merchandising agent. On the other hand, the merchant did not feel it profitable for him to purchase goods in Great Britain to sell in a foreign market when he might have to face the competition of the manufacturer himself, disposing of his surplus stocks. Hence we find the manufacturer necessarily assuming a larger proportion of the risks of marketing and the merchant to a greater degree than formerly, acting as a commission agent for the manufacturer.[58]

As in the earlier period, the pressure for manufacturers to export direct was particularly acute in depression years when stock lay on hand. Benjamin Gilpin, a manufacturer of Gildersome, sold some cloths on his own account in 1821, but 'only since the depression of the trade'. The same witness estimated that only a fifth of the cloth manufactured in the Leeds district by 1821 came to the halls.[59] The extension of the direct order system gave further impetus to the role of the merchant-manufacturer in credit provision by the 1820s.

A major development in the American and Far Eastern trades in the years following 1815 and associated with bulk selling by the manufacturers was the prevalence of the consignment system. Surplus stock was shipped, without direct orders being received, either to an agent abroad or to a merchant in Great Britain who consigned it. In either case the risks of loss were assumed by the manufacturer. A common form of organisation which developed was consignment by the manufacturer to a commission merchant who then reconsigned them to his agent abroad and settled with the manufacturer when he received the proceeds of their sale. Consignment to commission merchants became such a common method of exporting goods that a witness declared in 1834: 'from the best information there are now not more than three exporting merchants at Liverpool'.[60] The other houses had come to specialise in the commission business.

In theory, with this system the manufacturer was out of pocket – extending credit for lengthy time periods – until the proceeds from goods sold abroad arrived. In practice, however, consignment to commission merchants offered an advantage to the manufacturer over the system of direct consignment because, as earlier, the British commission merchants were usually willing to make advances to the amount of two-thirds or three-quarters of the value of goods so consigned. This practice of drawing bills of exchange against consignments now became almost a rule in the trade.

The commission merchants were only able to extend such advances by drawing on the facilities of their local bill and money market, a fact noted by contemporaries:

The growth of our commerce appears to have gradually led to a greater extension of credit facilities and pecuniary advances have increased in proportion as our trade generally has extended; and it is proved ... not only that the merchants of Great Britain are constantly in the habit of making advances on merchandise consigned to them for sale, to the extent of two thirds or three quarters of their value, but that they are also in the habit of obtaining advances themselves from bankers, corn factors, brokers and others upon the goods so consigned to them as well as upon their own merchandise ... and it is stated ... to be practiced to such an extent by all classes of merchants (not excepting houses of the highest respectability) that it may be considered essential to the carrying on of trade.[61]

Minute Books of the early nineteenth-century Liverpool banks illustrate and confirm the extent to which merchants could rely on overdrafts and loans on the security of merchandise and ships' lading papers.[62]

The consignment business was just as prominent in trade with the Far East as in trade with America. Again, advances were not made by British manufacturers and merchants alone. In some instances, consignments were made to the London branch house of a foreign concern or to his British agent. They allowed the manufacturer to draw on them for the amount of the advance and accepted the bill when drawn. In some cases the advances were in the form of cash, but usually bills were used – drawn by the manufacturer on the merchant and accepted by him. These bills could then be discounted in the general bill market and the manufacturer placed in possession of the ready cash. Sometimes the bills were of short date but more often they ran for several months. In the Indian trade the bills were generally for six, nine or twelve months and were renewable if the sale of goods had not been effected by the time that the bill matured.[63]

The merchants of the manufacturing localities commonly dealt with commission merchants in the ports. West Riding merchants dealt largely through Liverpool and London. Advances obtainable at the time the goods were shipped enabled the Yorkshire merchants to continue to buy cloths for cash or short credit but most cloths at this time were being bought with a trade acceptance at three or four months' sight.

The frequency with which merchants and manufacturers dealt in 'acceptances' in this period is symptomatic of the increasing importance of the banking structure and bill market in providing the linchpin of the credit system. 'Acceptances' were bills of exchange drawn upon a merchant and accepted by him. The whole purpose in drawing such bills was to put the manufacturer in the possession of immediate funds and thus to ease the burden of credit provision from the capital required for the cycle of production. This system relied on the existence of a large discount market supplied by banks and bill brokers and, except in times of panic, there seems to have been no real difficulty in getting bills discounted. Thomas Wiggin, foreign banker on American account, commented thus on the system prevailing in the 1820s: 'It would be no difficulty for a merchant receiving an order from New York to purchase goods at three months' credit on his own acceptance. He could then send them to Liverpool and get an acceptance for three quarters of the amount. Parties receiving advances could then get bills discounted at their bank.'[64]

As Buck has concluded: 'the importance of banking and credit facilities open to the British merchant and manufacturer and through them to the American merchant and even to the American consumer cannot be overestimated'.[65] The same could justifiably be said for all other branches of British trade in the period, especially outside of Europe.

The amount of direct trade undertaken by British manufacturers consigning goods to their own agents abroad increased remarkably in the years after 1815. The ending of hostilities saw a flurry of emigration of partners and relatives of Yorkshire manufacturers to the North American seaboard towns in particular. Joseph Dixon of Morley arrived in New York in 1815, Buckley Bent of Saddleworth was in Boston from 1816 to 1822, after which he moved to New York, and Samuel Buckley of Saddleworth sold cloth in three cities in the period 1822–9.[66] As Heaton has described, there was a veritable invasion of New York by Saddleworth manufacturers in 1825: '[they] had the smell of the mill rather than the warehouse about them . . . They belonged to manufacturing families which were stepping out into merchandising.'[67]

These manufacturers and their agents needed to ensure as quick a return as possible. Without the intermediary of the consignment agent to provide credit, the manufacturer could easily tie up funds for long periods in the trade and put his manufacturing business at risk. The need for quick returns, the growth of speculative consignments and competitive pressure for mass sales at low unit profit, together led to the development of the auction system which dominated sales in the distant trades, particularly on the American continent in these years.

Auctions became popular in America following the heavy influx of goods which had piled up in Canada and Liverpool during the war years. The success attending early auctions encouraged merchants and manufacturers to send fresh orders for speculative sale thus stimulating manufacturers to increase output. In an effort to dispose of their surplus production, manufacturers shipped more than had been ordered and the inherent result of the system was the periodic overstocking of the market. So long as auctions continued, even in slump years, it was possible to remit fairly regular cash advances back to England which enabled the manufacturer to continue to produce on a speculative basis.

By using the auction system, the larger British manufacturers began to assume a firm hold over the American trade, especially in New York, at the expense of the American and even the British merchant. Few could undercut the manufacturers' prices. A contemporary described the situation in New York:

The embarrassments of 1816–17 compelled the holders of merchandise to effect sales. This threw at one time into the hands of the auctioneers, almost the whole trade of the city. What accident gave them, they have been able to retain. They now possess the monopoly of a large part of the trade of New York. The foreign merchant and manufacturer, through them, has taken the trade out of our own hands.[68]

Auctions were driving the American importer out of business and by 1825 it was estimated that more than 75% of dry goods imported into New York were on foreign account.[69] English agents of manufacturers had several advantages over their American rivals especially if they used the auction system. They could practise fraudulent invoicing to avoid full payment of customs and they could avoid the costs of warehousing. Finally, as Buck stresses, the real success of the British merchant-manufacturer and the auction system was connected with competition and innovation in England. Each manufacturer rushed to secure for himself the profits which were possible if he could sell at the ruling market price, and at the same time lower his costs per unit by increasing his production. The American importer was competing with British manufacturers engaged in cut-throat competition, therefore it was not surprising that he found difficulty in purchasing in England at prices which would yield a profit when sold in America.

With the ubiquity of the auction system the turnover time of trading capital was quickening but who was now financing the delays in realisation? Buck characterises the period after 1815 as one of shortening credit given by the manufacturer to the merchant and by the British merchants to their foreign correspondents. In saying this he is, however, looking at all commodities and concentrating on the American trade. He relies heavily on evidence from Parliamentary Papers of 1828 and 1833 and it seems surprising that, in view of the limited evidence available to him from the earlier period, he can date the change so early. The evidence from business records of the wool textile trade suggests that although credit periods were slightly less after 1817 than during the war period, they remained long until the mid-1820s after which a really marked change took place in credit practices in both the home and the foreign trades.

This radical change in credit practice, and its timing, is particularly well illustrated in the papers of the Lupton concern of Leeds who were merchant-manufacturers. From 1826, and almost certainly associated with the financial crisis and trade collapse of late 1825, Lupton's trade terms in both the home and overseas markets came to be on a much shorter credit. In their trade with North America their practice of allowing nine to twelve months' credit had been replaced by the 1830s with credit periods of four months or less and this continued in the 1840s.[70]

In January 1826, Lupton's wrote to many of their American purchasers informing them of the new terms:

The various changes that of late have taken place have caused us to determine on restricting the terms of our business entirely to money transactions . . . that is to have authority to value upon a house in this country at three months from date of invoice, which we accept the same as cash, or we would allow interest for any time the bills may be shorter than three months or that the money may be lodged in our hands before the goods are sent off.[71]

In 1828 Jowitt, giving evidence before the Select Committee on the Wool Trade, indicated that Lupton's were not atypical and, in fact, a widespread change in the nature of credit terms had taken place: 'a great deal of the cloth of Leeds and Huddersfield was sold at 6 and 8 months credit which is now sold for money or at a month or two'.[72] Indicating that the trend was in part a response to the instabilities created by the earlier practice, Jowitt earlier mentioned: 'The trade is in a sounder state but the profits are very low.'[73] In the same year Lupton's bought over £20,000 worth of cloths from several hundred Leeds and Huddersfield clothiers with the following credit periods:

2–4 weeks:	63%
5–8 weeks:	17%
9–12 weeks:	13%
13–16 weeks:	3%
more than 4 months:	4%[74]

By 1833, John Brooke, woollen manufacturer of Armitage Bridge Mills near Huddersfield averred that the credit period on Yorkshire cloth had decreased and that it was customary to sell for cash or on short credit.[75] This he associated with low profits and intense competition. Even in the yarn trade by 1833 John Marshall stated that 'our credit is a bill at 2 months at the end of 4 months; we formerly gave 9 months'.[76] The evidence of a third witness before the 1833 committee confirms the impression that the change in credit practice dates from the late 1820s rather than earlier as Buck has suggested.

Have you ever known the kind of business referred to of goods purchased for acceptances and sent to Liverpool and the party immediately drawing for ¾ of the amount? I have heard of such transactions in former years but within the last two or three years my own correspondents have paid cash almost uniformly for their goods without their aid.[77]

Apart from the growth of the auction system after 1816, which obviously reduced the credit periods needed once goods reached their port of sale, there is little evidence to suggest that the new trend in credit practice became common before the late 1820s, certainly in the wool textile trade. The only indication found of earlier origins is contained in a letter from Lupton to Dexter & Almay, his Boston correspondents, in 1826: 'Business has been for a considerable time tending towards this mode and we are convinced it cannot now be carried on advantageously any other way.'[78]

Although the change in credit practice was pervasive, long credits did not entirely disappear in the trade of the Yorkshire manufacturers at this time. In the trade with South America one still finds examples of credits of twelve months or more from the 1820s to mid-century. John Anderton, a Keighley worsted manufacturer with a long involvement in the South American trade, sold on credits ranging from six to eighteen months in the 1830s and 1840s but this probably represents some reduction from the terms forced upon him in the Napoleonic War years.[79]

One cannot leave the period from 1815 to the 1830s without considering the pattern of development in the home trade particularly because here also from the late 1820s credit was being curtailed. The home market at this time took perhaps 40% overall of the Yorkshire cloths and a larger proportion of the milled broadcloths and the more expensive up-market cloths of the fancy areas. Auction selling and cut-throat price competition never became a feature of the home trade partly because products were less homogeneous and because trade relationships were more personalised and customatised.

Lupton started to deal on much shorter credit terms from 1826 when letters were sent to his major correspondents informing them of a general curtailment to five months: 'You will observe an alteration in the terms restricting credit to 5 months which the various changes that have lately taken place in the trade have induced us to adopt.'[80] By the 1830s Lupton further reduced his credit to three months and a few years later 'money' terms were made explicit on most domestic accounts, which in practice meant four to six weeks followed by cash or, more rarely, bills at three months.[81]

In the 1820s and 1830s Lupton's were cutting down their intricate network of trade with virtually all the Scottish towns and concentrating on the larger wholesalers in the county towns who had bigger resources and could afford to pay more promptly.[82] The task of supplying credit to retailers in the localities was devolving on the larger wholesalers and their banking facilities in the provincial towns. This was almost certainly a widespread trend with improving transportation and communication and the changing structure of retailing in the 1830s and 1840s.

To sum up, the period from 1815 to 1830 witnessed a switch from long to shorter credit in most trades, domestic and overseas. This seems to have been promoted in the short term by the instability of the mid-1820s and the losses which many merchants sustained in 1825. But it was also associated with the rise to prominence of new merchants, merchant-manufacturers and, especially, commission agents who relied heavily on a system of acceptances, bank accommodation and discount. Chapman associates this period not only with the rise of commission agents and acceptance houses but also with the decline of exporting on the part of manufacturers themselves and the rise of foreign agents resident in industrial areas.[83] The evidence from Yorkshire suggests, however, that the settlement of European and American commission merchants who were active in the textile area was much more a feature of the 1830s and 1840s than earlier.

The 1830s–1850: bank credit and speculation

From the late 1820s the local West Riding newspapers began to give considerable attention to banking activity and its relationship to trade conditions. The role of the banking system in determining the level of credit and, in the short run, commodity prices was becoming even more important. The changing structure of banking with the rapid growth of provincial joint stock banks and the development of the large Anglo-American and London-based foreign banking houses underlies much of the observable trends in the organisation and finance of commodity trade and credit in both the domestic and foreign markets in this period.

The stage of development of 'central banking' and the competitive climate of commercial banking resulted in periodic over-extensions of credit which had a strong impact on the state of trade. In 1837 the collapse of confidence and credit, which led to the massive trade recession of that year, followed from the reversal of central bank policy and the raising of the bank rate to 5%. This resulted in curtailment of accommodation by provincial banks and thus a deprivation of the normal amount of bank accommodation to manufacturers and merchants. The extent of the commercial and industrial recession which followed highlighted the dominant role which the banking structure now played in underpinning much of the rest of the economy. The monetary crisis of 1846–7 was similar in origin and violent fluctuations in bank rate were a feature of the years from the mid-1830s. Frequent complaints were heard from manufacturers about the government's mismanagement of the credit supply to the economy.[84]

Credit in the period to the late 1840s was characterised by the continuation of earlier trends in the direction of shorter credits between manufacturers and merchants and extended by British merchants to their correspondents at home and abroad. To understand why this occurred, it is necessary to consider developments in the organisation and finance of the domestic and overseas trades and their relationship to changes in the banking system.

The overseas trade in wool textiles was changing both in direction and organisation from the 1830s. America continued to be the most important single market taking about 30% by value of exports by 1850. This, however, represented a relative decline from the 1820s when 40% of British wool textiles found their markets there. Cheaper worsted cloths and blankets were particularly dependent on the Atlantic trade but other branches of production, such as fine milled woollens, fancy cloths and worsted yarn, concentrated more on the domestic and European market. The latter, especially the German and East European markets, was expanding again in these years partly under the impulse of freer trade. Other important markets continued to develop in India and the White Dominions and trade with Russia and China increased.

Competition between firms continued on an intense level and low prices remained a key to success. The use of increasing amounts of waste and rag wool and cotton warps, together with further mechanisation and the squeezing of labour costs, were features of this period. Some manufacturers were finding stability and success in specialisation in particular products for clearly defined areas of the market. This ensured disposal of products without cut-throat price competition. The massive recessions of

1837, 1842 and 1847, as well as seeing the demise of many fairly sound concerns, also weeded out those depending heavily on purely speculative production of cheap goods for consignment abroad.

The most important trend in the organisational structure of trade occurring in the 1830s and 1840s was the increasing importance of foreign and especially European and American merchants and their agents resident in Britain. By the 1840s:

> many foreign merchants who previously employed agents or obtained their supplies from consignments to them by English merchants, began to settle in the worsted districts of the West Riding. This circumstance undoubtedly had a great influence on the prosperity of our export trade, for the foreign merchant being on the spot could not only avail themselves of any advantages which offered in the market but also stimulated the manufacturers to make in the best manner, fabrics suited for the respective continental markets ... These merchants are a large and respected colony in Bradford.[85]

Even in the American trade the foreign merchant was becoming more prominent although the most important system of export continued to be that of consignment by the manufacturer or merchant to an agent in America who arranged sale in the auction room. The consignment system and auction sales in the American market were, however, becoming relatively less important than in the hectic years following 1815. By 1860 only 60% of textiles imported into the U.S. were consignments destined to be sold at auction.[86] The rest, as with the bulk of exports to other foreign markets, were sold privately as Joshua Bates described in 1833: 'manufacturers ... [are] ... in the habit of sending goods to foreign markets where they are placed in depot and held in stock for the demand as it occurs and where they employ an agent to effect a sale for them'.[87] Direct trade in response to orders received was becoming more important and the role of the foreign merchant in this was expanding.

Several factors encouraged this trend. Steam navigation lessened the uncertainties and inducements to speculation, the introduction of the bond and warehouse system enabled importers to hold stocks from auctions until the market could absorb them through private sale and the imposition of auction duties in America discouraged their use there. Also in America, indigenous manufacture was beginning seriously to compete with the British so that less of bulky low-value commodities were imported. The more varied the range of imports the less suitable they were for auction sale.

Perhaps the most important factor discouraging consignment sale after the mid-1820s, and one given little prominence in the historiography, seems to have been the revulsion of the larger, well-established manufacturers against the instability of concentrating on this type of trade. Consignments were coming to be seen by many manufacturers as a resort to be used only when alternatives were spent and when dumping abroad at a loss was less costly in the long run than selling cheaply in the home market and hence competing with one's own customers. In 1830 Hague, Cook & Wormald, who held about 40% of the total North American blanket market, wrote to Dixon their New York correspondent: 'The order business, although leaving only a small profit is better than the continuance of shipping goods which [in] the last two years has been hateful and never profitable.'[88] By the late 1830s even the home trade was being regarded as a better prospect than tying up capital for long periods in long distance consignments: 'having now as large a sum of money as we ought to have in this New York trade we ought not by a hope of profit to carry it larger as at home it may be turned over many times at 2½% before we can expect a return from the U.S.'.[89]

Consignments by British merchants and manufacturers remained a feature of the American and Far Eastern trades but the system was adopted mainly by the more speculative and unstable traders and was the cause of bankruptcy of a great many manufacturers in these decades. As it was easy for a manufacturer to get early advances amounting to a large proportion of the value of his goods, many firms shipped goods simply to realise the cash and it was possible for a manufacturer to maintain himself in business for a considerable time by these means.[90]

Some of the commission houses, especially speculative London concerns, were not content with accepting consignments but actively sought them. These were called 'slaughterhouses' from the effect which they had on smaller manufacturers (who became entirely dependent upon them) and on the trade in general. It was asserted by contemporaries that the slaughterhouses had been the cause of ruin of hundreds of manufacturers by selling goods at great sacrifice to meet the bills drawn on them by the manufacturing concerns.[91]

It seems that many British manufacturers and merchants were drawing in their horns and licking their wounds after the crises of the 1820s and 1830s, looking for safer risks and a more rapid turnover. Some of the gap left in the trade was being taken by foreign merchants with the aid of British banking houses. The increasing role of foreign merchants did not, however, mean that foreign capital was coming to play the dominant part in trade and credit finance, although as in Lancashire, it was of some considerable importance. In 1833 Joshua Bates, a partner in the house of Baring Bros. & Company, was asked if the capital employed in the export of British manufactures to America was almost entirely American. He replied that he believed it was and that some years before English capital had been much more employed. At the same time he did, however, infer that some of the 'American capital' was from advances raised in England.[92]

This appears to have been the key to the finance of trade and credit extension in these years: the combined role of British manufacturers and merchants and of foreign merchants drawing on the credit facilities of the growing British banks and finance houses. The overall effect upon the British manufacturer and merchant was to enable him effectively to continue a short credit trade which the traumas of recent crises and the decreasing turnover time of capital in manufacturing made highly desirable.

By the 1830s the operations of American importers were facilitated by the establishment in the United States of agents of large British banking houses with authority to grant letters of credit to merchants about to send abroad for a consignment. Thus an American merchant who wished to buy goods through his agent in England could secure from the representative of one of the large Anglo-American houses a letter of credit giving him the right to draw a bill usually at forty months on the house in London. The London branch of the house accepted the bill and paid it when due with the understanding that the American merchant should provide the house with cash to meet the bill at maturity.[93] The financing of American trade in this way became dominated by seven finance houses, six in London and one in Liverpool. The three biggest of these, the famous Wilsons, Wiggins & Wildes did an enormous business and had acceptances outstanding equal to £15–16 million in 1835–6. As Buck explains,

This method of conducting business was profitable to all concerned; to the British manufacturer, because he received a bill of exchange which could be turned into cash immediately; to the American importer, because he got the benefit of lower prices for prompt payment; and to the British banking house which received a commission for accepting the bills of exchange, without having advanced any actual funds.[94]

The same system of underwriting and providing credit by the big London finance houses was used increasingly also in the Far Eastern trades in these years. The problem was that the whole pyramid of credit was coming to rest on the narrow basis of confidence in the stability of a small number of houses who, in turn, relied upon the reactions of the Bank of England at different points of the trade cycle.

It was partly the periodically rising interest charges of the banks which made manufacturers and merchants reluctant to borrow in order to finance long credits. Lupton wrote to one of his main customers in Glasgow in 1837:

we do not see how we can charge the advance of bank interest upon our customers, on the contrary, we think we must hold out the inducement if possible for cash payments ... we shall draw at three months from the first of each month unless the parties signify their intention to pay in cash which, if done, we shall only allow interest for the time such payment may be earlier than the date of three months.[95]

Evidence from Parliamentary Papers and business records suggests that short credit terms were almost customary and uniform in the textile trades by the late 1830s and in the 1840s. A witness in 1847 described the practice in the Lancashire trade thus:

the mode of conducting business is this, the manufacturers in Lancaster sell to the Manchester houses at 4 months; they sell this month, and the goods are paid for the next, and the buyers have the option of paying in Bank of England notes and deducting interest at 5% or paying in a three months bill.[96]

Lupton's terms from the mid-1830s were exactly similar. In 1836 he wrote to John G. Stewart of Glasgow: 'we shall endeavour as much as possible to reduce all our accounts to three months net . . . commencing January next'.[97]

Hague, Cook & Wormald had the same terms with their American customers by 1844: 'The manner in which Henry and Co. and Crofts and Stell, and all our American customers, pay us is the first of the month for all goods in their hands before the 20th.'[98] The concern never gave more than six weeks' credit at this time except in the trade which they initiated themselves direct to China.[99] In most branches of the export trade three to four months became the most common maximum credit period offered by British manufacturers and merchants. Lupton's blamed this necessity on low profits and the danger of over-extension towards the peak of the trade cycle. In the difficult years of 1841 and 1842, they wrote to their British and American clients alike that they could not afford to exceed three months and that the times required more than extra caution.[100]

The ubiquity of payments in trade by bills at three months compared with the practice in earlier years is confirmed by the surviving Bill Books and bills of West Riding manufacturers[101] and by evidence of Adam Hodgson, director of the Joint Stock Bank of Liverpool. In 1847 he stated that he had £8–900,000 in bills lodged at under three months and £30–40,000 in bills at over three months. But in former times he had had £200–240,000 worth of bills at above three months.[102] The allowance of a discount of 5% for payment in cash was fairly general; this made it worthwhile for a merchant to pay cash when the rate of discount was lower than 5% otherwise it was in his interest to pay with a bill at three months.

Surviving sets of Sales Ledgers of two worsted firms Bairstow's of Sutton in Craven and Clough's of Keighley illustrate the widespread nature of short credits in the sale of West Riding cloths in the 1830s and 1840s. This applied equally to purchasers dealing in the home market and agents for the export trades.[103] Virtually all Bairstow's clients were allowed ½ or 1½% discount for cash payment before the expiration of four weeks and many of Bairstow's customers took advantage of this.

A really clear picture of some of the trends which characterised the period from the 1830s to mid-century is exhibited in Graph 7.1 which shows some features of the Lupton accounts in these years. The relative decline of the consignment business is mirrored and particularly interesting is its renewed prominence in the bad trading years of the early 1840s. The general tightening of credit terms is reflected in the lower absolute level of the firm's overall credits in the period from the early 1830s to 1843 although the trade cycle in the mid- and late 1840s interrupted the trend. The most interesting aspect illustrated in the graph, however, is the related movement of total trade credits and debts owed to clothiers before the 1840s. The causal connection and its direction is impossible to ascertain and probably varied depending on whether a buyers' or a sellers' market prevailed. Either the credit extended to their purchasers forced Lupton's to demand more in turn from their clothiers or, as the Letter Books suggest, tighter credit from clothiers prompted tightening of credit in the trade. A third possibility is that the two movements are quite independently related to some third factor such as the general state of trade or the conditions of the money market.

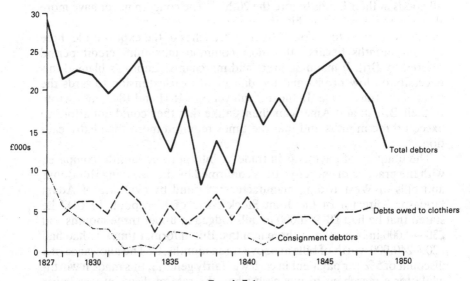

Graph 7.1
Some aspects of the accounts of Lupton & Company, woollen merchants, Leeds,
1827–50
Source: Lupton, Ledger balances, item 115 (B.).

After the crisis of 1847, a secular expansion in the length of trade credit began which accelerated to feed the periodic speculations of the following decades. By the mid-1850s credit of six months or more was commonly given once again by British manufacturers.[104] The woollen branch of the industry seems to have prolonged credit more than the worsted industry.[105] The trend was related to the continuing intense competition between manufacturers for business, to the further expansion of the banking sector and to the use of accommodation bills. The development of free trade and the growth of markets in Russia and China, which with distance and exchange problems were slow in making returns, endorsed the credit trend. A further factor stimulating this change in favour of longer credit was the upward movement of prices in the 1850s which particularly encouraged longer credits in the home trade. As the retail trade mushroomed with the growth of towns and shopping facilities, retailers multiplied, their wholesale suppliers continued to grant long credits and they in turn demanded longer credits from their suppliers. Perhaps credit from banks was not readily forthcoming for provincial wholesalers during the bank-amalgamation period.[106] In the more prosperous years of the mid-century many manufacturers and merchants were better able to give credit than earlier.

The story of this period is outside the scope of the present analysis but it is worth noting at this point that credit practice was now lengthening at a time when the turnover time of capital in the production and trade of textiles was generally quickening. This resulted in credit extension of an inflationary type which may have stimulated overcapacity, speculation and crises.

8

TRADE CREDIT AND GROWTH

What was the position of the manufacturer within the web of credit outlined in the preceding chapters? In order to understand the relevance and importance of trade credit to capital accumulation and to the course and extent of change in the industry, it is necessary to analyse the implications of both short-term cyclical movements and long-term trends in credit practice over time.[1]

The long-term movement of credit: the supply side

In Chapter 5 credit practice in the supply of raw wool was analysed and related to change in the organisation of trade in this commodity and to the changing sources of its supply. Several major points concerning the chronology of trends in wool trade credit in the period 1750–1850 were particularly emphasised.

First, growers of wool gave little credit to their purchasers. Most wool was sold for cash or short dated bills. Where trading relationships were long established, a maximum of three to four months' credit would be allowed but even this saw a marked decline in favour of strict cash terms from the mid-1820s.

Secondly it was noted that the tendency from the late eighteenth century to the 1820s was for most manufacturers to join the smaller concerns in relying more and more heavily on the staplers and dealers for their wool. In this way, although prices were often somewhat higher, specific types of wool, including imported wool, could be bought and an important measure of credit gained. From all the evidence available it appears that staplers' credit terms exhibit the longer-term trends outlined in Table 8.1, although terms varied a great deal between different customers and much depended on the build up of commercial and personal trust and knowledge.

Thirdly, as imported wool became important in the nineteenth cen-

Table 8.1 *Staplers' credit terms summarised*

Period	Most common range of credit
1770s–80s	4–8 months
1790s–1810s	3–6 months
1810s–c.1820	6–10 months
1820s	6–8 months
1830s–40s	3–4 months

Source: Staplers' business records, see Chapter 5.

tury, changes in credit practice occurred in this sphere. A large proportion of the manufacturers, especially the smaller concerns, were
dependent on staplers for their imported wool and obtained the usual
staplers' credit terms. Larger manufacturers buying direct from importers before the 1830s were able to obtain credits of six months or
more. However, from the 1830s, as Australian wool and auctioneering
became more important, manufacturers anxious to gain the cost advantage of buying direct decided or were forced to sacrifice their credit facilities and pay cash within fourteen days. Alternatively, purchasing
through London or Liverpool middlemen could secure lower prices than
the staplers' and a few weeks' credit more than direct purchase at the
auctions allowed.

By the 1830s and 1840s other fibre inputs were sufficiently important
for the effects of credit in their supply to be of note to the industry. Recycled wool seems generally to have reached the manufacturer on a
credit of three to four months by the 1840s and early 1850s, although it is
possible that credit was somewhat tighter than this in the early years of
its use. Cotton warps were sold on tighter credit terms than raw wool,
three to four months being most common. Worsted yarn, the crucial
material input of stuff-weaving concerns, was sold on credit of four
months generally in these decades. Other fibres of significance such as
silk and, to a lesser extent, alpaca and mohair were also sold on three to
four months' credit at this time. It is interesting to note that the surviving
ledgers of manufacturers and their suppliers indicate that during the
1830s and 1840s a large proportion of manufacturers, especially the
larger and longer-established concerns, were often paying for their basic
raw materials *within* the credit period allowed in order to gain the
discounts available which at this time ranged from 1½ to 5%.

Long credits of four to six months seem to have been common in the
supply of dyewares which were important to manufacturers who dyed
their own wool or, more rarely, their own pieces. It is, however, a little
difficult to assess the effects of changes in dyewares' credits on manufac-

turers as dyeing in the piece throughout the period was usually the province of specialised concerns. Before the 1820s dyeing concerns were allied to or employed by merchants rather than by the manufacturers. Even after this, when more manufacturers came to do their own merchanting, dyeing tended to remain a separate trade so that the credit which was important to the manufacturer was that allowed in the payment for dyeing services done on commission. Before the 1820s this seems to have been lengthy, six to twelve months being common. By the 1830s and 1840s dyeing credit seems to have been reduced to around four months on average. Dressing (finishing) credit, an important element in the costs of woollen manufacture, exhibited a similar trend.

The liquidity position of the woollen clothier was greatly influenced by his need to pay for fulling, scribbling and carding services (and sometimes also scouring and dyeing) at the local mill or company mill. Here, as we have seen, the custom until the 1820s and 1830s was the half yearly pay day which gave up to six months' free credit and was often exceeded. From the mid-1830s four-monthly or quarterly pay days became more common but again they were not rigidly adhered to and extra credit was often given for which a charge was made.

Only in that most important element of costs, the wage bill, is it difficult to isolate a general trend from the enormous changes which occurred in the way in which 'wage' labour was organised, employed and paid. Delayed wage payment and payment in kind were ubiquitous features of the late eighteenth, and early nineteenth centuries. This was particularly the case where journeymen, apprentices and family labour were employed in small workshops or households. In a period when few consumer goods were available and when manufacture was allied to a farm or subsistence plot, much labour payment within the artisan structure inevitably took the form of transfers and barter of services, food and shelter within the extended household. It is impossible to isolate the 'wage' let alone its method of payment and credit practice from the intricate structure of custom, perquisite and advances which were bound up with the traditional artisan order and also with putting-out systems of organisation.

Credit in wage payment attracted most contemporary comment in the competitive climate of the second quarter of the nineteenth century. By this time a larger proportion of the textile workforce were dependent solely on industrial earnings. Divorced from the traditions of perquisite and mutual interdependence of the proto-industrial household, 'truck' and delays now took on a different complexion. It seems that large-scale employers of domestic labour and early factory masters commonly were able to gain three to four months' credit in the payment of their wages bill by a combination of delays and payment in truck or shop notes. This may not have represented a major change from the perquisites and delays of pre-factory manufacture, but, stretched to its limits in the competitive struggle at low points of the trade cycle and in conditions of labour oversupply in many branches, this represented the one area of credit which was becoming relatively more, rather than less, important to the manufacturer before the mid-century. This helps to account for growing concern over the abuse of truck payments in the 1840s.

Thus, aside from the complex element of labour costs, the most important material inputs into wool textile manufacture in the period 1750–1850 exhibit a long-term trend (despite the fluctuations of the Napoleonic War period and its aftermath) in favour of shorter and more uniform credit allowances. Other inputs of more minor importance such as carriage, oil and coal supply also exhibited this credit trend. Credit of two to four months on most raw material and service purchases was becoming the rule by the 1830s and 1840s. Even commercial rentals seem to have been increasingly confined to quarterly rather than half yearly payments by this time.

The long-term movement of credit: the demand side

Unlike the supply side of the industry, the demand side does not exhibit a linear trend in internal credit practice before 1850. However, a secular trend becomes apparent if the whole of the nineteenth century is observed and when the mechanisms of external credit are considered.

Corresponding to the dominance of the smaller artisan concerns, especially in the woollen branch, and the concentration of cloth sales through the halls in the eighteenth century very short credit predominated in cloth sales: often cash within seven or fourteen days. Only where the direct order system was growing or where the larger putting-out concerns of the worsted branch sold direct to merchants at home and abroad was longer credit apparent. Even in the latter cases credit was most often under four months and could be reduced to less, if necessary, by the discount of the bill of sale.

In the last quarter of the eighteenth century a minority of manufacturers were entering merchanting for themselves and, in the difficult years of the 1760s and again after 1800, were venturing further afield to compensate for decline in traditional markets. Trade with areas such as South America tied up capital in long credits of twelve months and often more but it was fairly rare to find manufacturers who eschewed the cloth halls, and most of the worsted putting-out concerns dealt with Leeds merchants on credit of three to four months at the maximum.

The difficult years of trading during the Napoleonic War period disturbed the traditional pattern of organisation and credit in cloth sales by making the industry and the mercantile sector more competitive in the search for sales outlets. As a major aspect of competition was cost advantage, organisational economies were pursued which involved the elimination of middlemen and much of the traditional cloth hall trading.

At the same time competition between merchants, and to a lesser extent manufacturers, to maintain or increase their share of dwindling foreign and domestic markets also led to longer extension of credit. Thus the period of the first two decades of the nineteenth century saw manufacturers commonly extending longer credits to merchants and to their correspondents in the increasing amount of direct overseas trade in which they were being forced to participate. John Varley, woollen manufacturer of Stanningley, described his predicament and the way in which he was forced to merchant his goods himself to keep his men in work: 'In 1820 . . . I was not a merchant, I was a cloth manufacturer and I only exported goods then when I could not find a market at home for them, to give my poor men employment, and give them cheese and bread.'[2]

To some extent the effective credit granted by manufacturers who traded abroad direct was reduced by the common practice of advances given by the shipper. Of the 80% of cloths which were being sold outside the halls by the 1810s, a large proportion were sold on three to four months' credit either to local merchants or consigned through shippers on effectively similar credit terms. However, a significant quantity, perhaps as much as a quarter, was being sold direct in the home and foreign trades on credit of twelve months and sometimes more.

From the mid-1820s, manufacturers' credit in the sale of the various products of the woollen and worsted industries was generally curtailing. The late 1820s saw a reduction to four to five months even in direct branches of trade both domestic and foreign. This could be further reduced by bill discount. It seems that only a small minority of concerns continued the traditonal long credit terms with their distant connections. By the 1830s and 1840s, three to four months was the regular open credit period for the trade in commodities for both home and foreign sale. However, the incentive of discounts for payment within time or for cash enabled many manufacturers to secure really prompt payment from their clients in these decades, three to five weeks being most common.

The secular trend and the importance of external credit

Observed trends in credit practice before 1850 are illuminated by adopting a longer time perspective. It is thus fortunate that the only detailed study of nineteenth-century credit practice to date is that of A. J. Topham who concentrated on the West Riding trade from the 1830s and 1840s to 1914.[3] Topham used the Jowitt wool stapling accounts to analyse the credit period taken by wool purchasers from 1848 to 1905. Ignoring speculative short-term movements, his figures show two broad trends. Until the 1890s credit taken varied from two and a half to four months depending on the phase of the trade cycle (see pp. 203–7). From about 1896 credit lengthened noticeably, four to six months becoming most common.[4]

Lavington's much earlier study of trade credit implies that credit was contracting in the second half of the nineteenth century, even in the years before 1914.[5] Furthermore, although there is much contemporary comment on the wool trade in West Riding newspapers after 1850, no documentation has been found of a secular increase as opposed to a speculative or cyclical increase in wool credit in these years.

On the demand side of the industry, as we have seen, the very tight credits between manufacturers and their clients which had come to dominate the trade from the mid-1820s were undergoing some revision by the 1850s. A witness before Parliament in 1857 described the changes of the previous quarter century:

before 1825 a practice had prevailed to a great extent ... particularly in the woollen trade, of giving very long credits. At the time when our house sprang into evidence [1820] ... Mr. Morrison [late partner] ... established a new principle in trade, the principle of short credit, reducing trade almost to ready money, and of course the prices were in proportion; the prices were very moderate and low, and that led to a new era in trade altogether. In the course of a few years wholesale houses similar to our own established themselves in London upon this new principle of short credit, but in the course of time, as capital increased very considerably, surplus profits accumulated very largely, it led to the employment of a larger amount of money in trade and created an amount of competition which has been going on gradually ever since; and the consequence is that competition has not confined itself only to parties fighting against each other in prices, but has been of a worse character; it has extended credit to an enormous amount.[6]

In 1857 worsted piece manufacturers agreed to reduce credit from eight to four months[7] indicating that a rapid lengthening of credit must have occurred in this branch of trade in the years leading up to the Parliamentary Inquiry. Evidence from the Lupton, Clough and Bairstow Ledgers indicates the continuation of short credit trading in the 1830s and 1840s so it is likely that Slater's evidence quoted above and the Worsted Piece Agreement of 1857 were largely a reaction to developments of the 1850s, a decade marked by speculation and the inflation of external credit practices. Even in this decade clothiers gave no more than four to six weeks' credit.[8]

Evidence for the rest of the century suggests that credits in piece and yarn trades remained somewhat longer than in the 1830s and 1840s but that they were relatively short compared with the early years of the century. In the 1870s, for example, credit extension of two or three months in the woollen trade occasioned particular discussion by local Chambers of Commerce. The worsted and cotton trades were regarded as more stable because of the shorter and more uniform credits given. The Huddersfield Chamber of Commerce held an inquiry in 1877 'to ascertain whether any principle of giving credit in the [woollen] trade can be adopted'.[9] A movement was then afoot to regularise the woollen credit terms

and to eliminate credit competition between firms which had led to such
instability in the 1850s and 1860s.

Long credit in piece goods trade was not unknown in the second half of
the nineteenth century especially in the long distance trades. In the 1880s
trade with Russia, for example, necessitated two years' credit before
returns would be expected.[10] It was, however, unusual for West Riding
manufacturers to involve themselves in direct trade of this kind. Credits
of six to ten months were sometimes extended by manufacturers in this
period but if examined closely the mechanism whereby this was done
becomes clear and, in practice, the manufacturers were seldom out of
pocket for long. The system of giving long credits to shippers of textiles
in the 1870s was based on a practice of two months' initial book credit followed by a bill at six months often renewed for another three months.[11]
Much of the credit in the cloth trade from the 1830s and 1840s was similarly *external* rather than internal and turned on the ability to gain bank
accommodation to finance the external credit period.

Thus from the 1820s manufacturers themselves were rarely involved in
long credit extension. Once severe cost competition had taken hold of
much of the trade the accent was placed upon cheapness of both production *and* circulation costs, and credit was an expensive commodity.
Credit competition became restricted to periods of speculative activity
such as the 1850s in particular and declined noticeably after the agreements made between employers in 1857 and 1858. At the same time
mechanisation and vertical disintegration quickened the turnover time
of capital in production, facilitating the use of shorter credits, and
improvements in communications reduced the period of realisation. It
would appear that generally shorter internal credits ranging from two to
twelve weeks characterised the Yorkshire textile trades in this way until
the emergence of monopolistic and oligopolistic structures at the end of
the century began fundamentally to alter the structure of trade and competition once again.

As well as being related to the progress of technology and changing
organisation of production and commerce, the secular credit trend as
experienced by Yorkshire (and probably other) manufacturers was intimately linked with the growth of external finance and with the history of
the banking sector. Bank discount facilities were crucial in enabling
manufacturers to contract the amount of finance which they might formerly have been forced to devote to the sale of their commodities. Open
book credits had often been a lucrative form of investment in themselves
before the abolition of the Usury Laws in the 1830s, but other channels
of investment then became more attractive for the entrepreneur, including reinvestment in industrial capacity. The upsurge in banking and
discount activity must have facilitated this switch and certainly provoked
the extended use of the bill of exchange as primarily an instrument of
credit rather than of circulation.

The establishment of provincial branches of the Bank of England after 1826 did much to underpin and extend the supply of bank credit in industrial areas. The Leeds branch was opened in 1827 and its manager (until 1841), Thomas Bischoff, had the sort of mercantile connections which made him well placed to recognise and service the commercial needs of the industrial West Riding. Large firms with high status and 'respectability' were allowed discount accounts with the Leeds branch. These clients were mainly merchants but the numbers of substantial manufacturers opening such accounts increased in the 1830s.[12] Firms which were allowed discount accounts with the Bank were those estimated to have upwards of £25,000 invested in business and which had a local reputation for reliability.[13] These stipulations ruled out the majority of textile manufacturers who had to rely on private banks for their discount facilities. The Bank charged the going Bank rate on all bills which was usually less than the regular market rate. Private banks varied their charges in relation to the reliability of the commercial paper presented. It was thus much easier for the large concerns holding Bank of England and private accounts to discount a wide range of bills at a cheap rate giving them an advantage over other traders.[14]

A Bank of England account could also facilitate the transfer of money from London to the provinces[15] and some businessmen used their accounts to bolster the position of their private bank in which they often had a major shareholding. Bills were presented to the Leeds branch which had been endorsed by a private bank and which the trader had not received in the normal course of his business. This became a rather common method of bank access to Bank of England credit in the West Riding.[16] In 1836 the Bank was forced to recognise its importance to the stability of the local economy and allow the practice.[17]

The Bank of England was also active in bolstering the discount capability of private and joint stock banks directly: by allowing them discount accounts at 3%. These accounts were quite common in many areas of the country in the late 1820s and early 1830s.[18] They represented a method whereby the Bank succeeded in suppressing private note circulation as 3% accounts were not made available to note issuing banks.[19] The large extent to which banks used these 3% accounts created credit instability and by the mid-1830s branches were instructed to enquire very carefully into the capital and character of all banks applying and to place stricter limits on the availability of cheap discounts by stipulating the need for first class paper and by imposing a fixed amount of discount for circulation only.[20]

These cheap discount facilities may have been very important in enabling banks to extend accommodation to their customers but in the West Riding their role was minimal as far fewer banks held such accounts than was the case in most other areas.[21] The Yorkshire District Bank was the first to obtain a 3% account from the Leeds branch but this did not occur until 1841 by which time the Bank's policy on the granting of such accounts was very tight. The relatively small amount of Yorkshire bank note circulation may explain the small number of 3% accounts granted at the Leeds branch. The Yorkshire District Bank got an account largely because, with fifteen issuing branches, the Bank saw the opportunity to eliminate a large and unregulated source of circulation.[22]

Several of the well-established private banks in Yorkshire did have 'normal' discount and drawing accounts with the Bank by the late 1830s which must considerably have aided their ability to supply credit and advances to their clients.[23] But in the short term in periods of crisis, particularly 1832 and 1837, sudden changes in bank policy and interest rates could have a destabilising effect, as we shall see.[24]

The experience of different firms

How did these discernible long-term movements of internal and external trade credit, on the supply and the demand sides of the industry, affect the different types and sizes of manufacturing concern which made up the Yorkshire wool textile sector? The diversity of organisational and technological structures of production within the industry, coupled with the different raw materials used and the varying products and markets served, together ensured that credit practices would impinge differentially on different types of manufacturers. Diagrams 8.1 to 8.7 represent an attempt to illustrate some of the variations between different types of manufacturers in the composition of both their input costs and their sales outlets and the associated credit relationships. They are based on estimates of inputs and sales structures derived from a variety of primary and secondary sources. These diagrams simplify a very complex picture at the aggregate level for different broad types of manufacturing concern. The diagrams are intended as an aid to conceptualising the liquidity position of different sorts of manufacturers despite the impossibility of properly representing flows of finance in such a static form. Furthermore, in the real world firms would not just experience their position within a typology of manufacturing unit but would also feel the effect of personal and commercial relationships and the build-up of mutual trust between trading partners which seems to have been so important in the formation of the credit matrix.

It was a matter of note to contemporaries that the credit available on raw material supply in the late eighteenth and early nineteenth centuries made it very easy for the new entrant to set up in business in the woollen branch of the industry: 'It is one recommendation of the domestic system of manufacture that a young man of good character can always obtain credit for as much wool as will enable him to set up as a little master manufacturer.'[25] One witness before the 1806 Parliamentary Inquiry spoke of the ease with which a journeyman could become a sizeable

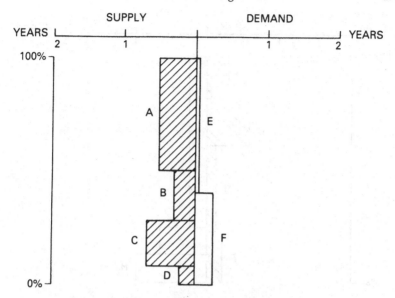

A   Purchase of wool from staplers at average of 6 months' credit
B   Labour payment (largely weaving and spinning) at 3–4 months' credit
C   Fulling, scribbling and carding at 6–8 months' credit
D   Other inputs, tools and rents at 2–3 months' credit
E   Sales at cloth halls at under 14 days' credit
F   Direct sales to merchants or middlemen for short bills at 3 months

Diagram 8.1
The credit matrix of the domestic artisan woollen manufacturer, pre-1815

master and attributed this to 'the facility of credit, as soon as they have accumulated a sum of money that they can procure material, they send it to the mill, and we scribble for them; or if they have not money, we give credit; and they have credit upon every operation it undergoes'.[26]

From the post-Napoleonic War deflation through the oscillations of trade and credit in the following decades, entry eased by generous credit terms began to disappear. Staplers' credit continued fairly long to the 1840s but from 1815 to the late 1820s the longer credits needed on the demand side to expedite sales made it more difficult to set up in business on a small scale except in very specialised branches of the trade sheltered from the brunt of competition. External credit obtained through the system of 'slaughterhouses' and immediate advances on consignments eased entry a little but it was conducive mainly to speculative activity on the part of new firms rather than to longer-term viability.

In the 1830s and 1840s the shorter credits common on cloth sales were facilitated, as we have noted, where a manufacturer could shift the burden by having access to bank discount and accommodation facilities

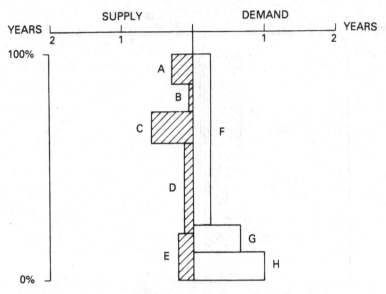

A Purchase of wool from growers and dealers at 3–4 months' credit
B Purchase of wool from growers and fairs at 14 days' credit or less
C Purchase of wool from staplers at 6–8 months' credit
D Labour payment at average of 1–2 months' credit
E Tools, carriage, oil, soap, etc., at 2–3 months' credit
F Cloths sold to Leeds merchants at 3 months' credit
G Cloths sold direct to Europe at average of 8 months' credit
H Cloths sold direct to American market and to the home trade at average of 12
   months' credit

Diagram 8.2
The credit matrix of the worsted putting-out manufacturer, *c.* 1780s–1810

or where he could afford to discount prices generously for prompt payment. At the same time wool credit was being curtailed and the cost
advantage of buying colonial wool at auction was high especially for
manufacturers of the woollen branch whose purpose it suited. Both these
factors ensured that the threshold of entry into the manufacture was
rising. Not only did the potential newcomer of the 1830s and 1840s need
higher initial fixed capital outlays, but he also needed the status to command extensive credit from the local financial sector. Despite the fact
that the rapid extension of joint stock banking at this time and the competition between banks for business made bank credit much easier to
obtain, the early nineteenth-century ideal of the self-employed manufacturing artisan gave way to the type of pessimism expressed by John
Varley before Parliament in 1828: 'Supposing you were to embark in
trade for the first time, what percentage on your capital would induce
you to embark on it? If I had to begin in the world again I should be a
farmer; I should not be a manufacturer.'[27]

Credit changes on both the supply and demand sides of the industry

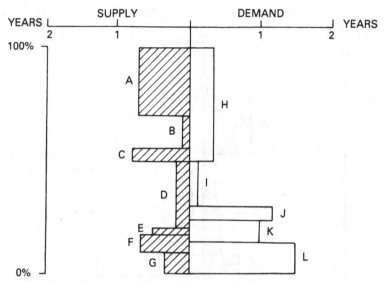

A   Purchase of wool from staplers at 6–10 months' credit
B   Direct purchase of wool from growers and middlemen at an average of 1 month's credit
C   Purchase of wool from importers at 6–11 months' credit
D   Labour, part centralised, part domestic, at an average of 2 months' credit
E   Rental of premises at 6 months' credit
F   Dyeing and dressing services at 6–12 months' credit
G   Other inputs: oil, soap, tools, carriage at an average of 4 months' credit
H   Sales to local merchants at 4 months' credit
I   Sales to shippers for advances at 6 weeks' credit
J   Direct sales to Europe at credit averaging 14 months
K   Sales to the home trade at credit averaging 12 months
L   Sales to North and South America at 18 months' credit

Diagram 8.3
The credit matrix of the large-scale manufacturer in the woollen branch,
c. 1800–20s

tended by the nineteenth century to favour the larger manufacturer at the expense of the smaller concern. The possibility of buying wool for cash at lower prices was most readily taken up by those who could afford to lose their credit terms with the staplers. Thus the position of the small clothiers was undermined by the use of cheaper wool on the part of their larger rivals. It was true of the general stabilisation of credit on the supply side that concerns with a greater liquidity margin gained more than the traditional small concerns who lived from hand to mouth and whose existence was predicated on the long open credits endemic in the earlier phase of manufacture. Furthermore, discount and external credit facilities were more easily available to larger concerns with some standing in the local commercial and financial community. The share registers

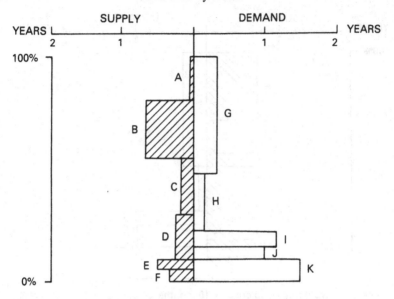

A Purchase of wool from growers at 2 weeks' credit
B Purchase of wool from staplers at 8 months' credit
C Labour at credit averaging 2 months
D Machinery, tools, equipment, oil at around 3 months' credit
E Rental of premises/fixed capital charges at 6 months' credit
F Dyeing and carriage at an average of 4 months' credit
G Cloths sold to merchants at 4 months' credit
H Sales to shippers for 'immediate' advances – 2 months' credit
I Cloths consigned direct to Europe to agents on commission at 14 months' credit
J Direct sales to the home trade at 12 months' credit or more
K Direct sales to North and South America at 18 months' credit

Diagram 8.4
The credit matrix of the worsted manufacturer with centralised, mechanised
spinning, pre-1830s

and directors' list of the Yorkshire banks of the 1830s and 1840s show the
dominance of medium- and large-scale industrialists on the boards and in
positions of directorial influence and only the largest concerns were
allowed discount facilities at the Bank of England.

The smaller-scale manufacturer or the newcomer had less sway in
local banking circles and hence could call upon only limited external
credit to expedite disposal of his product. Gervaise Walker, woollen
manufacturer of Horbury described his predicament to the Parliamentary Commission of 1828:

since the early 1820s ... my trade was better than at present. I am alluding to
myself as a domestic manufacturer; I do not mean to say trade is bad, but it has
changed hands considerably and we, attending the Cloth Hall, find it very diffi-

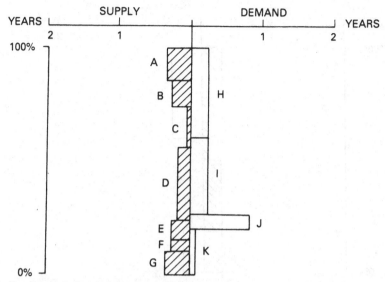

A   Purchase of recycled wool at 4 months' credit
B   Purchase of wool from staplers at 3 months' credit
C   Purchase of wool at auction at 2 weeks' credit
D   Labour at credit averaging 2 months
E   Dyeing and carriage at 3 months' credit
F   Rental of premises/fixed capital charges at an average of 3 months' credit
G   Machinery, tools, utensils, residual inputs at 4 months' credit
H   Direct sales or through intermediaries to the home trade at 3 months' credit
I   Direct sales abroad at 3 months' credit
J   Direct sales abroad on long credits
K   Direct sales to foreign houses in England for immediately discountable bills: 1
    month's credit

Diagram 8.5
The credit matrix of the factory woollen manufacturer, 1820s–40s

cult to meet the market, so that I am almost disposed to give up business. I have
cloth by me which I have had upon my hand two years.[28]

Walker's evidence indicates the difficulties of competing with the new
short (internal) credit trade at lower prices. However, it is too simplistic
to talk of the overwhelming advantages of large- over smaller-scale concerns especially in the 1840s and 1850s. The immense respiration of the
trade and credit cycles often affected the large concerns most adversely.
Apart from the need to keep fixed capital working through a slump, 'the
lengthening of credit of course adds very largely to the risk attendant
upon business; parties buying goods are not expected to pay for them for
a much longer period and consequently they are much more likely to be
influenced by a crisis'.[29] This susceptibility to crisis occurred whether
firms had extended open credit or whether they were heavily dependent
on discount facilities and their cost.

Until the difficult years of the 1800s the credit structure of trade in the

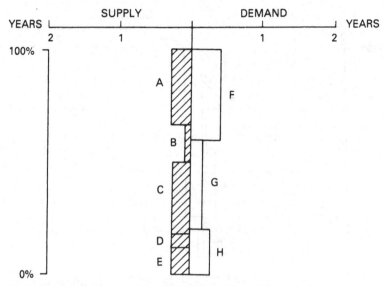

A Purchase of wool from staplers at 3–4 months' credit
B Purchase of wool from growers and at auction at 2–4 weeks' credit
C Labour payment (mainly factory female spinners) at 3 months' credit
D Rental of premises/fixed capital charges at 3 months' credit
E Machinery, tools, equipment at 3 months' credit
F Yarn sold to the home trade at 4–6 months' credit
G Yarn sold to merchants, including foreign merchants in England, at 6–8 weeks' credit
H Yarn sold direct abroad at 3–4 months' credit

Diagram 8.6
The credit matrix of the factory worsted manufacturer, *c.* late 1820s–40s
(spinning branch)

woollen branch tended certainly to *favour* the small clothier by ensuring ready cash for sale and long credit extended by the staplers and fullers. Furthermore, the turnover time of capital in production as well as sale was more rapid in the woollen than in the worsted branch at this time and net credit gained by the manufacturer could almost cover the time of production and circulation. This provided an environment for capital accumulation enabling the gradual evolution of larger concerns from the ranks of the manufacturers and the building of scribbling and carding mills on a joint stock basis. These developments are reflected in Graph 2.1.

The worsted putting-out capitalist by contrast generally purchased wool on short (often no) credit and sold at three or four months' credit at least. This credit position was one factor ensuring the domination of the industry by concerns of larger capital and perhaps contributed along with the disarray of markets in the early nineteenth century to the very slow build-up of fixed capital in the worsted branch before the 1820s (see Graph 2.1). The credit matrix together with the slow turnover time of

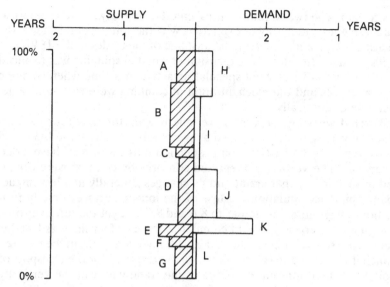

A Purchase of cotton warps at 3 months' credit
B Purchase of worsted yarn at 4 months' credit
C Purchase of other fibres at 3 months' credit
D Factory labour at 2–3 months' credit
E Rental of premises/fixed capital charges at an average of 6 months' credit
F Dyeing and carriage at 4 months' credit
G Machinery, engine, tools, etc., at 3 months' credit
H Direct sales to the home trade at 3 months' credit
I Direct sales to domestic merchants in home and foreign trades at 1 month's credit
J Direct sales abroad at 4 months' credit from invoice date
K Direct sales abroad, e.g. to South America, on long credits
L Direct sales to foreign houses in England for immediately discountable bills: 2 weeks' credit

Diagram 8.7
The credit matrix of the factory worsted manufacturer, *c.* late 1820s–40s
(weaving branch)

capital in the production and sale of worsted piece goods also possibly stimulated the vertical disintegration which was becoming a marked feature of this branch of trade by the early nineteenth century.

Until the 1820s the credit position on the supply side favoured the woollen branch of the industry with a large role being played by the credit of staplers, wool importers and fulling and scribbling millers. On the demand side the persistence of a portion of sales for cash through the cloth halls gave the woollen sector as a whole a better liquidity potential.

From the time of the spread of mechanised spinning in the worsted branch in the 1820s the situation changed. The turnover time of plain worsted production was halved in the space of a decade and increasing vertical disintegration radically affected the importance of input and sales credits. Staplers regarded spinners as less risky credit purchasers than manufacturers whose turnover was slower and whose markets were less certain. The two to four months' credit commonly available on wool purchase goes a long way to explaining why the spinning branch was the fastest growing and also the most unstable of the trades in the 1840s and 1850s. In the latter decade, expansion of worsted spinning was financed by the long credits of wool speculators active at a time when spinning improvements and the mechanisation of combing were cutting production time dramatically.

Worsted weaving concerns were able to gain three to four months' credit on yarn and warps but sold at even shorter credit in the 1830s and 1840s. Rapid turnover times on production must, however, have aided expansion. The vertically integrated concerns by contrast were organised in such a way that credit and its changes generally had less impact upon capital accumulation because of the longer turnover time in production. Diagram 8.5 is similar to 8.6 and 8.7 and yet the turnover time of capital in a vertically integrated mill was three or four times as lengthy, much more so if dyeing and finishing were involved. Thus in the worsted branch it is possible to see credit acting as an agency for the transport of capital between different branches of the trade whilst in the vertically integrated mills of both sectors this was not so important.[30]

Despite improvements in the credit matrix for worsted manufacturers, the build-up of fixed capital in the industry in the 1820s and 1830s was very volatile and did not match the expansion of woollen mill capacity (see Graph 2.1). Credit was a double-edged tool: an often dangerous and unstable aid to expansion from which the woollen sector was rather more immune. The greater expansion of fixed capital in the woollen branch in the 1820s and 1830s may owe something to its sounder credit foundations but the expansion of the transatlantic and domestic markets for woollen goods was a major factor. Not until the 1840s and 1850s did fixed capital embodied in worsted mills draw near to that represented in the woollen sector. By this time the European market for worsted yarn was providing a major fillip for mill construction in this rapid turnover branch.

Some case studies

Few sets of business records survive in sufficient detail to test the foregoing analysis at the level of the individual firm. Furthermore, credit is seldom merely a question of uniform or mechanical commercial practice but involves personal elements; knowledge and trust built upon the relationships of hundreds of different individuals often living within the same social, religious and commercial community. These elements of the credit matrix impinged in a random way and make it difficult to be confident in generalising about credit behaviour on the basis of a small sample.

Enough has been written about the woollen merchanting and manufacturing concern of Benjamin Gott to show that this giant firm was unusual in the nineteenth century. However, the mine of business records which survive, most of which have not been previously analysed, are a valuable source of information on more general commercial practice if used with care. Graph 8.1 shows some aspects of the Gott accounts in the period 1785 to 1838, although the series is unfortunately broken from 1820 to 1824 and from 1826 to 1834. The long-term movement of debts due to the firm (a reasonable proxy for the movement of credit extended) is quite clear with a sustained increase from the 1790s to 1815 and remaining high to the mid-1820s in line with the foregoing analysis.

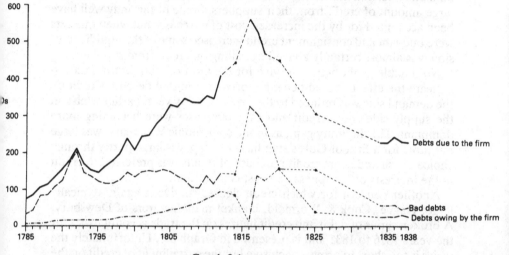

Graph 8.1
Some aspects of the accounts of Benjamin Gott & Company, 1785–1838
Source: Gott, item 20 (B.)

The most interesting feature of this graph, however, is the lack of correspondence of the trends of debts owing *by* and *to* the firm after the turn of the nineteenth century and until the 1820s when the downturn in both is obvious. Before the 1800s the correspondence is very close suggesting either a relationship between the two, or that the two were independently related to a third factor such as the state of the money market. From the mid-1790s the two trends separate and a widening gap develops between them. It seems that the difficulties of marketing goods in the war years and the tendency of merchant-manufacturers to extend their clientage further afield is here being reflected together with the growth of speculative consignments to America which reached a peak in 1815–16. To shift their goods a firm of Gott's resources could afford to become heavily involved in large-scale credit extension to purchasers and shippers both domestic and foreign, incurring increasing bad debts in the period. This picture of an untypically large and centralised concern almost certainly mirrors, in extreme form, the experience of the more typical medium-sized concerns in both woollen and worsted production who were being forced into directing merchanting in these years.

The 'success' of Gott's credit extension on the demand side seems to have been apparent until the trade blockades of 1806. Up to this point the profit rate was fairly steady (see Graph 10.2, p. 240). From 1805 credit seems to have been curtailed on the purchase of inputs which increased the 'liquidity gap' and probably aggravated the decline in profitability. In 1815, at the time when there was a rush to flood the newly opened American market, Gott's were able to wring an unprecedentedly large amount of credit from their suppliers. Some of this may well have been accounted for by the increased cost of purchases but when markets were buoyant and consignment credit increased some of the liquidity tension was almost certainly allayed by calling on credit from suppliers.

No reliable profit figures survive for the Gott concern in the 1820s to indicate the effect of credit changes occurring in that decade. Credit on the demand side was reduced to the levels of thirty years earlier whilst on the supply side short credit and cash purchases were becoming more dominant. The 'liquidity gap', as in the Napoleonic War years, was large but now, for a firm of Gott's standing, the gap was large partly through choice. Cash and short credit purchase of inputs was preferred to credit in the interests of cheapness and cost competition.

Another concern for which credit figures survive is again atypically large: Hague, Cook & Wormald, blanket manufacturers of Dewsbury. A broken series of debit and credit figures on the trade account exists for the years 1816 to 1831 and is presented in Graph 8.2. Unfortunately the series is too short to prove conclusive but the curtailment of credit on the demand side after the mid-1820s again seems obvious. As well as manufacturing and selling their own cloths the firm was buying significant amounts from clothiers throughout the period and it seems from the graph that clothiers may also have been extending less credit from the mid-1820s. It is difficult to explain the leap in wool debts which occurred in the early 1820s except by assuming some speculative activity in the upturn of the trade cycle. The concern avoided the staplers and bought most of their wool direct from the wool counties and from London at this time.

An even more complex picture is portrayed in the Marriner accounts illustrated in Graph 8.3. This, however, was quite a different concern from Cook's or Gott's. Marriner's were worsted as opposed to woollen manufacturers and were more typical in size of the worsted branch as a whole. In the 1820s combing and spinning were done on the premises and weaving sent out to outworkers. Spinning was mechanised at their mill in this decade and the weaving operations were gradually wound down. By the mid-1830s the concern was almost entirely concentrating on spinning.

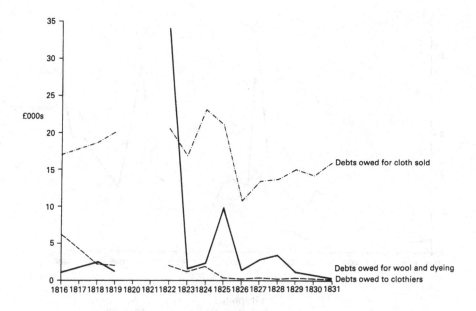

Graph 8.2
Some aspects of the accounts of Hague, Cook & Wormald, 1816–31
Source: Wormalds & Walker, items 1, 2 (B.).

The pattern of debts and credits falls into three chronological periods. First from 1818 to 1824 when trade debts owed to Marriner's were greater than debts owed by them. This squares with the experience of Gott's and with what we know of the long credits extended on the demand side of the industry. Nine months' credit was commonly given on worsted yarn sales at this time.[31] In the second period 1824–34 debts owed by the concern were much larger than debts owed to the concern, although the two tended to vary together. This was a period in which credit on the sale of yarn and piece goods was reduced. Marriner's expansion of productive capacity in these years must be seen in the light of their improved position within the credit matrix. Their net trade credit position was positive at a time when spinning mechanisation and specialisation in spinning was speeding the turnover of their capital.

From 1834 the relative levels of trade debts and credits changed once more so that their net position was negative. Except for 1843, this negative position was maintained to 1850 and became even more pronounced in the second half of the nineteenth century. It is a pity that so few series like Marriner's survive as they may indicate the sort of positive credit position which could be so important at a crucial stage of development. Even big concerns like Gott's could not afford to let too large a gap de-

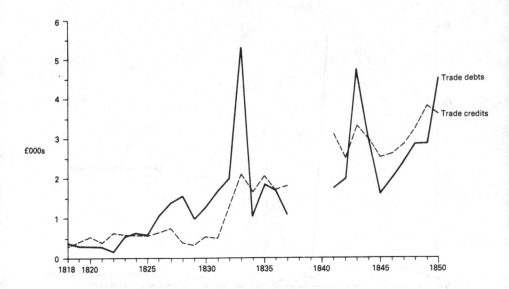

Graph 8.3
Trade debts and credits, B. & W. Marriner, 1818–50
Source: Marriner, item 47 (B.).

velop on a negative trade balance and it is interesting to note that both
Gott's and Marriner's had large bank overdrafts when their net trade
accounts were negative, which helped to finance the liquidity position.[32]

Two other fragments of information on trade credit balances are available. The first is for John Broadbent & Sons, a small-scale factory woollen manufacturer, who put out weaving and undertook commission milling in the period 1826 to 1833. The second is for Clay & Earnshaw (1812 and 1814), sizeable woollen manufacturers on a putting-out system, who also carried out the centralised preparatory processes and finishing in their mill. Both show a negative net trade balance which must have had adverse effects on their potential for financing production expansion. A marked relationship between debts owed and owing is indicated in the case of both concerns. Both were probably creating credit but it appears that this was accompanied by the necessity of keeping the net trade position under control.[33]

In the light of all the evidence it may be that Cottrell's considered comment concerning credit in the nineteenth century is a gross overstatement; certainly as far as the West Riding is concerned before the mid-century: 'Generally, it would appear that the power to create trade credit lay mainly in the hands of the merchants rather than the manufacturers and it was based on the accommodation given by the financial sector.'[34] Although the West Riding evidence confirms the importance of the banking sector, particularly after 1826, it fails to substantiate Cottrell's main assertion. The surviving business records of the first half of the nineteenth century in the wool textile trade all indicate the dominance of negative trade credit balances. Manufacturers were creating trade credit by allowing greater credits to be run up on the demand side than debts owed to their suppliers. In doing this they generally relied on their ability to draw short-term funds from the local banking sector. This situation is further substantiated by inspection of bankruptcy records. Many wool textile firms which failed in the 1820s, 1830s and 1840s did so because of liquidity problems rather than lack of assets or a negative balance sheet.[35] The extension of credit, largely as a form of competition in these decades, and bolstered by bank discount and accommodation, brought many firms to grief.

Short-term credit

As well as the long-term trends discernible in the movement of credit, there is much evidence of severe short-term fluctuations whose presence and effects need to be explained.

Short-term movements, often lasting as much as five years or so through the upturn or downswing of a Juglar cycle, as well as short-lived rapid escalations resulting from speculation were just as important to most manufacturing concerns as longer-term movements. At a time when bankruptcy rates were high and few firms had a long history the whole lifespan of a concern may have been conditioned by just one phase of a cyclical credit movement. Furthermore, as liquidity problems were a major cause of failure, the sudden tightening of credit at the downturn of a trade cycle is crucial to understanding the rate of exit from the industry.

Two questions need to be answered at this point. First, what was the mechanism of the short-term trends and fluctuations in credit and how did the conditions influencing this change over time? Secondly, how did these fluctuations affect the position of the manufacturer? Did credit circumstances in boom and slump aid the manufacturer to expand when times were propitious and in weathering the storms of commercial life or did volatile credit seal the fate of many concerns?

One noticeable feature of the various graphs showing the movement of trade debts and credits is their cyclical correlation, although this seems to have been less obvious in the Napoleonic War period when interruptions of trade caused perennial stockpiling of raw materials and finished products. In an upturn of the trade cycle staplers and raw material suppliers would increase their credit absolutely to cover the increased costs of manufacturers' purchases and manufacturers would tend to increase the absolute levels of credit extended to cover the increased cost of sales.

At the same time a period of increasing activity and confidence might create greater willingness to grant longer credit to buyers. Other forces, however, worked in the opposite direction at such times. Increased trade and profits would tend to give added power to the seller to demand prompt payment whilst buyers were better able to meet this demand.[36] If these forces were at work in the industry in our period it would seem that upturns until the early 1820s were generally dominated by the former impulse towards the lengthening of credit in boom periods whereas, although these influences continued strong, the contrary forces tending toward shorter internal credit became more prominent in the upturns of the second quarter of the nineteenth century. The next two decades and especially the 1850s saw some reversion to the former position (largely because of the force of speculative activity). This appears to have imposed itself anomalously upon the secular trend.

In addition to the forces outlined above the effect of external credit was felt particularly in the upturns of cycles which were fuelled by the growth of the discount and banking sector. This was especially important from the 1820s. In 1833, for example, at a time of heightened commercial activity and fixed capital expansion, open credits were said to be less than formerly but accommodation finance was rife.[37]

Bigger firms with greater call on the local and London financial community could allow their external credit to lengthen inordinately and it became common from the late eighteenth century and especially from the 1820s and 1830s to use accommodation bills whereby the credit of a house or individual was gradually separated from that of a particular transaction. This had the inherent problem of the ratio of the debt represented by the bills to the debtor's wealth getting out of hand in periods of euphoria towards the peak of the trade cycle. The greatest vice of the accommodation bill according to R. G. Hawtrey was its 'use for construction of fixed capital when the necessary supply of bona fide long run savings cannot be obtained from the investment market'.[38] Evidence from the 1820s suggests that many Manchester cotton mills were financed in this way whilst similar speculative building of industrial premises for hire was occurring in Huddersfield in the early 1830s.[39]

With accommodation bills many traders with little capital of their own were able to acquire the use, at least temporarily, of large volumes of borrowed funds. Around 1808, for example, Sir Francis Baring knew of clerks not worth £100 who were allowed discounts of £5,000 to £10,000.[40] By 1857, John Ball, a London accountant, reported knowing firms with capital of under £10,000 and obligations of £900,000 and claimed it was a fair illustration.[41] The trouble was that if one house failed the chain of credit would collapse and bring down good names (those with a reasonable ratio of debt to credit) along with the bad. The most notorious collapse affecting the West Riding trade was that of Hindes & Dereham, worsted spinners of Leeds and Dolphinholme, whose liabilities in 1839 at the time of their demise were £225,000, £97,000 of which were accommodation bills running at the time of their stoppage.[42] At least seven other important manufacturing and trading concerns were brought down by this collapse.

Each boom in trade and credit was, as we have noted, fed by the expansion of bank credit. The West Riding was an area of great expansion in the numbers of country banks from the 1770s and after the joint stock enabling legislation of 1826 it was one of the areas of the country which felt the sudden expansion of banking facilities with particular force. Competition in the discount market from the branch Bank of England in Leeds led to a reduction of the discount rate from 5 to 4% in 1831 which stimulated further discounting.[43] In the decade of the 1850s alone the value of discounts to traders given by the Leeds branch of the Bank of England rose fourfold. All firms discounting at the branch were given a limited accommodation on their own bills but there was no formal limit to the amount of bills of other parties which might be discounted there.[44] The problem with this was that although it created a stimulating environment during the upswing of the trade and investment cycle, over-trading and over-extension of credit was the perennial problem; the sudden contraction of bank credit and the rush for liquidity brought many firms to the ground.

The expansion of joint stock banking after 1826 did not necessarily lead to greater stability of the provincial banking structure. In fact, in the 1830s and 1840s the competition between banks for business led to easier acceptance of much unsafe commercial paper for discount. This, plus the expansion of rediscounting on the London money market, enabled banks to work with very small paid up capitals and to over-extend the amount of credit which they gave.[45] Many discounted six to eight times their paid up capital and, as uncalled capital could not be obtained quickly, banks had to rely on rediscounts in an emergency. This meant that the severity of crises in the London market were enhanced and communicated to the provinces. It may, however, be the case that the West Riding was less powerfully linked through interest rates and Bank of England note circulation to the policy of the Bank, and thus to the London money market, than other industrial areas.[46] As we have noted, the Leeds branch made few deals with local banks to suppress their note issue and 3% accounts were unimportant.[47]

Those concerns depending most heavily on bank accommodation fared worst in periods of financial panic. The problem was not just one of liquidity but of depreciation of assets upon which the credit was founded:

If a man is known to be possessed of, I will suppose, £10,000 of capital he can have no difficulty in commanding credit for £100,000 and I dare say that he may keep a stock of £100,000 in the course of his business. If the bank minimum rate rises as high as 10% ... the man's goods must drop 10–20% in value ... therefore he loses the whole of his capital and is compelled to go into bankruptcy.[48]

The losses from the sudden raising of the rate of discount were not solely attributable to the high rate of discount itself but to the depression of the value of goods and the increase in bad debts which followed from the accompanying alarm.

In the downturn of the cycle external credit was rapidly withdrawn and in the atmosphere of pessimism there was a marked increase in liquidity preference which translated itself to some extent into a restriction of book debts and internal credit. However, open credit may not have shortened markedly at such times as we have noticed in the case of staplers in particular. Declining prices and reduced markets promoted a competitive struggle for survival in which credit was a valuable weapon. Those concerns who could afford to do so tended to lengthen their open credit to retain their business and to bolster their customers. Credit as a form of competition to retain or increase custom was felt as acutely, if not more, in hard times than in good.

Graph 8.4 depicts the quarterly credit sales and cash sales of Jowitt's, wool staplers, in the period 1832 to 1843 which covers the long downswing of 1836 to 1839. Credit sales were restricted in the depression but only after a lag of twelve months or so. Even after this the change was not drastic. The movement depicted in the graph reflects the tendency to increase or be forced to increase open credit at least in the early stages of a cyclical downswing in activity. Those firms of some standing or of some long-term importance to their suppliers are likely to have been treated most favourably. Topham's analysis of the period from 1848 which shows the credit taken by three of Jowitt's customers through the cycles of the second half of the nineteenth century also indicates that the peaks of credit extension exhibited a lag of a year or so behind the general peaking of industrial activity.[49]

The need for manufacturers, particularly factory manufacturers, to produce through depressions often led to credit extension in order to shift their produce at a time when the market was already overstocked. It is not surprising that domestic and small-scale manufacturers often fared better in depressions than the larger concerns with more fixed capital charges and more wage labour. They had perhaps not over-extended themselves with their banks to the same extent because they had less security. Furthermore, they could rely on the continuation of credit from their staplers, bought little of their wool direct and could more easily cut down production or delay wage payments until conditions improved.[50]

In sum, cyclical fluctuations in credit fuelled the expansion of the industry at certain periods but contained the inherent danger of instability, speculation and crises. The tendency of open credit to react more slowly in an upswing, especially after the mid-1820s, and to contract less rapidly or even expand on the downswing, especially on the supply side of the industry, had a stabilising effect. The question to be asked is whether a less expansive but more stable system of credit would have

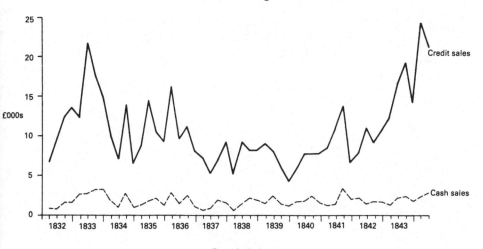

Graph 8.4
Quarterly cash and credit sales of Jowitt & Company, wool staplers, 1832–43
Sources: Jowitt, item 58 (B.).

been better for the industry than the one which prevailed. However, this question leads one into the realms of untestable hypothesis. The upswings of the cycle provided fertile conditions for entry into the trade and for the expansion of productive capacity. Crashes resulted in high rates of bankruptcy and chains of accommodation finance resulted in the downfall of many sound concerns. However, panics also weeded out speculators and unsound links in the commercial network and led to the adoption of agreements regarding credit in the late 1850s which were first steps in the longer-term stabilisation of the West Riding and the national economy.

PART 4
EXTERNAL AND INTERNAL FINANCE

Well. Some people talk of morality, and some of religion, but give me a little snug property.

Maria Edgeworth (1767–1849),
The Absentee

9
ATTORNEYS, BANKS AND INDUSTRY

The overwhelming feature of the capital market in Yorkshire throughout the period 1750–1850 was its very local and highly personal nature. The bulk of short- and long-term loan finance changed hands within a narrow radius of some 10–15 miles and most lenders were personally acquainted with the character and affairs of their debtors.[1] Usually they were related to each other through a family connection, by religion or through business – sometimes all three. The eighty-four loans, together worth over £89,000, which were raised by Gott and Wormald in the period 1780–1811 are a good illustration of these local relationships. Of the finance, 82% came from the West Riding, 67% from Leeds alone. The two biggest single sources of funds were individuals involved in the same line of business and relatives of the partners.[2]

The personal element and its influence on the size and direction of flow of loan capital in the community is particularly obvious in the business dealings of money scrivening attorneys and remained of overwhelming importance in the lending policies of banks until the mid-nineteenth century and beyond. Attorneys and banks were the two most important financial intermediaries at this time and warrant close attention in any study of the market for industrial capital.

Attorneys and industrial finance

Benjamin Gott & Company appear to have been by no means unusual among manufacturers in raising finance in the immediate locality, much of it through attorneys. It appears to have been rare in the West Riding, as in Lancashire, for much capital to flow to London to the safer arena of government securities, certainly before the second quarter of the nineteenth century. Attorneys like John Howarth of Ripponden and John Eagle of Bradford did buy government bonds on behalf of their clients but the bulk of investment negotiated through them went into local ventures – in agriculture and public utilities and to manufacturers and merchants.[3] The majority of potential investors in the West Riding appear to have preferred to know exactly to whom their savings were going and had a strong inclination towards dealing through the familiar and trusted figure of their local attorney.

Potential lenders were often already regular customers of the attorney's legal services and formed a fruitful circle of contacts through whom he could raise loan capital. There were two aspects of legal work in which the eighteenth-century attorney was particularly involved: estate stewardship and trusteeship. Thus a large number of lenders through attorneys were landowners or trustees and executors of wills. The extent to which landed capital found its way into industry and trade by these means was the subject of discussion in Chapter 4.

The rapid growth in the numbers and efficiency of trusts in the eighteenth century has been well documented by Anderson.[4] Trust money was a suitable source of longer-term loans since the complex and time-consuming legal processes involved, even in testate cases, meant that trustees were often in no hurry to withdraw the principal. Furthermore, attorneys themselves were commonly named as trustees in the wills of their clients and had a strong influence over the use to which the trusteeship funds were put. Thomas Edward Upton of Leeds, for example, was made trustee of a marriage settlement from which he loaned £1,000 to Gott's in 1803 for a period of twelve months. A proviso was made that the money should be recallable within two months.[5] Similarly John Howarth managed the trust of William Parker of Sowerby from 1787 to 1803 and invested hundreds of pounds of the money in various outlets during those years.[6]

Apart from large landowners and trusteeships, the most important single source of investment funds was spinsters and widows of the locality. Most of these had family connections with either landownership or merchanting and it was these areas of activity which had originally spawned the capital. About a third of John Howarth's clients providing loan capital in the period 1789–96 were widows and spinsters of this type.[7] The same names crop up regularly in his Cash Books indicating that the savings and capital of these people were available for loan again and again. One attraction for the lender was that a secure living could be gained from the interest. Many, in fact, demanded an annuity income rather than interest.

The attorney also mobilised many small and diverse hoards of cash, insignificant in themselves but important when added together and employed in the community. Surprisingly, one finds institutions such as the Ripponden Friendly Society among the clients appealing to Howarth to find a borrower, at interest, for their small cash holdings kept as a reserve to pay sickness benefits and burial fees.[8]

The links between local attorneys were strong and if they could find no suitable lender or borrower for a client themselves, they would invariably apply to their neighbours in the profession. Frequently a close working relationship appears to have existed between groups of attorneys, a relationship which was facilitated by regular contact in legal work especially at the Quarter Sessions. Howarth's contacts with other attorneys extended as far as London, Manchester and York but his most frequent contacts were within a narrower radius which took in Bradford and Wakefield.[9]

Some attorneys were very influential local figures and could cast their net wide in negotiating loans for clients. John Eagle, for example, had contacts with a large number of Lancashire businessmen and landowners through his position as law clerk to the Leeds and Liverpool Canal Company.[10] Although the vast majority of loans were procured by attorneys in their own localities most of these men had links with the London capital market and could call on funds from there. London capital was generally obtained through the relationship between the provincial attorney and his London agent. The London agents functioned primarily as conductors of litigation on behalf of their clients in the London courts but they could also be employed to secure loan capital. In November 1773, for example, John Howarth applied to his agent Mr Allen of Furnival's Inn asking him to procure £9,000 on mortgage for his friend George Stansfield, woollen merchant and manufacturer.[11] The close relationship between Robert Parker, a Halifax attorney, and Oliver Farrer, his London agent of Lincoln's Inn, resulted in many loans being procured including one of £3,000 in 1778.[12] The standard charge levied by attorneys for procuring money on loan in the late eighteenth century appears to have been 5s for every £100 borrowed.[13]

If the attorney's circle of contacts failed to result in a suitable loan transaction, the personal columns of the provincial press were used. Miles has studied the columns of the *Leeds Intelligencer* for information on this and found over 150 adverts in the second half of the eighteenth century. The lack of similar announcements on the part of other financial agencies indicates that attorneys were the most distinctive single group of local financiers in this period.[14]

The attorneys themselves appear to have been an important source of loan capital. In the case of Howarth, between a third and a half of loans arranged in the 1780s and 1790s ostensibly came out of his own pocket.[15] Attorneys were often men of some capital. Their business, both legal and financial, was expanding rapidly in the second half of the eighteenth century and so also were their profits. In addition attorneys were well placed to build up their landed assets.[16] When a debtor was compelled to put land on the market, the attorney was often given first refusal to purchase, and estate management for clients placed him in a good position to buy up land as it became available. Furthermore, it is likely that rentals, collected by an attorney in his capacity as estate agent, were often lodged with him for a period before being passed on to the estate owner and they could thus be utilised at least for short-term loans. Finally, the ability of the attorney himself to act as creditor in a loan derived from his activities as a deposit banker. Particularly where no sound local banking institution existed, small savers traditionally deposited their cash with the attorney who hastened to employ it in the locality.

It is much less easy to trace the nature of borrowers than of the lenders of sums negotiated by attorneys and it is impossible to assess the use to which these loans were put. Borrowers from Howarth included merchants, landowners and manufacturers and a large range of the more humble members of the community but most borrowers are only mentioned by name and it is not possible to trace the origin of more than 25–30%. In a sample of ninety-one of the hundreds of loans procured by John Howarth in the period 1789–96 about a quarter of the borrowers are readily identifiable. The largest single group of these were merchants but landowners also figure strongly and a handful of manufacturers are recognisable. The average size of loans was between £200 and £300 but they ranged in the period from £44 to over £4,000.[17] In addition many smaller short-term loans were made which did not enter the Cash Books as no interest was charged.[18]

It is obvious that some of these loans, large and small, long and short term, were directed into industry. Miles has shown the extent of involvement of John Eagle in colliery and mining finance in the Bradford area in the period.[19] Several of the merchants and manufacturers named as debtors in the Howarth accounts were involved in the textile trade but one can only speculate as to the precise importance of this source of loan capital to textile manufacture in the late eighteenth century. In this connection, however, it is surely no accident that one finds a large number of mortgage papers and promissory notes, witnessed by attorneys, amongst the archives of textile manufacturers.[20]

The duration of loans made by attorneys seems to have varied enormously. Howarth's Cash Books contain details of interest payments and it is therefore possible to see that some loans of considerable sums were for periods exceeding five years. These longer-period loans include some to merchants and manufacturers. For example, £400 was lent by Mrs Brisco, a landowning widow, to Joshua Norminton, a comb maker, in 1790 on security of a mortgage and the sum was still outstanding in 1795.[21] Similarly, £1,000 lent by John Howarth himself to Joseph Priestly, merchant and wool stapler, in 1793 was still outstanding four years later.[22] Richard Holroyd borrowed £1,000 from William Parker in 1790 on security of his mill and some cottages and there appears to be no record of the repayment before the series of Cash Books expires in 1796.[23]

The most common duration of loans of £50 and upwards appears to have been around two years in the case of Howarth and it is unlikely that his business was unusual in this respect. By the 1790s Howarth had an average of £5,260 of long-term securities lodged with him and only £200–£300 worth of short-term securities, which indicates where the bulk of his business lay.[24]

In addition to procuring substantial loans for long periods attorneys appear to have been active in short-term loan transactions for both large and small amounts. In their capacity as rent receivers and legal functionaries, they often held the precious idle cash balances of the locality for short periods and these were invariably put out on short-term loan. In his position as clerk to a Justice of the Peace, Howarth, for example, regularly received fines which he did not hesitate to put to temporary advantage.[25] Many of Howarth's short-term debtors were merchants and putting-out capitalists: for example, George Stansfield and Robert Butterfield, two local woollen merchants, who normally took loans of under £100 two or three times a year in the 1780s.[26] These loans were probably used either to buy wool at propitious times of the year and hence obtain the best prices or these individuals who were putting-out capitalists borrowed the sums to pay their spinners and weavers.

Small sums of a few shillings or pounds were frequently loaned by Howarth without interest for a few days or weeks. These loans were mainly to people of humble means – local tradesmen, craftsmen (including textile workers) or labourers, most of whom were known to Howarth personally as they had worked for him or supplied him with goods at some time. As long as the principal was promptly repaid Howarth was not concerned to make a profit on these loans. As Miles has rightly argued, '[His] attitude was possibly shared by other attorneys and businessmen and may have been part of a policy of communal self help in which all manner of people clubbed together to help each other in a situation of acute cash shortage.'[27] This is in marked contrast to the situation in south east Lindsey earlier in the century where Holderness found little evidence of 'social' or 'community' motives influencing the relationship between borrower and lender.[28]

There is no indication that the role and position of the attorney in the capital market changed significantly with the competing developments of the banking sector, certainly before the second quarter of the nineteenth century. The numbers of attorneys in the major West Riding towns expanded continuously as Table 9.1 indicates, although demands for their legal as opposed to their financial services must have played a large part in this. The number of private banks in Yorkshire expanded equally rapidly during this period, as Table 9.2 indicates.

It seems likely that the services of banks and attorneys as intermediaries in the capital market were complementary rather than directly competitive in the late eighteenth century. The main business of the banks was in bill-discount (and thus short-term accommodation) whereas, as we have seen, attorneys were skilled and practised in arranging longer-term loans and mortgages. Attorneys did discount bills but this was not a

Table 9.1 Number of attorneys in the principal towns of the
West Riding, 1793–1830s

	1793	1814–15	1816–17	1818	1830
Leeds	6	21	20	26	63
Halifax	5	12	14	13	16
Huddersfield	3	6	7	7	12
Bradford	1	8	8	10	19

Source: Contemporary directories (these give some indication of numbers but are by no means precisely accurate).

Table 9.2 Number of private banks founded
in Yorkshire[a]

By 1790	22
By 1800	49
By 1810	71
By 1826	83

[a] Includes those going out of business in the period.
Sources: Crick and Wadsworth, A Hundred Years of Joint Stock Banking, pp. 195–240; Matthews and Tuke, A History of Barclays Bank Ltd., pp. 208–49; Ling Roth, The Genesis of Banking in Halifax, passim; Hartley, Banking in Yorkshire, passim; records of private banks (Lloyds, Barclays, Midland); contemporary West Riding trade directories.

major part of their business. They also held deposits for their clients almost like bankers but, fearing robbery, surplus funds were usually banked with the attorney's banker.[29] Conversely, eighteenth-century banks were known to involve themselves heavily in medium- and long-term loans but this part of their business seems not to have been so important for most banks as it was to become in the 1830s and 1840s.

Before the more competitive phase of banking was initiated after 1826, there was so much scrivening work available, certainly in Yorkshire, that there was plenty of space for the activities of both attorneys and banks even where their functions overlapped. There is no evidence that attorneys moved into banking to any degree in the West Riding as they did in other areas[30] and even as late as the 1830s they appear to have been active as financial intermediaries and money lenders, along with their expanding legal work.[31] This was particularly the case concerning their landowning clients and widows and spinsters for whom they did business. These groups preferred to execute their financial affairs in the traditional manner through their attorney until the mid-nineteenth century and beyond.

The industrial origins of banks[32]

The growing use of bills and notes in the industrial regions in the late eighteenth century was part of the response by traders to the chronic shortage of exchange media, particularly acute in low denominations.[33] The use of the bill of exchange made every businessman a banker of sorts and the pressing need for circulating media was an inducement for some merchants and manufacturers to enter banking more formally. The need for safe remittance facilities, especially to London, also encouraged persons involved in inter-regional trade to extend into banking. This was particularly so where business necessitated having a London trade agent or partner. These manufacturers and merchants were well placed to become financial intermediaries for their wider business community. There are many examples of the eighteenth-century banker/industrialist in the West Riding. They issued notes, discounted bills and remitted money to London and other parts of the country via their London connections. In their capacity as bankers they also often accepted deposits which could be deployed in their non-banking business.[34]

The marked connection between West Riding banks and the expanding wool textile sector, the dominant industry of the area, is illustrated in

Table 9.3 *Commercial interests of private bankers in the West Riding of Yorkshire, 1758–1820s*

Town	Textile merchants	Textile manufacturers	Other industries and trades	Landowners, office-holders	Unidentified	Total
Leeds	1	—	1	1	4	7
Halifax	3	4	—	—	2	9
Huddersfield	—	2	1	1	5	9
Wakefield	—	1	—	1	1	3
Bradford	2	—	1	—	1	4
Other	8	5	9	2	8	32

Total number of private bank partners surveyed = 64
Number clearly connected with textiles = 26 (41%)

Note: Includes identifiable partners of all banks traced which were in existence more than two years (disregarding partnership changes).
— = none recorded.
Sources: As for Table 9.2.

Table 9.3. The table confirms that the majority of West Riding private bankers were simultaneously involved in a fairly narrow range of industrial production and trade, and were thus part of a close knit and localised framework of mutual trading and credit extension. Banks were spawned with the requisite local knowledge to assist them in assessing the credit-worthiness of their clients and, as one might expect, their partners' personal and business involvements coloured the nature and direction of their banking activities particularly in the granting of credit and loans to customers.

Some banker industrialists can be seen as pillars of the financial structure of local trading groups: so much so that it was common in times of panic and liquidity crisis for large groups of manufacturers and traders in the local community to pledge their loyalty and even their money in support of the bank.[35] The cohesion of the local banking and industrial sectors was further endorsed by the number of interlocking bank owners[36] and by the very limited growth of branch banking.[37]

The continuity of these close links between banking concerns and the local business community is evident in the dominance of local business interests in the ownership and directorship of the Yorkshire joint stock companies formed after 1826. At least until the second half of the nineteenth century, over 90% of shareholders lived in the immediate vicinity of the banks' offices. Indeed, some banks insisted on this as a principle.[38]

Geographical localisation resulted in narrow occupational groupings of shareholders in some cases. Of the ninety-four shareholders of the Bradford Banking Company in 1827 more than a third can be identified as wool textile manufacturers and, if wool staplers and textile merchants are added to this group, more than half of the shareholders can be seen to have been actively engaged in the same industry.[39] The involvement of local businessmen in the new banks is also apparent from lists of bank promoters and directors. Analysis of the directorates of eight West Riding joint stock banks in the 1820s and 1830s indicates a strong connection with textiles. Of a total of fifty-two directors, thirty-one were directly involved in textile manufacture and trade.[40] The continuity of links between banks and industry after 1826 was further reinforced by the representation of many of the old banking families on the boards of the new concerns. It frequently was the case that private bankers insisted on a large shareholding and overriding influence in the directorate when their firm was converted to joint stock. Thus, in many cases, rather than weakening the direct influence of the banker/industrialist figure, joint stock legislation resulted in many of the same people having control over the disposal of vastly increased resources.[41]

Banks and industrial finance

What were the implications of these close links between banks and industry throughout the period? What sort of financial inter-connections did they spawn? And to what extent did banks contribute to the finance of industrial production as well as trade?

The composition of a bank's asset portfolio depended on the ability to combine wisely the competing demands for liquidity and profit. The logical asset structure in ascending order of liquidity, descending order of earning power, would be advances and loans, then investment in government securities, bills and money at call and, finally, the cash reserve. However, there were several factors operating in our period which distorted the play-off between liquidity and profit for the provincial banker. First, both private and early joint stock banks were influenced largely by the whim of the partners or directors. The very local nature and the generally small scale of banking concerns resulted in much specialisation of investments on the basis of local economic life and the banker's personal and business connections and knowledge. There was, of course, a danger in overengagement in a narrow range of industry but this was often forgotten where the banker himself or a close relative was directly involved. Secondly, although it may be expected that the Usury Laws before the 1830s would put a ceiling upon local investment vis-à-vis the competing attractions of the London money market, the addition of commission and postage charges enabled the banker to charge 6–7% interest on an overdrawn account. In addition, a banker with his own manufacturing firm was unaffected by the Usury Laws in many respects; he was not controlled in the amount of profit he might put back into the bank in return for the use of its money.[42] For these reasons the asset structure of the West Riding 'industrial' banks before the mid-nineteenth century comprised mainly local investments and advances with money market assets held primarily for immediate purposes as money at call.[43]

Several forms of bank lending to West Riding industry were common in the period. First, although no complete set of records survive, scattered sources indicate that private banks may have significantly subsidised the manufacturing interests of their owners. The bank run by Hague & Cook, blanket manufacturers of Dewsbury, played a supportive role in the overall functioning of the concern in the period 1811–36.[44] In the ten years 1812–22, 26% of total profits had been made by the banking adjunct. This represented a higher and much more stable rate of return on capital than was made for the concern as a whole and was particularly higher in the difficult years following the French wars. In 1813 an agreement was signed with Smith, Payne & Smith of London who agreed to underwrite the country banking business for £15,000 in return for a mortgage on the Dewsbury Mills' premises. It seems likely that this money was regarded as a reserve for the business as a whole. The bank accounts were not separated from the other accounts of the firm until 1824 so it was difficult to distinguish the banking capital as a separate entity. The firm was accommodated by Smith's in 1812 to the extent of £1,372 and in 1823 to £5,833. In the latter year new weaving sheds, warehouses and a drying shop were being erected and gas lighting installed in response to an increase in trade. The mortgage of the mills to Smith's was not redeemed until 1843, seven years after the sale of the banking business to the West Riding Union Bank. The wind-up of the bank resulted in a massive injection of capital, some £15,000, into the manufacturing concern. In addition no limits were set to Hague's overdraft allowance by the joint stock concern which bought out their bank.[45]

The Bros. Swaine & Company of Halifax, bankers from 1779, were simultaneously engaged in worsted manufacture and trade, owning three large mills by the early nineteenth century.[46] Their bankruptcy broadsheet published in 1807 reveals that again the trades of banker and manufacturer were not separated in the partnership accounts. The £40,000 lodged with them in their capacity as bankers would obviously provide useful credit for their trade as a whole. Only 1.7% of their total assets was held in London as a cash reserve, a large proportion of the remaining £523,000 (excluding mills and estates worth £90,000) were employed actively in the locality and £204,000 of this was tied up in drafts of the textile firm W.S. & J. Crossley with whom they presumably did a great deal of trade.[47] Their successors in the banking business in Halifax, Rawsons Rhodes & Briggs, were concurrently in partnership as wool merchants; the Rawson family were heavily engaged in woollen manufacture and Briggs was connected with a worsted spinning firm.[48] In 1809 James Hartley was a partner in this firm and arranged for an additional advance of £1,000 to his family's firm of cotton warp manufacturers on security of their cotton mill and its contents. Nine years later, following a bankruptcy petition, Chas. Hartley & Company still owed the bank £2,410.[49]

There are several examples of bankers who failed in the early nineteenth century through tying up too large a proportion of their assets in illiquid manufacturing capital. One such was run by Joshua Taylor at Gomersal, a concern which collapsed in 1825. The bankruptcy hearing emphasised 'over-engagements in woollen manufactures'[50] as the reason for the bank's demise. Taylor owned extensive mills and was involved in the army-cloth trade.[51]

In analysing the extent to which private bankers engaged in credit provision and longer-term advances to other members of their business communities one is aided by the survival of more complete evidence. The bill account or current account kept with the local bank frequently became a source for the longer-term extension of funds. These extensions might be seasonal or of a longer-term nature, but, whichever, it was common for overdraft limits to be agreed in advance and they were often secured by the deposit of collateral. By taking full advantage of these agreements it was possible in practice for local businessmen to obtain advances for fairly long periods.

In 1809, Rawsons Rhodes & Briggs were listing securities valued at between £1,000 and £15,000 for each of eleven debtor accounts covering unspecified overdrafts. Five years later seven of the same eleven concerns still owed amounts varying from £1,711 to £3,403 (average £2,055). In the years 1818–22, six of the same concerns persistently had a substantial debit balance of £1,000–£3,000.[52] It seems that little security was demanded for these loans and although it is difficult to trace the nature of all the debtor concerns, about a third were local firms involved, like the bankers themselves, in the wool textile sector.

The same firm was heavily tied up with loans to woollen firms which suffered in the crisis of 1815. By 1814 advances extended for a limited period were not being reduced and securities were arranged for a number of accounts to regularise the overdrafts on a more permanent basis.[53] In the case of loans to James Moore & Sons of Brockwell, woollen manufacturers, sums of several thousand pounds were extended on security of woollen goods. Their bankruptcy resulted in the bank having full rights to the mill, estates and goods in Halifax, New York, London and in shipment, to the value of £14,700. The lengthy process of selling the goods and the estates meant that the advance was not redeemed for at least two years.[54] The experience of this bank was not unusual. Many loans which started as short-term overdraft facilities became longer term by default.

Wentworth, Chaloner & Rishworth of Wakefield, bankers from 1814, whose notorious collapse in 1825 brought down a number of other firms and had a serious effect on commercial life in the region, were found to be deeply overengaged in illiquid investments in their locality. Well over three-quarters of their total assets were held as loans and overdrafts. Whether through default or design, they owned at least four textile mills by the early 1820s which they leased out to manufacturers or managed themselves.[55] As late as 1830, five years after their bankruptcy, their assignees were managing Union Mills at Ossett – a substantial concern.[56] The solicitor's Bill Books of the bankruptcy period show that Wentworth, Chaloner & Rishworth were considerable owners of industrial and other properties, and that they had regularly lent money on security of estates.[57] At the bankruptcy hearing in Wakefield it was obvious that the partners had advanced money to industrial concerns and although the duration of the loans is not detailed, the amounts were large. Four concerns between them owed £183,700. The bankers themselves owned two of these which were woollen mills.[58]

Wentworth, Chaloner & Rishworth may have been atypical as an example of lending policies by the private banks in this period. William Beckett, private banker of Leeds, when asked by Parliamanet if he considered that they had conducted their business 'upon any principles of common sense or common safety', replied 'None whatever.'[59] Nor were the 1820s necessarily a typical period of bank lending as much speculative activity was occurring. In Manchester, for example, mill building was commonly financed by bank accommodation given in the form of renewal of bill-discount in that decade. Sums were also loaned on mortgage by the Manchester banks expressly for the extension of productive capacity.[60] Examples of 'wild' lending by certain banks in the periods of speculative mill building raises the question of to what extent they were aberrations from 'normal' banking practice.

That they were merely extreme examples of what was more general banking activity is evidenced when one considers material relating to three very reputable private banking firms in this period. Two, Beckett & Company of Leeds, and Leatham, Tew & Company of Wakefield and Pontefract, prospered until the twentieth century while the third, Benjamin Wilson & Son of Mirfield and Dewsbury became a stable joint stock concern in 1833.

In his evidence before the 1832 Committee on the Bank of England Charter, Beckett leaves one in no doubt as to his bank's lending policies over previous decades. He frequently advanced money to customers, loans being determined by the character and credit of the parties and a variety of securities both real and personal. We 'generally advance money to merchants and manufacturers ... to manufacturing firms who keep accounts with us and consequently they are often for a long time owing us money which varies in amount'. He was not in the habit of refusing advances on good security to anyone in Leeds who came to him. Sometimes the loan was for a fixed period but most were on current account and therefore 'not closed for any certain stated time'.[61] That some of these loans were extended in time through default is evidenced by bankruptcy accounts of local firms. In the difficult years 1839–43 six failed wool textile concerns alone owed Beckett's £20,700 at the time of their demise and only a fraction was recovered by the bank.[62]

Leatham & Company of Wakefield regularly lent amounts varying between a few hundred and several thousand pounds for periods as lengthy as several years in the first half of the nineteenth century.[63] Some loans were clearly short term, e.g. the £25,000 lent to Steer & Aldman, wool staplers, in 1833 which account was marked: 'will soon come down by sales of wool'.[64] Often, however, it is possible to trace loans for several years, some unsecured, and others secured by a variety of personal bonds, mortgages, life policies and deed deposits. Around 1830 there was £92,000 outstanding on only twenty-three accounts, £32,000 of which represented doubtful debts. About half of these debtors were connected with the wool textile trade. The partners' minutes of the succeeding nine years show the longer-term nature of many of these loans. For example, Halliley Brooke & Company, blanket manufacturers of Dewsbury, first secured overdraft limits with Leatham & Company in 1811.[65] By 1833 their debit balance was £12,466 and was tending to stay above the agreed limit of £10,000 which was backed by two mortgages. By

December 1834 they were bankrupt, owing the bank £9,900. Some accounts had overdraft limits as high as £15,000, e.g. Thos. Taylor & Sons, linen and worsted manufacturers of Barnsley.[66] Allowed limits were generally related to the returns on a customer's account and agreed periodically. It was only when a client reduced his business with the bank or had an overdraft at or near the limits without alteration for a number of years that the bank expressed concern unless economic circumstances intervened to determine the bank's revision of its asset structure. This situation left plenty of scope for *de facto* long-period loans. No doubt many of the hundred local overdrafts totalling £153,788 in 1837 were of this nature.

Benjamin Wilson & Son, woollen manufacturers and bankers probably had similar policies. At the time of their transition to a joint stock concern in 1832 accounts and overdraft limits were examined. Overdraft limits had been arranged on 216 accounts and varied from £50 to £5,000; fifty-nine of these were allowed over £500 and twenty-six more than £1,000. The highest limit was £5,000 to Joseph Lee, a neighbouring woollen manufacturer. All told, 203 firms were allowed a total of £75,000 and a further thirteen concerns were allowed advances equivalent to securities deposited. About a half the debtors are identifiable as local textile manufacturers, reflecting the personal knowledge and business connections of Wilson's.[67]

Further evidence in the Directors' Minute Books of joint stock concerns discussing the continuation of overdrafts allowed previously by private banks endorses the same picture.[68] In general, private bankers lent substantial sums of money often for lengthy periods, but mainly on current account both with and without security depending on the status of the customer and the amount to be advanced. Loans and the assessment of the credit-worthiness of clients tended to reflect the nature of the business involvement of the private banking partners.

This picture changes little when one examines the policies and lending practice of the joint stock banks up to the 1850s except that these concerns were generally able to mobilise greater resources.[69] The Deeds of Settlement of all indicate that loans were expected to be an important element in the banks' business and most put this high on their proposed list of functions.[70]

Joint stock banks

Medium- and longer-term loans, particularly to shareholders, were definitely common among the West Riding joint stock banks. It seems likely that investment in bank shares was made more attractive by the knowledge that favourable treatment would be accorded in the procurement of overdraft facilities. Despite principles expressed to the contrary in the 1836 Committee Report on Joint Stock Banks,[71] the banks commonly regarded the paid up capital on shares as security for an advance to that amount and such overdraft facilities were generally made automatic at the time of opening the account and purchasing the shares. In addition, bank shares were commonly pledged as collateral security for loans.[72]

There are examples of shareholders and especially directors being treated very favourably with respect to loans; sometimes to such an extent as to operate against the banks' interests.[73] The Halifax Commercial Banking Company provides an example of the dangerous effect of this policy of favouring bank directors. In 1848 the woollen merchanting firm of bank partners Bernard & Thomas Hartley failed owing the bank nearly £10,000 on current account and more than £11,000 on bills discounted. It is not certain whether they were overdrawn above agreed limits but the account was only secured for £2,843 until after the liquidation when further estates were quickly transferred to the bank to the consternation of the other creditors.[74]

It seems that most bank lending to directors, their relatives and acquaintances was consistent with safe banking practice but three major failures occurred among the West Riding joint stock banks before 1850.[75] One of these, the Yorkshire District Bank, liquidated in 1843, had extended advances and loans to industrialists and traders well beyond safe limits. Despite a proviso in the Deed of Settlement that no director could vote advances to himself or his relatives,[76] the Committee of Investigation discovered serious mismanagement and excessive local advances amounting to £2 million. The bank had extended £121,500 to fourteen wool textile concerns all of which failed in the period 1839–43.[77] The Committee referred to 'misplaced confidence in their manager which enabled parties to obtain advances for most incredible amounts'.[78] Three banks with branches in the West Riding also failed in the period, partly it seems because remoteness from head office meant that it was more difficult for branches correctly to assess the credit-worthiness of parties applying for loans. The recklessness and independence of the branch managers in extending advances to their personal acquaintances was partly blamed for the notorious failure of the Northern and Central Bank in 1836. One manager had accumulated, in just two months, bad debts to the extent of £40,000. Other reasons for the failure were declared to be that the interests of the shareholders were preferred to those of the general public and that the directors and their friends had overdrawn themselves to the extent of £1,556,000.[79] Despite these failures the majority of West Riding joint stock banks were sound concerns and paid dividends of 5½% or more in most years in addition to building up reserve funds.

As with the private banks, fears of liquidity crises dictated the popularity of bill-discounting as a form of credit extension on the part of the joint stock concerns but loans and especially the more flexible overdrafts were very common. While there are major problems in using nineteenth-century balance sheet data, it is possible to calculate the proportion of assets held as loans and overdrafts for seven West Riding banks for various years within the period 1837–50. The average proportion was around 57% which for most banks represented more than twice the amount of money tied up in bills.[80] Most of these advances were extended to local enterprises in the period before mid-century.[81]

In distinguishing between the role of banks as providers of short-period credit and their role in financing, directly or indirectly, the production of commodities, the loan period is critical. Examination of the Minute Books and other papers of five joint stock and one private bank in the period 1826–1840s[82] and consideration of references to more than 1,000 accounts leaves the conclusion in little doubt: lending most commonly took the form of overdrafts rather than fixed period loans but in all banks chronic overdrafts were very common. Contrary to accepted views this seems to have been particularly so in the case of account-holders in their early years of business and during periods of expansion of their productive and trading capacities. In theory the overdraft was regarded by banks as a fairly liquid asset but too often they found it difficult to draw in their commitments in a deflationary phase or decided that it would only damage their business in the long run to do so.[83] A system similar to the Scottish 'cash credits' thus seems to have spread to England despite avowed principles to the contrary aired before the Parliamentary Committees. In addition, in the West Riding it was the practice to utilise 'the 10% rule', that is to allow bank customers overdraft facilities to the limit of 10% of the turnover on their current account.[84] Further overdraft limits could be granted and were determined by the financial or personal standing of the clients involved or the offer of a variety of collateral securities.[85]

Unfortunately, only one West Riding bank Ledger survives which covers the year by year movements on customers' accounts. This is for the Bradford Banking Company 1827–30.[86] The Ledger details one hundred and fourteen accounts, fifty-two of which are concerned with wool textile production or trade. Of those fifty-two, thirty were persistently in debt to amounts varying up to £5,500 and averaging £1,500. Six were persistently in debit well over £3,000 including four manufacturers.[87] Only in the case of five textile accounts did a net credit position obtain over the period 1827–30 as a whole. These were either old-established firms or those with substantial land-owning interests in addition to textiles.[88] Table 9.4 details forty-eight of the textile accounts and using Directors' Minute Books for the succeeding ten-year period one can clearly see the existence of chronic debit balances commonly for periods of three to ten years. Thirty-six of the forty-eight account-holders were shareholders in the bank and twenty-two of them had pledged their shares as partial security. Some accounts were also secured by property deeds or bonds but persons of some standing in the community or associates of the directors had less security demanded of them.[89]

Some examples from Table 9.4 will illustrate the nature of bank lending. Number 13 represents the firm of William & Thomas Marshall, woollen manufacturers. They opened their account in 1827 and were allowed an advance of £2,500 without security, partly because they had obtained a similar facility from their previous bank, Briggs & Company. In 1828 a personal bond and mortgage were deposited to cover the account to £4,000. They utilised this allowance virtually in full for the next five years. The bank allayed any fears after one of the directors discovered that Marshall's owned their mill. They were thus deemed to be of substance. However, by 1832 they were bankrupt. By 1834 the bank still had a 4/9ths share in their mill which was being leased for the benefit of creditors. The account was not finally settled until 1871.

Number 27 represents William Rouse & Son, worsted spinners and manufacturers of Bradford. This large concern was allowed 10% of turnover in 1827 which amounted to £5,000 unsecured. In the early 1830s deeds to property were deposited and, in return, a further £2,000 was allowed plus £5,000 'occasionally' on top of the chronic 'overdraft'. In February 1833 the bank allowed them a further advance on the same title deeds expressly to enable them to extend their premises. On this additional £5,000 advance the bank agreed to give twelve months' notice of the need to repay.

Account number 3 is that of the firm Illingworth, Murgatroyd & Company, woollen and worsted spinners. By 1830 their overdraft limit had been increased from £3,000 to £4,000 and it was larger than their profits during 1828–32.[90] In the early 1830s the overdraft limit was raised again and only in 1833 did profits begin to exceed it. In 1828 considerable additions had been made to the firm's premises[91] and it must be the case that their overdraft played a role in this.

A Securities Register[92] which survives for the period covered by the Ledger and Minute Books of the Bradford Banking Company shows that it was common for deposits of collateral to stay with the bank for several years. The most common period was three to five years, but some were left for more than ten years. A similar but less complete picture is obtained from the records of other banks. The Mirfield & Huddersfield District Banking Company operated a 'cash credits' type of system. Overdraft limits were agreed when an account was opened and were related primarily to turnover although offers of collateral and personal standing or influence also played a part in determining allowances. Overdraft limits ranged up to £12,000 in 1830. It is possible to trace some firms with frequent overdrafts through much of the period for which records exist (1833–40s) but they are mentioned only sporadically as their account position changed, and it is thus difficult to be certain for what periods they used their overdraft facility.[93]

The Halifax Commercial Banking Company, like the Bradford Banking Company, declared openly their adherence to the 10% rule. They generally did not require security up to that amount of advance but above it security was almost always demanded and a higher interest rate was charged. The bank took care to agitate if advances grew inconsistent with the returns made on accounts but, as mentioned earlier, the directors were treated as special cases.[94]

The Huddersfield Banking Company also allowed 'cash credits' on personal bond and there are examples, in the Minute Books of the period 1827–38, of the deposit of less-liquid collateral to secure longer-term overdraft limits.[95] Firms regularly took advantage of their overdraft facilities. The illiquidity of some of the loans granted in the first years of the bank's existence can be gleaned from the third Annual General Meeting report July 1830, announcing heavy bad debts.[96] In the 1830s the bank became a little more cautious and kept a wary eye on what were termed 'dead' advances.[97] Hugh Watt, manager of the bank and formerly branch inspector of the Perth and Arbroath banks in Scotland, wrote an extensive thesis on the practice of banking which acknowledged the practice of advances up to a tenth or even an eighth of returns.

These credits are often granted by the English banks . . . without any security at all and the bankers are therefore much in the habit of inquiring whether the persons keeping accounts with them are doing well or ill in their business. In Scotland the banks require security for all advances and therefore trouble themselves less with such inquiries into their customers' business.[98]

Thorough knowledge of customers' affairs was the essential element in loan decisions. The wool textile connections on the board of the Huddersfield bank, as in the case of other banks, may explain some of the heavy lending to woollen concerns.

The evidence of business and bankruptcy records

Unfortunately only eight wool textile firms' records have survived which include bank accounts for a period of years. These are detailed in Table 9.5. Although small, the sample includes both large and small firms with different mixes of merchanting and manufacture at different periods and with different banks. In all, debit balances significantly outweighed credit balances although, in the cases of Jowitt's and Lupton's, credit balances were built up in the later years of the firms' existence. When the concerns were relatively new and expanding rapidly, debit balances were significantly large and exceeded 10% of turnover in all cases.

Robert Clough built Grove Mill in 1822. The years of highest debit balance with his bank were 1822–3. Further extension of plant took place in the 1820s.[99] He applied to open a second account with the Bradford Banking Company in 1829 with an advance of £800 but was refused –

Table 9.4 Details of the bank balances of wool textile manufacturers and merchants with the Bradford Banking Company, 1827–30[a]

No. of firm	No. of debit balances	No. of credit balances	A Average debit balance (or credit C.R.) (£)	B Average turnover on account in debit years (£)	A/B (%)	Share-holder	Partial security	Chronic similar or increasing overdrafts 1830–8
1	2	—	3,363	28,590	11.8	→	→	→
2	4	—	3,809	26,103	14.6	→	→	→
3	2	1	1,590	15,382	10.3	→	→	→
4	3	1	4,110	42,687	9.6	→	→	?
5	4	—	901	3,602	25.0	→	→	→
6	4	—	3,334	26,503	12.6	→	→	?
7	4	—	632	8,430	7.5	→	→	
8	1	—	476	926	51.4	—	—	—
9	3	—	155	965	16.1	→	→	→
10	3	—	1,569	5,335	29.4	→	→	?
11	1	—	11	1,182	0.9	→	→	→
12	1	—	90	4,442	2.0		→	→
13	4	—	4,154	38,370	10.8	→	→	→
14	4	—	503	7,901	6.4	→	→	→
15	2	—	304	13,408	2.3	→	→	→
16	2	—	630	3,733	16.9	→	→	?
17	4	—	359	1,350	26.6		—	→
18	2	1	169	1,465	11.5	→	→	→
19	2	2	(283 C.R.) 803	4,487	17.9		→	→
20	3	—	244	1,414	17.3	→	—	→
21	1	—	246	5,889	4.2		→	?
22	1	3	443	1,708	25.9	→	→	?
23	3 (very small)	—	267	3,360	7.9	→	→	→
24	3	—	261	3,025	8.6	→	→	?
25	4	—	264	1,419	18.6		—	?
26	2 (very small)	2	70	1,010	6.9		—	?

					Check columns
27	4	—	4,805	59,867	8.0
28	1	2	1,188	8,216	22.8
			(581 C.R.)		
29	—	3	1,022 C.R.	8,947	—
30	1	—	54	3,157	1.7
31	1	1	560	624	89.9
			(130 C.R.)		
32	3	1	260	2,542	10.2
33	—	3	477 C.R.	3,590	—
34	4	—	2,038	21,504	9.5
35	1	2	255	2,201	11.6
			(170 C.R.)		
36	3	—	350	644	54.3
37	2	—	183	2,060	8.9
38	1	2	174	5,831	3.0
			(175 C.R.)		
39	2	1	1,405	27,698	5.1
			(303 C.R.)		
40	1	1	1,580	63,705	2.5
41	2	2	79	745	10.6
			(344 C.R.)		
42	—	2	1,060 C.R.	3,724	—
43	1	1	605	9,335	6.5
44	1	2	1,093	2,969	52.8
		(small)			
45	3	—	1,161	5,822	19.9
46	1	2	104	1,865	5.6
47	2	—	259	1,062	24.4
			(88 C.R.)		
48	—	3	1,516 C.R.	9,532	—

a 1827 balance is for less than half a year.

— = None.

? = No information.

Sources: Bradford Banking Company: Ledger 1827–30 (B38), Securities Register from 1827 (B28), Deed of Constitution 1 June 1827 (B1), Order Books 1827–38 (B2, B3, B4), Deed of Covenants 1831 (B46) (Midland); Cudworth, Round about Bradford; Jenkins, The West Riding Wool Textile Industry, Appendix; Baines, History, Directory and Gazetteer of the County of York.

Table 9.5 *Bank lending on advance or chronic overdraft: the case of eight textile firms*

Name of firm	Name of bank	Period/no. of balances	No. of balances in debit	No. of balances in credit	A Average debit balance (£)	B Average turnover (£)	A/B (%)
Robert Clough, Keighley Worsted spinners	Chippendale & Company, Skipton	1820–33 26	24	2	595 (1820–8) 125 (1828–33)	3,093 1,262	19.2 9.9
Kellett, Brown & Company, Calverley Commission fullers, spinners	Bradford Banking Company	1835–48 21	16	5	467	1,730	17.1
John Broadbent & Sons, Longwood Woollen manufacturers	Halifax & Huddersfield Union Banking Company	1841–7 14	12	2	553	1,356	40.8
	Yorkshire Banking Company	1857–62 11	11	None	2,440	4,580	53.3
John Jowitt & Sons, Bradford Combers, scourers	Beckett, Calverley & Lodge, Leeds	1790–7 8	6	2	1,447	11,610	12.5
	Beckett, Calverley & Beckett	1798–1805 8	5	3	2,794	12,975	21.5
	Beckett Blayde & Company	1812–24 12	12	None	1,684	19,579	8.6
	Beckett & Company	1825–60 68	47	21	3,033	19,133	15.9
William Lupton & Company, Leeds Woollen and worsted manufacturers and traders	Beckett Blayde & Company	1811–19 9	7	2	3,610	27,332	13.2
		1819–21 3	3	None	3,305	25,854	12.8
		1828–52 25	6	19	*credit* 4,650		

William Brooke (John Brooke & Sons), Armitage Bridge Woollen manufacturers	Beckett Blayde & Company	1824-30	11	8	3	6,575	42,744	15.4
B. & W. Marriner, Keighley Worsted spinners	Alcock & Company, Skipton	1842-60	19	19	None	10,930	—	
John Foster & Son, Black Dyke Mills Worsted spinners	Bradford Banking Company	1831-53	44	38	6	2,828	20,189	14

— = information not recorded.

Sources: Clough, items 221, 222 (B.); Kellett, Brown & Company, item 1 (B.); Broadbent, items 46, 47 (B.); Jowitt, items 2, 3, 12, 13, 14 (B.); Lupton, items 9, 10, 11, 12, Box 116 (B.); Brooke, Bank Book 1824-30 (the home of the Brooke family, Armitage Bridge); Foster items 4, 73 (B.); Ingle, 'A History of R. V. Marriner Ltd.'.

probably because his main business was with Chippendale's. Kellet, Brown & Company were established in 1834. They twice applied for an advance of £5,000 in 1834 and in 1838 but were refused.[100] Despite this they still retained a chronic debit balance through the period 1835–48. John Broadbent built mills in 1847 and 1849. He continued a large debit balance relative to turnover until the 1860s which elicited sharp letters from the Yorkshire Banking Company demanding a formal loan or mortgage agreement.[101] The wool stapling firm of Jowitt's had a bank overdraft at least twice as large as the level of their profits 1832–44 and Marriner's bank debit was five times larger than profits in all years to 1866. The latter's highest overdraft figure of nearly £18,000 in 1852 coincided with heavy losses made by the firm.[102] John Brooke & Sons built and fitted out a new mill in 1828 at a cost of some £20,000. Their overdraft was obviously important in this expansion.[103]

In 1832 just before the main period of construction at Black Dyke Mills, John Foster was asked to give security for his overdraft but there is no record of deposit of collateral. He was a substantial shareholder in the Bradford Banking Company from 1831 and possibly received favourable treatment because of this. In the 1840s his bank debts were half the level of the firm's yearly profits.[104]

One final source for study of the extent to which banks were active in financing their industrial clients is bankruptcy records.[105] When Richard Mathewman of Leeds, clothier merchant and dealer, failed in April 1820, he had proved debts against him totalling £12,044. He owed £2,920 of this to Perfect, Hardcastle & Company of Leeds arising from his bank account with them. He had an overdraft agreement up to £1,000 but had clearly been allowed to draw well above that by the time of his demise.[106]

The case of Joseph Harrop is also detailed in the London Court of Bankruptcy files. He was a Saddleworth clothier and owed considerable debts to bankers when he failed in 1826. Total debts amounted to £57,329 of which £23,656 was owed to his family's bank, £450 to Stephen Pattishall, a London banker; £538 to Thomas Wilson, banker of Huddersfield; £500 to Charles Holloway, Hereford banker; £300 to William Wardell, Liverpool banker; and £353 to Dainty Royal & Company, Middlesex bankers.[107] Although the majority of these debts are marked as arising out of bills payable, the fact that Harrop was being bolstered in his circulating capital requirements to such an extent prompts the suggestion that his position as a manufacturer was underpinned through this. He had two sizeable mills in Saddleworth (Royal George and Throstle Nest), two warehouses, a dyehouse, a residence and considerable land.[108]

A notebook on local bankruptcies kept by Jowitt, the Leeds wool stapler, gives further details of the indebtedness to bankers in the period 1839–47.[109] Although the details are far from complete, the notebook covers over 300 West Riding textile industry bankruptcies naming the major creditors involved. In the eight years covered by the notebook, six Yorkshire banks were left with debts of £211,226 on their hands after the demise of just thirty textile concerns.

Table 9.6 gives a breakdown of bankrupts by type of concern showing the average level of their debts to banks. It can be seen that around a quarter of bankrupts had outstanding bank debts of over £500. Manufacturers appear commonly to have benefited from bank finance although to a lesser extent than mercantile concerns. Worsted spinners had particularly heavy debts: perhaps they represented less risk because of their more rapid turnover of capital. Only the smaller clothier concerns, as one might expect, exhibit an unwillingness, or inability, to get much in the way of advances from their banks.

Table 9.6 *Bank debts of bankrupts by type of concern, 1839–47*

Type of concern	% proportion of bankrupts with significant debts to banks[a]	Average debt (£)
Clothiers	12	1,346
Cloth manufacturers	32	3,567
Worsted spinners	23	49,000
Merchant-manufacturers	25	9,500
Wool staplers	24	24,600
Cloth and yarn merchants	22	86,375

[a] More than £500.
Source: Jowitt, item 62 (B.). For fuller details see Hudson, 'The West Riding Wool Textile Industry', Appendix A.

Of course, the bankruptcy figures detailed in Table 9.6 give no indication of the nature of the indebtedness – whether advances or overdrafts had been envisaged as short, medium or long term or whether debts had arisen out of bill-discount. Furthermore, it is not possible from this source to get any idea of the use to which the loans were put. If, as seems likely, some of the loans had developed into longer-term arrangements by default, it seems not unreasonable to suggest that they contributed to the finance of manufacturing as well as trading irrespective of the original intention on the part of both lender and borrower.

The various Directors' Minute Books of the banks indicate a tendency to lend more in the upturn of cycles of industrial trading activity thus boosting trade expansion and no doubt underpinning decisions about the extension of productive capacity.[110] At the downturn of cycles, however, it was not easy for banks to draw in their horns particularly when doing so might force bankruptcy on their clients. Bankruptcy rarely resulted in recovery of more than 10s in the £ in the textile area by the 1840s.[111]

There is also some evidence that banks actually conceived of their role as bolstering 'trusted' customers through hard times. At the Seventh Annual General Meeting of the Mirfield & Huddersfield District Banking Company in February 1840 the following was recorded: 'At no period in the annals of banking has the monetary system of this country been so deranged as during the last 12 months ... [but] ... the bank is still able to give such aid and assistance to customers as they are properly entitled.'[112] A year later: 'Profits have lessened but no customer has been refused accommodation if he was justly entitled.'[113] At this time at the Dewsbury branch alone fifty customers were indebted to the bank for sums over £500. At least a quarter of these are identifiable as textile manufacturers.[114]

Thus one can discern throughout the entire period a continuity of banking practice which included a fairly liberal attitude to the granting of *de facto* medium- and longer-term loans to local industry and commerce. The majority of these loans were made on current account and were, in theory, short term and easily recallable. Others were understood as longer-term advances from the start particularly where bank partners, directors and proprietors were involved. Whether through design or default asset portfolios before the mid-nineteenth century were heavily biased in favour of local involvements many of which were, in practice, relatively illiquid. In some cases one can trace a relationship between bank advances and the extension of productive capacity but it is not necessary to do this in order to emphasise the role of banks in the expansion of industry. Bill-discount with medium-term overdraft facilities could significantly release the manufacturers' own capital for fixed investment.

If, as George Rae pointed out in 1850,[115] bankers had made loans that should never have been made, accepted securities that should never have been touched by a banker, one must go along with Pressnell in suggesting two justifications for this.[116] First, the range of securities and the general mobility of capital were very limited before the 1840s. Secondly, the characteristics of early financial activities tended to linger as a family firm graduated from amateur quasi-banking into full banking. The death of old habits was postponed by the very personal character of banking prior to the amalgamation period and the close knit nature of industrial and commercial communities such as those which grew in the West Riding valleys.

10

PLOUGHED-BACK PROFITS

'Industrial Capital has been its own chief progenitor', wrote T. S. Ashton in 1948.[1] Historiographical opinion has changed little since: in 1972 Crouzet was moved to remark that 'This fact is so obvious to be almost a cliché and the point is not worth labouring.'[2] It seems generally agreed that, in England in particular, the role of ploughed-back profits was of overriding importance in industrial expansion but this view prevails despite the absence of reliable data on profitability and reinvestment in different sectors. How did ploughed-back profits compare with finance obtained from other sources? What personal and impersonal forces determined both the level of profitability and the extent to which profits were retained in a business rather than spent or invested elsewhere?

The purpose of this chapter is to study the genesis of profit and reinvestment in the wool textile sector in order to explain both the relative importance and the mechanics of plough-back. Before proceeding, however, it is important to say something about the concept of profit and its measurement at this time.

Profit and its measurement

The small size of fixed compared with circulating capital in most branches of industry before the mid-nineteenth century encouraged industrial entrepreneurs to follow their mercantile predecessors in regarding profitability as a product of business acumen rather than the return on capital employed.[3] A distinction was usually drawn between interest on capital and the profits of the business. The resultant treatment of capital in the accounts, as an auxiliary to entrepreneurship rather than the central motive force behind the firm, appears to have been general throughout the nineteenth century.[4] Plentiful capital, and interest fixed at 5% before 1832, encouraged contemporaries to regard profit as the surplus after interest was charged and to regard capital as a tool for which one paid the going rate.

There appears to have been no clear attempt before the late nineteenth century to adapt accounting practice to the notion of capital as a general depersonalised property seeking the highest return.[5] The most common form of partnership determination of profits in the West Riding and elsewhere before the later nineteenth century took the form of periodic inventories. These were a particular feature of advanced single entry systems of book-keeping, which were prevalent at the time. All claims except for the original partners' capital were deducted from total assets and the difference was regarded as capital plus profits.[6] This, compared with the previous year's total, showed the profitability although few firms made the comparison or stated a profit figure. Profit as an isolated entity was usually regarded as relatively unimportant by the businessman who was closely and continuously concerned, on a personal level, with his business operations. Before the separation of ownership from management, entrepreneurs were much more concerned with cash flow and with inventory figures which represented their future earnings. Furthermore, the desire for confidentiality and secrecy of affairs meant that most businessmen preferred to do their own accounting and the sheer burden which this involved militated against the adoption of more tedious profit calculations and double entry methods.

There was little external pressure to involve a firm in accurate or regular demonstrations of its profit or loss until the limited liability joint stock legislation of 1856 and 1862 after which a small minority of firms became incorporated and disclosed their accounts regularly in accordance with statutory recommendations.[7] The only West Riding examples of earlier external pressures resulting in more regular and formal accounting practice regarding profits are found in the case of company mills which had a wide responsibility to shareholders. With these mills dividends were calculated and provision made for shareholders to examine the accounts at regular intervals. It seems, however, that dividends were not generally calculated from profits as such but from the profit realised on the commission services performed, ignoring fixed capital costs and charges.[8]

For the bulk of firms, the nearest one gets to profit measurement in the surviving Ledgers are the annual statements of affairs. It is possible, with careful use, to derive profit figures and hence profit rates from these but many difficulties arise in so doing. The most intransigent problem is that this form of accounts procedure often distorts profit levels. There was a tendency to ignore fixed equipment altogether. Additions to fixed assets, as well as repairs or replacement were normally entered into the current accounts.[9] Thus where large capital equipment was bought out of revenue, profits would take a dive but would recover quickly because no phasing of capital outlays occurred. Chronic under-estimation of profits might occur where a long period of re-equipping was taking place. This may well have encouraged the ploughing-back of funds never properly assigned to profits.[10]

Other elements of early accounting procedure resulted in wild fluctuations of capital from year to year affecting 'profitability' and reinvestment. Three main factors were usually involved here: the method of asset valuation and the treatment of depreciation, the provision for bad debts and variations in partnership and interest-withdrawal arrangements.

There seems to have been no consistent policy towards asset valuation and depreciation among firms or even, very often, within a single concern from year to year. The paucity of evidence of valuation and depreciation practice before the 1840s leads one to suppose that few firms thought it important enough to be worthy of note! Where evidence does exist, the immense variety of practice is the most notable feature. Some concerns valued their plant and equipment at cost until bad trade conditions forced a revaluation of assets.[11] Others, such as Wormalds & Walker, allowed depreciation on the basis of historic cost[12] and some such as Foster's of Queensbury calculated depreciation as a somewhat arbitrary percentage of the previous year's value.[13] Most concerns which had a definite policy tended to differentiate between the depreciation of buildings and machinery and power plant. Depreciation of machinery varied enormously between 5 and 20% per year whereas buildings warranted 2 or 2½% if anything at all.[14] There is little evidence of how these sums were arrived at except some reference to depreciation being equal to money spent on repairs or on new machinery. At Black Dyke Mills, for example, buildings were depreciated by 2½% annually in the 1840s, machinery at an average of 12½%, and the engine and shafting at very variable rates averaging 2%.[15]

Evidence is particularly absent on the treatment of stock valuations in the first half of the nineteenth century. Most firms seemed to value finished goods at cost price but others may have considered stock value on the basis of what the market would bear. It is thus impossible to determine to what extent profit estimates include capital gains or losses arising from any appreciation or depreciation of the value of stocks. Raw material stocks, especially raw wool, seem often to have been depreciated or appreciated in line with price changes.[16]

The most salient feature of all the surviving valuation and depreciation records is the predominance of ad hoc measures. Depreciation often consisted merely of a rounding down to a 'tidy' sum for arithmetical convenience and asset valuations altered most often as a sudden rather than a gradual recognition of changes in market circumstances and market prices.[17]

The provision for bad debts was similarly erratic. One would expect this at a time when trade credit was lengthy and when book debts, and the interest payable on them, were an important part of the business operations of all manufacturers. Outstanding debts of two years or more were usually still considered good and bad debts were often left on the books for a large number of years before being written off. Sudden revision of the bad debts account and inconsistent policy regarding the writing off of debts radically affected the comparability of periodic valuations of the trade account and hence of any measures of profitability.

A final factor contributing to erratic fluctuations in stated profitability concerns the practice of charging interest on capital. The common practice in established firms, family businesses and those with several partners by the early nineteenth century was to allow partners to withdraw their interest. In the case of the Gott concern the partners started freely to withdraw their interest of 4½% in 1791 and this was raised to 5% from 1800. The usual interest charged on capital in textile concerns was 5% throughout the nineteenth century.[18] Some firms in their early stages of development did not permit interest to be withdrawn as of right and others forbade interest withdrawals in years of low profits or of loss which resulted in an underestimation of the effects of hard times upon profitability.

The many distortions of capital assets and hence profit figures found in manufacturers' Account Books means that the profit rate estimates used later in this chapter should be regarded with caution. This, coupled with the problem of typicality of the surviving records, necessitates a very wary approach to generalising, from the sample available, about the level of profitability in the industry as a whole. What can be relied on with a little more certainty, and what is more important for present purposes than the profit rates themselves, is the direction and timing of changes in profitability and their relationship to other variables.

Before discussing this question it is necessary to comment on the method of derivation of the profit rate figures included in Graphs 10.1 and 10.2 and used in the later analysis of this chapter. Where possible, the practice adopted was to regard the profit rate as:

$$\frac{\text{Profit (less depreciation)}}{\text{Net tangible assets}}$$

Profit includes any interest which the partners expect and take from the business. Net tangible assets include fixed assets, stock and work in progress, trade and other debtors, bills and cash (including bank deposits) *less* current liabilities (creditors, loans, bank overdrafts, etc.). Where the statements of affairs did not yield the above information in sufficient detail, net worth figures were used instead of net tangible assets. Net worth was calculated as share capital and capital reserves plus retained profits, on the assumption that these should equal net tangible assets, as both exclude liabilities.

Graphs 10.1 and 10.2 show the movement of profit rates for those concerns and over those periods for which figures are obtainable separating

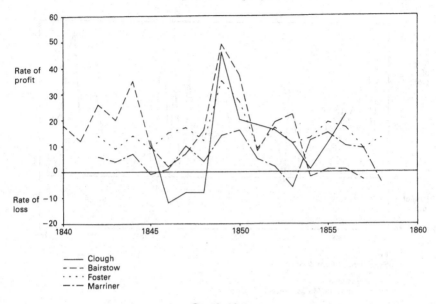

Graph 10.1
Profit rates in the worsted industry, 1840–58
Source: See Appendix.

woollen from worsted producing firms. There are obvious problems about the extent to which this sample of concerns was typical of the industry as a whole. The sample is indeed heavily biased in favour of the larger, more successful firms but it does also include smaller businesses and is certainly the most representative attempt available to examine profitability in any sector for the industrial revolution period. The comforting feature of these graphs for present purposes is the extent to which the movement of profit rates of the different concerns exhibits a similar pattern over time. This is particularly apparent in the case of the worsted firms whose profit rate series exhibit a significant positive correlation.[19] This would indicate that the dominant influences on the movement of the profit rates were a common set of factors external to the individual firms themselves.

The generation of profits

It is misleading to consider profit as a source of industrial expansion as if it were independently generated. Profit rates depend on raw material and finished goods prices, on innovation, on the extension of the market, on wage costs and on a large number of other variables. If one factor in particular can be shown to have dominated the movement of profit rates

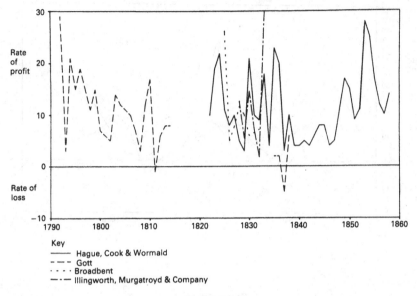

Key
— — Hague, Cook & Wormald
– – – Gott
· · · · Broadbent
—·— Illingworth, Murgatroyd & Company

Graph 10.2
Profit rates in the woollen industry, 1790–1860
Source: See Appendix.

in any period, then that factor must be isolated as a major variable in the accumulation process.

On a hypothetical plane several factors stand out as being potentially important determinants of the level of profitability and most of these are quantifiable to some degree. Tables containing the relevant series of variables are collected in the Appendix with an indication of their method of calculation and sources. They include export levels, wool prices, monetary variables, real and money wage trends. Most of the information relates to the second quarter of the nineteenth century as it is not readily available in the earlier period.

Unfortunately, no accurate output figures for the industry or its different branches exist.[20] The only quantifiable variables concerning output are the indices of exports by value and by volume. These official sources are far from fully accurate but probably reflect fluctuations in demand sufficient for our purposes. The wool price series are those of English wool varieties derived from Parliamentary Papers. As mentioned in Chapter 5, these seem to be a reasonable reflection of wool prices in the West Riding but must be regarded as being less accurate for the woollen branch by the 1840s when so much foreign and recycled wool was being used. Even in the worsted branch the extended use of cotton warps by that decade lowered raw material costs very significantly and reduced the importance of raw wool prices to the manufacturer.

The state of the money market and the movement of discount and interest rates may well have been a crucial determinant of profitability. Three series are used as measures of different aspects of the condition of the money market: Overend Gurney's discount rate on first class bills at three months, bank rate and the yield on consuls. These series are useful indicators of the general state of the money market nationally but, of course, the West Riding was also subject to local influences which are not possile to measure accurately.

Finally, taking advantage of Johnstone's work on the movement of money wages and living standards of workers in Keighley worsted mills, an index of money wages for the factory industry in the 1840s and 1850s was constructed. This was then converted using Rousseaux, and Gayer, Rostow and Schwartz price series into two different indices of real wages. These then formed perhaps the most accurate foundation on which to assess the relative movement of real wages and industrial profitability in any single sector of industry in the crucial decade of the 'hungry' '40s'.

Bearing in mind the shortcomings of the data and thus the limited accuracy of any statistical analysis based upon it, it was decided to test for correlation between the different variables and the profit rate figures.[21] Obviously, the correlations even if proved significant can comment only on the strength of observed relationships. They can say nothing about causality but may provide us with some clues to this.

Dealing with the woollen sector first, no significant correlation was found between the movement of profit rates and the indices of the state of the money market. This may merely mean that the series used were insufficiently accurate to reflect monetary conditions in the West Riding. Topham has suggested that the peculiar conduct of the Leeds branch of the Bank of England meant that the West Riding was less powerfully linked to the national interest movements than many industrial areas.[22] This, together with the localised nature of financial and credit markets, may help to explain why there is no indication of profit rates being influenced by such overall monetary indicators.

During the period 1792–1814, Gott's profitability shows a significant negative correlation with the movement of English wool prices if a lag of one year is introduced into the wool price series (-0.460, n = 22). This indicates that wool prices may have been a significant influence on the profitability of woollen production in the 1790s and 1810s but that variations took several months to affect profit rates. This may have been the result of the slowness of trade and the extent of stockholding. Later the woollen sector became heavily dependent on imported and recycled wool and large concerns like Hague, Cook & Wormald were involved in speculative buying which may explain why no relationship is found between the movement of English short wool prices and the profitability of woollen manufacture in the 1830s and 1840s.

242 External and internal finance

Table 10.1 *Correlation of profit rates with export levels, 1822–58*

Time period	Variables	n	Correlation coefficient	Significant at 5% level
1822–55	BLANK on H	34	0.55	YES
1840–55	BLANK on H	16	0.83	YES
1828–33	BLANK on I	6	0.87	YES
1822–9	EXPO 1 on H	8	0.55	NO
1825–9	EXPO 1 on BAI	5	0.86	NO
1826–58	EXPO 2 on H	33	0.44	YES
1828–33	EXPO 2 on I	6	0.68	NO
1842–50	YARN on F	9	0.76	YES
1842–50	YARN on MA	9	0.70	YES
1840–50	TOT on B	11	0.60	YES
1842–50	TOT on F	9	0.67	YES
1842–50	TOT on MA	9	0.70	YES
1845–56	TOT on CLO	12	0.51	NO

Key:

n	= number of observations.
BLANK	= blanket exports from U.K. by volume.
EXPO 1	= exports of wool goods from Great Britain at current prices.
EXPO 2	= exports of wool goods from U.K. at current prices.
YARN	= yarn exports by volume.
TOT	= total cloth exports by volume.
H	= Hague, Cook & Wormald profit rate.
I	= Illingworth profit rate.
BAI	= Bairstow profit rate.
F	= Foster profit rate.
MA	= Marriner profit rate.
B	= Broadbent profit rate.
CLO	= Clough profit rate.

Sources: See Appendix.

Interestingly, the most significant correlations occurred between the woollen profit rates and indices of export levels, as shown in Table 10.1. The volume of blanket exports correlated very significantly with profitability in the case of Hague, Cook & Wormald for 1822–55 and there was a particularly close relationship in the 1840s and 1850s. Illingworth, Murgatroyd & Company also show a strong and significant correlation between profit rates and the state of the blanket export market. Hague, Cook & Wormald were the biggest single exporters of blankets to the Americas at this time and were peculiarly dependent on the trade.[23] The same concern shows a marked and significant correlation between profitability and the *value* of exports of woollen goods from the U.K. over the whole period 1826–58. Illingworth and Broadbent profit figures show positive correlations with indices of the value of woollen goods exports at current prices but the data runs are too short to show a significance at the 5% level. Thus, as one might expect, it would appear that export fluctuations may have been an important determinant of profit rates especially for those concerns heavily involved in the overseas market.

Turning to the worsted sector one finds even more interesting results. Before 1850, as with the woollen trade, correlation of profitability with measures of export levels is clearly significant. Foster's and Marriner's profitability move with the index of yarn exports by volume. Both these concerns specialised in spinning and Foster's in particular relied heavily on foreign demand. During the 1850s yarn export movements ceased to be reflected in the profit rates of these firms indicating the possibility that other variables were becoming more important in influencing profitability. Bairstow's, Foster's and Marriner's profit rates all exhibit a significant correlation with the movement of total cloth exports by volume in the period before 1850, as indicated in Table 10.1.

English long wool prices are likely to be fairly accurate as an index of wool input costs for the worsted branch as it used largely domestic supplies before the mid-century. It is thus perhaps not surprising to find negative correlations between worsted profit rate movements and movement in the price of wool. This is significant in the case of half-hog prices and Bairstow's profit rate figures. A composite profit rate (CA), based on an average of the Bairstow, Foster and Marriner figures, also correlates significantly with Lincoln half-hog prices.

Table 10.2 *Correlation of profitability and wool prices, 1840–58*

Time period	Variables	n	Correlation coefficient	Significant at 5% level
1840–58	L on BAI	19	−0.61	YES
1842–58	L on CA	17	−0.56	YES
1845–50	L on BAI	11	−0.66	YES
1842–50	L on CA	9	−0.67	YES

Key: n = number of observations.
L = price of Lincoln half-hogs.
BAI = Bairstow profit rate.
CA = composite profit rate A.

Sources: See Appendix.

The state of the money market as reflected in the movement of the interest rate series shows little correlation with profit rates in the worsted branch. The exception is the Bairstow profit rate which shows a significant negative correlation with Overend Gurney's rates on first class bills at three months (r = −0.65, n = 11). This correlation may be associated with Bairstow's concentration on the home market and their direct dealings with London and Manchester retailers and wholesalers which was largely carried out in short dated bills at this time.[24] This may have made Bairstow's and firms like them particularly dependent on the state and cost of credit in internal trade.

No significant correlation shows up between worsted profit rates and money wage movements when the series are compared without a lag. If the wage series is lagged a year the correlations are uniformly negative although none reach the significant level, suggesting that only a very weak causal relationship, if any, existed between money wages and profit levels. It is, however, possible that the line of causal connection ran from profitability to wage levels and this does seem to be suggested in the presence of significant positive correlation results when a year lag is introduced into the profit series.

Most interesting is the existence of significant positive correlations when the lagged profit rates are compared with real wage indices. As profit rates rose so the purchasing power of wages appears to have increased. Workers were in a stronger bargaining position after a year of higher profits and employers had more to lose from troublesome labour relations but movements of the cost of living must also have played a role. At the same time, the fact that real wages may have declined in response to the lowering of profits possibly indicates the extent to which employers were able to press down on wages in the face of declining profit and stable or rising prices of provisions. This would fit the hypotheses of Foster and Hobsbawm concerning the 1840s in particular.[25] It is possible that employers were able further to reduce the movement of wage costs in hard times by truck payments which were such a feature of the worsted area at this time. Workers were of course also laid off in slump periods which, unlike short-time working, does not show up in the wage index. By this means the living standards and incomes of labour in the textile localities were reduced to the benefit of profits in a way which escapes precise record or quantification.

These results are very interesting and prompt some contentious questions about the nature of capitalist accumulation. However, in the present state of knowledge, and allowing for the imperfections of the data, they cannot be stretched to provide any more sophisticated analysis or conclusions.[26] The most one can say is that if the various significant correlations do indicate a degree of causal connection, it is possible to isolate some variables which appear to have been of major importance in the movement of profitability. As one would expect in an industry heavily dependent on external trade, export fluctuations appear to have had an important effect on the profit rate of the majority of firms. This would tend to support the notion of growth being export-led in the second quarter of the nineteenth century. The movement of domestic wool prices also seems to have been of some importance, particularly in the worsted sector. Profits were boosted in years when supplies of wool were plentiful and prices lower. The extent to which wool prices are

Table 10.3 *Correlation of profitability and wage movements, 1840–58*

Time period	Variables	n	Correlation coefficient	Significant at 5% level
1845–56	MW on CLO (−1)	11	0.40	NO
1840–58	MW on BAI (−1)	18	0.69	YES
1842–58	MW on F (−1)	16	0.47	ALMOST
1842–58	MW on MA (−1)	16	0.15	NO
1842–58	MW on CA (−1)	16	0.62	YES
1845–56	MW on CB (−1)	11	0.67	YES
1845–56	R on CLO (−1)	11	0.52	NO
1840–58	R on BAI (−1)	18	0.76	YES
1842–58	R on F (−1)	16	0.58	YES
1842–58	R on MA (−1)	16	0.29	NO
1842–58	R on CA (−1)	16	0.82	YES
1845–56	R on CB (−1)	11	0.71	YES
1844–9	GRS on CLO (−1)	5	0.69	NO
1841–50	GRS on BAI (−1)	10	0.84	YES
1841–9	GRS on F (−1)	8	0.51	NO
1841–9	GRS on MA (−1)	8	0.60	NO
1841–9	GRS on CA (−1)	8	0.83	YES

Key:
n	=	number of observations.
MW	=	money wages.
R	=	real wage index using Rousseaux price series.
GRS	=	real wage index using Gayer, Rostow and Schwartz price series.
CLO	=	Clough profit rate.
BAI	=	Bairstow profit rate.
F	=	Foster profit rate.
MA	=	Marriner profit rate.
CA	=	composite profit rate A.
CB	=	composite profit rate B.

Source: See Appendix.

reflected in the movement of profit rates is important in considering the effect of introducing cheaper inputs as a substitute for new wool. Recycled wool and cotton warps, so much cheaper than the raw wool, must have had a marked effect on profitability at least in the short term. Finally it is possible to discern from the correlations that periods of low profitability may have been met by controlling wage costs relative to price movements which may have helped to minimise the downward trend of profit in years of bad trade or high wool prices.

The reinvestment of profits

Just as discussion of 'profit' usually neglects the nature of profit generation so also allusions to the importance of ploughed-back profits obscure the complex nature of the reinvestment process. The retention of profits came about in a number of different ways, being strongly influenced by accounting procedures, by competition and by the life-cycles of firms and their proprietors.

Most firms drew up their statements of affairs yearly although a significant number only got round to this tedious and time-consuming business every two years or so.[27] Until a profit estimate was made the bulk of a firm's revenue was continuously used to buy current factors. Thus, whether accounts were taken every twelve or twenty-four months, all firms tended to reinvest their profits at least in the short term through the continuous employment of revenue in the acquisition of raw materials and labour. The effect of this was sometimes modified by partners' withdrawals during the year in anticipation of the profit available. However, drawings were commonly based on the previous year's profits, a practice which tended to inhibit withdrawals by proprietors during the upturn of a profit cycle.[28]

Other practices common in nineteenth-century accounting, particularly those arising from the confusion of the capital and revenue accounts, tended to underestimate profits, and hence encouraged an unconscious reinvestment of profit back into the business. Furthermore, the small partnership or family business, which characterised the period, tended to minimise withdrawals more than larger proprietorships where more individuals were dependent on the profits for their livelihood.

By far the most important factor affecting the extent and importance of ploughed-back profit was, of course, the conscious decision of proprietors to withdraw amounts smaller than the return on their capital. It is this which requires most detailed examination. Since internal investment was first studied by historians of the industrial revolution, analysis has commonly taken the form of an examination of the personalities and social values of the entrepreneurs. These have been related to the contemporary ideology of thrift, self-help, self-denial and industriousness and particularly associated with religious dissenting sects to which a large proportion of entrepreneurs belonged. Typical of this approach is the following:

The widespread practice of systematically ploughing back profits is, of course, related to specific psychological attitudes and to a certain pattern of mentality: it is largely due to the 'frugality' of the pioneers of the Industrial Revolution. Their origins were often humble, and they were as hard on themselves as they were on others; business was their consuming interest and they continued to lead the simple lives to which they had early been accustomed, practising a stringent personal economy and a rigid austerity, which maximised their savings.[29]

The Yorkshire textile industry was by no means short of the sort of

RODS MILL 1800.

RODS MILL 1866.

10
The expansion of mill-building in the first half of the nineteenth century:
Rods Mill, Morley
Source: William Smith, *Rambles about Morley with Descriptive and Historical
Sketches: Also an Account of the Rise and Progress of the Woollen Manufacture
in This Place* (1866).

Smilesian characters to which Crouzet refers above and which historians of other industrial sectors have studied. Individuals were known to rise from the ranks of small-scale manufacturers to become important names in the factory industry. However, the majority of the substantial manufacturers of the early decades of the nineteenth century appear to have been possessed of capital or mercantile wealth before embarking on factory manufacture.[30] Nebulous ideas concerning moral and religious motivations leave one with the feeling that capitalist accumulation is obscured more than it is illuminated by explanations which employ them. Other determinants of reinvestment were much more important. Three factors in particular are worthy of close examination: competitive pressures, reinvestment related to the life-cycle of the firm and of the individual entrepreneur and the attraction of other outlets for accumulated profits.

In an industry experiencing rapid technological change, it was necessary to conduct business finance with a view to the constant pressure to innovate in order to retain a competitive position in the industry. Entrepreneurs, far from choosing to live a frugal life, could easily have become enmeshed in a dynamic that was not of their own choosing. As Sweezy has pointed out, 'The habit of ploughing profits into the firm is partly due to the pressure of competition for any business which is not constantly struggling to expand, is liable to shrink and collapse.'[31] This view of capitalist profit and competition endorses the importance of self-finance but doubts the economic and socio-psychological motivation which is commonly ascribed to this behaviour.

If Jenkins' estimates of fixed capital formation in the Yorkshire wool textile industry before 1835 sufficiently reflect the general timing of expansion, it is obvious that the growth of productive capacity was not confined to boom periods (see Graph 2.1). This is the case even when a twelve-month time lag is introduced to represent the gestation of investment plans. During a slump, the availability of both trade credit and bank accommodation would be generally curtailed so that contracyclical investment activity must have been heavily dependent on reinvestment. If the available yearly profit rates for the woollen sector are indicative of the general state of the industry, there is further indication that fixed capital expansion occurred in bad times as well as good. Allowing a year for profitability to translate itself into fixed capital construction, correlation coefficients of profitability and fixed capital formation in the woollen branch show no significance.[32] These findings together with scattered references in business records[33] confirm that a major motive for reinvestment was defensive: a response to hard times and competition from rivals.

Life-cycle factors also prevent any simplistic view of reinvestment. While a business was still small there was every discouragement to proprietors to make more than minimal drawings. Liquidity problems were a major cause of bankruptcy and the more cash that could be left on hand, the better placed a firm would be to ride out commercial storms. This was particularly so in the early years of a business or with very small concerns whose standing with the local financial community may have been weak. We have seen that domestic clothiers and fullers of the eighteenth century led very frugal lives in terms of their personal consumption; a fact reflected in the paucity of household furniture and possessions left in wills and not specifically related to manufacture or farming. To keep a domestic business going the maximum capital had to be tied up in raw materials and equipment and in credit granted to purchasers in all but the best years.

For the newly established firm, retention of profits was a matter of how little it was necessary to draw, rather than how much to leave in. This was particularly so when funds for expansion of enterprise from other sources were few. A firm had to build up a name for itself in the trade and a reputation for stability before calls upon credit and capital from external sources would materialise. Until then internal or self-finance would inevitably be a major source of funds.

Apart from the withdrawal from the partnership of John Wormald in 1786 and Joseph Fountaine in 1797, the net amount withdrawn from Wormald, Fountaine & Gott in the early years of their transition from merchanting to manufacture remained under £5,000 until the late 1800s. Although hardly an abstemious income for the four partners, it was considerably less than the £10,000 which was regularly drawn each year thereafter.[34] The Broadbent brothers started in the woollen industry in 1825 with £4,500 which their father gave them and a further £6,000 which he loaned to the concern at interest. Until 1832 interest payments to the father were delayed and still outstanding at each year end. Furthermore, the brothers appear to have made no withdrawals before 1834 when their first account book terminates.[35] Foster's records show withdrawals above interest and rent charges seldom exceeding £1,000 per annum in the 1840s, a decade after their mill was built. In the 1850s withdrawals rapidly increased reaching a peak of over £130,000 in 1859–60.[36]

Once an enterprise and its partners became more firmly established commercially and financially, it was no longer imprudent to make larger withdrawals. In the surviving business records it is possible to discern marked increases in withdrawals as a firm matured. Gott & Company's net withdrawals exceeded £50,000 a year in the early 1820s but were more than £130,000 per annum by the mid-1830s. Foster's regularly withdrew over £30,000 a year by the 1860s.[37] However, other firms such as Hague & Cook had an erratic pattern of drawings in their 'mature years'.[38]

Several factors modified the extent to which established firms experienced regular heavy withdrawals. First, as partners expanded the amount of capital they invested in an enterprise, their income from the interest alone increased and sometimes this was sufficient to meet most of their living expenses. Sigsworth has noted that interest income invariably covered the withdrawals of the Foster partners after 1846 so that the whole of the profits made, plus a varying proportion of the interest paid on the capital, henceforward remained in the business.[39]

Secondly, the effect of partners withdrawing from the business sometimes modified the drawing activities of the remaining proprietors. Partnership changes radically altered the capitalisation and the financial standing of a firm. The twelve partnership changes of the Gott concern over the period 1786 to 1838 affected net worth by up to 50%.[40] In the case of Gott's, drawings do not seem to have been radically affected by partners pulling out but this may not be typical of wider practice as the firm was by far the largest in the entire Yorkshire industry. The low drawings from Hague, Cook & Wormald in 1838 following John Wormald's retirement from the firm in that year may well be more characteristic. Wormald had taken his £5,000 of capital with him which represented 7% of the total capital of the enterprise.[41]

A further factor modifying the extent of withdrawals from established manufacturing firms is that years of parsimony at the start of an enterprise could well have placed the first generations of industrial capitalists into a distinctly abstemious mould. It is interesting that one finds much greater evidence of conspicuous consumption on the part of the later generations of textile entrepreneurs who had generally been expensively educated and had been subject to different stimuli and horizons. It may well be, as Cairncross has suggested, that 'the faith and outlook that expressed themselves in thrift were born of economic expansion and the growth of capital and the line of causation was from accumulation to thrift rather than the other way round'.[42] Pankhurst completes this picture: 'By the time an enterprise was firmly established and it was no longer imprudent for the proprietors to make continuous withdrawals, they tended to be in receipt of an income which it was difficult to spend ... heavy investment throughout the economy left no resources for the production of a wide variety of consumer goods.'[43] This absence of consumer goods may well have been a factor of note, particularly in the rural industrial areas away from the urban centres of conspicuous consumption. Also, when the individual entrepreneur or small partnership was responsible for so many aspects of business organisation, the time left for socialising and spending may have been slight. In Yorkshire the extent of manufacturers' spending on ornate housing, on churches, schools and other buildings not strictly industrial was limited before the mid-century.[44]

The barriers to conspicuous spending may also have affected accumulation indirectly as significant withdrawals appear to have gone into private savings or local property and landholdings rather than being spent.[45] Here, although not ploughed-back, they formed an external reserve, available to the firm in time of need, and could be used as collateral for industrial loans.

The life-cycle of the individual businessman also seems to have been an important factor in reinvestment decisions. Most businessmen early in their manufacturing careers drew little and built up their industrial investment. This seems to have been the case irrespective of whether the start of an individual's career coincided with that of his firm. Later, as he married and developed a range of family responsibilities, the income needs of the partner grew as did his drawings. Towards retirement from active business drawings were often particularly heavy perhaps representing a diversion of funds into secure forms of investment. This cycle of drawing activity related to the life of the businessman is clearly evidenced in the case of partners in Hague, Cook & Wormald from the 1810s to the mid-century. John Hague Jnr gradually built up his investment from £1,977 in 1812 to £8,664 in 1819 by ploughing-back his returns. A period of slower growth followed but from the late 1830s further increases occurred. His capital stood at over £13,000 by 1832 and £21,000 in the early 1840s. After this his investment fell to £15,000 where it remained during the later decades of this career. Similarly Edwin Hague ran down his investment from a high point of £18,464 in 1846 to just over £1,000 by the early 1850s, and Percy Wormald reduced his from over £29,000 in 1844 to £22,000 in the early 1850s.[46]

Benjamin Gott provides perhaps the clearest example of this sort of activity: his drawings show an upward trend throughout his lifetime. In the 1790s and 1800s they were limited but by the 1830s they were regularly over £120,000 a year! At this time he owned a sumptuous residence, a wide range of real estate in the locality, and had seen to the education of his several children. Growing withdrawals in middle life can be related to increased conspicuous consumption, particularly in the case of entrepreneurs of the second and third generations. William Gott withdrew £15,000–£17,000 each year from joining the firm in the 1830s. Much of this appears to have been spent on the refinements of upper middle class life. He had an array of property investments, a well-stocked wine cellar and a notable collection of fine art.[47] The partners of John Foster & Sons and of Marriner's similarly seem to have been indulging in the material benefits of success by the 1850s and 1860s,[48] but insufficient evidence survives of the smaller, more typical concerns whose partners were probably forced to keep withdrawals to a minimum throughout their lifetime in order to avoid bankruptcy.

Increasing withdrawals by partners of successful firms in later life also seem to be related to a common desire to spread investments – perhaps in order to ensure a safer rentier income after retirement or for dependents and heirs. William Gott and Benjamin Gott both had extensive shareholdings in railway companies and public utilities as well as investments in the property market.[49] The diversion of textile profits into other sectors of the economy and into foreign bonds and stock was a marked feature in the case of larger concerns by the 1840s and 1850s and became increasingly common later in the century.[50]

Graphs 10.1 and 10.2 indicate that profits in the industry, although they could be very high, fluctuated wildly in the first half of the nineteenth century. Decisions about alternative investments may thus have been influenced more by a desire for security and stability than for higher returns. However, it does appear that the start of major diversion of funds from the industry by its more substantial proprietors coincides with a period, from the late 1830s through the 1840s, when the rate of profit was generally lower. By the 1850s the more substantial manufacturers all seem to have employed stock brokers and had an active interest in the movement of stock and share prices.[51] The major areas of alternative investment chosen by textile manufacturers appear to have been railways, public utilities and foreign government stocks. Few of these in the longer term proved capable of yielding a higher rate of return than that possible in textile manufacture but their yield was generally more stable. It would seem to be no coincidence that the increasing volatility of trade and the intensification of competition in the 1840s seems to have precipitated a notable spread of investments on the part of the larger textile entrepreneurs.

Series of profit and drawings figures survive for only two concerns: T. & M. Bairstow, worsted spinners of Sutton in Craven (covering the period 1846–58), and Hague, Cook & Wormald, woollen manufacturers of Dewsbury (1832–58). Neither of these show any significant correlation between profitability and the level of partners' drawings and indicate that drawings were frequently far from frugal in years of low profit.[52] This was particularly the case for Hague, Cook & Wormald, the older-established of the two firms.

The newer-established factory concern of Bairstow's, still in the early stages of expansion of productive capacity, shows low drawings, especially in the first decade, and in years when new additions were being made to fixed capital. For example, in 1844 when the profit rate was as high as 35%, £1,407 was invested in a new shed and cottages leaving little surplus to withdraw. Again in 1853 with profit at 22% drawings were only £931. In this year £2,076 was spent on enlarging the mill and sheds.[53] The experience of these two firms suggest that reinvestment may have been a more important source of finance during the period of initial fixed capital outlays than it became in the later years of a firm's existence.

It is difficult to establish with any precision the importance of ploughed-back profits compared with other sources of finance throughout the life-cycles of different firms. Business accounts do not often reveal the sources of capital injections other than reinvestment, and the reinvestment figures themselves are difficult to isolate because of partnership changes. Some clues can, however, be obtained from the evidence of bonds, promissory notes, mortgages and bank accounts which indicate the relative size of loans and overdrafts compared with profits at particular points.

The level of loans and capital from new partners of the Gott concern together with the size of ploughed-back profits is indicated in Table 10.4. The reinvestment figures are reasonably reliable but the loan figures are based on surviving bonds and promissory notes which may be incomplete. They should thus be regarded as an underestimate.

It can be seen that in the years preceding 1792 and during that year, when factory building really got underway, loans generally exceeded ploughed-back profits by a factor of three or four and capital from new partners was also highly significant. This was followed by a decade in which loans were insignificant compared with reinvestment except in the year 1800 when loans were three times higher. The firm made losses in 1807 and 1808 and these losses do not appear to have been compensated by borrowing. Unfortunately there are no comparable figures for the succeeding decades except for odd years of the 1820s and 1830s when withdrawals were far in excess of profits in all years, indicating the importance of life-cycle factors in determining the level of reinvestment.

Bank overdraft and profit statistics covering the same periods survive only for four firms. Jowitt's, the wool stapling concern had a chronic bank overdraft which exceeded twice the level of profits throughout the period 1832–44 for which figures are available.[54] This may have been typical of a mercantile rather than a manufacturing enterprise but the figures from Marriner's and Foster's and Illingworth's confirm that reinvestment was by no means the most important pillar of financial support for manufacturers, particularly during the years of expansion of fixed capacity. In the case of B. & W. Marriner, worsted spinners, chronic bank debts alone were five times as large as net profit figures in all years from 1842 to 1866 during which period much re-equipping and expansion took place.[55]

The case of Foster's shows most clearly changes in the relative importance of bank overdrafts and profits during the life-cycle of the firm. Black Dyke Mills were built during the period 1834–5 at a cost of some £10,000 in all, including machinery. In the 1840s further capital expenditure was taking place in the replacement of hand by power looms. Bank debit totals were larger than profits in the period 1831–5 and remained about half the level of profits until the late 1840s after which they declined to around a fifteenth. Net of withdrawals, profits were a less important source of capital than the bank throughout the main period of mill construction and re-equipping.[56]

Illingworth, Murgatroyd & Company had their bank overdraft limit increased from £3,000 to £4,000 in 1830. This allowance was larger than their profits in the period 1828–32, during the first two years of which

Table 10.4 *Ploughed-back profits, new partners and loans of Benjamin Gott & Company, 1787–1808*

Year	Ploughed-back profits[a] (£)	Capital from new partners (£)	Loans (£)
1787	4,220	—	11,600
1788	4,659	—	3,860
1789	1,507	—	4,200
1790	2,292	7,270	10,070
1791[b]	—	—	17,150
1792	5,418	—	16,600
1793	−3,605 (loss)	5,241	—
1794	3,724	—	600
1795	5,052	—	—
1796	10,218	—	100
1797	8,734	—	170
1798	6,331	—	400
1799	14,046	—	—
1800	5,116	—	16,400
1801	3,015	—	660
1802	3,475	—	400
1803	19,425	—	1,000
1804	15,943	—	—
1805	17,480	—	2,100
1806	11,085	—	—
1807	−4,502 (loss)	—	—
1808	−18,243 (loss)	—	—

[a] Omits interest on capital withdrawn which increases in 1799 from 4½ to 5%.
[b] 1791 figures complicated by the withdrawal of Joseph Fountaine from the partnership taking £33,400.
— = information not recorded.
Source: Gott, item 20 (B.), item 1 (J.G. MSS).

considerable additions were being made to the firm's premises. In the period 1828–30 the *use* of their overdraft facility was equivalent to half of the profit figure. Although the firm's records do not reveal the extent to which these profits were being reinvested at the time it is unlikely that plough-back was any more important than the bank overdraft.[57]

Thus, although the information available is somewhat fragmentary, it is difficult to trace any general or overriding reliance on reinvestment as a means of expansion. Even in newly centralising concerns, profits may have played only a subsidiary role. Major capital extension or re-equipping requires large sums of money in a relatively short time period whereas profits represent a continuous income over the longer term. Thus even where minimal withdrawals were made, profits themselves were often insufficient to finance industrial transition. For later expansion as opposed to initial outlay, reinvestment of profit and a cautious withdrawal policy seems, where it occurred, to have been related more to the scope of alternative investment outlets and to the size and life-cycles of firms and businessmen rather than to the mentality or religious morality of the latter. It may, however, be that the crude accounting of the time, particularly the treatment of depreciation, under-estimated profitability and resulted in the retention of profits which were never defined as such. Finally, if retained profits were of importance at some stages in a firm's life, it must be remembered that profitability for most concerns was related to an ability to achieve export success and to juggle with the main input costs of fibres and labour.

PART 5
SUMMARY AND CONCLUSION

Come wealth or want, come good or ill
Let young and old accept their part
And bow before the Awful Will,
And bear it with an honest heart.
Who misses or who wins the prize –
Go, lose or conquer as you can.
But if you fail, or if you rise,
Be each, pray God, a gentleman.

W. M. Thackeray, cited by Samuel
Smiles in *Life and Labour or
Characteristics of Men of Industry,
Culture and Genius* (1887)

11
THE GENESIS
OF INDUSTRIAL CAPITAL

Following a brief summary of the findings of each major section of the thesis, this Part draws some conclusions whilst also highlighting the remaining gaps in our knowledge.

Primary accumulation

The essential prerequisite of the development of industrial capitalism is the concentration of ownership of the means of production and the emergence of a landless 'free' proletariat. By examining this gradual development as it affected one region and one industrial sector, interesting features of the initial accumulation process have been revealed.

The classical Marxist questions about the nature of 'primitive accumulation', together with the recent proto-industrialisation debate have drawn attention to three factors in particular which have been highlighted in the present study. First, the relationship between industrial capital formation and the changing nature of landholding. Secondly, the varying role of artisan capital, and thirdly, the place of merchant capital in industrial transformation: was mercantile accumulation a revolutionising influence?

On the question of land distribution, a number of interesting points have emerged from the current research. It has been argued that the nature of landholding associated with both the agrarian and the institutional environment was a crucial determinant of the organisational structure of proto-industry. The varying rural industrial structures in turn conditioned the accumulation of capital and the timing and nature of the transition to factory production.

The artisan structure of the woollen sector generally retained its dominance in the eighteenth century in areas of later enclosure, of larger landholdings and where considerable land remained leasehold and copyhold. The putting-out systems of worsted manufacture emerged in areas such as Halifax Parish and the Manors of Bradford and Keighley where soils were poor, where enfranchisement was a feature of the early and mid-seventeenth century and where social polarisation and partible inheritance resulted in the early emergence of a considerable landless and cottager class.

For the old-established woollen sector, traditionally closely tied to agrarian practices, the role of finance from landed sources would appear to have been crucial in the early stages of transition to the factory. A significant proportion of the fulling and later carding, scribbling and even spinning mills were owned and financed by estate owners, long after the decline of manorial monopolies. Once the expansion in numbers of scribbling mills got underway from the 1790s direct investment by landowners was joined by capital from artisan and other sources. Thus landed finance declined in importance relative to capital from elsewhere. In the eighteenth and nineteenth centuries the majority of the large landed families of the West Riding were absentees with little direct interest in the development of either industry or agriculture on their estates.

The landholdings of the clothiers themselves appear to have been a major key to the finance and expansion of their enterprise. In this connection the active land market and, particularly, the increasing popularity of the medium- and long-term mortgage was of immense importance. Study of both the freehold and copyhold land transactions of clothiers in a sample township indicated that even during the Napoleonic War period sale and mortgage of land was an important source of industrial finance: both a major element in the accumulation process and a valuable reserve used to combat difficult economic circumstances. Complementary information from deeds surviving in the business archives of both woollen and worsted concerns confirm that lands and properties were a dominant form of security for longer-term loans, especially during periods of the construction of industrial capacity to the mid-nineteenth century and beyond.

The role played by capital from the artisan sector in the transition to centralised and mechanised production was also predicated on the nature of the proto-industrial structure. In the woollen branch the artisan turning over his own capital and working within a dual household economy had the prospect of accumulation and of riding out the storms of commercial life by a careful balancing of his activities. The upward economic mobility to which this could give rise is illustrated by the importance of the larger artisans in the finance and ownership of many of the early woollen mills. Nowhere was this more true than in the case of the company mills which form a unique example of 'the energy amongst the smaller capitalists of the manufacturing districts'.[1] The company mill was a product of the peculiarly artisanal nature of proto-industrial production in the woollen branch and spawned a form of 'co-operative capitalism' rather different from the norm. The organisation of company mills and their financial and credit dealings embodied a collective and communitarian spirit whose aim tended toward stability rather than radical change.

The worsted sector in Yorkshire exhibited more features of a classic proto-industrial development based on the 'functional inter-relationship between the family economy and merchant capital'[2] found in the putting-out system. Rural mass production of worsteds expanded in Yorkshire outside of the traditional guild and artisan regulations and structures, and its success was predicated upon the absorption of unapprenticed and cheap labour scattered over wide areas of poor soils and small agricultural holdings. These households, rather than accumulating capital, were vastly more likely, through natural increase, partible inheritance and increasing dependence on the capitalist, to become 'proletarianised'. More research is required on the social and demographic characteristics of the woollen and worsted areas of the West Riding in the period of proto-industry. As was indicated in Chapter 3, although the domestic worsted workers were not prominent in mill renting or finance in any way, they did not either readily provide the mass of wage labour for the factory system. The worsted mills seem to have drawn young female labour from areas well beyond the confines of the proto-industrial region.

With respect to the role of merchant capital, this study has shown that there was great variation in the importance of this source of finance in the transition to factory production. Where, as in the woollen sector, proto-industrial expansion was not characterised by extensive putting-out systems, the emergence of the merchant-manufacturer would appear to have been primarily a result of developments within the ranks of the manufacturers. This would agree with Wilson's findings about the very limited role played by the traditional mercantile community in Leeds.[3] Even in cloth finishing in the eighteenth century, Dickenson had shown that merchants generally played only a small part in direct financing.[4] Factory building and financing was dominated by manufacturers who eased their way into centralised production via tenancy and multiple tenancy of mills and via maximum use of credit facilities. Their task was aided by relatively slow technical innovation and the resultant slow growth of the (fixed) capital threshold of entry into the trade.

In the worsted sector, mill ownership in the first half of the nineteenth century was dominated by merchant-manufacturers, including former putting-out capitalists, wool staplers and manufacturers previously engaged in other sectors, especially cotton spinning. The relatively high threshold of entry into factory production, together with the accumulation of capital in the putting-out sector, dictated a more important role for mercantile capital. But even here it is doubtful whether this formed a dominant source of funds for fixed capital investment. The majority of the putting-out capitalists of the later eighteenth century seem to have arisen from the local landowning and rural craft communities rather than from the ranks of the traditional urban merchant groups. Their initial capital came from farming, from land dealing and from putting-out production, and their expansion arose from profits earned in both manufacture and trade. The majority of eighteenth-century Yorkshire worsted entrepreneurs dealt through Blackwell Hall or other merchants and factors and were themselves merely middlemen in the chain of trade. Only for a minority were the profits earned from exchange of dominant importance compared with the income earned in manufacture and farming.

The exception to this limited extension of merchant capital into fixed capital investment and production lies in the frequency with which wool staplers turned to factory manufacture. This occurred particularly in the worsted branch and after the 1820s when the role of the wool stapler in the West Riding economy was radically changing. It seems that as many as 15–20% of pre-1850 worsted mills were owned or part-owned by wool staplers or by persons whose capital had been accumulated in this trade. Even here, however, it appears that commercial contacts, status in the local financial community and hence calls upon loan finance and credit were the most important advantages begot by a background in stapling.

On the whole, *direct* involvement and transfer of merchants into factory entrepreneurship and their finance of fixed capital in centralised production was not of major importance. The first generations of Yorkshire mills were founded primarily by manufacturers who, through their increasing control over the process of production, represented a direct challenge to the systems of scattered production inspired and endorsed by merchant capital. In financing these mills the manufacturers relied on their backgrounds in landholding, farming and artisan production and on their standing in the local community. To be known and trusted in the locality and to have some form of property or security were *the* vital elements in procuring a lifeline to the capital and credit markets.

The credit matrix

The analysis of credit in the Yorkshire woollen and worsted trades identified some important and interesting shifts in terms and their implications for the finance of industry during the period 1750–1850.

In raw material supply the long credits of the eighteenth century were gradually superseded by shorter and more uniform credit terms. By the 1830s and 1840s credit of two to four months was becoming the rule with most raw material and service purchases which represented a very significant shift from the six to eighteen months or more so common in the eighteenth century and during the Napoleonic Wars. This may have left labour as the most flexible element in total costs in terms of credit (worked through delays and the truck system) as well as in real terms by the 1830s and 1840s, as Hobsbawm and Foster have suggested.[5]

On the demand side of the industry cash and short credit sales were replaced by very long credit terms from the later 1790s. This was associated with the evolution of the merchant-manufacturer and the struggle to gain a competitive position in volatile and, especially, in long-distance trades. From the 1820s credit extended in the sale of yarn and cloths was curtailing once more from the extremes reached in the first two decades of the nineteenth century. This stabilisation and reduction of credit terms seems to have remained a characteristic feature of the trade through much of the rest of the nineteenth century although it was interrupted as in the 1850s by cyclical and speculative activity.

By the 1830s and 1840s the curtailment of open or internal credit in the trade in raw materials and manufactures was eased by the expansion of external credit associated with the growth of banking facilities. This may well have placed the larger and more influential concern, with links to the local banking fraternity, at an advantage *vis-à-vis* the smaller manufacturer or the new entrant to the industry. However, the volatility of external finance was a common cause of failure and bankruptcy for those firms tempted to overcommit themselves to accommodation finance.

There is a great difficulty in attempting meaningful generalisations regarding the effects of these open and external credit trends and their cyclical fluctuations upon the finance of production in the crucial period of industrialisation. There is probably no such thing as an average concern at this time: all were differentiated in terms of products, markets, size, degree of technological advance, entrepreneurial standing and other features. These affected such major variables as the call upon credit and the need for it as well as the period of realisation – an important factor in determining the impact of credit changes on the finance of production. Were manufacturers able to exert a favourable influence on the credit matrix for themselves and how was this related to the expansion of fixed capital in the industry and to the turnover time of capital?

In the domestic systems the artisan producer was generally able to gain credit from staplers, other suppliers and from his labour force to a much greater extent than he was forced to extend credit to the merchant. Furthermore, the turnover time of capital in production as well as in trade in the woollen branch was more rapid than in the worsted sector in the eighteenth century and the net credit gained by the manufacturer could cover the time of production and circulation. This provided an environment for capital accumulation enabling the gradual evolution of larger concerns from the ranks of the domestic manufacturers.

The worsted putting-out capitalist by contrast often bought his wool on shorter or no credit and sold at three or four months at least. This may well have been a factor, along with the slower turnover time, in ensuring that the sector was dominated by concerns of larger capital than the woollen branch. This, with the disarray of markets, especially for worsted products, in the early nineteenth century may account for the very slow build-up of fixed capital in the industry before the 1820s.[6] The credit matrix, together with the slow turnover time of production and sale of worsted piece goods, also possibly stimulated the vertical disintegration which was becoming a marked feature of this branch of the trade by the second quarter of the nineteenth century.

It is possible that before the 1820s the credit matrix favoured the woollen rather than the worsted branch of the industry, with a large role being played by staplers, wool importers and fulling and scribbling millers. On the demand side the traditional possibilities of selling for cash or on short credit remained. From the 1820s mechanical innovation in worsted spinning and the accelerated trend to vertical disintegration increased the turnover speed of capital in that branch at a time when the period of realisation was also shortening because of transportation, mercantile and financial improvements. In the climate of generally reducing open credits after the mid-1820s it would seem that the firms best placed to take advantage, and to expand their fixed capital, were those capable of reducing turnover speeds by mechanical or organisational innovation whether in the woollen or in the worsted branch.

It would appear from the case studies undertaken in Chapter 8 that credit extended by successful *factory* manufacturers in the early nineteenth century was generally greater than that extended to them by their suppliers. This seems to have been true of woollen and worsted merchant-manufacturers and manufacturers alike in the difficult years of the Napoleonic Wars and their aftermath. From the mid-1820s when credit in sales was curtailing it was possible, using staplers and delays in wage payments, to gain from the credit position without losing a competitive foothold in the trade. Many concerns, like Marriner's, may have used this to aid the expansion of their productive capacity. This is substantiated by the bankruptcy records of the period which show that a good deal of failures were caused by liquidity problems rather than lack of assets. These records and other Business Ledgers of the period also show the enormous importance of staplers and bankers as creditors. The former were the major source of book credit while the latter fuelled the external credit possibilities.

Short-term credit fluctuations were also important in conditioning the environment for capital accumulation. It appears that internal credit cycles before the 1820s were dominated by the impulse towards the lengthening of credit in boom periods. Credit was here being used very positively by manufacturers and merchants as a form of competition in securing markets. In the second quarter of the nineteenth century periods of increased prosperity and profits tended to give added power to the seller to demand prompt payment whilst buyers were in a better position to meet this demand. Credit was coming to be regarded as an expensive luxury in an era of greater innovation, market expansion and cost competition.

In cyclical downswings open credit tended to stabilise or contract but usually there was a delay prompted by the fear of merchants and manufacturers that they would cause the liquidation of clients and further undermine their own position particularly in the longer term. There was always the chance that greater open credit, if it could be afforded, would help to retain custom during hard times and periods of intense competition for dwindling markets. Factory manufacturers were further pressured to maintain or advance their credit allowances in depressions as they continued to manufacture through the slumps and became desperate to shift their produce at a time when the markets were already overstocked.

Superimposed on these fluctuations was the effect of external credit which in cyclical upturns was fuelled by activity in the discount and banking sector particularly after the 1820s. The problem with this is that although it created an environment of great stimulus during the upswings of the trade and investment cycles, over-trading and over-extension of credit was a perennial problem. The sudden contraction of bank credit at the peak of activity, the consequent rush for liquidity and the loss of confidence brought many firms to ruin.

Thus open credit, particularly after the mid-1820s tended to have a stabilising effect on cyclical activity whilst external credit tended to aggravate the dangers of instability, speculation and crises, weeding out sound as well as unsound concerns until the gradual maturation of monetary policy ameliorated such problems later in the century.

The capital market

The present study has indicated that the capital market of the West Riding region was overwhelmingly a local phenomenon. However, by the 1840s investment outlets outside the area were tempting capital away.

The textile industry appears to have attracted its finance largely from the cash and savings generated within the textile communities and there is little evidence of long-term funds being drawn from outside the area. Local finance found its way into productive investment via an array of conduits; informal personal and social relationships being of undoubted importance in directing flows of funds. Connections through family, church or chapel arise again and again in examining the business papers of the textile concerns and are sufficient to warrant a separate study. The present analysis concentrates more on the formal channels whereby finance found its way from lender to borrower within the textile communities but even here the crucial importance of personal and social contacts is overwhelmingly apparent.

Investigation has shown that the main institutional links of the local capital market in the West Riding in the late eighteenth century were the money scrivening attorneys and the private banks. Many of the latter had emerged as an adjunct to the business dealings of the textile merchants and manufacturers themselves.

The attorney's role at the centre of local financial business – estate stewardship, rent collecting, testation and land transfer – made him the major holder of the precious idle cash balances in the communities. These were used to provide both long- and short-term loans to clients in all spheres. In addition, the attorney's wide circle of business and legal contacts made him a linchpin in matching lender to borrower. The extended use of the mortgage in the eighteenth century and the establishment of the West Riding Registry of Deeds encouraged and gave security to these operations.

Whilst the attorney remained the major intermediary in loan transactions it is likely that landed capital played an important role in local finance. The most important clients of the attorney's legal services were landowners and these provided his first source of loan capital. It is, however, more difficult to assess the major direction of flow of funds handled by the attorneys. Much of the money involved in short-term transactions went to artisans and small traders and to the more sizeable merchants and putting-out capitalists. Attorneys were thus helping to finance trade. At the same time there is evidence of major longer-term lending, as found by Anderson in Lancashire in the eighteenth century.[7] These included loans to industrialists. In the case of John Howarth of Halifax long-term lending was important although the proportion going to industrialists was much less than that going to landowners and merchants at the end of the eighteenth century. Complementary evidence of mortgage and loan transactions arranged by attorneys is to be found in the textile business archives, indicating that this source was of some importance for many industrial concerns but that its importance was declining with the development of other organs of the capital market by the 1820s and 1830s.

Unlike the attorney, whose role in long-term finance of industrial as opposed to trading or agricultural ventures may have been somewhat limited, the evolution of banks in the West Riding was from the start closely related to the needs of the dominant mercantile and industrial developments of the region. Textile merchants and manufacturers figured prominently among the founders of both private and joint stock banks. Shareholders of the later banks were also overwhelmingly drawn from the immediate locality and from the textile and trading interests.

These close links appear to have proved decisive in influencing the flow of short- and long-term accommodation from the banks to the local economy. In the case of longer-term finance, the use of bill re-discount, overdraft practices, the 10% rule and the generally favourable treatment of partners, directors, shareholders and others known to those in positions of authority within the banks ensured that the local industrial and trading circles were generally well supplied with funds. So much so that the liquidity position of banks was frequently placed in jeopardy, particularly in the cycles of the 1830s when competition between the increasing number of joint stock banks accelerated.

The private banks from the eighteenth century were invariably involved in long-term commitments to industrial ventures – often their own. From their inception the later joint stock banks also saw a major element of their business as being the supply of loan capital to industry as well as trade as an examination of the Deeds of Settlement and Minute Books prove. The chronic overdraft was the major means by which funds were in practice extended by banks to local trade and industry over the long term. Most industrial shareholders had a perpetual overdraft and business records show that these overdrafts were frequently larger than annual profits during the 1830s and 1840s. Bank finance must therefore have been more important than self-finance for at least some firms in some phases of their development.

Bank loans can be related to periods of expansion of productive capacity and of mill building indicating their major role here. This seems to have been particularly prevalent in the 1830s and 1840s especially among established concerns who were regarded as a sound risk. Bank loans as a source of initial capital for a firm launching into centralised production in the industry would seem to have been less important although a good reputation in the locality, a bank shareholding, landed property as security or a friend on the directorate of the bank could radically alter the position of the new entrant as a potential borrower.

Self-finance

It has long been accepted that internal self-finance was *the* dominant form of industrial finance during the industrial revolution in England. Evidence for the West Riding confirms the importance of this source but questions its *dominance* in the finance of both the transition to factory production and of the later expansion of centralised capacity in the industry.

New entrants to factory industry generally had to call upon resources from a vast array of external sources, although the prevalence of renting and the ubiquity of company mills in the woollen branch eased the threshold of entry sufficiently for self-finance to have played a prominent role. Among the larger factory manufacturers of the 1830s and 1840s and the second or third generations of textile entrepreneurs, finance from other sources, particularly banks, would appear to have been of more importance than plough-back in periods of fixed capital expansion. Investment is discontinuous whereas profit income is more gradual. Big investment projects, such as that required to build an Arkwright-type mill by the 1820s and 1830s, invariably required concentration of investment far beyond that capable of being found from internal sources. Furthermore, by the 1840s, alternative investment opportunities, particularly the stable returns of domestic and foreign railways and public utilities, were important in tempting profits away from reinvestment in the industry. Later generations of textile entrepreneurs also seem to have developed greater commitments to conspicuous consumption and philanthropic spending than their predecessors.

Apart from analysing the importance of ploughed-back profit in industrial finance it is crucial to understand the factors and variables which governed the movement of profitability. The accumulation process can be little understood by invoking the idea of self-finance unless it is acknowledged that profitability in turn is a dependent variable: dependent on both personal and impersonal forces.

Insofar as these forces can be identified it would appear that export fluctuations were a major determinant of profitability for the majority of textile concerns by the second quarter of the nineteenth century. Wool price movements were also important giving emphasis to the search for cost reducing innovation in raw material inputs which characterised these decades. The degree to which the wage bill in real terms could be squeezed to accommodate the trade cycles through truck, delays and other devices also shows up as an important determinant of profitability.

It must be acknowledged that the analysis of self-finance presented here is dogged by the restrictions of the available data. Profit rates are only available in significant quantity for the 1830s–50s (and later). Furthermore, these may be biased in favour of the larger, more successful concerns and could also be distorted by the vagaries of early industrial accounting. Despite these disabilities, the data would at least appear to be a considerable improvement upon that used in previous attempts to comment on the reinvestment process. The current study has drawn attention to the need to subject such a crucial aspect of accumulation to rigorous analysis across the different sectors of the economy and over time. It may well be that previous generalisations about the importance of self-finance may obscure more than they reveal about the nature and motivation of industrial expansion.

Conclusion

It would appear useful to think in terms of three time periods in suggesting the hierarchy of importance of the various sources of finance used in the industry and in considering how this hierarchy may have changed over time.

Before the mid-1790s the most crucial source of funds was probably land mortgage and sale coupled with staplers' credit, the credit and contacts acquired by the putting-out capitalists and reinvestment.

During the war period and to the early 1820s land mortgage and sale appear to have continued, enclosure awards favouring some manufacturers at the expense of others. This, overall, was a period of mixed fortunes in the industry. Those substantial firms able to extend credit, to obtain bank finance and government contracts and to seek out new distant markets were well placed to gain and expand their fixed capital. For the more typical concerns, staplers' credit, quick sales for cash, a squeezing of the living standards of the proto-industrial household, and property holdings as financial security were the key to survival and growth.

From the mid-1820s substantial changes took place in the financial and economic environment. Open credit contracted on trend whilst bank finance expanded rapidly and innovation in the industry accelerated. With a quickening of the turnover time of capital and vertical disintegration some firms could gain a positive stimulus from the credit matrix but in circumstances of cyclical volatility much depended on the manufacturer's ability to juggle with costs and prices and to guard against financial overcommitment and heavy withdrawals.

Through the whole period, in gaining access to both credit and capital, the personal and property assets of manufacturers were of crucial importance. The close knit communities of the West Riding with their complex networks of familial, religious, personal and business affiliations formed the markets within which manufacturers sought to raise finance. With unlimited liability, lenders were reassured if they knew what private means and property a borrower had and if they had a reputation for sober conduct. The importance of immediate commercial intelligence encouraged the highly localised nature of financial dealings.

Contemporary business and bank records abound with assessments of the degree of 'respectability' of their clients.[8] Being respectable had little to do with social morality but had everything to do with property and with a reputation for regularity in paying debts and avoiding speculation. The 'respectable' were the propertied (especially with land or tangible assets outside of those sunk in business), the well known in the neighbourhood, the native, the naturalised or the long-resident and those who avoided accommodation bills or similar improper commercial dealings. If a manufacturer gained respectable status he could be assured of continuing support from institutions of the capital market and from lenders or suppliers even in hard times. Similarly local banks could enjoy pledges of support from their community in periods of liquidity problems once they had established a sound reputation.[9]

Local commercial intelligence contributed to the stability of business but could and did come unstuck where firms regarded as 'unexceptionable' nevertheless crashed. A notable example occurred with the bankruptcy of Hindes & Dereham in 1839. They, doubtless like others, had managed to hide their true situation from the financial community, especially from banks and staplers, to the consternation and shock of many, including Thomas Bischoff of the Bank of England: 'it never occurred to me that the manager of so long-established and so respectable a concern should keep a false set of books'.[10]

At the level of the small semi-rural clothiers, who continued as a characteristic feature of the woollen branch until well into the second half of the nineteenth century, community spirit, affiliations and loyalties expressed themselves in mutual co-operation and trust among the stratum of respectable concerns. This enabled them to build mills and to weather the storms of commercial life. But for those regarded as outside the financial fraternity, and without land or property assets, the door to proletarianisation was the only one open.

Thus capital sources altered considerably over time and varied a great deal between different sorts of concerns. When bankruptcies were ubiquitous and volatility the norm, there were few constant elements in the capital and credit matrix of any manufacturer. The one enduring feature appears to have been the importance of maintaining a trusted, respected and propertied status in the eyes of the local business community.

APPENDIX
TABLES RELATING TO CHAPTER 10

Table 1 *Profit rates in the worsted industry, 1840–58*

Year ending	Clough	Bairstow	Foster	Marriner	Composite[a] (A)	(B)
1840		18				
1841		12				
1842		26	14	6	15.3	
1843		20	9	4	11.0	
1844		35	14	7	18.6	
1845	12	10	9	−1	6.0	10.0
1846	−12	2	15	1	6.0	1.5
1847	−8	7	17	10	4.6	1.5
1848	−8	16	12	4	10.6	6.0
1849	46	49	35	14	32.6	36.0
1850	20	37	27	16	26.6	25.0
1851	18	8	9	5	18.7	10.0
1852	16	19	17	2	12.7	13.5
1853	11	22	11	−6	9.0	9.5
1854	1	−2	13	12	7.7	6.0
1855	11	1	19	15	11.7	11.5
1856	22	1	17	10	9.3	12.5
1857		−3	9	9	5.0	
1858		16	13	−4	8.3	

[a] Composite A is the mean of Bairstow, Foster and Marriner.
Composite B is the mean of Clough, Bairstow, Foster and Marriner.
Sources: Clough, item 230 (B.); Bairstow, item 3 (L.); Foster, items 4, 5 (B.); Ingle, 'A History of R. V. Marriner Ltd.', p. 157.

Table 2 *Wool prices for the worsted sector, 1840–58 (pence per lb)*

Year	Lincoln half-hog	Year	Lincoln half-hog
1840	14.0	1850	11.0
1841	12.5	1851	12.5
1842	11.0	1852	13.6
1843	10.0	1853	16.0
1844	11.0	1854	15.5
1845	13.0	1855	13.0
1846	13.0	1856	16.0
1847	12.0	1857	20.5
1848	11.0	1858	15.6
1849	10.0		

Source: Mitchell and Deane, *Abstract of British Historical Statistics*, pp. 495–6.

Table 3 *Yarn exports and cloth exports by volume, 1840–58*

Year	Yarn exports (000 lbs)	Total wool manufactures including carpets (000 yds)
1840	3,797	68,675
1841	4,903	77,962
1842	5,962	75,285
1843	7,410	96,314
1844	8,272	112,367
1845	9,406	106,382
1846	8,631	87,949
1847	10,065	98,953
1848	8,429	84,792
1849	11,773	124,035
1850	13,794	150,520
1851	14,671	151,231
1852	14,220	165,527
1853	13,965	168,561
1854	15,733	153,325
1855	20,408	133,042
1856	27,340	156,461
1857	24,654	177,132
1858	24,070	166,142

Source: Mitchell and Deane, *Abstract of British Historical Statistics*, p. 195.

Appendix

Table 4 *Financial data, 1822–50*

Year	Overend Gurney's rates for first class bills at three months (market rate of discount) (%)	Bank rate yearly average (%)	Yield on consols (%)
1822		4.00	3.8
1823		4.00	3.8
1824	3.50	4.00	3.3
1825	3.88	4.00	3.5
1826	4.50	5.00	3.8
1827	3.25	4.50	3.6
1828	3.04	4.00	3.5
1829	3.38	4.00	3.3
1830	2.81	4.00	3.5
1831	3.69	4.00	3.8
1832	3.15	4.00	3.6
1833	2.73	4.00	3.4
1834	3.38	4.00	3.3
1835	3.71	4.00	3.3
1836	4.25	4.50	3.4
1837	4.44	5.00	3.3
1838	3.00	4.00	3.2
1839	5.13	5.50	3.3
1840	4.98	5.00	3.4
1841	4.90	5.00	3.4
1842	3.33	4.25	3.3
1843	2.17	4.00	3.2
1844	2.13	3.25	3.0
1845	2.96	3.00	3.1
1846	3.79	3.00	3.1
1847	5.85	5.75	3.4
1848	3.21	3.50	3.5
1849	2.31	3.00	3.2
1850	2.25	2.50	3.1

Source: Mitchell and Deane, *Abstract of British Historical Statistics*, pp. 455–7, 460.

Table 5 *Money wage rate index in the worsted industry, 1840–58*

Date	Wage rate index	Date	Wage rate index
1840	100.0	1850	110.4
1841	102.9	1851	106.8
1842	97.3	1852	90.8
1843	94.0	1853	98.9
1844	110.4	1854	89.7
1845	110.7	1855	93.3
1846	87.8	1856	97.0
1847	103.3	1857	84.5
1848	89.0	1858	75.4
1849	100.2		

Source: Derived from information in Johnstone, 'The Standard of Living of Worsted Workers', Chs. 3 and 4. The wage data is from Clough's and Brigg's converted to indices and reduced to a common base of 1840 = 100. Spinners' wages are not available before the 1870s. The following weights were used:

1842–7	power loom weavers	75
	mill hands	10
	handloom weavers	15
1848–58	power loom weavers	90
	mill hands	10

Table 6 *Real wage indices for the worsted industry, 1840–58*

Year	Using Rousseaux	Using G.R. & S.[a]
1840	100.0	100.0
1841	111.0	107.3
1842	112.5	112.7
1843	117.3	122.9
1844	130.8	140.1
1845	130.0	132.9
1846	104.9	99.8
1847	116.6	100.0
1848	117.3	103.6
1849	138.6	136.0
1850	158.8	157.5
1851	160.1	
1852	136.1	
1853	123.5	
1854	101.2	
1855	102.7	
1856	106.8	
1857	91.6	
1858	96.7	

[a] Gayer, Rostow and Schwartz.
Source: Rousseaux and G.R. & S. from Mitchell and Deane, *Abstract of British Historical Statistics*, pp. 470–1. Corrected to base 1840 = 100.

Table 7 *Profit rates in the woollen industry, 1822–40*

Year Ending	Wormalds & Walker	Broadbent	Illingworth Murgatroyd & Company[a]	Gott
1822	10			
1823	19			
1824	22			
1825	11	26.2		
1826	8	5.0		
1827	10	7.8		
1828	5	11.7	12.7	
1829	3	10.1	5.5	
1830	21	6.0	14.7	
1831	10	6.6	7.2	
1832	9	7.2	1.8	
1833	18		29.8	
1834	4			
1835	23			2
1836	20			2
1837	3			−5
1838	10			6
1839	4			
1840	4			

Sources: Wormalds & Walker, items 2 and 3 (B.), also Glover, 'Dewsbury Mills', pp. 374 and 510; Broadbent, item 1 (B.); Holly Park Mill, item 1 (L.); Gott, item 20 (B.).
[a] Also worsted spinners.

Table 8 *Additional profit rate figures for the woollen industry,*
1792–1858

Year	Gott	Year	Wormalds & Walker
1792	29	1840	4
1793	3	1841	5
1794	21	1842	4
1795	15	1843	6
1796	19	1844	8
1797	15	1845	8
1798	11	1846	4
1799	15	1847	5
1800	7	1848	11
1801	6	1849	17
1802	5	1850	15
1803	14	1851	9
1804	12	1852	11
1805	11	1853	28
1806	10	1854	25
1807	7	1855	17
1808	3	1856	12
1809	12	1857	10
1810	17	1858	14
1811	− 1		
1812	6		
1813	8		
1814	8		

Source: Gott, items 20, 21 (B.); Wormalds & Walker, item 3 (B.); and Glover, 'Dewsbury Mills', p. 510.

Appendix

Table 9 *Wool prices for the woollen industry, 1792–1845*
(pence per lb)

Year	Southdown	Year	Southdown
1792	15.00	1819	20.50
1793	11.50	1820	16.50
1794	12.50	1821	14.25
1795	15.00	1822	14.00
1796	16.00	1823	14.75
1797	15.25	1824	12.50
1798	14.50	1825	16.00
1799	19.00	1826	10.00
1800	17.00	1827	9.00
1801	18.00	1828	8.00
1802	18.50	1829	6.00
1803	18.75	1830	10.00
1804	21.00	1831	13.00
1805	23.50	1832	12.00
1806	21.50	1833	17.00
1807	21.50	1834	19.00
1808	20.00	1835	18.00
1809	27.50	1836	20.00
1810	30.00	1837	15.00
1811	19.00	1838	16.00
1812	18.75	1839	16.00
1813	21.00	1840	15.00
1814	25.25	1841	12.00
1815	23.50	1842	11.50
1816	16.50	1843	11.25
1817	19.50	1844	14.00
1818	26.00	1845	16.00

Source: Mitchell and Deane, *Abstract of British Historical Statistics*, pp. 495–6.

Table 10 *Exports from U.K. by volume, 1815–55*

Year	Blankets (m yds)	Year	Blankets (m yds)
1815	3.4	1836	4.3
1816	1.9	1837	2.4
1817	2.3	1838	2.6
1818	2.7	1839	3.1
1819	1.8	1840	2.2
1820	1.3	1841	2.1
1821	1.4	1842	1.4
1822	1.9	1843	1.7
1823	2.1	1844	3.3
1824	2.0	1845	2.4
1825	2.2	1846	2.2
1826	1.1	1847	—
1827	1.9	1848	4.1
1828	2.1	1849	5.7
1829	1.8	1850	6.4
1830	2.2	1851	5.7
1831	2.5	1852	9.8
1832	1.7	1853	9.8
1833	3.1	1854	9.4
1834	2.5	1855	5.0
1835	3.1		

Source: Mitchell and Deane, *Abstract of British Historical Statistics*, p. 293.

Table 11 *Exports at current prices: wool goods from Great Britain, 1814–29 (£m)[a]*

Year	£m	Year	£m
1814	6.4	1822	6.5
1815	9.3	1823	5.6
1816	7.8	1824	6.0
1817	7.2	1825	6.2
1818	8.1	1826	5.0
1819	6.0	1827	5.3
1820	5.6	1828	5.1
1821	6.5	1829	4.7

[a] Excludes exports to Ireland.
Source: Mitchell and Deane, *Abstract of British Historical Statistics*, pp. 302–3.

Appendix

Table 12 *Exports of woollen and worsted yarn and manufacture,*
1792–1812 (official values in £000s)

1792	5,154	1803	5,303
1793	3,547	1804	5,694
1794	4,126	1805	6,006
1795	5,096	1806	6,248
1796	5,677	1807	5,373
1797	4,625	1808	4,854
1798	6,177	1809	5,416
1799	6,435	1810	5,774
1800	6,918	1811	4,376
1801	7,321	1812	5,085
1802	6,687		

Source: Mitchell and Deane, *Abstract of British Historical Statistics*, pp. 294–5.

Table 13 *Exports at current prices: wool goods from U.K., 1826–1858*
(£m)

1826	5.0	1843	7.5
1827	5.3	1844	9.2
1828	5.1	1845	8.8
1829	4.7	1846	7.2
1830	4.9	1847	7.9
1831	5.4	1848	6.5
1832	5.5	1849	8.4
1833	6.5	1850	10.0
1834	6.0	1851	9.9
1835	7.2	1852	10.2
1836	8.0	1853	11.6
1837	5.0	1854	11.7
1838	6.2	1855	9.7
1839	6.7	1856	12.4
1840	5.8	1857	13.5
1841	6.3	1858	12.5
1842	5.8		

Source: Mitchell and Deane, *Abstract of British Historical Statistics*, pp. 302–3.

NOTES

The following abbreviations are used in the notes

B	Brotherton Library, University of Leeds
Barclays	Barclays Bank Archives
B.E.R.	*Bulletin of Economic Research*
B.H.R.	*Business History Review*
B.O.	*Bradford Observer*
D.E.T.	Dartmouth Estate Terriers, Dartmouth Estate Office, Slaithwaite
E.H.R.	*Economic History Review*
E.J.	*Economic Journal*
Ha.	Calderdale District Archives, Halifax
H.O.	Home Office Papers
Hu.	Dewsbury Public Library (Kirklees District Archives)
J.E.H.	*Journal of Economic History*
J.G. MSS	John Goodchild Manuscripts housed in Wakefield District Library
L.	Leeds District Archives
L.I.	*Leeds Intelligencer*
Lloyds	Lloyds Bank Archives
L.M.	*Leeds Mercury*
Midland	Midland Bank Archives
P.P.	Parliamentary Papers (followed by date, command and volume number and page or question reference)
P.R.O.	Public Record Office
T.H.	*Textile History*
T.H.A.S.	*Transactions of the Halifax Antiquarian Society*
T.S.	*Thorseby Society*
W.R.R.D.	West Riding Registry of Deeds, West Yorkshire Archive Service Head Quarters, Wakefield
Y.A.S.	Yorkshire Archaeological Society
Y.B.E.S.R.	*Yorkshire Bulletin of Economic and Social Research*

PART 1 INTRODUCTION
I THE STUDY OF CAPITAL ACCUMULATION

1. J. Robinson, *The Accumulation of Capital* (1956). S. Kuznets, 'Quantitative Aspects of the Economic Growth of Nations', *Economic Development and Cultural Change*, VIII, 4, 1960, pp. 1–96. S. Kuznets, *Modern Economic Growth: Rate, Structure and Spread* (1966). See also R. M. Solow, 'Technical Progress, Capital Formation and Economic Growth', *American Economic Review*, LII, 1, 1962. A. K. Cairncross, *Factors in Economic Growth* (1962). W. A. Lewis, *The Theory of Economic Growth* (1955).
2. W. W. Rostow, 'The Take-Off into Self-Sustained Growth', *E.J.*, LXVI, 261, 1956, pp. 33–8. W. W. Rostow (ed.), *The Stages of Economic Growth* (1960). P. Deane and H. J. Habbakkuk, 'The Take-Off in Britain', in W. W. Rostow (ed.), *The Economics of Take-Off into Sustained Growth* (1963), pp. 63–82. P. Deane, 'Capital Formation in Britain before the Railway Age', *Economic Development and Cultural Change*, IX, 3, 1961. P. Deane, 'New Estimates of Gross National Product for the United Kingdom, 1830–1914', *Review of Income and Wealth*, XIV, 1968. S. Pollard, 'The Growth and Distribution of Capital in Great Britain, c. 1770–1870', in *Proceedings of the Third International Conference of Economic History, Munich, 1965* vol. 1 (1965). C. Feinstein, 'Capital Formation in Great Britain', in *Cambridge Economic History of Europe*, vol. 7, part 1, ed. P. Mathias and M. M. Postan (Cambridge, 1978).
3. See, for example, S. Pollard, 'Investment, Consumption and the Industrial Revolution', *E.H.R.* XI, 2, 1958. J. Saville, 'Primitive Accumulation and Early Industrialisation in Britain' *Socialist Register*, VI, 1969. P. Kriedte, H. Medick and J. Schlumbohm, *Industrialisation before Industrialisation* (1982), provides a recent interesting extension of the 'transition debate' so prominent among Marxist historians of the 1950s and early 1960s. See R. Hilton, *The Transition from Feudalism to Capitalism* (1976), which collects together some of the more important early contributions. R. Brenner has rejuvenated this debate in recent years: 'Agrarian Class Structure and Economic Development in Pre-Industrial Europe', *Past and Present*, LXX, 1976. Critiques of Brenner are found in contributions to a symposium on Agrarian Class Structure and Economic Development in Pre-Industrial Europe published in *Past and Present*, 1978–80. See, for example, J. Hatcher and M. M. Postan, 'Population and Class Relations in Feudal Society', *Past and Present*, LXXVIII, 1978; Patricia Croot and David Parker, 'Agrarian Class Structure and Economic Development', *ibid.*, Guy Bois, 'Against the Neo-Mathusian Orthodoxy', *ibid.*, LXXIX, 1978. Brenner's reply to various critiques appears as 'The Agrarian Roots of European Capitalism', *ibid.*, XCV, 1982. On profits and reinvestment, see P. Sweezy, 'Schumpeter's theory of Innovation', in *The Present as History* (1953). On merchant capital, see M. Dobb, *Studies in the Development of Capitalism* (1946), and, most recently, E. Fox-Genovese and E. Genovese, *The Fruits of Merchant Capital* (1983), and Hisao Otsuka *The Spirit of Capitalism* (Tokyo, 1982).
4. Rostow, 'The Take-Off into Self-Sustained Growth', pp. 33–8. See also Lewis, *The Theory of Economic Growth*.
5. Deane and Habakkuk, in Rostow, *The Economics of Take-Off*, pp. 63–82 (Rostow's take off period for Britain is 1783–1803).
6. Kuznets, 'Quantitative Aspects'. Kuznets, *Modern Economic Growth*. Solow, 'Technical Progress'. Cairncross, *Factors in Economic Growth*.
7. S. Kuznets, 'Capital Formation in Modern Economic Growth (and Some Implications for the Past)', in *Proceedings of the Third International Conference of Economic History, Munich, 1965*, pp. 30–1, 33–5.
8. Kuznets, *Modern Economic Growth*; J. P. P. Higgins and S. Pollard (ed.), *Aspects of Capital Investment in Great Britain, 1750–1850* (1971), pp. 6–7, 27, 150, 186–7.
9. Kuznets, *Modern Economic Growth*, p. 243.
10. Pollard, in *Proceedings of the Third International Conference of Economic History*.
11. Feinstein, in *Cambridge Economic History of Europe*, Ch. 2, pp. 28–96.
12. *Ibid.*, pp. 73ff.
13. *Ibid.*, pp. 83–92.

14. Crafts has recently criticised Feinstein's calculation of pre-1831 investment proportions for relying on Deane and Cole's inaccurate measures of economic growth. His reworked estimates show a more rapid rise in investment proportions in the second decade of the nineteenth century following very gradual growth through the eighteenth century. He does not, however, comment on the fixed capital proportions or on domestic reproducible capital. See N. F. R. Crafts, 'British Economic Growth 1700–1831: A Review of the Evidence', *E.H.R.*, XXXVI, 2, 1983, pp. 194–5.
15. Feinstein in *Cambridge Economic History of Europe*, p. 87.
16. A point stressed by Domar in his analysis of the 'residual': E. D. Domar, 'On the Measurement of Technological Change', *E.J.* LXXI, 1961.
17. Feinstein, in *Cambridge Economic History of Europe*, p. 161; Crafts, 'British Economic Growth', pp. 197–8.
18. H. Perkin, *Origins of Modern English Society* (1969), pp. 138–9.
19. E. J. Hobsbawm, *Industry and Empire* (1968), p. 57.
20. S. Shapiro, *Capital and the Cotton Industry in the Industrial Revolution* (Ithaca, 1967), Ch. 4.
21. J. Foster, *Class Struggle in the Industrial Revolution* (1974) (draws heavily in his analysis of crisis in the cotton sector on Hobsbawm, *Industry and Empire*).
22. W. A. Lewis, 'Economic Development with Unlimited Supplies of Labour', *Manchester School*, XXII, 1954.
23. C. P. Kindleberger, *Europe's Post War Growth: The Role of Labour Supply* (1967).
24. Feinstein, in *Cambridge Economic History of Europe* Table 27, pp. 88, 90.
25. *Ibid.*, p. 89.
26. See Chapter 2.
27. M. M. Edwards, *The Growth of the British Cotton Trade, 1780–1815* (Manchester, 1967), pp. 213–14, 257–9, Appendix E, Tables 1–7.
28. L. Weatherill, 'Capital and Credit in the Pottery Industry before 1770', *Business History*, XXIV, 3, 1982.
29. Saville, 'Primitive Accumulation'. Brenner, 'Agrarian Class Structure', and 'The Agrarian Roots'.
30. G. Mingay and others rather stress the role of demographic increase in the countryside in creating a surplus labour force. G. E. Mingay, *Enclosure and the Small Farmer in the Age of the Industrial Revolution* (1968); J. D. Chambers and G. E. Mingay, *The Agricultural Revolution* (1966). For works on rural domestic industries and their implications, see notes to Chapter 3.
31. M. Berg, P. Hudson and M. Sonenscher (eds.), *Manufacture in Town and Country before the Factory* (Cambridge, 1983), the introduction surveys the literature on these issues.
32. Feinstein, in *Cambridge Economic History of Europe*, pp. 88–9.
33. Dobb, *Studies in the Development of Capitalism*, Ch. 5.
34. Saville, 'Primitive Accumulation'.
35. K. Marx, *Capital*, vol. 3 (Lawrence and Wishart edn, 1959), p. 393.
36. Dobb, *Studies in the Development of Capitalism*, Chs. 3 and 5. R. Brenner, 'The Origins of Capitalist Development: A Critique of Neo-Smithian Marxism', *New Left Review*, CIV, 1977.
37. Fox-Genovese and Genovese, *The Fruits of Merchant Capital*.
38. K. Polanyi in particular has emphasised the need to study economies within their own cultural and temporal environments. The 'substantivist' approach highlights the inextricable mix of economic and 'non-economic' relationships. K. Polanyi, *The Great Transformation* (1944), K. Polanyi (ed.), *Trade and Market in the Early Empires* (1957).
39. For a typical example, see F. Crouzet (ed.), *Capital Formation in the Industrial Revolution* (1972), p. 188.
40. K. Marx, *Capital*, vol. 1 (Penguin edn, 1976), *passim*. Sweezy, *The Present as History*.
41. J. Schumpeter, *Theory of Economic Development* (Cambridge, Mass., 1953).
42. F. F. Mendels, 'Proto-Industrialisation: The First Phase of the Industrialisation Process', *J.E.H.*, XXXII, 1, 1972. Kriedte, Medick and Schlumbohm, *Industrialisation*

before Industrialisation. For a survey of the broader range of literature on proto-industry, see Berg, Hudson and Sonenscher, *Manufacture in Town and Country*, Introduction.
43. Kriedte, Medick and Schlumbohm, *Industrialisation before Industrialisation*.
44. F. F. Mendels, 'Seasons and Regions in Agriculture and Industry', in S. Pollard (ed.) *Region und Industrialisierung* (Göttingen, 1980). H. Medick, 'The Proto-Industrial Family Economy: The Structural Function of Household and Family during the Transition from Peasant Society to Industrial Capitalism', *Social History*, I, 3, 1976.
45. Mendels, 'Proto-Industrialisation', p. 246.
46. The best existing survey of capital sources remains Crouzet, *Capital Formation*. There has been little substantial new work in the area since.
47. M. M. Postan, 'Recent Trends in the Accumulation of Capital', *E.H.R.*, VI, 1, 1935, reprinted in Crouzet, *ibid.*
48. H. Heaton, 'Financing the Industrial Revolution', *Bulletin of the Business History Society*, XI, 1, 1937. p. 2.
49. *Ibid.*, p. 2.
50. On machinery values as an indication of prices see inventories and machinery prices listed in P. Hudson *The West Riding Wool Textile Industry: A Catalogue of Business Records* (Edington 1975). On sales of second-hand machinery, see *L.M.*, 1790s–1840s, *passim.*
51. See correspondence in the Boulton & Watt Collection, Birmingham City Library, and Chapter 6 below.
52. These various points with reference to the wool textile industry are substantiated in later chapters.
53. Heaton, 'Financing the Industrial Revolution', p. 4.
54. Crouzet, *Capital Formation*, p. 164.
55. Examples quoted in *ibid.*, p. 169
56. S. D. Chapman, 'Fixed Capital Formation in the British Cotton Industry, 1770–1815', *E.H.R.*, XXIII, 1970, pp. 248–9. S. D. Chapman, 'The Peels in the Early English Cotton Industry', *Business History*, XI, 2, 1969, p. 62. S. D. Chapman, *The Early Factory Masters*, (Newton Abbot, 1967), pp. 19–20, 23–6.
57. Crouzet, *Capital Formation*, pp. 17–174.
58. R. G. Wilson, *Gentlemen Merchants: The Merchant Community in Leeds, 1700–1830* (Manchester, 1971), Chs. 3 and 7.
59. S. Pollard 'Fixed Capital in the Industrial Revolution in Britain', *J.E.H.*, XXIV, 3, 1964, pp. 305–14 (reprinted in Crouzet, *Capital Formation*). For examples of the importance of credit to industrialists, see Crouzet, *Capital Formation*, pp. 191–4.
60. S. D. Chapman, 'Financial Restraints on the Growth of Firms in the Cotton Industry, 1790–1850', *E.H.R.*, XXXII, 1979.
61. Pollard, 'Fixed Capital', p. 313.
62. Crouzet, *Capital Formation*, p. 159.
63. *Ibid.*, p. 178.
64. Chapman, *Early Factory Masters*, p. 65.
65. Crouzet, *Capital Formation*, p. 180.
66. I. Donnachie, 'Sources of Capital and Capitalisation in the Scottish Brewing Industry c. 1750–1830', *E.H.R.*, XXX, 2, 1977.
67. See Mendels, 'Proto-Industrialisation'; and Medick, 'The Proto-Industrial Family Economy'.
68. For detailed analysis see Chapter 4 below.
69. B. L. Anderson, 'The Attorney and the Early Capital Market in Lancashire', in Crouzet, *Capital Formation*, pp. 223–57; B. L. Anderson, 'Provincial Aspects of the Financial Revolution of the 18th Century', *Business History*, XII, 1969; B. A. Holderness, 'Credit in Rural Community, 1660–1800', *Midland History*, III, 1975.
70. L. S. Pressnell, *Country Banking in the Industrial Revolution* (Oxford, 1956). R. Cameron (ed.), *Banking in the Early Stages of Industrialisation: A Study in Comparative Economic History* (New York, 1967). P. Mathias, *The First Industrial Nation: An Economic History of Britain, 1700–1914* (1969), Ch. 5, p. 13.

71. For research on these questions see Chapter 9.
72. Crouzet, *Capital Formation*, p. 188.
73. Heaton, 'Financing the Industrial Revolution', pp. 8–9.
74. E. J. Hamilton, 'Profit Inflation and the Industrial Revolution, 1751–1800', *Quarterly Journal of Economics*, LVI, 2, 1942, pp. 256–73. For an interesting discussion of Hamilton, see Shapiro, *Capital and the Cotton Industry*, pp. 214–15, 221–5.
75. D. S. Landes, *The Unbound Prometheus* (1969), p. 74.
76. For the best criticism of the Hamilton thesis, see P. Deane, *The First Industrial Revolution* (Cambridge, 1965), p. 163. D. Felix, 'Profit Inflation and Industrial Growth: The Historic Record and Contemporary Analogies', *Quarterly Journal of Economics*, LXX, 3, 1956, pp. 441–63.
77. See n. 17, n. 18, and Pollard 'Investment, Consumption and the Industrial Revolution'.
78. Crouzet, *Capital Formation*, p. 195. Crouzet here quotes Arthur John's work on South Wales iron masters, R. P. Beckingsale on Trowbridge textile manufacturers and P. Mathias on brewers of the period.
79. Foster, *Class Struggle, passim*.
80. A. D. Gayer, W. W. Rostow and A. J. Schwartz, *The Growth and Fluctuation of the British Economy, 1790–1850* (Oxford, 1953), *passim*.
81. Feinstein, in *Cambridge Economic History of Europe*, pp. 87–94.
82. T. S. Ashton, *The Industrial Revolution 1760–1830* (1948), pp. 9–11, 58. T. S. Ashton, *Economic Fluctuations in England, 1700–1800* (Oxford, 1959).
83. Shapiro, *Capital and the Cotton Industry*, pp. 61–9.

2   AN INDUSTRY IN TRANSITION: THE WEST RIDING WOOL TEXTILE SECTOR, 1750–1850

1. H. Heaton, *The Yorkshire Woollen and Worsted Industries from Earliest Times up to the Industrial Revolution* (Oxford, 1920; 2nd edn. Oxford, 1965). D. T. Jenkins, *The West Riding Wool Textile Industry 1770–1835: A Study of Fixed Capital Formation* (Edington 1975). Where there are no other notes, much of the general description of the industries in this chapter is derived from these two sources.
2. J. H. Clapham, 'Industrial Organisation in the Woollen and Worsted Industries of Yorkshire', *E.J.* XVI, 1906, pp. 515–22.
3. For a detailed account of the development of the worsted branch see J. James, *History of the Worsted Manufacture in England from the Earliest Times* (1857); and E. M. Sigsworth, *Black Dyke Mills: A History with Introductory Chapters on the Development of the Worsted Industry in the Nineteenth Century* (Liverpool, 1958).
4. Compare, for example, the trade of Joseph Jackson, Wakefield wool stapler, with wool buying by B. & W. Marriner or John Foster from surviving business collections catalogued by P. Hudson, *The West Riding Wool Textile Industry: A Catalogue of Business Records* (Edington, 1975), pp. 142–73, 289–90, 362–86.
5. Several of these points are raised by R. G. Wilson, 'The Supremacy of the Yorkshire Cloth Industry in the Eighteenth Century', in N. B. Harte and K. G. Ponting (eds.), *Textile History and Economic History: Essays in Honour of Miss Julia de Lacy Mann* (Manchester 1973).
6. P.P. 1806 (268) III, pp. 8–9.
7. For interesting detail on these see M. J. Dickenson, 'The West Riding Woollen and Worsted Industries 1689–1770: An Analysis of Probate Inventories and Insurance Policies', unpublished Ph.D. thesis, University of Nottingham, 1974, Chs. 3, 4.
8. J. Lawson, *Letters to the Young on Progress in Pudsey during the Last Sixty Years* (Stanningley 1887), p. 27.
9. Dickenson, 'The West Riding Woollen and Worsted Industries'.
10. Fuller details of Dickenson's analysis of the regional variations in types and sizes of domestic manufacturers are contained in Chapter 3, Tables 3.1–3.3.
11. P.P. 1806 (268) III, *passim*.
12. See E. M. Carus-Wilson, 'An Industrial Revolution of the 13th Century', *E.H.R.*, XI, 1941.

13. Dickenson, 'The West Riding Woollen and Worsted Industries', Ch. 3. See also his 'Fulling in the West Riding Woollen Cloth Industry, 1689–1770', *T.H.*, X, 1979.
14. See Chapter 3 below.
15. West Riding Quarter Sessions Papers (West Yorkshire Archive Service Head Quarters, Wakefield).
16. For detailed list of fulling mills and their output in the period 1805–21, see William Lupton & Company Ltd, Quarterly Broadcloth Accounts, item 113 (B.).
17. See, for example, records of J. & J. Holroyd, Leeds, dyers (L.), and Grace & Jepson, drysalters (L.).
18. Dickenson, 'The West Riding Woollen and Worsted Industries', Ch. 5.
19. *Ibid.*, p. 155.
20. *Ibid.*, Ch. 5.
21. R. G. Wilson, *Gentlemen Merchants: The Merchant Community in Leeds, 1700–1830* (Manchester, 1971), p. 71.
22. See Chapter 6 below and W. B. Crump (ed.) *The Leeds Woollen Industry, 1780–1820*, Thoresby Society (Leeds, 1931).
23. W. B. Crump and G. Ghorbal, *History of the Huddersfield Woollen Industry* (Huddersfield, 1935), p. 69.
24. See Chapter 3.
25. See evidence of Law Atkinson, P.P. 1806 (268) III, p. 220.
26. Most of the fancy cloths were produced in the Huddersfield area and the tendency towards centralisation is described by Crump and Ghorbal, *History of the Huddersfield Woollen Industry*, Chs. 9, 10 and 11.
27. *Leeds Guide* (Leeds, 1806), p. 28.
28. P.P. 1806 (268) III, p. 16. See also evidence of Robert Cookson, pp. 70–6.
29. Heaton, *The Yorkshire Woollen and Worsted Industries*, pp. 300, 388. See also P. Mantoux, *The Industrial Revolution in the Eighteenth Century: An Outline of the Beginnings of the Modern Factory System in England* (1961 edn), p. 271.
30. Wilson, *Gentlemen Merchants*, p. 59 and *passim*.
31. Crump and Ghorbal, *History of the Huddersfield Woollen Industry*, p. 90.
32. P.P. 1806 (268) III, p. 9.
33. *Ibid.*, p. 159.
34. Crump and Ghorbal, *History of the Huddersfield Woollen Industry*.
35. P.P. 1833 (690) VI, p. 118.
36. *Ibid.*, p. 646.
37. P.P. 1840 (43–II) XXIII, pp. 527–63.
38. Letter from W. Aldham Esq. to W. E. Gladstone, quoted in P.P. 1844 (119) VII, p. 366.
39. For details, see Dickenson, 'The West Riding Woollen and Worsted Industries', Ch. 4.
40. See records and references cited in Hudson, *The West Riding Wool Textile Industry*; also E. M. Sigsworth 'William Greenwood and Robert Heaton', *Bradford Textile Society Journal*, 1951–2, pp. 61–72.
41. Analysis of the development of the worsted branch is derived from Heaton, *The Yorkshire Woollen and Worsted Industries*; Dickenson, 'The West Riding Woollen and Worsted Industries'; and James, *History of the Worsted Manufacture*.
42. Sigsworth, *Black Dyke Mills*.
43. See tables and analysis in Chapter 3, derived from Dickenson, 'The West Riding Woollen and Worsted Industries'.
44. W. Cudworth, *Round About Bradford: A Series of Sketches of Forty Two Places Within Six Miles of Bradford* (Bradford 1876), *passim*.
45. Jenkins, *The West Riding Wool Textile Industry*, Ch. 5.
46. D. T. Jenkins, 'The Cotton Industry in Yorkshire', *T.H.*, X, 1979.
47. See more detailed analysis of mill ownership and occupancy in Chapter 3.
48. Crump and Ghorbal, *History of the Huddersfield Woollen Industry*, p. 66.
49. S. D. Chapman, 'The Pioneers of Worsted Spinning by Power', *Business History*, VII, 1, 1965.

50. Jenkins, *The West Riding Wool Textile Industry*, Ch. 5.
51. P.P. 1806 (268) III, *passim*; P.P. 1802–3 (71) V.
52. Jenkins, *The West Riding Wool Textile Industry*, p. 10.
53. *Ibid.*
54. Chapman, 'The Pioneers', pp. 116–17.
55. Sigsworth, *Black Dyke Mills*, Ch. 1 and *passim*.
56. Jenkins, *The West Riding Wool Textile Industry*.
57. Lawson, *Letters to the Young*, p. 93.
58. S. D. Chapman, 'Fixed Capital Formation in the British Cotton Industry, 1770–1815', *E.H.R.*, XXIII, 1970, p. 239.
59. P.P. 1833 (690) VI, p. 163.
60. *Ibid.*, pp. 117–18, 549.
61. Factory Returns, P.P. 1839 (41) (135) XLII, 1850 (745) XLII.
62. Lawson, *Letters to the Young*, p. 118.
63. These changes are analysed in detail in Part 3, in which a large number of businesss records are used.
64. These points are the subject of attention in Topham's analysis which concentrates on the later nineteenth century: A. J. Topham, 'The Credit Structure of the West Riding Wool Textile Industry in the 19th Century', unpublished M. Phil. thesis, University of Leeds, 1953.
65. By 1836, fifteen joint stock banks had been established in the West Riding, and the Leeds branch of the Bank of England was opened in 1827.
66. F. J. Glover, 'Dewsbury Mills: A History of Messrs. Wormalds and Walker Ltd.', unpublished Ph.D. thesis, University of Leeds, 1959, Ch. 5. Sigsworth, *Black Dyke Mills*. Foster, items 10–17 (B.).
67. J. Maitland, *An Account of the Proceedings of the Merchants and Manufacturers, and Others Concerned in the Wool and Woollen Trade of Great Britain* (1800), pp. 100, 109.
68. Dickenson, 'The West Riding Woollen and Worsted Industries', Appendices and Chs. 3, 4.
69. Foster, items 15–17 (B.).

PART 2 THE PRIMARY ACCUMULATION OF CAPITAL
INTRODUCTION

1. K. Marx, *Capital*, vol. 1 (Penguin edn, 1976), Part 8.
2. D. S. Landes, *The Unbound Prometheus* (1969).
3. A. Gerschenkron, *Economic Backwardness in Historical Perspective* (1962).

3 PROTO-INDUSTRIALISATION

1. The seminal works in the evolution of this model are F. F. Mendels: 'Industrialisation and Population Pressure in 18th Century Flanders', unpublished Ph.D. thesis, University of Wisconsin, 1969, 'Proto-Industrialisation: The First Phase of the Industrialisation Process', *J.E.H.*, XXXII, 1, 1972, 'Recent Research in European Historical Demography', *American Historical Review*, LXXV, 1970. H. Medick, 'The Proto-Industrial Family Economy: The Structural Function of Household and Family during the Transition from Peasant Society to Industrial Capitalism', *Social History*, I, 3, 1976. P. Kriedte, H. Medick and J. Schlumbohm, *Industrialisation before Industrialisation* (Cambridge 1982). It must be emphasised here that these works are informed by a body of writing on rural industry which has a much earlier history. Furthermore, the above-cited authors vary a great deal in their ideas concerning the phase of proto-industry particularly regarding its systemic qualities and its political and cultural corollaries.
2. Kriedte, Medick and Schlumbohm, *Industrialisation before Industrialisation*.
3. In this connection, the work of Herbert Kisch has been given renewed prominence. See Herbert Kisch, 'The Textile Industries of Silesia and the Rhineland: A Comparative Study of Industrialisation', *J.E.H.*, XIX, 1959, and 'The Growth Deterrents of a

Medieval Heritage: The Aachen Area Woollen Trades before 1870', *J.E.H.*, XXIV, 1964. Mendels pays much less attention to exogenous variables.

4. F. F. Mendels, 'Agriculture and Peasant Industry in 18th Century Flanders', in W. N. Parker and E. L. Jones (eds.). *European Peasants and Their Markets* (Princeton, 1975), 'Seasons and Regions in Agriculture and Industry', in S. Pollard (ed.), *Region und Industrialisierung* (Göttingen, 1980). E. L. Jones, 'The Agricultural Origins of Industry', *Past and Present*, XL, 1968.

5. Mendels, 'Seasons and Regions'. For a full discussion of the role of 'Z goods' (craft goods) in the economic development of peasant societies see S. Hymer and S. Resnick, 'A Model of an Agrarian Economy with Non-Agricultural Activities', *American Economic Review*, LIX, 1969; and Jan de Vries, 'Labour/Leisure Trade Off', *Peasant Studies*, I, 1972. The proto-industrialisation theorists generally ignore the fact that rural industry and commercial agriculture could co-exist in the same region.

6. It is interesting to note that Mendels contrasts the seasonality of labour requirements of mixed/arable temperate agriculture with the Mediterranean crop regimes, such as viticulture, which require a more constant labour input throughout the year. He attributes the very limited growth of proto-industry in Southern Europe to these differences in the structure of peasant agriculture. Mendels, 'Seasons and Regions'.

7. The current debate is informed by numerous earlier attempts to conceptualise 'cottage industry' systematically as an historical category. The work of several German historians and philosophers of the late nineteenth century has been particularly influential: Werner Sombart, 'Die Hausindustrie in Deutschland', *Archiv für soziale Gesetzgebung und Statistik*, IV, 1891, pp. 103–56; also works of W. Roscher, A. Schäffle and G. Schmoller reviewed in Kriedte, Medick and Schlumbohm, *Industrialisation before Industrialisation*, Introduction.

8. For recent critiques of the ascription to rural industry of these and other dynamics see M. Berg, P. Hudson and M. Sonenscher (eds.), *Manufacture in Town and Country before the Factory* (Cambridge 1983), Introduction. R. Houston and K. Snell 'Proto-Industrialisation? Cottage Industry, Social Change and Industrial Revolution', *Historical Journal*, XXVII, 2, 1984. *Proceedings of the Eighth International Conference of Economic History, Budapest 1982, A2: Protoindustrialisation* (1982). D. C. Coleman, 'Protoindustrialisation: A Concept Too Many?', *E.H.R.*, XXXVI, 3, 1983.

9. In the Yorkshire worsted industry the problems of embezzlement were met by united action on the part of employers in forming the Worsted Committee in 1775 to prevent and prosecute frauds and embezzlement in England; see J. Styles, 'Embezzlement, Industry and the Law in England, 1500–1800', in Berg, Hudson and Sonenscher, *Manufacture in Town and Country*.

10. This behaviour of the peasant economy was first analysed by A. V. Chayanov. See his *The Theory of Peasant Economy*, ed. D. Thorner, B. Kerblay and R. E. D. Smith (Homewood, Illinois, 1966). See also comments by Medick, 'The Proto-Industrial Family Economy', p. 299.

11. The classic example here is perhaps that of the Midlands metalware trades composed of both centralised and dispersed forms of industry and trading mass-produced goods in large quantities to the American market by the mid-eighteenth century.

12. Kriedte, Medick and Schlumbohm, *Industrialisation before Industrialisation*, Ch. 4. P. Hudson, 'From Manor to Mill: The West Riding in Transition', in Berg, Hudson and Sonenscher, *Manufacture in Town and Country*, p. 125.

13. There are many examples of this. J. Schlumbohm points to some of the north European cases: Kriedte, Medick and Schlumbohm, *Industrialisation before Industrialisation*, Ch. 4. Worsted production in the West Riding was organised in this way as early as the late seventeenth century in some areas.

14. R. G. Wilson, 'The Supremacy of the Yorkshire Cloth Industry in the Eighteenth Century', in N. B. Harte and K. G. Ponting (eds.), *Textile History and Economic History: Essays in Honour of Miss Julia de Lacy Mann* (Manchester, 1973).

15. J. de L. Mann, *The Cloth Industry in the West of England from 1640 to 1880* (Oxford, 1871), p. 116.

16. Wilson, in Harte and Ponting, *Textile History*, p. 232.
17. As, for example, in the Leeds and Wakefield areas.
18. Seven were consulted in all: A. Young, *A Six Months Tour through the North of England*, vol. 1 (1771); W. Marshall, *Rural Economy of Yorkshire* (1788); Messrs Rennie, Brown and Shirreff, *A General View of the Agriculture of the West Riding of Yorkshire* (1794); Robert Brown, *General View of the Agriculture of the West Riding* (1799); J. Hausman, *A Topographical Description of Cumberland, Westmorland, Lancashire and a Part of the West Riding of Yorkshire* (1800); John Bigland, *A Topographical and Historical Description of the County of York*, 5 vols. (1812); G. A. Cooke, *Topographical and Statistical Description of the County of York* (1818).
19. Rennie, Brown and Shirreff, *A General View*, p. 13.
20. Bigland, *A Topographical and Historical Description*, p. 604.
21. Rennie, Brown and Shirreff, *A General View*, p. 14.
22. Bigland, *A Topographical and Historical Description*, p. 604.
23. Some idea of the importance of using land in this way is gained from a survey of deed transactions in the West Riding Registry of Deeds, Wakefield, established in 1704 specifically to ease the raising of money by manufacturers through the mortgage of their land. Many surviving business records also contain evidence of substantial mortgaging: see P. Hudson, *The West Riding Wool Textile Industry: A Catalogue of Business Records* (Edington, 1975), *passim*.
24. Bigland, *A Topographical and Historical Description*, p. 601.
25. *Ibid.*, p. 601.
26. Rennie, Brown and Shirreff, *A General View*.
27. D. Defoe, *A Tour Through the Whole Island of Great Britain*, vol. 3 (1724), p. 135, quoted by H. Heaton, *The Yorkshire Woollen and Worsted Industries from Earliest Times up to the Industrial Revolution* (Oxford, 1920; 2nd edn Oxford, 1965), p. 290.
28. M. J. Ellis, 'A Study of the Manorial History of Halifax Parish in the 16th and Early 17th Centuries', *Yorkshire Archaeological Journal*, XL, 1962, pp. 250–420.
29. 2 & 3 Philip and Mary, c. 13, quoted in Heaton, *The Yorkshire Woollen and Worsted Industries*, p. 94.
30. J. Thirsk (ed.), *The Agrarian History of England and Wales*, vol. 4, 1500–1640 (Cambridge, 1967), p. 9.
31. Heaton, *The Yorkshire Woollen and Worsted Industries*, p. 95–6.
32. Crop rotations and land usages in different areas of the Riding are admirably described in Brown, *General View*, pp. 89–94.
33. Rennie, Brown and Shirreff, *A General View*, p. 25.
34. *Ibid.*, p. 11.
35. *Ibid.*
36. For a fuller examination of the manorial history of the region, see Hudson, 'From Manor to Mill', in Berg, Hudson and Sonenscher, *Manufacture in Town and Country*, and 'The Environment and Dynamic of Proto-Industry: Some Considerations', in *Proceedings of the Eighth International Conference of Economic History*.
37. A. Betteridge, 'A Study of Halifax Administrative Records 1585–1762', unpublished Ph.D. thesis, University of Leeds, 1979.
38. *Ibid.*, p. 66.
39. Copyhold land remained common in the Manor of Wakefield (outside of the sub-manor of Halifax) until 1922. Rating valuations for this area suggest a more equitable distribution of land among the population.
40. See Table 3.4.
41. D. F. E. Sykes, *The History of Huddersfield and the Valleys of the Colne, the Holme and the Dearne* (Huddersfield, 1898); E. Baines, *History, Directory and Gazetteer of the County of York*, vol. 1 (Leeds, 1822).
42. Sykes, *Huddersfield*, p. 43.
43. Quote from The Lord Chancellor in a court case, 1866, cited by Sykes, *ibid.*, p. 43.
44. Described by Isaac Horden, Ramsden's estate agent, 1846, in 'Notes Relating to the Ramsden Estate and Huddersfield', manuscript notebook (Leeds City Reference Library).

45. C. Stephenson, *The Ramsdens and Their Estate in Huddersfield* (Almondbury, 1982).
46. S. H. Waters, *Wakefield in the Seventeenth Century: A Social History of the Town and Neighbourhood, 1550–1710* (Wakefield, 1933), Ch. 1.
47. See J. Goodchild, 'The Tammy Hall at Wakefield', *Bulletin of the Wakefield Historical Society*, 1974, pp. 24–30.
48. H. Clarkson, *Memories of Merrie Wakefield* (Wakefield, 1877), p. 44.
49. *Wakefield Journal*, 4 January 1850.
50. J. Aiken, *A Description of the Country from Thirty to Forty Miles around Manchester* (1795), p. 560.
51. See Hudson, *The West Riding Wool Textile Industry, passim.*
52. For the different technologies of woollen and worsted production, and particularly the adaptability of worsted production to mechanisation, see E. M. Sigsworth, *Black Dyke Mills: A History with Introductory Chapters on the Development of the Worsted Industry in the Nineteenth Century* (Liverpool, 1958), Introduction; and S. D. Chapman, 'The Pioneers of Worsted Spinning by Power', *Business History*, VII, 1, 1965, pp. 97–116.
53. J. H. Clapham, *An Economic History of Modern England*, vol. 2 (1932), p. 83.
54. For a convincing argument regarding this see S. Marglin, 'What Do Bosses Do?', in A. Gorz (ed.), *The Division of Labour* (1976).
55. P.P. 1840 (203) X, Qu. 2911. See P.P. 1841 (311) X, for many examples of this.
56. Figures are averages derived from surviving business records and the records of landed estates which rented out mills. Hudson, *The West Riding Wool Textile Industry*, esp. p. 342. D.E.T. and Savile Estate Papers (Hu.).
57. W.R.R.D. and Wakefield Manor Court Rolls (Y.A.S.) provide evidence of the mortgaging of freehold and copyhold land, respectively. See Chapter 4.
58. P.P. 1844 (119) VII, p. 366.
59. Leeds branch, Letters 1832, no. 246 (Bank of England).
60. Evidence of Law Atkinson, clothier and merchant of Bradley Mills near Huddersfield: P.P. 1802–3 (71) V, p. 380.
61. Diary of Thomas Cook, Dewsbury Mills, 14 February 1820, quoted by F. J. Glover in 'Dewsbury Mills: A History of Messrs. Wormalds and Walker Ltd.', unpublished Ph.D. thesis, University of Leeds, 1959.
62. P.P. 1833 (690) VI, *passim*, esp. Qu, 2317 (evidence of John Brooke). Leeds branch, Letter Books 1 and 2, esp. letters of 6 October 1841 and 21 August 1844 (Bank of England).
63. P.P. 1833 (690) VI, Qu. 1096 (evidence of Henry Hughes).
64. J. Lawson, *Letters to the Young on Progress in Pudsey during the Last Sixty Years* (Stanningley, 1887), p. 119.
65. Heaton, *The Yorkshire Woollen and Worsted Industries*, pp. 418–21.
66. The Worsted Committee had powerful rights of search and could call on heavy legal penalties, more so than any similar employer's organisation before the late 1840s: H.O. 45, 1925 (P.R.O.).
67. J. Hodgson, *Textile Manufacture and Other Industries in Keighley* (Keighley, 1879), *passim.* See also D. T. Jenkins, 'The Cotton Industry in Yorkshire', *T.H.*, X, 1979.
68. This point is stressed by K. V. Pankhurst, 'Investment in the West Riding Wool Textile Industry in the Nineteenth Century', *Y.B.E.S.R.*, VII, 1955, pp. 93–116.
69. Hudson, *The West Riding Wool Textile Industry*, pp. 9, 92, 142, 362, *et seq.*
70. Hodgson, *Textile Manufacture*. W. Cudworth, *Round About Bradford: A Series of Sketches of Forty Two Places Within Six Miles of Bradford* (Bradford, 1876), *passim.*
71. This impression is gained from descriptions of factory entrepreneurs given in insurance records: I am grateful to Dr D. T. Jenkins, University of York, for allowing me to use his working papers on the Royal Exchange and Sun policies (Guildhall Library). Local directories were also used to form a Card Index for mills and their ownership/occupancy details.
72. Insurance valuations, *ibid.*, Card Index. The statistical information which forms the basis of analysis of mill finance in both branches of industry in the preceding pages is derived from details of all mills traced before 1850. The information is much

more complete to 1835 as it includes the research on insurance policies undertaken by Jenkins. It may be that undue emphasis on the pre-1835 mills does not give a fully accurate picture of different types of mill building and occupancy to the mid-century. Mill size and cost were increasing in both branches of the trade in the 1840s, but there is no evidence to suggest that this was sufficient radically to change the nature of factory ownership. A further problem is that, although the index contains details of more than 850 mills, it is only possible to trace the background and occupations of mill builders, or purchasers, and occupiers for about 25% of concerns.

73. Letters from John Nussey, woollen manufacturer of Bristol, 9 August 1843, quoted in P.P. 1844 (119) VII, 366.
74. P.P. 1844 (119) VII. Hudson, *The West Riding Wool Textile Industry*, pp. 203–4, 271–80, 313–18, 360, 403–6, 452, 466, 523. J. Goodchild, 'The Ossett Mill Company', *T.H.*, I, 1, 1968; and Hudson, 'From Manor to Mill', in Berg, Hudson and Sonenscher, *Manufacture in Town and Country*. Insurance records also bear witness to the proliferation of company mills. I am grateful to Dr D. T. Jenkins for the loan of his notes on the Sun and Royal Exchange policies.
75. Leatham & Company Mss, Colvard drafts, in Ossett Mill Papers, quoted by Goodchild, 'The Ossett Mill Company', pp. 47–8.
76. Goodchild, 'The Ossett Mill Company', pp. 46–7.
77. Ossett Mill Company, item 1 (J.G. MSS), Ossett Township Valuation 1801 (J.G. MSS).
78. Ossett Mill Company (J.G. MSS), item 3. The lease refers to Healey Mill.
79. The 1844 House of Lords Papers quote the example of an unnamed mill established in 1825 which stipulated that partners must reside within one and a half miles: P.P. 1844 (119) VII, 366.
80. *Ibid.*: 'It is understood that partners send all their work to their own mill.' See also Rawden Low Mill Company, Committee Minute Book 1843–5 (Ha.).
81. Factory Inspector's letter, 1843, quoted by E. Lipson, *History of the Woollen and Worsted Industries* (1921), pp. 177–9.
82. *Ibid.*
83. P.P. 1844 (119) VII, p. 366.
84. Goodchild, 'The Ossett Mill Company', p. 50.
85. Kellett, Brown & Company Ltd, item 1 (B.).
86. See Chapter 9.
87. Bradford Banking Company, Order Book 1834–8 (B4) (Midland).
88. Kellett, Brown & Company, item 1 (B.).
89. *Ibid.*, item 1 and contemporary directories.
90. For example, Hannah Whitely a local widow loaned £500 at 4%, Gill Royd Mill Company, Minute Book 1835–61, in John Hartley & Sons Ltd, item 3 (L.).
91. *Ibid.*, 27 April 1838.
92. *Ibid.*, 9 May 1836, 30 January 1837. (£4,000 requested from Beckett Blayd & Company, Leeds bankers.)
93. Rawden Low Mill Company, Committee Minute Book 1843–51, Articles of Partnership 1847, Share Book 1860s (Ha.).
94. For a further good example of the raising of finance in this way by a company mill, see records of Ossett Mill Company (J.G. MSS).
95. For example in 1847 Rawden Low Mill insisted that partners were not to employ other mills and in April 1847 Samuel Gray was only allowed shares if he could provide £5 of custom per share yearly: Articles of Partnership 10 April 1847, Minute Book 1843–51 (Ha.).
96. Although complaints of delays and monopoly pricing seem to have declined by the 1820s, it is possible that company mills, favouring their own shareholders, worked partly to the disadvantage of those clothiers excluded from participation in them.
97. Rawden Low Mill Company, Committee Minute Book 30 December 1844 (Ha.).
98. See Chapter 6 and Hudson, 'From Manor to Mill', in Berg, Hudson and Sonenscher, *Manufacture in Town and Country*, pp. 136–7.
99. Letter from Mr Baker, Factory Inspector, 1843, quoted in P.P. 1844 (119) VII, 366.

100. Pankhurst, 'Investment in the West Riding Wool Textile Industry', p. 95.
101. See especially P.P. 1806 (268) III, *passim*.
102. P.P. 1828 (515) VIII, p. 258.
103. For the period before 1830, see E. P. Thompson *The Making of the English Working Class* (1963): Yorkshire references.

4   LAND AND INDUSTRY

1. It seems that in this respect the West Riding was very similar to South Lancashire: see B. L. Anderson, 'The Attorney and the Early Capital Market in Lancashire', in J. R. Harris (ed.), *Liverpool and Merseyside: Essays in the Economic and Social History of the Port and Its Hinterland* (1969).
2. P. Hudson, *The West Riding Wool Textile Industry: A Catalogue of Business Records* (Edington, 1975), index, p. 556.
3. H. Heaton, *The Yorkshire Woollen and Worsted Industries from Earliest Times up to the Industrial Revolution* (Oxford, 1920; 2nd edn Oxford, 1965), pp. 290–1.
4. Messrs Rennie, Brown and Shirreff writing in 1794 stated that much of the land of the West Riding was let without lease at all, occupiers being removable at six months warning. Rennie, Brown and Shirreff, *A General View of the Agriculture of the West Riding of Yorkshire (1794)*, p. 12. See also G. A. Cooke, *Topographical and Statistical Description of the County of York* (1818), on leases and tenures.
5. P.P. 1806 (268) III, pp. 444–5, Heaton, *The Yorkshire Woollen and Worsted Industries*, pp. 291–2.
6. 'An Act for confirming certain Leases granted by Sir James Graham', 1835, quoted in M. F. Ward, 'Industrial Development and Location in Leeds North of the River Aire 1775–1914', unpublished Ph.D. thesis, University of Leeds, 1972, p. 158. Title Deeds of Estates in Kirkstall and Schedule of Tenants, 1849 (L.).
7. P.P. 1806 (268) III, pp. 444–7.
8. The geographical spread of the rate valuations used here is not very wide but it does include contrasting areas of production.
9. See those references mentioned frequently in Chapter 3.
10. Several contemporary sources stress this, see, e.g., Cooke, *Topographical and Statistical Description of Yorkshire*, p. 63.
11. Savile Estate Papers, National Register of Archives List, document 79 (Hu.).
12. *Ibid.*, Valuation Books: Elland and Southowram (1839), Emley and Skelmanthorpe (1840), Golcar, Stainland, Barkisland and Ovenden (1839), Rishworth (1839), and Thornhill (1840).
13. The D.E.T. are housed in the Dartmouth Estate Office, Slaithwaite.
14. D.E.T., Slaithwaite Book, 1828.
15. D.E.T., Register, Survey and Rental of the Earl of Dartmouth's Estate in the West Riding of the County of York (1805), pp. 81–2.
16. See the case of Waterside Mill described in *ibid.*, p. 45.
17. D.E.T., Morley Book.
18. D.E.T., Register, Survey (1805), p. 45.
19. D.E.T., Memos of Changes in Leases, etc., 1840–50.
20. *Ibid.*
21. All information in this paragraph is from D.E.T., Register, Survey (1805).
22. These details rely heavily on information from insurance valuations collected by Dr D. T. Jenkins, University of York. These together with rate valuations, title deeds and factory returns form the basis for information on mill ownership which is gathered on a Card Index possessed by the author.
23. See Chapter 9.
24. Papers of John Howarth, Halifax attorney (Ha.). For a fuller analysis of his activities see Chapter 9.
25. There are several other collections of attorneys' papers which have survived for the West Riding, e.g. those of Robert Parker (Ha.) and John Eagle of Bradford (Brad-

ford District Archives). These are the subject of M. Miles, 'Eminent Attorneys: Some Aspects of West Riding Attorneyship, *c.* 1750–1800', unpublished Ph.D. thesis, University of Birmingham, 1983.
26. See John Howarth, Cash Books 1780s, 1790, and Day Book 1781–3 (Ha.).
27. *Ibid.*
28. See, for example, *ibid.*, Day Book 22 February 1780–1, July 1783, 30 May 1780.
29. Gott's bonds and promissory notes, item 1 (J.G. MSS).
30. R. V. Marriner Ltd., Box 26 (B.).
31. Benjamin Hallas collection (J.G. MSS). See also J. Goodchild, 'Pildacre Mill: An Early West Riding Factory', *T.H.*, I, 3, 1969, p. 341.
32. Information derived from mortgage deeds listed in Hudson, *The West Riding Wool Textile Industry*, and indicated in the index, p. 556.
33. Quoted in W. E. Tate, 'The Five English District Statutory Registries of Deeds', *Bulletin of the Institute of Historical Research*, XX, 1943–5, p. 98.
34. Andrew Yarranton, *England's Improvement by Sea and Land: To Out-Do the Dutch without Fighting etc.* (1677), pp. 7–12.
35. For details of the early history of this and the other registries, see Tate, 'The Five English District Statutory Registries of Deeds'; and F. Sheppard and V. Belcher, 'The Deeds Registries of Yorkshire and Middlesex', in *Journal of the Society of Archivists*, VI, 5, 1980.
36. Ossett-cum-Gawthorpe Enclosure Award, 1813 (J.G. MSS).
37. Ossett Rate Valuation, 1819 (J.G. MSS).
38. See F. Sheppard, V. Belcher and P. Cotterell 'The Middlesex and Yorkshire Deeds, Registries and Study of Building Fluctuations', *London Journal*, V, 2, 1979, pp. 176–217.
39. *The Poll of the Knights of the Shire, 1807* (York, 1807).
40. W.R.R.D., Vol., GA, 580, 696, 1814.
41. *Ibid.*, Vol., E2, 499, 746, 1807.
42. *Ibid.*, Vol., ES, 285, 391, 1804; FK, 331, 414, 1810; Vol., GC, 469, 556, 1815; ER, 375, 509, 1804; Vol., GC, 587, 693, 1815.
43. Goodchild, 'Pildacre Mill', p. 451.
44. W.R.R.D., Vol., GM, 301, 293, 1817.
45. Ossett Rate Valuation, 1819 (J.G. MSS).
46. W.R.R.D., Vol., GD, 564, 643, 1815. The purchasers were Thomas Burdett of Emley, Joseph Gaunt of Penistone and Isaac Armitage of High Hoyland.
47. *Ibid.*, Vol., GM., 301, 293, 1817.
48. See D. T. Jenkins, 'The West Riding Wool Textile Industry, 1770–1835: A Study of Fixed Capital Formation', unpublished D.Phil, thesis, University of York, 1970, Appendix: mill number 18 (published under the same title, without the Appendix).
49. W.R.R.D., Vol., GM, 300, 292, 1817.
50. Jenkins, 'The West Riding Wool Textile Industry', Appendix: mill number 18.
51. D.E.T., Register, Survey (1805), p. 80.
52. W.R.R.D., Vol., FI, 26, 29, 1811.
53. M. M. Postan, 'Recent Trends in the Accumulation of Capital', *E.H.R.*, VI, 1, 1935, p. 3, reprinted in F. Crouzet (ed.), *Capital Formation in the Industrial Revolution* (1972).

PART 3   THE WEB OF CREDIT

INTRODUCTION

1. J. Maitland, *An Account of the Proceedings of the Merchants and Manufacturers, and Others Concerned in the Wool and Woollen Trade of Great Britain* (1800), p. 34.
2. All wool textile business records covering the period 1780–1850 are surveyed in P. Hudson, *The West Riding Wool Textile Industry: A Catalogue of Business Records* (Edington, 1975).
3. Trade ledgers listed in *ibid.*

5.WOOL PURCHASE

1. Estimates of Forbes (1851) and James (1857), see E. Baines, *Account of the Woollen Manufacture of England* (1858; repr. 1970), pp. 139–40.
2. See Table 5.1, and F. J. Glover, 'Dewsbury Mills: A History of Messrs. Wormalds and Walker Ltd.', unpublished Ph.D. thesis, University of Leeds, 1959, Ch. 1, section (a).
3. For a much fuller account of the history of the English wool supply than is possible here, see J. Bischoff, *A Comprehensive History of the Woollen and Worsted Manufacture*, 2 vols. (1842, repr. 1968), *passim*; and H. Heaton, *The Yorkshire Woollen and Worsted Industries from Earliest Times up to the Industrial Revolution* (Oxford, 1920; 2nd edn. Oxford, 1965), Ch. 10. On the changing quality of English fleeces in the eighteenth century, see J. de L. Mann, *The Cloth Industry in the West of England from 1640 to 1880* (Oxford, 1871), p. 255; J. Maitland, *An Account of the Proceedings of the Merchants and Manufacturers, and Others Concerned in the Wool and Woollen Trade of Great Britain* (1800), *passim*; and retrospective remarks in P.P. 1828 (515) VIII.
4. P.P. 1828 (515) VIII, evidence of John Brooke, pp. 218–27, Thos. Cooke, p. 209, Benjamin Gott, pp. 279–92, and *passim*. See also the official tables of imports (though unreliable in their precision) reproduced in Bischoff, *A Comprehensive History*, vol. 2, appendix, and elsewhere.
5. For the classic account of the development of the Australian wool trade see A. Barnard, *The Australian Wool Market 1840–1900* (Melbourne, 1958).
6. S. Jubb, *The History of the Shoddy Trade: Its Rise, Progress and Present Position* (Batley, 1860).
7. There are no comprehensive series for wool prices in the West Riding. Business records indicate similar trends to those experienced nationally but often show slightly lower prices probably indicating the extent to which Yorkshire utilised lower sorts of wool. See e.g., John & William Emmett, Letter Books 1785–1816 (L.). See also Heaton, *The Yorkshire Woollen and Worsted Industries*, p. 325.
8. Bischoff, *A Comprehensive History*, vol. 2, Appendix Table VI.
9. Maitland, *An Account of the Proceedings*, p. 84.
10. *Ibid.*, pp. 120, 131.
11. *Ibid.*, p. 120.
12. For a full discussion of imported wool and tariff changes see Barnard, *The Australian Wool Market*, pp. 218ff; Baines, *History of the Woollen Manufacture*, pp. 78–9; Bischoff, *A Comprehensive History*, vol. 2, Appendix.
13. See H. Heaton (ed.), *The Letter Books of Joseph Holroyd and Sam Hill* (Halifax, 1914), Introduction; F. Atkinson (ed.) *Some Aspects of the Eighteenth Century Woollen and Worsted Trade in Halifax* (Halifax, 1956); Samuel Hill, Letter Book 1737 (Ha.); John Sutcliffe, Day Book 1791–3 (Ha.).
14. Atkinson, *Some Aspects*.
15. Maitland, *An Account of the Proceedings*, p. 98.
16. See R. V. Marriner Ltd, Correspondence, *passim* (B.); Robert Clough, Keighley Ltd, item 134 (1840s) (B.); Thomas Marriott & Son, item 9 (1850s) (J.G. MSS).
17. Retrospective comments in P.P. 1828 (515) VIII, evidence of Charles Bull, wool stapler, p. 171, and John Jowitt, wool stapler, p. 135.
18. Heaton, *The Yorkshire Woollen and Worsted Industries*, p. 330; Robert Jowitt & Sons Ltd, Ledgers 1775–1840s (B.).
19. Business monographs such as those of E. M. Sigsworth, *Black Dyke Mills: A History with Introductory Chapters on the Development of the Worsted Industry in the Nineteenth Century* (Liverpool, 1958) and Glover, 'Dewsbury Mills', can be misleading on this as they are concerned with large firms (who bought much wool direct) rather than with those firms more typical of the industry as a whole.
20. P.P. 1828 (515) VIII, evidence of John Lucas Calcraft, Lincoln, p. 29.
21. Maitland, *An Account of the Proceedings*, p. 109.
22. Atkinson, *Some Aspects*, Appendix. Jowitt, item 47 (B.). The Yorkshire trade used the bottom five sorts largely.
23. John Dauber, Brigg, to Joseph Jackson 1 July 1815 (J.G. MSS).

24. Richard Fisher, Newark, to Jackson 22 June 1815 (J.G. MSS).
25. J. Hodgson, *Textile Manufacture and Other Industries in Keighley* (Keighley, 1879), *passim*; Marriner, Correspondence 1820s (B.).
26. E.G. Titus Salt and Thos. Cook imported wool direct from Odessa in 1830s, the latter dealt with importers in London and Hull, Glover, 'Dewsbury Mills', p. 744.
27. See the example of Reuben Gaunt of Farsley below, n. 62.
28. Enquiries made of Record Offices in the wool counties yielded surprisingly little of value.
29. See, e.g., Emmet, Letter Books (L.); and Jowitt, items 1–5 (B.).
30. Joseph Jackson of Wakefield and Jowitt's of Leeds and Bradford sold wool on commission in this way in the early nineteenth century. Jackson, Correspondence (J.G. MSS); Jowitt, Ledgers (B.). See also Heaton, *The Yorkshire Woollen and Worsted Industries*, p. 329.
31. Jackson, Correspondence 1809–24, *passim* (J.G. MSS).
32. Richard Fisher of Newark (commission agent) to Jackson 22 June and 11 October 1815 (J.G. MSS). Jackson's incoming correspondence is replete with reference to the cash purchase of wool from the growers.
33. James Liptaft to Jackson 7 April 1821 (J.G. MSS).
34. P.P. 1828 (515) VIII, evidence of James Fison, pp. 196–7.
35. Jowitt's of Bradford and Leeds 1770s–1840s (B.); David Spencer, Keighley, 1790–1816 (Marriner, B.); and Joseph Jackson of Wakefield 1809–24 (J.G. MSS).
36. David Spencer, Account Books 1798–1816 (Marriner, B.).
37. Jowitt, Ledgers 1775–1815, items 1–3 (B.).
38. See Jackson, Correspondence, *passim*, especially James Lupton to Jackson 30 November 1811 (J.G. MSS).
39. R. Hanson to Jackson 22 February 1815 (J.G. MSS). See also R. Hanson to Jackson 16 March 1815 re. purchase of marsh wool for cash.
40. Robert Cropper, Lacely Hill, Lincs., to Jackson 24 July 1821 (J.G. MSS).
41. See, e.g., J. Watmuff, Bourne, to Jackson 6 February and 11 August 1809, Geo. Barkin, Kirton, to Jackson 19 March 1815, Wm Hall, Lincoln, to Jackson 11 September 1815 (J.G. MSS).
42. P.P. 1828 (515) VII, p. 135.
43. *Ibid.*, pp. 166–73.
44. Jowitt, Ledgers 1802–15 and 1817–40 (B.).
45. Jowitt, Letter Book A 1802–5 and Ledgers 1790–1830s (B.).
46. Benjamin Hallas, Account Book 1789–1819 (J.G. MSS).
47. William Haigh, Papers 1826–32 DD96/16 (Y.A.S.).
48. Emmet, Letter Books, *passim* (L.).
49. Jowitt to Geo. Overitt, Letter Book A, 7 and 16 July 1802 (B.).
50. Jowitt, Letter Book A 1802–5, *passim*, and Ledger 1802–15, item 3 (B.).
51. Jackson, Letters May-June 1810 and July 1815 (J.G. MSS).
52. Richard Hanson to Jackson July and September 1815 (J.G. MSS).
53. Glover, 'Dewsbury Mills', Ch. 1, section (a).
54. See estimates, Table 5.2.
55. Jowitt, Ledgers 1802–34, items 3 and 4, *passim* (B.).
56. Jowitt, Ledger 1802–15, item 2 (B.).
57. Thos. Roberts, Leeds agent for Maitlands Sherry & Nettleship of London, to Wm Clay, J. T. Clay & Sons Ltd, item 1 (Ha.). Glover, 'Dewsbury Mills', chs. 1 and 10.
58. William Willans & Company Ltd, Book of Invoices and Correspondence 1825–31, item 4 (B.).
59. *Ibid.*
60. Jowitt, item 13, Ledger 1830–48 and item 58 (B.).
61. For the best account of these developments see Barnard, *The Australian Wool Market*.
62. For an interesting account of these auction visits by a small manufacturer see Reuben Gaunt, Diary 1841–54 (L.).
63. See Chapter 10, *passim*; and Barnard, *The Australian Wool Market*, p. 101.

64. Barnard, *The Australian Wool Market*, p. 132.
65. Jowitt, 'L Ledger B' 1830–48, item 13 (B.), shows that Jowitt's were importing consignments worth over £1,000 at their own risk but this was unusual.
66. For a more detailed account of the Australian side of the wool trade see Barnard, *The Australian Wool Market*, pp. 92–103.
67. For information on Liverpool banks acting in this manner, see M. Collins and P. Hudson, 'Provincial Bank Lending: Yorkshire and Merseyside, 1826–1860', *B.E.R.*, XXXI, 2, 1979.
68. *Ibid.*, and Chapter 9.
69. Jowitt, Ledgers, items 4 and 12 (B.); Haigh, Papers 1826–32, DD96/16 (Y.A.S.).
70. R. Campbell, *London Tradesman* (1757), p. 199 and 340, quoted by Heaton, *The Yorkshire Woollen and Worsted Industries*, p. 330. D. Defoe, *Complete Tradesmen*, vol. 2 (1737?; 1841 edn.), pp. 188–9.
71. Campbell, *London Tradesman*, p. 199.
72. Jowitt Jnr, Ledger 1775–1815, item 1 (B.). Comments in the following two paragraphs are based on this source.
73. Jowitt, Ledger 1791–1802, item 2 (B.).
74. John & William Emmet to Sumner 17 March 1797 (L.).
75. *Ibid.*, 4 November 1799.
76. *Ibid.*, 25 October 1803.
77. *Ibid.*, 2 December 1803.
78. *Ibid.*, 6 April 1806.
79. Jowitt, Ledger B 1812–34, item 4 (B.).
80. *Ibid.*, Ledger C 1829–54, item 5.
81. David Spencer, Account Books 1797–1816 (Marriner, B., Box 5a).
82. Letter from Dawson, Humble & Son to Richard Fox Lister, June 1796 (Marriner, B., Box 8).
83. James Hoyle to Jackson 15 June 1809 (J.G. MSS).
84. Jackson to Tweedy, Anderson & Son 29 December 1815 (J.G. MSS).
85. John Brigg & Company, bills for wool and oil purchases, 1822–38 (L.).
86. This conflicts with some contemporary opinion on general trends: see P.P. 1857–8 (381) V.
87. Clough, item 134 (B.).
88. T. & M. Bairstow Ltd, items 28, 29, 35 (L.).
89. Marriner, Accounts 1818–41, Box 68 (B.). These accounts are used surprisingly little by Ingle.
90. J. James, *History of the Worsted Manufacture in England from the Earliest Times* (1857), pp. 428–50; *L.M.*, 1832–6, *passim*.
91. Estimate based on evidence from business records primarily J. Foster & Son (B.) and T. & M. Bairstow Ltd (L.).
92. Information from Hague & Cook, Balance Sheets 1816–31 (Wormalds & Walker Ltd, B.).
93. Court of Bankruptcy, B1 and B3 (P.R.O.).
94. *Ibid.*, B3, 2414–16, 20 April 1826.
95. *Ibid.*, file 5336, 4 November 1829. John Williamson, Keighley, worsted spinner, whose major creditors were staplers in Halifax, Huddersfield and Wakefield. Leeds branch, Letter Books (Bank of England), give full commentaries on local bankruptcies, particularly in 1840s. These confirm the importance of debts to staplers.
96. Jowitt, item 62 (B.).
97. See Chapter 9 below.
98. Bradford Banking Company, Ledger 1827–30 (B38) and Order Books 1830s, 1840s, (B3–B6) (Midland). Some of the information is detailed in Table 9.4.
99. Jowitt, items 2–4, 14 (B.).
100. Court of Bankruptcy, B3, file 428 (P.R.O.). See also Jowitt, item 62 (B.).

6 MATERIALS, PLANT, SERVICES AND LABOUR

1. These are rough figures based on the contemporary estimates of Behrens (1858),

James (1857) and Forbes (1851), quoted in E. Baines, *Account of the Woollen Manufacture of England* (1858; repr. 1970), pp. 139–40.

2. For the best account of cotton warp introduction see E. M. Sigsworth, *Black Dyke Mills: A History with Introductory Chapters on the Development of the Worsted Industry in the Nineteenth Century* (Liverpool, 1958), Introduction.

3. F. J. Glover, 'Dewsbury Mills: A History of Messrs. Wormalds and Walker Ltd.', unpublished Ph.D. thesis, University of Leeds, 1959, p. 204.

4. Robert Clough, Keighley Ltd, item 124 (B.).

5. J. T. Clay & Sons Ltd, item 1 (Ha.).

6. The suppliers were: John Dewhirst of Skipton, James Lees of Oldham, Ashworth's of Turton near Bolton and Hugh Shaw & Company, Manchester. Clough, items 118, 119, 134 (B.).

7. T. & M. Bairstow Ltd, item 37 (L.).

8. J. James, *History of the Worsted Manufacture in England from the Earliest Times* (1857), p. 512.

9. Glover, 'Dewsbury Mills', p. 321; and P. P. 1850 (10) XLII.

10. Bairstow, items 28, 35, 37 (L.).

11. J. Malin, 'The West Riding Recovered Wool Industry, ca. 1813–1939', unpublished Ph.D. thesis, University of York, 1979, Ch. 4.

12. *Ibid.*

13. J. T. & J. Taylor Ltd, item 1 (Sheffield University Library), quoted *ibid.*

14. Malin, 'The West Riding Recovered Wool Industry', Ch. 4.

15. Calculation based on *ibid.*, table of blends of heavy woollens and cost of inputs.

16. S. Jubb, *The History of the Shoddy Trade: Its Rise, Progress and Present Position* (Batley, 1860), p. 24.

17. See, e.g., W. White, *Directory and Topography of the Borough of Leeds and the Whole Clothing District of the West Riding* (1842 and 1847).

18. Jubb, *The History of the Shoddy Trade, passim*; and *ibid.* Malin, 'The West Riding Recovered Wool Industry', p. 32.

19. See retrospective comments in E. Fox & Sons, item 11 (B.); and Henry Day's book 1843–58, in hands of Henry Day & Son Ltd, Savile Bridge Mills, Dewsbury.

20. Malin, 'The West Riding Recovered Wool Industry', pp. 260–2.

21. 'Notice of An Agreement of the Shoddy and Rag Wool Merchants of the Dewsbury district about alteration of the system of credit and discounts, 4 February 1858', preserved in the business records of E. Fox & Sons, Fox, item 11 (B.).

22. *Ibid.*

23. The main users of alpaca were G. & J. Turner, John Foster & Son and Titus Salt & Company; and of mohair: Mitchell Bros., Salt and Foster. On production and raw material costs see Sigsworth *Black Dyke Mills*, p. 242; and John Foster & Son, items 61, 62 (B.).

24. Foster, items 103–10 (B.).

25. Sigsworth, *Black Dyke Mills*, p. 240.

26. *Ibid.*, p. 244.

27. Baines, *Account of the Woollen Manufacture*, pp. 103, 139–40.

28. J. C. Waddington & Sons Ltd, item 1 (B.).

29. J. & J. Holroyd, item 1 (L.).

30. See accounts of Grace & Jepson, drysalters of Leeds, with London importers, 1807–30, Grace & Jepson, item 1 (L.).

31. Emily Hargrave and W. B. Crump, 'The Diary of Joseph Rogerson, Scribbling Miller of Bramley, 1808–1814', in W. B. Crump (ed.), *The Leeds Woollen Industry, 1780–1820*, Thoresby Society (Leeds, 1931); hereafter Rogerson.

32. Grace & Jepson, item 2 (L.).

33. Clay, item 1 (Ha.).

34. Bairstow, items 28 and 29 (L.); Kellett, Brown & Company Ltd, item 1 (B.); Clough, item 241 (B.).

35. R. V. Marriner Ltd, Box 68 (B.); Bairstow, item 35 (L.).

36. Clay, item 1 (Ha.).

37. William Willans & Company Ltd, item 4 (B.).
38. Bairstow, item 28 (L.); Clough, item 241 (B); John Brigg & Company, bills for wool and oil purchase, 1822–38 (L.).
39. Holroyd, item 1 (L.).
40. Rogerson, 11 October 1808.
41. Foster, items 128, 129, 130, 131 (B.).
42. Kellett, Brown & Company, item 1 (B.).
43. For agricultural practice, see W. Marshall, *Rural Economy of Yorkshire* (1788), p. 41. For industrial and commercial properties see references cited in index of P. Hudson, *The West Riding Wool Textile Industry: A Catalogue of Business Records* (Edington, 1975), p. 558.
44. The Ossett Valuation of 1837 explicitly states this practice (J.G. MSS).
45. Comments based on Rate Valuations of Ossett, 1801, 1819, 1837 (J.G. MSS); Survey and Valuation of the Township of Warley, 1805, OR 147 (Ha.); and D.E.T., Register, Survey and Rental of the Earl of Dartmouth's Estate in the West Riding of the County of York (1805), p. 45.
46. *Ibid.*
47. Ossett and Warley Valuations, *ibid.*
48. In fact, only two of the ten mills in Ossett in 1837 were rented but the rental calculations based on all ten mills gives one some idea of the average magnitude of mill rentals, Ossett and Warley Valuations, *ibid.*
49. D.E.T., Surveys of 1805, 1828.
50. Savile Estate Papers, item 272 (Hu.).
51. Title Deeds of Estates in Kirkstall and Schedule of Tenants, July 1849 (L.).
52. See Hudson, *The West Riding Wool Textile Industry*, references cited on p. 558, especially pp. 342, 344.
53. P.P. 1840 (203) X, Qu. 2911. For the ubiquity of multiple tenancy, see also P.P. 1841 (311) X, *passim*.
54. G. Ingle, 'A History of R. V. Marriner Ltd., Worsted Spinners, Keighley', unpublished M.Phil. thesis, University of Leeds, 1974, p. 85. See also John Broadbent & Sons, item 74 (B.).
55. D.E.T., Memorandum Book of Changes in Leasing Arrangements 1840–50 (Dartmouth Estate Office, Slaithwaite).
56. This is a rough estimate based on knowledge of rate valuations, insurance records and estate papers.
57. Bairstow, items 17–20 (L.); Foster, item 1 (B.); Broadbent, item 83 (B.); Benjamin Gott & Company, item 8 (J.G. MSS), item 25 (B.). Foster, item 1 (B.), includes details of payments for building work made in cloth and agricultural produce.
58. William Lupton & Company Ltd, item 119 (L.); Gott, item 6 (J.G. MSS).
59. M. J. Dickenson, 'The West Riding Woollen and Worsted Industries 1689–1770: An Analysis of Probate Inventories and Insurance Policies', unpublished Ph.D. thesis, University of Nottingham, 1974.
60. *Ibid.*
61. See, for example, archives of John Foster & Son, and of Hattersley & Son, Keighley and Haworth.
62. L.I. 18 November 1793. For many other similar adverts collected in easily available form, see Emily Hargrave and W. B. Crump, 'Trade, Notices, Newspaper Advertisements and Extracts', in Crump, *The Leeds Woollen Industry*, pp. 313–27.
63. *Ibid.*
64. Ingle, 'A History of R. V. Marriner Ltd.', p. 49.
65. Brigg, item 4 (Keighley Public Library, Bradford District Archives).
66. Lupton, item 9 (B.).
67. See P. L. Cottrell, *Industrial Finance 1830–1914* (1980).
68. D. T. Jenkins, *The West Riding Wool Textile Industry, 1770–1835: A Study of Fixed Capital Formation* (Edington, 1975), pp. 191–2.
69. Gott, item 7 (J.G. MSS).
70. See Foster, item 1 (B.).

71. Jenkins, *The West Riding Wool Textile Industry*, pp. 191–2.
72. *Ibid.*, p. 192.
73. Foster, item 1 (B.).
74. Derived from Jenkins, *The West Riding Wool Textile Industry*, p. 165, Table 25.
75. *Ibid.*, pp. 165–6.
76. M. J. Dickenson, 'Fulling in the West Riding Woollen Cloth Industry, 1689–1770', *T.H.*, X, 1979, pp. 81–2
77. *Ibid.*, pp. 86–7.
78. See following analysis.
79. J. Goodchild, 'The Ossett Mill Company', *T.H.*, I, 1, 1968, p. 52.
80. Dickenson, 'The West Riding Woollen and Worsted Industries', pp. 79–80.
81. See lists of mills traced in Jenkins, *The West Riding Wool Textile Industry*, pp. 208–20.
82. See *ibid.*, Notes and References.
83. Marshall, *The Rural Economy of Yorkshire*, p. 41.
84. Rogerson, Diary references.
85. *Ibid.*, 6 November 1811.
86. *Ibid.*, 7 February 1811.
87. *Ibid.*, 2 November 1808.
88. *Ibid.*, 9 November 1809, 29 November 1809. Pay days improved somewhat in 1813.
89. *Ibid.*, 20 February 1808, 12 October 1810.
90. *Ibid.*, 12 July 1809.
91. *Ibid.*, 20 January 1808.
92. *Ibid.*, 8 October 1808.
93. *Ibid.*, 5 July 1809.
94. *Ibid.*, entries for 1811, 1812.
95. Glover, 'Dewsbury Mills', Ch. 5.
96. *Ibid.*, p. 370.
97. Diary of Thomas Cook, 8 July 1819, quoted in *ibid.*, p. 373.
98. See Chapter 3. The sub-inspector of West Riding factories in 1844, Mr Baker, maintained that Idle, Eccleshill, Batley and Dewsbury were areas dominated by company mills, P.P. 1844 (119) VII, 366.
99. This was explicitly stated in the case of the Holly Park Mill Company in their Articles of Association in 1867 (item 1 (L.)) but it was the case also with earlier concerns.
100. Holly Park Mill Company, item 1 (L.).
101. See resolution of 26 January 1838 in the Gill Royd Mill Company, Minute Book 1835–44, in John Hartley & Sons Ltd, item 3 (L.).
102. P.P. 1844 (119) VII, 366; Kellett, Brown & Company had forty-four shareholders and eighty-four customers in 1838, Kellett, Brown & Company, item 1 (B.).
103. P.P. 1844 (119) VII, 366.
104. Kellett, Brown & Company, item 1. (B.).
105. Hartley, item 3 (L.).
106. Resolution of 26 January 1838 in the Gill Royd Mill Company, Minute Book 1835–44, in Hartley, item 3 (L.).
107. Rawden Low Mill Company, Committee Minute Book 18 June 1845 (Ha.).
108. Rawden Low Mill Company, Articles of Partnership 10 April 1847 (Ha.).
109. Dickenson, 'The West Riding Woollen and Worsted Industries', p. 147.
110. Holroyd, item 1 (L.).
111. *Ibid.*
112. See P. Hudson, 'The Genesis of Industrial Capital in the West Riding Wool Textile Industry c. 1770–1850', unpublished D.Phil. thesis, University of York, 1981, Table 6.5. Based on *ibid.*
113. Henry & Andrew Peterson, item 5 (J.G. MSS).
114. William Haigh, clothier, Saddleworth, Papers 1826–32 DD96/16 (Y.A.S.).
115. Marriner, Box 68 (B.).
116. Bairstow, items 28, 29 (L.).
117. Dickenson, 'The West Riding Woollen and Worsted Industries', Appendix, Tables XXI, XXII.

118. Peterson, item 5 (J.G. MSS).
119. Robert Jowitt & Sons Ltd, item 2 (B.).
120. *Ibid.*
121. *Ibid.*
122. Joseph Jackson, items 8–10 (J.G. MSS).
123. Estimates based on correspondence of Joseph Jackson (Jackson, items 9–22 (J.G. MSS)) and Jowitt, items 2–4 (B.).
124. See constant comment in Jackson, items 8–10 (J.G. MSS); and John & William Emmett, Letter Books 1785–1816 (L.).
125. Figures based on Jowitt, item 2 (B.); and Jackson, items 8–10 (J.G. MSS).
126. Lupton, items 9, 15 (B.).
127. Lupton, item 15 (B.); Foster, item 1 (B.).
128. *Ibid.*; and Clough, items 118, 134 (B.).
129. No mention is made of significant credit being given by early railway companies in the major secondary sources. See, for example, G. R. Hawke, *Railways and Economic Growth in England and Wales, 1840–1870* (Oxford, 1970).
130. Rogerson, 31 December 1812, 1 January 1814.
131. Prime cost calculations based on estimates of Forbes (1851), Behrens (1858) and James (1857), detailed in Baines, *Account of the Woollen Manufacture*, pp. 103, 139–40.
132. G. N. von Tunzelmann, *Steam Power and British Industrialisation to 1860.* (1978), p. 244.
133. H. Heaton, *The Yorkshire Woollen and Worsted Industries from Earliest Times up to the Industrial Revolution* (Oxford, 1920; 2nd edn Oxford, 1965), p. 313. There is evidence of payment practice in surviving Settlement Certificates and Examinations and in Apprenticeship Indentures.
134. See, for example, T. S. Ashton, *England in the 18th Century* (1955), pp. 215–16.
135. P.P. 1842 (471) IX, *passim*, especially Qu. 62.
136. *Ibid.*, Qu. 637.
137. *Ibid.*, *passim*
138. Marriner, items 1 and 2 (B.); Foster, item 1 (B.).
139. *Ibid.*, especially Foster (B.), item 1.
140. P.P. 1834 (556) X, 1835 (341) XIII, *passim*; and P.P. 1842 (471) IX.
141. Foster, item 1 (B.).
142. P.P. 1842 (471) IX, Qu. 613.
143. See following analysis and in P.P. 1842 (471) IX, *passim*.
144. Ossett Mill Company, item 2 (J.G. MSS).
145. Rogerson, 7 October 1809.
146. C. Johnstone, 'The Standard of Living of Worsted Workers in Keighley in the Nineteenth Century', unpublished Ph.D. thesis, University of York, 1978, p. 100.
147. See many references cited in Hudson, *The West Riding Wool Textile Industry*, p. 559, especially Broadbent, item 24 (B.); Edward Ripley & Son, items 1–4 (B.); Foster, items 98–9 (B.).
148. Discussions in *L.M.*, 1824–6, *passim*.
149. See references to this speculative production in P.P. 1834 (556) X, p. 598.
150. *L.M.*, 1 April 1826.
151. *L.M.*, 13 May 1826.
152. *L.M.*, 2 May 1829.
153. P.P. 1842 (471) IX, *passim*.
154. *Ibid.*, Qu. 613.
155. *Ibid.*, QQ. 457ff.
156. *Ibid.*, Qu. 298.
157. *Ibid.*, Qu. 15.
158. *Ibid.*, Qu. 5.
159. *Ibid.*, Qu. 52.
160. *Ibid.*, Qu. 637.
161. *Ibid.*, Qu. 613.

162. *Ibid.*, Qu. 648.
163. *Ibid.*, evidence of Squire Auty, QQ. 92–149.

7 THE TRADE IN WOOLLEN AND WORSTED PRODUCTS

1. N. S. Buck, *The Development of the Organisation of Anglo-American Trade, 1800–1850* (Yale, 1925).
2. S. D. Chapman, 'British Marketing Enterprise: The Changing Roles of Merchants, Manufacturers, and Financiers, 1700–1860', *B.H.R.*, LIII, 2, 1979.
3. Estimate of Thomas Wolrich, Leeds merchant, 1772, quoted in J. Bischoff, *A Comprehensive History of the Woollen and Worsted Manufacture*, 2 vols. (1842, repr. 1968), pp. 187–9.
4. 'Extracts from an Old Leeds merchant's Memorandum Book: 1770–1786' in *T.S.*, *Miscellanea*, XXIV, 1915–18, pp. 36–7.
5. R. G. Wilson, *Gentlemen Merchants: The Merchant Community in Leeds, 1700–1830* (Manchester, 1971), pp. 37–9.
6. C. Gill, 'Blackwell Hall Factors, 1795–99', *E.H.R.*, VI, 2, 1953, p. 274. Much of the information in the following paragraphs on the activities of Hanson & Mills is derived from this source.
7. *Ibid.* See also Ledgers of William Lupton & Company Ltd (L.) which clearly indicate the credit periods in the home and foreign markets in these years.
8. Court of Bankruptcy, B1 E112/1820/74465 (P.R.O.). I am indebted to S. D. Chapman for this reference.
9. Gill, 'Blackwell Hall Factors', pp. 279–80.
10. Wilson, *Gentlemen Merchants*, p. 75.
11. Lupton, item 19 (L.).
12. *Ibid.*, item 2.
13. *L.I.*, 16 July 1782, quoted in H. Heaton (ed.), *The Letter Books of Joseph Holroyd and Sam Hill* (Halifax, 1914), Introduction.
14. Wilson, *Gentlemen Merchants*, p. 66.
15. Lupton, item 2 (L.).
16. Wilson, *Gentlemen Merchants*, p. 78, on rules of Ibbetson & Koster, Lupton's predecessors.
17. These terms seem to have prevailed in the Iberian trade at this time, *ibid.*, p. 79.
18. *Ibid.* p. 79.
19. D. Defoe. *A Tour Through the Whole Island of Great Britain* (1927 edn.), quoted in *ibid.*, pp. 81–2.
20. Lupton, item 19 (L.).
21. See evidence of Jeremiah Naylor, Wakefield merchant, in J. Maitland, *An Account of the Proceedings of the Merchants and Manufacturers, and Others Concerned in the Wool and Woollen Trade of Great Britain* (1800), p. 134.
22. Lupton, item 19 (L.).
23. *Ibid.*, Copy Letter Book 1801–5, item 71, 30 December 1803, and see also 30 June 1804.
24. *Ibid.*, 4 November 1814.
25. *Ibid.*, *passim*.
26. *Ibid.*, 4 May 1815.
27. *Ibid.*, item 19.
28. *Ibid.*, Copy Letter Book 1801–5, item 71, 22 February 1816.
29. Maitland, *An Account of the Proceedings*, p. 135.
30. Evidence of John Oxley, Wakefield cloth merchant, P.P. 1808 X, pp. 83, 86.
31. Much of the general detail of Anglo-American trade in this and other sections of this chapter is derived from Buck, *Anglo-American Trade*.
32. H. Heaton, 'Yorkshire Cloth Traders in the United States, 1770–1840', *T.S.*, XXXVII, 1941.
33. P.P., 1808 X, p. 50.

34. Information derived from *The Trade and Commerce of New York from 1815 to the Present Time by an Observer* (New York, 1820), p. 28, quoted in Buck, *Anglo-American Trade*, p. 112.
35. Buck, *Anglo-American Trade*, p. 113.
36. P.P. 1808 X, Papers.
37. *Ibid.*, pp. 2ff.
38. *Ibid.*, pp. 33–5, 52.
39. *Ibid.*, pp. 46–51.
40. *Ibid.*, pp. 33–5.
41. See, for example, Lupton, items 1–5 (L.), Grace & Jepson, item 1 (L.). See also R. G. Wilson 'The Fortunes of a Leeds Merchant House, 1780–1820', *Business History*, IX, 1967.
42. P.P. 1808 X, p. 52.
43. *Ibid.*, p. 57.
44. P.P. 1810–11 (52) II, p. 4.
45. P.P. 1823 (452) IV, p. 79.
46. P.P. 1819 (202) III, p. 105.
47. Buck, *Anglo-American Trade*, p. 125.
48. P.P. 1810–11 (52) II, p. 2, evidence of Mr Gordon.
49. Lupton, item 74, letters to Henry George Barclay, New York, and Oliver, Borland & Abbot, Boston, March and August 1818 (L).
50. H. Heaton, 'A Merchant Adventurer in Brazil, 1808–18', *J.E.H.* VI, 1, 1946, pp. 1–23.
51. Emily Hargrave and W. B. Crump, 'The Diary of Joseph Rogerson, Scribbling Miller of Bramley, 1808–1814', in W. B. Crump (ed.), *The Leeds Woollen Industry, 1780–1820*, Thoresby Society (Leeds, 1931), 28 February 1808.
52. William Rhodes to Henry Glover 1 May 1809, quoted by Wilson, 'The Fortunes of a Leeds Merchant House', p. 78.
53. *Ibid.*, p. 82.
54. Figure derived from Lupton, items 4, 9 (L.).
55. On the 'Bradford Principle' see E. M. Sigsworth, 'The West Riding Wool Textile Industry and the Great Exhibition', *Y.B.E.S.R.* IV, 1952, p. 27.
56. H. Forbes, *Lectures on the Results of the Great Exhibition of 1851* (1853), p. 325.
57. Thomas Hopkins, *Great Britain for the Last Forty Years* (1834), pp. 232–3.
58. Buck, *Anglo-American Trade*, p. 121.
59. P.P. 1821 (437) VI, p. 435, evidence of Benjamin Gilpin.
60. P.P. 1834 (556) X, p. 424, quoted in Buck, *Anglo-American Trade*, p. 125.
61. P.P. 1823 (452) IV, p. 11.
62. See M. Collins and P. Hudson, 'Provincial Bank Lending: Yorkshire and Merseyside, 1826–1860', *B.E.R.*, XXXI, 2, 1979.
63. Buck, *Anglo-American Trade*, p. 128.
64. P.P. 1833 (690) VI, p. 123.
65. Buck, *Anglo-American Trade*, p. 134.
66. Heaton, 'Yorkshire Cloth Traders', pp. 268–9.
67. *Ibid.*, p. 269.
68. *The Trade and Commerce of New York*, p. 25, quoted in Buck, *Anglo-American Trade*, p. 139.
69. Buck, *Anglo-American Trade*, p. 140.
70. Lupton, items 21, 23 and 73 (L.). P. Hudson, 'The Genesis of Industrial Capital in the West Riding Wool Textile Industry c. 1770–1850', University of York, D.Phil., 1981, Tables 7.2 and 7.3, pp. 360–1.
71. Lupton to Edward Clarke & Company, Boston, 1 January 1826, Lupton, item 79 (L.).
72. P.P. 1828 (515) VIII, p. 136.
73. *Ibid.*
74. Lupton, item 115, Ledger balances 1828 (L.).
75. P.P. 1833 (690) VI, p. 118.
76. *Ibid.*, p. 161.

77. *Ibid.*, p. 123, evidence of Thomas Wiggin.
78. Lupton to Dexter & Almay 12 January 1826, Lupton, item 79 (L.).
79. R. V. Marriner Ltd (B.), item 46.
80. Lupton to William Craig, Glasgow, 11 January 1826, Lupton, item 79 (L.).
81. *Ibid.*, items 21 and 23; Lupton to John G. Stewart, Glasgow, 23 November 1836, item 79.
82. *Ibid.*, item 35, *passim.*
83. S. D. Chapman, 'Financial Restraints on the Growth of Firms in the Cotton Industry, 1790–1850', *E.H.R.*, XXXII, 1979, pp. 217–25.
84. For details of the ways in which monetary and industrial conditions were linked in the West Riding see Leeds branch, Letter Books (Bank of England).
85. J. James, *History of the Worsted Manufacture in England from the Earliest Times* (1857), p. 411.
86. Buck, *Anglo-American Trade*, p. 151.
87. P.P. 1833 (690), VI, pp. 61–2.
88. Hague, Cook & Wormald to T. Dixon, New York, 1 June 1830, quoted by F. J. Glover, 'Dewsbury Mills: A History of Messrs. Wormalds and Walker Ltd.', unpublished Ph.D. thesis, University of Leeds, 1959, p. 421.
89. Hague, Cook & Wormald to Van Arsedale & Company, New York, 25 August 1838, Wormalds & Walker Ltd, Letter Books (B.).
90. See P.P. 1847–8 (565) VIII, p. 234.
91. The term slaughterhouse first seems to appear in the 1830s. See Buck, *Anglo-American Trade*, p. 123.
92. P.P. 1833 (690), VI, p. 59.
93. See Buck, *Anglo-American Trade*, p. 153–4.
94. *Ibid.*, p. 156.
95. Lupton to John G. Stewart, Glasgow, 11 February 1837, Lupton, item 85 (L.).
96. P.P. 1847–8 (31), XXIV, p. 253, quoted by Buck, *Anglo-American Trade*, p. 158.
97. Lupton to John G. Stewart, Glasgow, 23 November 1836, Lupton, item 85 (L.).
98. Hague, Cook & Wormald to Reiss Bros., Manchester, 5 February 1844 (Wormalds & Walker Ltd, B.).
99. Glover, 'Dewsbury Mills', p. 630.
100. Lupton, item 85, *passim* (L.).
101. See P. Hudson, *The West Riding Wool Textile Industry: A Catalogue of Business Records* (Edington, 1975), list on p. 555.
102. P.P. 1847–8 (565) VIII, pp. 2–3.
103. P. Hudson, 'The Genesis of Industrial Capital', Tables 7.7 and 7.8, pp. 374–5. T. & M. Bairstow Ltd, items 28, 29, 35, 37 (L.). Robert Clough, Keighley Ltd, item 172 (B.).
104. See A. J. Topham, 'The Credit Structure of the West Riding Wool Textile Industry in the 19th Century', unpublished M.Phil. thesis, University of Leeds, 1953, Ch. 3.
105. See discussion of the situation in the 1870s *Textile Manufacturer*, January 1877. I am indebted to Dr D. T. Jenkins for this reference.
106. For some discussion of this see P. Hudson, 'The Role of Banks in the Finance of the West Riding Textile Industry', *B.H.R.*, LV, 3, 1981.

8   TRADE CREDIT AND GROWTH

1. Much of this chapter summarises the finding and arguments of Chapters 5 to 7, thus notes here are kept to a minimum.
2. P.P. 1828 (515) VIII, p. 142.
3. A. J. Topham, 'The Credit Structure of the West Riding Wool Textile Industry in the 19th Century', unpublished M.Phil. thesis, University of Leeds, 1953.
4. *Ibid.*, pp. 195–6.
5. F. Lavington, *The English Capital Market* (1921), p. 267.
6. P.P. 1857–8 (381) V, evidence of Robert Slater of Morrison, Dillon & Company, p. 159.

7. Topham, 'Credit Structure', p. 98.
8. P.P. 1857–8 (381) V, p. 382.
9. *Textile Manufacturer*, November 1876 and January 1877 – references provided by Dr D. T. Jenkins.
10. P.P. 1886 (4715) XXII, Second Report Appendix E. pp. 288 *et seq.* – reference provided by D. T. Jenkins.
11. *Textile Manufacturer*, January 1877.
12. Leeds branch, Letters, 1830s, *passim* (Bank of England).
13. *Ibid.*
14. Most really large concerns held accounts with both the Bank of England and their own banks and could combine discounts at the two establishments to maximum pecuniary advantage.
15. Leeds branch, Letters and Letter Books, 1830s and 1840s (Bank of England).
16. *Ibid.*
17. *Ibid.*, 3 December 1836.
18. Leeds branch, branch correspondence and miscellaneous files (Bank of England). I am grateful to David J. Moss (currently researching the Bank of England and its branches) for details of these 3% accounts.
19. This was a matter of repeated stress in the London correspondence with the Leeds branch (Bank of England).
20. General Memorandum in London–Manchester, Private Letter Book 3, 12 July 1834 (Bank of England).
21. I am indebted to David J. Moss for this point.
22. Leeds branch, Letter Book 1 1840–1 15 September 1841 (Bank of England). The Yorkshire District Bank was allowed discounts up to £100,000.
23. See Chapter 9.
24. See section on short-term credit.
25. P.P. 1806 (268) III, Report, p. 10.
26. *Ibid.*, evidence of James Walker, Wortley, p. 182.
27. *Ibid.*, 1828 (515) VIII, evidence of John Varley, Stanningley, p. 147.
28. *Ibid.*, evidence of Gervaise Walker of Horbury, p. 258.
29. *Ibid.*, 1857–8 (381) V, evidence of Robert Slater, p. 159.
30. Topham, 'Credit Structure', p. 66.
31. P.P. 1833 (690) VI, evidence of John Marshall, p. 161.
32. P. Hudson, 'The Genesis of Industrial Capital in the West Riding Wool Textile Industry c. 1770–1850', unpublished D.Phil., University of York, 1981, Table 10.4, pp. 491–2.
33. *Ibid.*, Graphs 8.4 and 8.5, p. 419.
34. P. L. Cottrell, *Industrial Finance 1830–1914* (1980), p. 251.
35. Court of Bankruptcy, B1 and B3 (P.R.O.). Robert Jowitt & Sons Ltd, item 62 (B.).
36. Topham discusses these theoretical relationships in 'Credit Structure', pp. 172 *et seq.*
37. P.P. 1833 (690) VI, evidence of John Brooke, p. 118.
38. R. G. Hawtrey, *Currency and Credit* (New York, 1930), p. 224, quoted in C. P. Kindleberger, *Manias, Panics and Crashes* (1978), p. 62.
39. P.P. 1833 (690) VI, evidence of Henry Hughes, p. 80.
40. Kindleberger, *Manias, Panics and Crashes*, p. 62.
41. P.P. 1857–8 (381) V, pp. 113, 115.
42. Jowitt, item 62 (B.); reports in *L.M.* 1839; and Leeds branch, Letter Book 1 1840–1 (Bank of England).
43. P.P. 1831–2 (722) VI, evidence of William Beckett, QQ. 1380–4.
44. Topham, 'Credit Structure', p. 67.
45. See *ibid.*, p. 34.
46. The bulk of the Leeds branch discount business was with traders not bankers. Topham, 'Credit Structure', p. 20; and Leeds branch, Letters, *passim* (Bank of England). See also P.P. 1847–8 (395) VIII, evidence of James Morris, Qu. 2678.
47. Leeds branch, Letter Books 1830s and 1840s (Bank of England).
48. P.P. 1857–8 (381) V, evidence of Robert Slater, p. 161.

49. Topham, 'Credit Structure', p. 195.
50. Thomas Bischoff reported on the ability of small domestic manufacturers to produce low qualities of cloth most cheaply during a slump: Leeds branch, Letters, 1832, No. 246 (Bank of England).

PART 4   EXTERNAL AND INTERNAL FINANCE
9   ATTORNEYS, BANKS AND INDUSTRY

1. Remarks based on study of wide range of business papers and attorneys' archives.
2. Benjamin Gott & Company (J.G. MSS).
3. John Howarth, Cash Books and Day Books 1740s–90s (Ha.); and Papers of John Eagle (Bradford District Archives) survive to give a fairly representative picture of the role of the attorney. The author has undertaken a study of the former collection but complementary information from the latter and much other useful information was obtained from M. Miles, 'Eminent Attorneys: Some Aspects of West Riding Attorneyship c. 1750–1800', unpublished Ph.D. thesis, University of Birmingham, 1983.
4. B. L. Anderson, 'Law, Finance and Economic Growth in England: Some Long-Term Influences', in B. N. Ratcliffe (ed.), *Great Britain and Her World* (Manchester, 1975), pp. 99–106.
5. Gott, item 1 (J.G. MSS).
6. John Howarth, Ledger 1791–1805 (Ha.).
7. *Ibid.*, Cash Book 1789–96.
8. *Ibid.*, 1 June 1789 and 20 May 1793.
9. See *ibid.*, Day Books, *passim*.
10. M. Miles, 'The Money Market in the Early Industrial Revolution: The Evidence from West Riding Attorneys, 1750–1800', *Business History*, XXIII, 1981, pp. 130ff.
11. *Ibid.*, p. 132.
12. *Ibid.*
13. Miles, 'Eminent Attorneys', and discussion.
14. *Ibid.*
15. John Howarth, Cash Books 1780s–97 (Ha.).
16. See B. L. Anderson, 'The Attorney and the Early Capital Market in Lancashire', in J. R. Harris (ed.), *Liverpool and Merseyside: Essays in the Economic and Social History of the Port and Its Hinterland* (1969), and reprinted in F. Crouzet (ed.), *Capital Formation in the Industrial Revolution* (1972), pp. 230–2; B. A. Holderness, 'Credit in a Rural Community, 1660–1800', *Midland History*, III, 1975, pp. 109–10.
17. John Howarth, Cash Book 1789–96 (Ha.), and contemporary directories.
18. See, for example, *ibid.*, Day Book 1780–3.
19. Miles, 'The Money Market', p. 134.
20. P. Hudson, *The West Riding Wool Textile Industry: A Catalogue of Business Records* (Edington, 1975), *passim*.
21. John Howarth, Cash Book 1789–96 (Ha.).
22. *Ibid.*
23. *Ibid.*
24. Miles, 'The Money Market', p. 141; John Howarth, Cash Book 1789–96 (Ha.).
25. John Howarth, Day Books (Ha.).
26. *Ibid.*
27. Miles, 'The Money Market', p. 136.
28. Holderness, 'Credit in a Rural Community', p. 97.
29. Miles, 'The Money Market', p. 141. John Howarth Cash Book 1755–66, p. 350, Cash Book 1774–7, p. 206 (Ha.).
30. The only West Riding attorney to be traced turning banker is Lucas Nicholson of Leeds who became a partner in the Leeds Commercial Bank in April 1792. See W. C. E. Hartley, *Banking in Yorkshire* (Clapham, 1975).
31. See, for example, bill to Marriner's from Christopher Netherwood, Keighley attorney, R. V. Marriner Ltd, Box 25 (B.).

32. For earlier investigation of this topic more generally, see L. S. Pressnell, *Country Banking in the Industrial Revolution* (Oxford, 1956), pp. 284–343; R. Cameron (ed.), *Banking in the Early Stages of Industrialisation: A Study in Comparative Economic History* (New York, 1967), Ch. 2, especially pp. 49ff; P. Mathias, *The First Industrial Nation: An Economic History of Britain, 1700–1914* (1969), pp. 176–7; M. Collins and P. Hudson, 'Provincial Banking Lending: Yorkshire and Merseyside, 1826–1860', *B.E.R.*, XXXI, 2, 1979.

33. T. S. Ashton, 'The Bill of Exchange and Private Banks in Lancashire, 1790–1830', in T. S. Ashton and R. S. Sayers (eds.), *Papers in English Monetary History* (Oxford 1954), pp. 37–49. P.P. 1831–2 (722) VI, evidence of Henry Burgess, Qu. 5331. W. Newmarch, 'An Attempt to Ascertain the Magnitude of Fluctuations of the Amount of Bills of Exchange', *Journal of the Statistical Society*, XIV, 1851, p. 153, on Sir George Saville's Small Notes Bill of 1775. Also H. Ling Roth, *The Genesis of Banking in Halifax* (Halifax, 1914).

34. For example, Ingram Kennet & Company 1773–6, Bros. Swaine & Company, 1802–7, Rawson Rhodes & Briggs, 1807–16, and John Williams & Christopher Rawson & Company, 1811–36, all of Halifax; Leach, Pollard & Hardcastle, 1777–81, of Bradford; Benjamin Wilson & Sons, 1802–32, of Mirfield; Nicholson Brown & Company, 1813–1900, of Leeds; Hague & Cook, 1810–36, of Dewsbury.

35. On 26 May 1803, 148 merchants and manufacturers publicly offered to accept the notes of Bros. Swaine & Company, bankers of Halifax, to allay panic after the resumption of war with France: *Halifax Guardian Historical Almanack* (Halifax, 1892). In the crisis of 1825 seventy local businessmen signed a statement of confidence in the stability of Messrs Leatham Tew & Company's bank in Wakefield. P. W. Matthews and A. W. Tuke, *A History of Barclays Bank Ltd.* (1926), p. 247. In the same crisis a large petition was produced in Bradford in support of Harris & Company. Its signatures included the foremost names in industry and commerce in the town and they declared that their joint worth of over £2m was pledged in support of the bank. *Centenary Souvenir of Bradford Old Bank* A50/10 (Barclays); (see also 'Declaration in Support of Whitby Old Bank 22nd February 1797' (Barclays); and 'Petition in Support of Leeds Banks', *L.M.* 17 December 1825.

36. William Pollard was a partner in a banking business in Halifax as well as a founder of the first Bradford Bank in 1779. Ling Roth, *The Genesis of Banking in Halifax*, Ch. 1. The main banking families in Halifax formed an interlocking group in the early decades of the nineteenth century. Records of Rawson & Company, Rawsons Rhodes & Briggs, Rhodes Briggs & Company (Barclays). Hague & Cook, blanket manufacturers and bankers of Dewsbury, were also partners in a bank at Malton 1816–25. F. J. Glover, 'Dewsbury Mills: A History of Messrs Wormalds and Walker Ltd.', unpublished D.Phil. thesis, University of Leeds, 1959, Ch. 5. These close relationships between bankers of the area are illustrated by the formation in 1824 of the Committee of the Association of Bankers in Yorkshire. The aim was mutually to protect against forgery and frauds. At least twenty-three different banks were involved: Haxby & Scholey, solicitors, Bill Book A (J.G. MSS).

37. Few West Riding banks had branches prior to the third quarter of the nineteenth century.

38. For detailed analysis of the localisation of shareholders see Collins and Hudson, 'Provincial Bank Lending'. A further example is provided by the Halifax Joint Stock Banking Company's Deed of Settlement, 25 November 1829 (Lloyds), which shows that almost 50% of shareholders lived in Halifax itself and less than 1% resided outside the West Riding. The Mirfield & Huddersfield District Banking Company agreed that no one should own a share unless his residence or place of business was within 20 miles of Mirfield or Huddersfield. G. Chandler, *Four Centuries of Banking* (1968), vol. 2, p. 265.

39. Bradford Banking Company, Deed of Constitution, 1 June 1827 (B1) (Midland). This was the subject of some anxiety – the fear of potential bank customers that commercial rivals may be on the board of a bank and thus have access to details of their accounts. The Bradford Joint Stock Bank, for example, would not have as Director

anyone interested in the spinning trade, the main industry of the town (Lloyds, Halifax file). Other banks got round the problem by insisting on oaths of secrecy or by denying the full board access to accounts, e.g. Leeds Banking Company 1832, Hartley, *Banking in Yorkshire*, p. 52.

40. For details of this analysis see Collins and Hudson, 'Provincial Bank Lending', pp. 5–9.
41. See Ling Roth, *The Genesis of Banking in Halifax*, Ch. 1; Halifax and Huddersfield Union Banking Company Ltd, Deed of Settlement, 1836 (Ha.). Chandler, *Four Centuries of Banking*, vol. 2, Ch. 5. Mirfield & Huddersfield District Banking Company, Directors' Minute Books 1836–40s (Barclays). Leeds Commercial Banking Company, Deed of Settlement, 1836 (J.G. MSS).
42. On the tendency for the Usury Laws to encourage the reinvestment of profits, see S. Shapiro, *Capital and the Cotton Industry in the Industrial Revolution* (Ithaca, 1967), pp. 10–22, 56–74, *passim*.
43. This section owes much to Pressnell, *Country Banking*, pp. 284–9.
44. The following section is based upon material in F. J. Glover, 'Dewsbury Mills: A History of Messrs. Wormalds and Walker Ltd.', unpublished Ph.D., University of Leeds, 1959, and in the archives of Wormalds & Walker Ltd (B.).
45. Chandler, *Four Centuries of Banking*, vol 2, pp. 270–2. Mirfield & Huddersfield District Banking Company, Directors' Minute Book 1833–42 (Barclays).
46. Ling Roth, *The Genesis of Banking in Halifax*, Ch. 1.
47. Bros. Swaine & Company, Accounts 1807 (Barclays).
48. Ling Roth, *The Genesis of Banking in Halifax*, Ch. 1.
49. J. W. Buck, *Cases in Bankruptcy*, vol. 1, *1816–20* (1820), p. 368. Rawson Rhodes & Briggs, General Balance 1818–23 (Barclays).
50. Anon., *British Losses by Bank Failures, 1820–57* (1858). See also case of Wentworth & Company, in *ibid.*, and Harrop & Company in Hartley, *Banking in Yorkshire*, pp. 36–8.
51. D. T. Jenkins, *The West Riding Wool Textile Industry, 1770–1835: A Study of Fixed Capital Formation* (Edington, 1975), pp. 208, 247. P.P. 1835 (342) XL.
52. Rawsons Rhodes & Briggs, Accounts 1809, 1818–23 (Barclays).
53. Rhodes, Briggs & Garlick, Accounts 1814 (Barclays).
54. *Ibid.*, Moore Papers, 1815–16 (Barclays).
55. *L.M.*, 14 March 1826; Hartley, *Banking in Yorkshire*, p. 41; Pressnell, *Country Banking*, p. 530. D. T. Jenkins, 'The West Riding Wool Textile Industry, 1770–1835: A Study of Fixed Capital Formation', unpublished D.Phil. thesis, University of York, 1970, vol. 2, Appendix A.
56. Jenkins, 'The West Riding Wool Textile Industry', vol. 2, Appendix A.
57. Haxby & Scholey, Bill Book *c.* 1819–20s, various mortgage agreements (J.G. MSS).
58. *L.M.*, 14 March 1826.
59. P.P. 1831–2 (722) VI, Qu. 1414.
60. *Ibid.*, evidence of John B. Smith of the Joint Stock Bank, Manchester, QQ. 4360, 4377. Loans were made 'in many cases on the security of the mills that were built with the money so lent'.
61. *Ibid.* QQ. 1238–436.
62. 'Account of Failures in and Connected with the Wool and Woollen Trade, 1839–48', handwritten account in Robert Jowitt & Sons Ltd, item 62 (B.).
63. Various mortgage agreements (J.G. MSS). Leatham, Tew & Company, records of half-yearly meetings of partners 1833–41 (Barclays).
64. *Ibid.*, first half-year report, 1833.
65. Bond of Halliley, Brooke and others to Messrs'Richard B. Milnes for securing monies on a banking account 1811, Leatham, Tew & Company (J.G. MSS).
66. Leatham, Tew & Company, records of half-yearly meetings of partners 1833–41 (Barclays).
67. Chandler, *Four Centuries of Banking*, vol. 2, Ch. 5. Mirfield & Huddersfield District Banking Company, Directors' Minute Book 1833–42 (Barclays).
68. E.g. Bradford Banking Company, Order Book 1827–30, 19 July 1827, 6 September 1827, 17 January 1828, 14 February 1828 (Midland).

69. For comparison of the lending policies of joint stock banks in the West Riding and Merseyside in this period see Collins and Hudson, "Provincial Bank Lending'.
70. See, e.g. Halifax Joint Stock Bank, Deed of Settlement, 1829 (Lloyds); and Yorkshire District Bank, Deed of Settlement, 1834, DB 255 (L.).
71. P.P. 1836 (591) IX, *passim*.
72. Bank Order Books (Barclays); Directors' Minute Books (Lloyds); Directors' Minute Books (Midland); and Bradford Banking Company, Securities Register (B28) (Midland).
73. For general discussion of this see Collins and Hudson, 'Provincial Bank Lending'.
74. Halifax Commercial Banking Company, Minutes 1844–50s, Letters 1847–52, Report of Meeting of Creditors 14 January 1848 (Barclays). See also Minutes 14 November 1841, 6 February 1839, which document large loans to other directors.
75. Leeds and West Riding Banking Company and Leeds Commercial Banking Company both failed in 1846. For comments on these failures see Anon., *British Losses by Bank Failures*.
76. Yorkshire District Bank, Deed of Settlement, 1834 DB 255 (L.).
77. Jowitt, item 62 (B.).
78. Quoted in W. F. Crick and J. E. Wadsworth, *A Hundred Years of Joint Stock Banking* (1958), p. 213.
79. See comments on failure of Northern and Central Bank of England which failed 1836 and Commercial Bank of England which failed 1840 in Anon., *British Losses by Bank Failures*.
80. The major problem is that the figures exclude 'rediscounts' and therefore would tend to underestimate the total volume of credit financed through bill-discounting. For further details for the balance sheet calculations see Collins and Hudson, 'Provincial Bank Lending'. The banks examined were Yorkshire Banking Company 1843–52, York City and County Banking Company 1839–42, 1844, 1846–52, Leatham, Tew & Company 1838–42, 1849–52, Beckett Blayd & Company, 1839–44, 1847–52, West Riding Union Banking Company 1837–50, Wentworth & Company 1826, Halifax Joint Stock Banking Company 1830. See also C. A. E. Goodhart, *The Business of Banking 1891–1914* (1972), pp. 15–39; S. Nishimura, *The Decline of Inland Bills of Exchange in the London Money Market 1855–1913* (Cambridge, 1971), *passim*.
81. See, e.g., West Riding Union Banking Company, Book of Accounts 1833–77 (Barclays). Local overdrafts were four times larger than money at call and invested in London in 1830s. By 1850 debit balances on bank accounts were still almost twice as large as cash at brokers. See also Halifax Joint Stock Banking Company, Letter Book 1830 (Lloyds). Letter to Jones Lloyd & Company, London of 2 February 1830 requests them to invest a few thousand pounds for a short time 'after which we hope to find better employment for it here'.
82. The banks surveyed are the following: Bradford Banking Company, Huddersfield Banking Company, Halifax Joint Stock Banking Company, Halifax Commercial Banking Company, West Riding Union Banking Company, Leatham, Tew & Company.
83. See various Directors' Minute Books, in particular that of West Riding Union Banking Company including Reports of Annual General Meetings 1840, 1841 (Barclays).
84. For explicit statements see Halifax Commercial Banking Company, Minutes 21 June 1836 (Barclays), and Bradford Banking Company, Order Books 21 June 1827, 27 June 1838, 28 November 1838 (B2, B4) (Midland). See also *Circular to Bankers*, 763, 14 October 1842, pp. 137–9.
85. Collins and Hudson, 'Provincial Bank Lending'.
86. Bradford Banking Company, Ledger 1827–30 (B38) (Midland).
87. The six were Daniel Salt & Son, wool staplers, Thomas Milthorp, wool stapler, Cousen, Leach & Company, worsted spinners and weavers, William Akroyd, worsted spinner, William & Thos. Marshall, woollen manufacturers, and William Rouse & Son, worsted spinners and manufacturers.
88. E.g. E. C. Lister (firm no. 48, Table 9.4) and Thomas Gill, Baildon (firm no. 42), who had a discount account only with the bank.

89. E.g. Turner, Mitchell & Company, Horton, worsted spinners (firm no. 39), had a verbal guarantee from Henry Leah, bank director, to secure their account to £2,000.
90. Holly Park Mill Company item 1 (B.).
91. *Ibid.*
92. Bradford Banking Company, Securities Register 1827–74 (B28) (Midland).
93. West Riding Union Banking Company, Directors' Minute Books 1833–45.
94. Halifax Commercial Banking Company, Directors' Minute Books 1836–55 (Barclays).
95. Huddersfield Banking Company, Minute Books 1827–38 (H4, H5) (Midland); see also Securities Register 1842–1850 (H24).
96. *Ibid.*, 28 July 1830 (H4). In the previous year, bad debts had amounted to almost £2,000: 17 July 1829 (H4).
97. *Ibid.*, Securities Register, 6 September 1844 (H25).
98. H. Watt, *The Practice of Banking in Scotland and in England* (Glasgow, 1833), p. 36.
99. Information in this section on mill building and extension and on profit figures, unless otherwise specified, is obtained from the business records in the Brotherton Library, see P. Hudson, *The West Riding Wool Textile Industry: A Catalogue of Business Records* (Edington, 1975).
100. Bradford Banking Company, Order Book 18 February 1834, 18 April 1838 (B4) (Midland).
101. John Broadbent & Sons, item 47 (B.).
102. Quoted in G. Ingle, 'A History of R. V. Marriner Ltd., Worsted Spinners, Keighley', unpublished M.Phil. thesis, University of Leeds, 1974.
103. W. B. Crump and G. Ghorbal, *History of the Huddersfield Woollen Industry* (Huddersfield, 1935), pp. 118–19. Religious affiliation between the Brookes and the Becketts was of importance here: interview with Mr Edward Brooke, 1979.
104. E. M. Sigsworth, *Black Dyke Mills: A History with Introductory Chapters on the Development of the Worsted Industry in the Nineteenth Century* (Liverpool 1958). List of new shares allotted 1 July 1831; Bradford Banking Company (B46) (Midland).
105. Court of Bankruptcy (B1 and B3) (P.R.O.).
106. *Ibid.*, B3, file 3417.
107. *Ibid.*, files 2414 and 2415.
108. *Ibid.*, file 2414, evidence of Joseph Harrop.
109. Jowitt, item 62 (B.).
110. See bibliography for full range of bank records used.
111. Jowitt, item 62 'Remarks', *passim* (B.).
112. Mirfield & Huddersfield District Banking Company, Minute Book 1833–42, February 1840 (Barclays).
113. *Ibid.*, February 1841.
114. *Ibid.*, 3 March 1841 (Dewsbury branch).
115. 'Thomas Bullion', *Letters on the Internal Management of a Country Bank* (1850), Letters IX–XIII.
116. Pressnell, *Country Banking*, pp. 295–6.

10 PLOUGHED-BACK PROFITS

1. T. S. Ashton, *The Industrial Revolution 1760–1830* (1948), p. 97.
2. F. Crouzet, 'Capital Formation in Great Britain during the Industrial Revolution', in F. Crouzet (ed.), *Capital Formation in the Industrial Revolution* (1972), p. 188.
3. For discussion of this and related aspects of accounting in the industrial revolution, see S. Pollard, 'Capital Accounting in the Industrial Revolution', *Y.B.E.S.R.*, XV, 2, 1963, reprinted in Crouzet, *Capital Formation*, pp. 119–44; P. Hudson, 'Some Aspects of 19th Century Accounting Development in the West Riding Textile Industry', *Accounting History*, II, 2, 1977; A. C. Littleton and B. S. Yamey (eds.), *Studies in the History of Accounting* (1956); Werner Sombart, *Der Moderne Kapitalismus*, 6th edn (Munich and Leipzig, 1924), vol 2, pp. 118–25; B. S. Yamey, 'Accounting and the rise of Capitalism: Further Notes on a Theme by Sombart', *Jour-*

nal of Accounting Research, II, 2, 1964. R. P. Brief, 'The Origin and Evolution of Nineteenth Century Asset Accounting', *B.H.R.*, XL, 1966.

4. S. Pollard, *The Genesis of Modern Management: A Study of the Industrial Revolution in Great Britain* (1965), p. 274.
5. Crouzet, *Capital Formation*, p. 35.
6. See for example records of John Barran & Sons Ltd, item 1 (1845–69) (L.); T. & M. Bairstow Ltd, items 3, 6, 78, 237, 241 (1839–1882) (L.); John Broadbent & Sons, items 1–5 (1826–73) (B.); J. T. Clay & Sons Ltd, item 1 (1812, 1814) (B.) and item 10 (1814) (Ha.) – all listed in P. Hudson, *The West Riding Wool Textile Industry: A Catalogue of Business Records* (Edington, 1975).
7. The mandatory provisions of the 1844 Act were subsequently dropped but the 1856 and 1862 Acts recommended fairly sophisticated disclosures with regular audit, double-entry and allowances for depreciation. See. H. C. Edey and Prot. Panitpakdi, 'British Company Accounting and the Law 1844–1900', in Littleton and Yamey, *Studies in the History of Accounting*, pp. 356–79.
8. See records of Ossett Mill Company, items 1, 2 (1786–1892) (J.G. MSS); John Hartley & Sons Ltd, item 1 (1835–61) (L.); Kellett, Brown & Company Ltd, item 69 (1845–75) (B.) – all listed in Hudson, *The West Riding Wool Textile Industry*.
9. Crouzet, *Capital Formation*, p. 35.
10. For fuller discussion of this see A. C. Littleton, *Accounting Evolution to 1900* (New York, 1933; repr. 1966), p. 350.
11. Gott's wrote down the value of their mills and machinery by more than 50% in 1816, see Benjamin Gott & Company item 20 (B.).
12. Wormalds & Walker Ltd, item 3 (1851–70) (B.).
13. John Foster & Son, item 4 (1841–9) (B.).
14. These figures are derived from studying all West Riding textile firms' records which yield evidence on depreciation. Most are referenced in Hudson, *The West Riding Wool Textile Industry*, Index.
15. I am grateful to D. T. Jenkins for this information derived from business records of John Foster & Son, notably item 4 (B.).
16. See for example records of Wormalds & Walker (B.), especially item 2.
17. This was common in the last quarter of the nineteenth century and must have been even more prevalent earlier. See J. T. Clay & Sons Ltd, item 301 (1882–92) (Ha.), Marshall, Kay & Marshal, items 30–3 (1880–1900) (Hu.).
18. Gott, item 20 (B.), see various balance sheets and partners' accounts detailed in Hudson, *The West Riding Wool Textile Industry*, Index.
19. All pairs of worsted profit rate series excluding Marriner's exhibit a significant positive correlation, and Marriner's correlates significantly with Foster's.
20. For discussion of the problems of the fulling returns see R. G. Wilson, *Gentlemen Merchants: The Merchant Community in Leeds, 1700–1830* (Manchester, 1971), pp. 39–41.
21. All correlations were set against the one-tail t-test at the 5% level. Where the word 'significant' is used in the analysis it indicates significance on the t-test at this level. Correlations were tried both with and without suitable lags.
22. A. J. Topham, 'The Credit Structure of the West Riding Wool Textile Industry in the 19th Century', unpublished M.Phil thesis, University of Leeds, 1953, p. 13. The Leeds branch negotiated few 3% discount accounts: Leeds branch, Letter Books 1827–44 (Bank of England).
23. See F. J. Glover, 'Dewsbury Mills: A History of Messrs Wormalds and Walker Ltd.', unpublished Ph.D. thesis, University of Leeds, 1959, Ch. 9.
24. Bairstow, section IV items (L.), and see Chapter 7.
25. See E. J. Hobsbawm, *Industry and Empire* (1968), Chs. 3 and 4; John Foster, *Class Struggle in the Industrial Revolution* (1974), Chs 4, 5 and 6.
26. Many non-quantifiable elements fundamental to an understanding of the accumulation process remain outside of the exercise. We have no reliable series for the output of the industry or of its different branches and no reliable measure of the movement of prices of outputs or inputs other than English wool. There is also no way of integrating

technological change or the rate of innovation into the study of profit generation, and the number of overlapping observations is too small to allow multiple regression analysis. Finally, yearly indices may be a rather clumsy and blunt instrument to use for these purposes but there is no alternative.

27. See, for example, records of Clay & Earnshaw and Jowitt's detailed in Hudson *The West Riding Wool Textile Industry.*
28. K. V. Pankhurst mentions this in 'Investment in the West Riding Wool Textile Industry in the Nineteenth Century', *Y.B.E.S.R.*, VII, 1955, p. 101.
29. Crouzet, *Capital Formation*, p. 188.
30. See Chapters 2 and 3.
31. For full discussion of this point see P. M. Sweezy, 'Schumpeter's Theory of Innovation', in P. M. Sweezy, *The Present as History* (1953), pp. 274–82.
32. Jenkins' original estimates were used (D. T. Jenkins, *The West Riding Wool Textile Industry, 1770–1835: A Study of Fixed Capital Formation* (Edington, 1975, p. 175) and compared in turn with the profit series lagged one year. The absence of significant correlation may reflect the problems of using insurance data as a guide to the timing of construction but these problems are more likely to influence the precision of the capital estimates than the chronology of their growth.
33. See business records indexed under inventories, machinery and steam engines in Hudson, *The West Riding Wool Textile Industry.*
34. Gott, item 20 (B.).
35. Broadbent, item 1 (B.).
36. E. M. Sigsworth, *Black Dyke Mills: A History with Introductory Chapters on the Development of the Worsted Industry in the Nineteenth Century* (Liverpool, 1958), p. 226.
37. Gott, item 20 (B.), and Sigsworth, *Black Dyke Mills*, p. 226.
38. Glover, 'Dewsbury Mills', Appendix.
39. Sigsworth, *Black Dyke Mills*, p. 221.
40. Gott, item 20 (B.).
41. Glover, 'Dewsbury Mills', Appendix.
42. A. K. Cairncross, *Home and Foreign Investment* (1953), p. 1.
43. Pankhurst, 'Investment in the West Riding Wool Textile Industry', pp. 101–2.
44. See various local histories cited in the bibliography. Surviving business records bear this out.
45. The ubiquity of land and property holdings of textile entrepreneurs and their use as security for industrial loans is illustrated in title deeds which survive among business archives and in the West Riding Registry of Deeds. On the former see Hudson, *The West Riding Wool Textile Industry*, Appendix.
46. Glover, 'Dewsbury Mills', Appendix; and Wormalds & Walker, items 2 and 3 (B.).
47. Gott, items 16 and 17 (J.G. MSS).
48. Sigsworth, *Black Dyke Mills*, *passim*; G. Ingle, 'A History of R. V. Marriner Ltd., Worsted Spinners, Keighley', unpublished M.Phil. thesis, University of Leeds, 1974; and R. V. Marriner Ltd, family papers, *passim* (B.).
49. Gott, item 17 (J.G. MSS).
50. Hudson, *The West Riding Wool Textile Industry*, pp. 155–6, 158–71, 300–6, 332, 344, 349, 376, 392, 433, 468, 471. See also references in the index.
51. See references in *ibid.*
52. Coefficients of 0.306 and 0.136 on 22 and 20 observations respectively. See P. Hudson 'The Genesis of Industrial Capital in the West Riding Wool Textile Industry c. 1770–1850', unpublished D.Phil. thesis, University of York, 1981, pp. 543–5. The results remain insignificant when a lag is introduced into the profit rate series.
53. Bairstow, item 3 (L.).
54. Robert Jowitt & Sons Ltd, items 2, 3, 12, 13, 14 (B.).
55. Quoted in Ingle, 'A History of R. V. Marriner Ltd.'.
56. Sigsworth, *Black Dyke Mills*, Ch. 7, and Foster, items 4, 73 (B.).
57. Bradford Banking Company, Ledger (B38) (Midland); Holly Park Mill Company, item 1 (L.).

PART 5   SUMMARY AND CONCLUSION
I I   THE GENESIS OF INDUSTRIAL CAPITAL

1. Factory Inspector's letter, 1843, quoted by E. Lipson, *History of the Woollen and Worsted Industries* (1921), pp. 177–9, and included in P.P. (119) VII, 1844.
2. H. Medick, 'The Proto-Industrial Family Economy: The Structural Function of Household and Family during the Transition from Peasant Society to Industrial Capitalism', *Social History*, I. 3, 1976, p. 269.
3. R. G. Wilson, *Gentlemen Merchants: The Merchant Community in Leeds, 1700–1830* (Manchester, 1971), p. 59 and *passim*.
4. M. J. Dickenson, 'The West Riding Woollen and Worsted Industries 1689–1770: An Analysis of Probate Inventories and Insurance Policies', unpublished Ph.D. thesis, University of Nottingham, 1974, Ch. 5.
5. E. J. Hobsbawm, *Industry and Empire* (1968), p. 47; J. Foster, *Class Struggle in the Industrial Revolution* (1974), Ch. 4.
6. See D. T. Jenkins, *The West Riding Wool Textile Industry, 1770–1835: A Study of Fixed Capital Formation* (Edington, 1975), p. 176, and Graph 2.1.
7. B. L. Anderson, 'The Attorney and the Early Capital Market in Lancashire', in J. R. Harris (ed.), *Liverpool and Merseyside: Essays in the Economic and Social History of the Port and Its Hinterland* (1969), *passim*.
8. See especially Minute Books of Bradford Banking Company (Midland) and Huddersfield Banking Company (Midland). Correspondence of John Foster & Son, Isaac Holden and Hague, Cook & Wormald listed in P. Hudson, *The West Riding Wool Textile Industry: A Catalogue of Business Records* (Edington, 1975), and Leeds branch, Letters 1830s and 1840s (Bank of England).
9. See Chapter 9, n. 35.
10. Leeds branch, Letter Book 1, 2 January 1840 (Bank of England).

BIBLIOGRAPHY

PRIMARY SOURCES

I.   MANUSCRIPT SOURCES

Leeds District Archives

Records of the following textile concerns:

T. & M. Bairstow Ltd
John Barran & Sons Ltd
Booth Bros. (Drighlington) Ltd
John Brigg & Company
John & William Emmet
Reuben Gaunt
Gill Royd Mill Company
Grace & Jepson
John Hartley & Sons Ltd
Hebblethwaite Hall Mill
Holly Park Mill Company
J. & J. Holroyd
David Jennings
William Lupton & Company Ltd
Josiah Oates & Son
Oates, Ingham & Sons
Potterdale Mill
Albert Rhodes & Company
William Rhodes
William Smith & Son
Wrigglesworth, Kent & Company

Other papers:

The Coloured Cloth Hall, Leeds
Gomersal Cloth Hall
Miscellaneous items listed in Hudson, *The West Riding Wool Textile Industry*,
pp. 521–3
Yorkshire District Bank

Brotherton Library, University of Leeds

Records of the following textile concerns:

William Ackroyd Ltd
Airedale Mill Company Ltd
Jonathan Akroyd
Jeremiah Ambler & Sons Ltd
Henry Booth & Sons Ltd
John Broadbent & Sons
William & John Clarkson Ltd
J. T. Clay & Sons Ltd
Robert Clough, Keighley Ltd
George Crowther & Company
John Foster & Son
E. Fox & Sons
Benjamin Gott & Company
George Hattersley & Sons Ltd
Isaac Holden & Sons Ltd
Holly Park Mill Company
Robert Jowitt & Sons Ltd
Kellett, Brown & Company Ltd
Joseph Lee
William Lupton & Company Ltd
R. V. Marriner Ltd
J. Marshall & Company
William Rhodes Ltd
Edwart Ripley & Son
J. C. Waddington & Sons Ltd
William Willans & Company Ltd
Wormalds & Walker Ltd

Other papers:

White Cloth Hall, Leeds

Calderdale District Archives, Halifax

Records of the following textile concerns:

Cornelius Ashworth
J. T. Clay & Sons Ltd
Chapel Field Mill Company
Isaac, Samuel & John Firth
John Firth
Hill family
Samuel Hill
Rawden Low Mill Company
John Sutcliffe

Records of the following attorneys:

John Howarth
Robert Parker

Civil Township Surveys and Valuations:

Barkisland
Halifax
Northowram
Ovenden
Skircoat
Warley

Halifax & Huddersfield Union Banking Company Ltd
Stansfeld Estate Papers
Title Deeds

John Goodchild manuscripts, Wakefield District Library

Records of the following textile concerns:

Aldham, Pease & Company
Claughton Garth Mill Company
Dudfleet Mill
Flanshaw Mill
Benjamin Gott & Company
Benjamin Hallas
Joseph & Thomas Hebblethwaite
Holdsworth family
Joseph Jackson
Thomas Marriot & Son
Ossett Mill Company
Ossett Union Mill Company
Henry & Andrew Peterson
Messrs Poppleton
M. P. Stonehouse
Whitely Mill
Thomas Wood
Wormald, Fountaine & Gott.

Other papers:

Committee of the Association of Bankers in Yorkshire
Deeds and other Papers relating to Wakefield Tammy Hall
Haxby & Scholey, Solicitors
Miscellaneous textile references listed in Hudson, *The West Riding Wool Textile Industry*, pp. 525–31
Ossett Surveys and Valuations 1801, 1819, 1830
Ossett-cum-Gawthorpe Enclosure Award, 1813

Papers relating to the following banks:

Barnsley Banking Company
Ingram Kennet & Company
Leatham, Tew & Company
Leeds Commercial Banking Company
Yorkshire Banking Company

316   *Bibliography*

Yorkshire Archaeological Society

Records of the following textile concerns:

J. T. Clay & Sons Ltd
William Haigh
Joseph Rogerson

Other papers:

William Foster Greenwood Papers
Slingsby Family and Estate Papers
Wakefield Manor Court Rolls

Dewsbury Public Library (Kirklees District Archives)

Benjamin Eastwood & Nephew records
Marshall, Kaye & Marshall
Savile Estate Papers: Estate Surveys and Valuations

Tolson Memorial Museum, Huddersfield (Kirklees District Archives)

J. T. Clay & Sons Ltd
Miscellaneous textile records as listed in Hudson, *The West Riding Wool Textile Industry*, pp. 534–7

Keighley Public Library (Bradford District Archives)

John Brigg & Company, Papers

Bradford University

Records of the following textile concerns:

I. & I. Calvert Ltd
Isaac Holden & Sons Ltd

Bradford District Archives

Robert Heaton Papers
Textile archives DB 17/24/5. See listing in Hudson, *The West Riding Wool Textile Industry*, p. 519

Saddleworth Public Library

James Lees, clothier, Papers
Saddleworth Clothiers' Society, Minute Book
Victoria Mill, Upper Mill, Deeds and Papers

Kirklees District Archives, Huddersfield

G. & J. Stubley, business records

Sheffield University Library

J. T. & J. Taylor Ltd, business records

Sheffield City Library

Miscellaneous textile records as listed in Hudson, *The West Riding Wool Textile Industry*, pp. 523–5

West Yorkshire Archive Service
Head Quarters, Wakefield

Quarter Sessions Order Books and Rolls
Returns of cotton and other mills for 1803 and 1804
The West Riding Registry of Deeds

Dartmouth Estate Office, Slaithwaite

The Dartmouth Estate Terriers

The home of the Brooke family, Armitage Bridge

Papers relating to Armitage Bridge Mills and The Hudderfield Banking Company

The home of the Edwards family, Sowerby Bridge

Papers relating to John Edwards & Son and to F. W. Cronhelm

Public Record Office

Records of the Court of Bankruptcy:

Order Books (B1)
Commissions of Bankruptcy (B3)

Home Office papers H.O. 45

Midland Bank Archives

Records of the following Yorkshire banks:

Barnsley Banking Company
Bradford Banking Company
Huddersfield Banking Company
Leeds and County Bank
York City and County Banking Company
Yorkshire Banking Company

318   *Bibliography*

Barclays Bank Archives

Records of the following Yorkshire banks:

Bradford Old Bank Ltd
Halifax Commercial Banking Company
Ingram Kennet & Ingram
Lancashire & Yorkshire Banking Company
Leatham, Tew & Company
Mirfield & Huddersfield District Banking Company
Peckover, Harris & Company
Rawson & Company
Rawsons Rhodes & Briggs
Rhodes Briggs & Company
Rhodes, Briggs & Garlick
Richmond Bank
Richmond & Swaledale Bank
Bros. Swaine & Company
Swaledale & Wensleydale Banking Company
Wakefield Banking Company
West Riding Union Banking Company
Whitby Old Bank
York Union Banking Company

Lloyds Bank Archives

Records of the following Yorkshire banks:

Halifax Joint Stock Banking Company
Leeds Union Bank
William Williams Brown & Company

Bank of England

Records relating to the Leeds branch, 1827–50.

2. PARLIAMENTARY PAPERS
Reports

First Report from the Select Committee on the Present State of Commercial
    Credit: 1793 (23) X.
Report from the Select Committee on the Petitions of Merchants and Manufac-
    turers Concerned in the Woollen Manufacture in the County of York and
    Town of Halifax: 1802–3 (71) V.
Report from the Select Committee on the Petition of the Manufacturers of
    Woollen Cloth in the County of York: 1803–4 (66) IV.
Report from the Select Committee on the Petition of the Clothworkers, Shear-
    men, Weavers and Clothiers of the Counties of York, Somerset, Gloucester
    and Wilts, and Other Parts of the United Kingdom: 1805 (105) III.
Report from the Select Committee Appointed to Consider the State of the
    Woollen Manufacture of England: 1806 (268) (168a) III.

Report from the Select Committee on the State of Commercial Credit: 1810–11 (52) II.

Report of the Minutes of Evidence taken before the Select Committee on the State of Children Employed in the Manufactories of the United Kingdom: 1816 (397) III.

Report on Cash Payments: 1819 (282) III.

Report from the Select Committee to Inquire into the Present State of Laws Regulating the Stamping of Woollen Cloths: 1821 (437) VI.

Report from the Select Committee on the Law Relating to Merchants, Agents and Factors: 1823 (452) IV.

Report from the Select Committee of the House of Lords on the State of the British Wool Trade, with Minutes of Evidence: 1828 (515) VIII.

Report from the Select Committee to whom the Bill to Regulate the Labour of Children in Mills and Factories of the United Kingdom was Referred: 1831–2 (706) XV.

Report from the Committee on Renewing the Bank of England Charter: 1831–2 (722) VI.

Report from the Select Committee Appointed to Inquire into the Present State of Manufactures, Commerce and Shipping in the United Kingdom: 1833 (690) VI.

Report from Commissioners Appointed to Collect Information in the Manufacturing Districts Relative to Employment of Children in Factories and as to the Propriety and Means of Curtailing the Hours of their Labour with Minutes of Evidence and Reports of District Commissioners:

First Report 1833 (45) XX
Second Report 1833 (519) XXI
Supplementary Reports 1834 (167) XIX, XX

Reports from the Select Committee on Handloom Weavers' Petitions: 1834 (556) X, 1835 (341) (492) XIII, 1842 (471) IX.

Report by Inspectors of Factories: 1835 (342) XL.

Report from the Select Committee on Joint Stock Banks: 1836 (591) IX.

Reports of the Assistant Commissioner on the West Riding of Yorkshire and Ireland: 1840 (43-II) XXIII.

Report of the Select Committee on the Regulation of Mills and Factories: 1840 (203) X.

Special Reports of Inspectors of Factories Relating to Accidents with Machinery: 141 (311) X.

Report from the Select Committee on the Payment of Wages: 1842 (471) IX.

Statements as to the Joint Stock Woollen Mills in the West Riding of Yorkshire: 1844 (119) VII (House of Lords).

Reports from the Select Committee on Commercial Distress: 1847–8 (565) (565-II) (395) VIII.

Report from the Select Committee on Commercial Distress: 1847–8 (395) VIII.

Report from the Select Committee on the Operation of the Bank Acts and the Causes of Commercial Distress: 1857–8 (381) V.

Accounts and papers

Minutes of Evidence Respecting Orders in Council, March 1808: 1808 X.

Account of Cotton and Woollen Mills and Factories Entered in Epiphany Sessions in Each Year 1803–18: 1819 CVIII.

Return of Numbers of Commissions of Bankruptcy Issued Each Year 1790–1818 Distinguishing those of Bankers: 1819 XCVIII.

Account of Woollen Cloths Milled in the West Riding of Yorkshire 1791–1819: 1820 (193) CXIX.

Account of Number of Bankruptcies in England Each Year 1819–1826, and in March-June 1793 Distinguishing those of Bankers: 1826 CCVIII.

Persons Employed in Mills and Factories of the United Kingdom Distinguishing Ages: 1836 (138) XLV.

Returns of Mills and Factories: 1835 (342) XL; 1839 (41) XLII; 1839 (135) XLII; 1850 (745) XLII.

Census abstracts

Census abstracts for 1801, 1811, 1821, 1831, 1841, 1851

3. CONTEMPORARY NEWSPAPERS AND JOURNALS

Bradford Observer
Leeds Intelligencer
Leeds Mercury
Textile Manufacturer
Woollen, Worsted and Cotton Journal

4. COMMERCIAL DIRECTORIES

Baines, E., *Directory of Leeds* (1809, 1814, 1817).

   History, Directory and Gazetteer of the County of York, vol. 1 (Leeds, 1822).

Baines and Newsome, *General and Commercial Directory of Leeds* (1834).

Barfoot, P., and Wilkes, J., *The Universal British Directory*, vol. 3, (1793).

Binns and Brown, *A Directory for the Town of Leeds* (1800).

Ibbetson, J., *General and Classified Directory of Bradford* (1852).

Parson, W., *General and Commercial Directory of Leeds* (1826).

Parson and White, *Directory of the Borough of Leeds and the Clothing District of Yorkshire* (1830).

Pigot and Co., *Commercial Directory* (1829).

Pigot and Dean, *A Commercial Directory of the West Riding* (1814–15, 1818 and 1820).

Ryley, J., *Leeds Directory for the Year 1798*.

White, W., *History Gazetteer and Directory of the West Riding* (1837).

   Directory and Topography of the Borough of Leeds and the Whole Clothing District of the West Riding (1842 and 1847).

5. MAPS AND PLANS

(Other than those found in business records.)

A Map of the Parish of Borough of Leeds ... from an Actual Survey by John Tuke, 1781.

'A Map of Ten Miles Round Leeds', in G. Wright, *A History of the Town and Parish of Leeds ...* (Leeds 1797).

A Map of Near 10 miles Round Leeds, published by E. Baines, 1817.
Plan of the Township of Dewsbury, J. Walker, 1833.
Map of the Parish of Halifax . . ., J. F. Myers, 1834–5.

MAJOR SECONDARY SOURCES
I. UNPUBLISHED THESES

Anderson, B. L., 'Aspects of Capital and Credit in Lancashire during the Eighteenth Century', University of Liverpool, M.A., 1966.

Betteridge, A., 'A Study of Halifax Administrative Records 1585–1762', University of Leeds, Ph.D., 1979.

Connell, E. J., 'Industrial Development in South Leeds, 1790–1914', University of Leeds, Ph.D., 1974.

Dickenson, M. J., 'The West Riding Woollen and Worsted Industries 1689–1770: An Analysis of Probate Inventories and Insurance Policies', University of Nottingham, Ph.D., 1974.

Glover, F. J., 'Dewsbury Mills: A History of Messrs. Wormalds and Walker Ltd., Blanket Manufacturers, of Dewsbury. With an Economic Survey of the Yorkshire Woollen Cloth Industry in the Nineteenth Century', University of Leeds, Ph.D., 1959.

Hartwell, R. M., 'The Yorkshire Woollen and Worsted Industries 1800–1850', University of Bristol, Ph.D., 1955.

Hudson, P., 'The Genesis of Industrial Capital in the West Riding Wool Textile Industry c. 1770–1850', University of York, D. Phil., 1981.

Ingle, G., 'A History of R. V. Marriner Ltd., Worsted Spinners, Keighley', University of Leeds, M. Phil., 1974.

Jenkins, D. T., 'The West Riding Wool Textile Industry, 1770–1835: A Study of Fixed Capital Formation', University of York, D.Phil., 1970.

Johnstone, C., 'The Standard of Living of Worsted Workers in Keighley in the Nineteenth Century', University of York, D.Phil., 1978.

Malin, J., 'The West Riding Recovered Wool Industry c. 1813–1939', University of York, D. Phil., 1979.

Mee, L. G., 'The Earls Fitzwilliam and the Management of the Collieries and Other Industrial Enterprises on the Estate, 1795–1857', University of Nottingham, Ph.D., 1975.

Mendels, F. F., 'Industrialisation and Population Pressure in 18th Century Flanders', University of Wisconsin, Ph.D., 1969.

Miles, M., 'Eminent Attorneys: Some Aspects of West Riding Attorneyship, c. 1750–1800', University of Birmingham, Ph.D., 1983.

Roberts, D., 'The Development of the Textile Industry in the West Craven and the Skipton District of Yorkshire', London School of Economics, M.Sc., 1956.

Roberts, J. S., 'The Bradford Textile Warehouse 1770–1914', University of Bradford, M.Sc., 1976.

Topham, A. J., 'The Credit Structure of the West Riding Wool Textile Industry in the 19th Century', University of Leeds, M.Phil., 1953.

Ward, M. F., 'Industrial Development and Location in Leeds North of the River Aire 1775–1914', University of Leeds, Ph.D., 1972.

2. BOOKS

(Place of publication London, unless otherwise stated.)

Aiken, J., *A Description of the Country from Thirty to Forty Miles around Manchester* (1795).

Anon., *British Losses by Bank Failures, 1820–57* (1858).

Ashton, T. S., *The Industrial Revolution 1760–1830* (1948).
England in the 18th Century (1955).
Economic Fluctuations in England, 1700–1800 (Oxford, 1959).

Atkinson, F. (ed.), *Some Aspects of the Eighteenth Century Woollen and Worsted Trade in Halifax* (Halifax, 1956).

Baines, E., *History of the Cotton Manufacture in Great Britain* (1835).
Account of the Woollen Manufacture of England (1858; repr. 1970).

Barnard, A., *The Australian Wool Market 1840–1900* (Melbourne, 1958).

Baumber, M. L., *A Pennine Community on the Eve of the Industrial Revolution* (Keighley, 1977).

Beresford, M. W., and Jones, G. R. J. (eds.), *Leeds and Its Region* (Leeds, 1967).

Berg, M., Hudson, P., and Sonenscher, M., (eds.), *Manufacture in Town and Country before the Factory* (Cambridge, 1983).

Bigland, John, *A Topographical and Historical Description of the County of York*, 5 vols. (1812).

Bischoff, J., *A Comprehensive History of the Woollen and Worsted Manufacture*, 2 vols. (1842, repr. 1968).

Brook, R., *The Story of Huddersfield* (Huddersfield, 1968).

Brown, Robert, *General View of the Agriculture of the West Riding* (1799).

Buck, J. W., *Cases in Bankruptcy*, vol. 1, *1816–20* (1820).

Buck, N. S., *The Development of the Organisation of Anglo-American Trade, 1800–1850* (Yale, 1925).

'Bullion, Thomas', *Letters on the Internal Management of a Country Bank* (1850).

Burnley, J., *History of Wool and Wool Combing* (1889).

Cairncross, A. K., *Factors in Economic Growth* (1962).
Home and Foreign Investment (1953).

Cambridge Economic History of Europe, vol. 7, ed. P. Mathias and M. M. Postan (Cambridge, 1978).

Cameron, R. (ed.), *Banking in the Early Stages of Industrialisation: A Study in Comparative Economic History* (New York, 1967).

Camidge, C. E., *A History of Wakefield . . .* (1866).

The Century's Progress, Yorkshire (1893).

Chambers, J. D., and Mingay, G. E., *The Agricultural Revolution* (1966).

Chandler, G., *Four Centuries of Banking*, vols. 1 and 2 (1968).

Chapman, S. D., *The Early Factory Masters* (Newton Abbot, 1967).

Chayanov, A. V., *The Theory of Peasant Economy*, ed. D. Thorner, B. Kerblay and R. E. D. Smith (Homewood, Illinois, 1966).

Circular to Bankers

Clapham, J. H., *An Economic History of Modern England*, vol. 2 (1932).
The Woollen and Worsted Industries (1907).

Clarkson, H., *Memories of Merrie Wakefield* (Wakefield, 1877).
Collier, Frances, *The Family Economy of the Working Classes in the Cotton Industry* (Manchester, 1965).
Collinson, E., *History of the Worsted Trade and Historic Sketch of Bradford* (1845).
Cooke, G. A., *Topographical and Statistical Description of the County of York* (1818).
Cottrell, P. L., *Industrial Finance 1830–1914* (1980).
Crick, W. F., and Wadsworth, J. E., *A Hundred Years of Joint Stock Banking* (1958).
Cronhelm, F. W., *Double Entry by Single* (1818).
Crouzet, F., (ed.), *Capital Formation in the Industrial Revolution* (1972).
Crump, W. B. (ed.), *The Leeds Woollen Industry, 1780–1820*, Thoresby Society (Leeds, 1931).
Crump, W. B., and Ghorbal, G., *History of the Huddersfield Woollen Industry* (Huddersfield, 1935).
Cudworth, W., *Round About Bradford: A Series of Sketches of Forty Two Places Within Six Miles of Bradford* (Bradford, 1876).
Worstedopolis: A Sketch History of the Town and Trade of Bradford, the Metropolis of the Worsted Industry (Bradford, 1888).
Histories of Bolton and Bowling (Bradford, 1891).
Manningham, Heaton and Allerton Treated Topographically (Bradford, 1896).
Deane, P., *The First Industrial Revolution* (Cambridge, 1965).
Defoe, D., *A Tour Through the Whole Island of Great Britain*, vol. 3 (1724).
Complete Tradesmen, vol. 2 (1737?; 1841 edn).
Dobb, M., *Studies in the Development of Capitalism* (1946).
Edwards, M. M., *The Growth of the British Cotton Trade, 1780–1815* (Manchester, 1967).
Fitton, R. I., and Wadsworth, A. P., *The Strutts and the Arkwrights, 1758–1830* (1958).
Fong, H. D., *The Triumph of the Factory System* (Tientsin, 1930).
Forbes, H., *Lectures on the Results of the Great Exhibition of 1851* (1853).
Fortunes Made in Business, vols. 1 and 2 (1884, 1888).
Foster, J., *Class Struggle in the Industrial Revolution* (1974).
Fox-Genovese, E., and Genovese, E., *The Fruits of Merchant Capital* (1983).
Garnett, W. Onslow, *Wainstalls Mills: The History of I. and I. Calvert Ltd., 1821–1951* (Halifax, 1951).
Gaunt, Reuben, & Sons Ltd., *Springfield and Broom Mills: A Record of Three Centuries' Connection with the Woollen Industry* (Farsley, 1923).
Gayer, A. D., Rostow, W. W., and Schwartz, A. J., *The Growth and Fluctuation of the British Economy, 1790–1850* (Oxford, 1953).
Gerschenkron, A., *Economic Backwardness in Historical Perspective* (1962).
Goodhart, C. A. E., *The Business of Banking 1891–1914* (1972).
Gorz, A. (ed.), *The Division of Labour* (1976).
Gulvin, C., *The Tweedmakers: A History of the Scottish Fancy Woollen Industry, 1600–1914* (Newton Abbot, 1973).
Halifax Guardian Historical Almanack (Halifax, 1892).
Hanson, T. W., *The Story of Old Halifax* (Halifax, 1920).

324 Bibliography

Harte, N. B., and Ponting, K. G., (eds.), *Textile History and Economic History: Essays in Honour of Miss Julia de Lacy Mann* (Manchester, 1973).
Hartley, W. C. E., *Banking in Yorkshire* (Clapham, 1975).
Hausman, J., *A Topographical Description of Cumberland, Westmorland, Lancashire and a Part of the West Riding of Yorkshire* (1800).
Hawke, G. R., *Railways and Economic Growth in England and Wales, 1840–1870* (Oxford, 1970).
Hawtrey, R. G., *Currency and Credit* (New York, 1930).
Head, George, *A Home Tour Through the Manufacturing Districts of England in the Summer of 1835* (1836).
Heaton, H., *The Yorkshire Woollen and Worsted Industries from Earliest Times up to the Industrial Revolution* (Oxford, 1920; 2nd edn Oxford, 1965).
(ed.), *The Letter Books of Joseph Holroyd and Sam Hill* (Halifax, 1914).
Hicks, J., *Capital and Labour* (Oxford, 1965).
Higgins, J. P. P., and Pollard, S. (eds.), *Aspects of Capital Investment in Great Britain, 1750–1850* (1971).
Hills, R. L., *Power in the Industrial Revolution* (Manchester, 1970).
Hilton, R. (ed.), *The Transition from Feudalism to Capitalism* (1976).
Hirst, W., *History of the Woollen Trade for the Last Sixty Years* (Leeds, 1844).
The History of Batley, Birstall and Heckmondwike: With Notices of Gomersal, Cleckheaton, Batley Carr and Carlinghowe (Batley, 1860).
Hobsbawm, E. J., *Industry and Empire* (1968).
Hodgson, J., *Textile Manufacture and Other Industries in Keighley* (Keighley, 1879).
Hopkins, Thomas, *Great Britain for the Last Forty Years* (1834).
Hudson, P., *The West Riding Wool Textile Industry: A Catalogue of Business Records* (Edington, 1975).
James, J., *The History and Topography of Bradford with Topographical Notices of Its Parish* (1841).
History of the Worsted Manufacture in England from the Earliest Times (1857).
The History of Bradford and Its Parish with Additions and Continuation to the Present Time (1866).
Jenkins, D. T., *The West Riding Wool Textile Industry, 1770–1835: A Study of Fixed Capital Formation* (Edington, 1975).
Jenkins, D. T., and Ponting, K. G., *The British Wool Textile Industry, 1770–1914* (1982).
Jones, J. G., *Jones's English System of Book-keeping* (1896).
Jubb, S., *The History of the Shoddy Trade: Its Rise, Progress and Present Position* (Batley, 1860).
Kindleberger, C. P., *Europe's Post War Growth: The Role of Labour Supply* (1967).
Manias, Panics and Crashes (1978).
Kriedte, P., Medick, H., and Schlumbohm, J., *Industrialisation before Industrialisation* (Cambridge, 1982).
Kuznets, S., *Modern Economic Growth: Rate Structure and Spread* (1966).
Landes, D. S. *The Unbound Prometheus* (1969).
Lavington, F., *The English Capital Market* (1921).
Lawson, J., *Letters to the Young on Progress in Pudsey during the Last Sixty Years* (Stanningley, 1887).

Leatham, W., *Letters on the Currency* (1840).
Leeds Guide (Leeds, 1806).
Lewis, W. A., *The Theory of Economic Growth* (1955).
Ling Roth, H., *The Genesis of Banking in Halifax* (Halifax, 1914).
Lipson, E., *History of the Woollen and Worsted Industries* (1921).
Littleton, A. C., *Accounting Evolution to 1900* (New York, 1933; repr. 1966).
Littleton, A. C., and Yamey, B. S. (eds.), *Studies in the History of Accounting* (1956).
Maitland, J., *An Account of the Proceedings of the Merchants and Manufacturers, and Others Concerned in the Wool and Woollen Trade of Great Britain* (1800).
Mann, J. de L., *The Cloth Industry in the West of England from 1640 to 1880* (Oxford, 1871).
Mantoux, Paul, *The Industrial Revolution in the Eighteenth Century: An Outline of the Beginnings of the Modern Factory System in England* (1961 edn).
Marshall, W., *Rural Economy of Yorkshire* (1788).
Marx, K., *Capital*, vol. 1 (Penguin edn, 1976), vols. 2 and 3 (Lawrence and Wishart edns, 1956 and 1959 respectively).
Mathias, P., *The First Industrial Nation: An Economic History of Britain, 1700–1914* (1969).
Matthews, P. W., and Tuke, A. W., *History of Barclays Banks Ltd.* (1926).
Mayhall, J., *Annals of Leeds and the Surrounding District* (Leeds and London, 1860).
Men of the Period: England (1897).
Mingay, G. E., *Enclosure and the Small Farmer in the Age of the Industrial Revolution* (1968).
Mitchell, B. R., and Deane, P., *Abstract of British Historical Statistics* (Cambridge, 1962).
Nishimura, S., *The Decline of Inland Bills of Exchange in the London Money Market 1855–1913* (Cambridge, 1971).
Norton, G. P., *Textile Manufacturers' Book-keeping* (Huddersfield, 1889).
Cost Accounting and Cost Control (1931).
Otsuka, Hisao, *The Spirit of Capitalism* (Tokyo, 1982).
Parsons, E., *The Civil, Ecclesiastical, Literary, Commercial and Miscellaneous History of Leeds, Halifax, Huddersfield, Bradford, Wakefield, Dewsbury, Otley and the Manufacturing Districts of Yorkshire* (London and Leeds, 1834).
Peel, F., *Spen Valley: Past and Present* (Heckmondwike, 1893).
Perkin, H., *Origins of Modern English Society* (1969).
The Poll of the Knights of the Shire, 1807 (York, 1807).
Pollard, S., *The Genesis of Modern Management: A Study of the Industrial Revolution in Great Britain* (1965).
Region und Industrialisierung (Göttingen, 1980).
Polyani, K., *The Great Transformation* (1944).
(ed.), *Trade and Market in the Early Empires* (1957).
Ponting, K. G., *A History of the West of England Cloth Industry* (London, 1957).
The Woollen Industry of South West England (1971).
(ed.) *Baines's Account of the Woollen Manufacture of England* (Newton Abbot, 1970).

Porter, G. R., *The Progress of the Nation* (1836).
Pressnell, L. S., *Country Banking in the Industrial Revolution* (Oxford, 1956).
Proceedings of the Second International Conference of Economic History, Aix en Provence (1962).
Proceedings of the Third International Conference of Economic History, Munich 1965, vol. 1 (1965).
Proceedings of the Eighth International Conference of Economic History, Budapest 1982, A2: Protoindustrialisation (1982).
Rennie, Brown and Shirreff, Messrs, *A General View of the Agriculture of the West Riding of Yorkshire* (1794).
Rimmer, W. G., *Marshalls of Leeds: Flax Spinners, 1786–1886* (Cambridge, 1960).
Robinson, J., *The Accumulation of Capital* (1956).
Rose, G. E., *Cases in Bankruptcy*, 2 vols. (1813).
Rose, H. B., *The Economic Background to Investment* (London, 1960).
Rostow, W. W. (ed.). *The Stages of Economic Growth* (1960).
The Economics of Take-Off into Sustained Growth (1963).
Schumpeter, J., *Theory of Economic Development* (Cambridge, Mass., 1953).
Scruton, W., *Pen and Pencil Pictures of Old Bradford* (Bradford, 1889).
Shapiro, S., *Capital and the Cotton Industry in the Industrial Revolution* (Ithaca, 1967).
Sigsworth, E. M., *Black Dyke Mills: A History with Introductory Chapters on the Development of the Worsted Industry in the Nineteenth Century* (Liverpool, 1958).
Singer, C. (ed.), *A History of Technology* (Oxford, 1957).
Smith, A., *An Inquiry into the Nature and Causes of the Wealth of Nations* (1850 edn).
Smith, William, *Rambles About Morley, with Descriptive and Historical Sketches: Also an Account of the Rise and Progress of the Woollen Manufacture in This Place* (1866).
The History and Antiquities of Morley (1876).
Morley Ancient and Modern (Morley, 1886).
Smith, William & Company, *A List of Bankrupts, 1786–1806* (1806).
Sombart, Werner, *Der Moderne Kapitalismus*, 6th edn (Munich and Leipzig, 1924).
Stephenson, C., *The Ramsdens and Their Estate in Huddersfield* (Almondbury, 1982).
Strickland, H. E., *General View of the Agriculture of the East Riding of Yorkshire* (1812).
Sweezy, P. M., *The Present as History* (1953).
Sykes, D. F. E., *The History of Huddersfield and the Valleys of the Colne, the Holme and the Dearne* (Huddersfield, 1898).
The History of the Colne Valley (Slaithwaite, 1906).
Tann, J., *The Development of the Factory* (1970).
Thirsk, J., (ed.), *The Agrarian History of England and Wales*, vol. 4, *1500–1640* (Cambridge, 1967).
Thompson, E. P., *The Making of the English Working Class* (1963).
The Trade and Commerce of New York from 1815 to the Present Time by an Observer (New York, 1820).
von Tunzlemann, G. N., *Steam Power and British Industrialisation to 1860* (1978).

Ure, A., *The Philosophy of Manufactures* (1835).

Wadsworth, A. P., and Mann, Julia de L., *The Cotton Trade and Industrial Lancashire, 1600–1780* (Manchester, 1931).

Walker, G., *The Costume of Yorkshire* (1814).

Walker, J., *Fortunes Made In Business* (1884).

Walker, J. W., *Wakefield: Its History and People* (Wakefield, 1939).

Ward, J. T., and Wilson, R. G., *Land and Industry: The Landed Estate and the Industrial Revolution* (Newton Abbot, 1971).

Waters, S. H., *Wakefield in the Seventeenth Century: A Social History of the Town and Neighbourhood, 1550–1710* (Wakefield, 1933).

Watson, J., *The History and Antiquities of the Parish of Halifax in Yorkshire* (1775).

Watt, H., *The Practice of Banking in Scotland and in England . . .* (Glasgow, 1833).

Williams, J., *Batley Past and Present: Its Rise and Progress since the Introduction of Shoddy* (Batley, 1880).

Wilson, E., *Our Village* (Bramley, 1860).

Wilson, R. G., *Gentlemen Merchants: The Merchant Community in Leeds, 1700–1830* (Manchester, 1971).

Wright, G., *A History of the Town and Parish of Leeds . . .* (Leeds, 1797).

Yarranton, Andrew, *England's Improvement by Sea and Land: To Out-Do the Dutch without Fighting etc.* (1677).

Young, A., *A Six Months Tour through the North of England*, vol. 1 (1771).

3. ARTICLES

Anderson, B. L., 'The Attorney and the Early Capital Market in Lancashire', in J. R. Harris (ed.), *Liverpool and Merseyside: Essays in the Economic and Social History of the Port and Its Hinterland* (1969).

'Provincial Aspects of the Financial Revolution of the 18th Century', *Business History*, XII, 1969.

'Law, Finance and Economic Growth in England: Some Long-term Influences', in B. N. Ratcliffe (ed.), *Great Britain and her World* (Manchester, 1975).

Ashton, T. S., 'The Bill of Exchange and Private Banks in Lancashire, 1790–1830', in T. S. Ashton and R. S. Sayers (eds.), *Papers in English Monetary History* (Oxford, 1954).

Barnard, A., 'Wool Buying in the Nineteenth Century: A Case History', *Y.B.E.S.R.*, VIII, 1956.

Beckwith, F., 'The Population of Leeds during the Industrial Revolution', *T.S.*, XLI, Part II, 1948.

Blaug, M., 'The Productivity of Capital in the Lancashire Cotton Industry during the Nineteenth Century', *E.H.R.*, XIII, 1961.

Bois, Guy, 'Against the Neo-Malthusian Orthodoxy', *Past and Present*, LXXIX, 1978.

Brenner, R., 'Agrarian Class Structure and Economic Development in Pre-Industrial Europe', *Past and Present*, LXX, 1976.

'The Origins of Capitalist Development: A Critique of Neo-Smithian Marxism', *New Left Review*, CIV, 1977.

'The Agrarian Roots of European Capitalism', *Past and Present*, XCV, 1982.

Brief, R. P. 'The Origin and Evolution of Nineteenth Century Asset Accounting', *B.H.R.* XL, 1966.

Carus-Wilson, E. M., 'An Industrial Revolution of the 13th Century', *E.H.R.*, XI, 1941.

Chapman, S. D., 'The Pioneers of Worsted Spinning by Power', *Business History*, VII, 1, 1965.

'The Peels in the Early English Cotton Industry', *Business History*, XI, 2, 1969.

'Fixed Capital Formation in the British Cotton Industry, 1770–1815', *E.H.R.*, XXIII, 1970.

'The Cost of Power in the Industrial Revolution in Britain: The Case of the Textile Industry', *Midland History*, I, 2, 1971.

'British Marketing Enterprise: The Changing Roles of Merchants, Manufacturers, and Financiers, 1700–1860', *B.H.R.*, LIII, 2, 1979.

'Financial Restraints on the Growth of Firms in the Cotton Industry, 1790–1850', *E.H.R.*, XXXII, 1979.

Clapham, J. H., 'Industrial Organisation in the Woollen and Worsted Industries of Yorkshire', *E.J.*, XVI, 1906.

'The Transference of the Worsted Industry from Norfolk to the West Riding', *E.J.*, XX, 1910.

'Of Empty Economic Boxes', *E.J.*, XXXII, 1922.

Coleman, D. C., 'Protoindustrialisation: A Concept too Many?', *E.H.R.*, XXXVI, 3, 1983.

Collins, M., and Hudson, P., 'Provincial Bank Lending: Yorkshire and Merseyside, 1826–1860', *B.E.R.*, XXXI, 2, 1979.

Crafts, N.F.R., 'British Economic Growth 1700–1831: A Review of the Evidence, *E.H.R.*, XXXVI, 2, 1983.

Croot, Patricia, and Parker, David, 'Agrarian Class Structure and Economic Development', *Past and Present*, LXXVIII, 1978.

Davis, K. G., 'Empire and Capital', *E.H.R.*, XIII, 1960.

Deane, P., 'The Output of the British Woollen Industry in the Eighteenth Century', *J.E.H.*, XVII, 1957.

'Capital Formation in Britain Before the Railway Age', *Economic Development and Cultural Change*, IX, 3, 1961.

'New Estimates of Gross National Product for the United Kingdom, 1830–1914', *Review of Income and Wealth*, XIV, 1968.

Dibden, A. A., 'Title Deeds from the 13th to 19th Centuries, *Historical Association*, 1971.

Dickenson, M. J., 'Fulling in the West Riding Woollen Cloth Industry, 1689–1770', *T.H.*, X, 1979.

Domar, E. D., 'On the Measurement of Technological Change', *E.J.*, LXXI, 1961.

Donnachie, I., 'Sources of Capital and Capitalisation in the Scottish Brewing Industry c. 1750–1830', *E.H.R.*, XXX, 2, 1977.

Ellis, M. J., 'A Study of the Manorial History of Halifax Parish in the 16th and Early 17th Centuries', *Yorkshire Archaeological Journal*, XL, 1962.

Felix, D., 'Profit Inflation and Industrial Growth: The Historic Record and Contemporary Analogies', *Quarterly Journal of Economics*, LXX, 3, 1956.

Garside, M., 'The Halifax Piece Hall', *T.H.A.S.*, 1921.

Gatrell, V. A. C., 'Labour, Power and the Size of Firms in Lancashire Cotton in the Second Quarter of the Nineteenth Century', *E.H.R.*, XXX, 1, 1977.

Gill, C., 'Blackwell Hall Factors, 1795–99', *E.H.R.*, VI, 2, 1953.

Glover, F. J., 'The Rise of the Heavy Woollen Trade of the West Riding of Yorkshire in the Nineteenth Century', *Business History*, IV, 1961.

Goodchild, J., 'The Ossett Mill Company', *T.H.*, I, 1, 1968.

'Pildacre Mill: An Early West Riding Factory', *T.H.*, I, 3, 1969.

'On the Introduction of Steam Power into the West Riding', *South Yorkshire Journal*, 1971.

'The Tammy Hall at Wakefield', *Bulletin of the Wakefield Historical Society*, 1974, pp. 24–30.

Hamilton, E. J., 'Profit Inflation and the Industrial Revolution, 1751–1800', *Quarterly Journal of Economics*, LVI, 2, 1942.

Hartwell, R. M., 'Good Old Economic History', *J.E.H.*, XXXI, 1, 1973.

Harwood, H. W., 'Peel House Mills', *T.H.A.S.*, 1946.

'Wainstalls Mills', *T.H.A.S.*, 1953.

Hatcher, J., and Postan, M.M., 'Population and Class Relations in Feudal Society', *Past and Present*, LXXVIII, 1978.

Heaton, H., 'Benjamin Gott and the Anglo-American Cloth Trade', *Journal of Economic and Business History*, II, 1, 1929.

'Financing the Industrial Revolution', *Bulletin of the Business History Society*, XI, 1, 1937.

'Yorkshire Cloth Traders in the United States, 1770–1840', *T.S.*, XXXVII, 1941.

'A Merchant Adventurer in Brazil, 1808–18', *J.E.H.*, VI, 1, 1946.

'Benjamin Gott and the Industrial Revolution in Yorkshire', *E.H.R.*, III, 1973.

Holderness, B. A., 'Credit in a Rural Community, 1660–1800', *Midland History*, III, 1975.

Houston, R., and Snell, K., 'Proto-Industrialisation? Cottage Industry, Social Change and Industrial Revolution', *Historical Journal*, XXVII, 2, 1984.

Hudson, P. 'Some Aspects of 19th Century Accounting Development in the West Riding Wool Textile Industry', *Accounting History*, II, 2, 1977.

'Proto-industrialisation: The Case of the West Riding Wool Textile Industry in the Eighteenth and Early Nineteenth Centuries', *History Workshop Journal*, XII, 1981.

'The Role of Banks in the Finance of the West Riding Textile Industry', *B.H.R.*, LV, 3, 1981.

Hymer, S., and Resnick, S., 'A Model of an Agrarian Economy with Non-Agricultural Activities', *American Economic Review*, LIX, 1969.

Jenkins, D. T., 'The Validity of the Factory Returns 1833–50', *T.H.*, IV, 1973.

'The Cotton Industry in Yorkshire', *T.H.*, X, 1979.

Jones, E. L., 'The Agricultural Origins of Industry', *Past and Present*, XL, 1968.

Kisch, Herbert, 'The Textile Industries of Silesia and the Rhineland: A Comparative Study of Industrialisation', *J.E.H.*, XIX, 1959.

'The Growth Deterrents of a Medieval Heritage: The Aachen Area Woollen Trades before 1870', *J.E.H.*, XXIV, 1964.

Kuznets, S., 'Quantitative Aspects of the Economic Growth of Nations', *Economic Development and Cultural Change*, VIII, 4, 1960.

Law, B. R., 'The Calder Millowners and the Rochdale Canal', *T.H.A.S.*, 1954.
Levine, D., 'The Demographic Implications of Rural Industrialisation: A Family Reconstitution Study of Shepshed, Leicestershire, 1600–1851', *Social History*, I, 2, 1976.
Lewis, W. A., 'Economic Development with Unlimited Supplies of Labour', *Manchester School*, XXII, 1954.
Maffey, J., 'On Some of the Decayed Families in Bradford', *Bradford Antiquary*, I, 1888.
Medick, H., 'The Proto-Industrial Family Economy: The Structural Function of Household and Family during the Transition from Peasant Society to Industrial Capitalism', *Social History*, I, 3, 1976.
Mendels, F. F., 'Recent Research in European Historical Demography', *American Historical Review*, LXXV, 1970.
'Proto-Industrialisation: The First Phase of the Industrialisation Process', *J.E.H.*, XXXII, 1, 1972.
'Agriculture and Peasant Industry in 18th Century Flanders', in W. N. Parker and E. L. Jones (eds.), *European Peasants and Their Markets* (Princeton, 1975).
'Seasons and Regions in Agriculture and Industry', in S. Pollard (ed.), *Region und Industrialisierung, Studien zur Rolle der Region in der Wirtschaftsgeschichte der letzten zwei Jahrhunderte* (Göttingen, 1980).
Miles, M., 'The Money Market in the Early Industrial Revolution: The Evidence from West Riding Attorneys, 1750–1800', *Business History*, XXIII, 1981.
Millmore, W. R., 'Jeremiah Ambler & Sons Ltd.: Glimpses of Foundation in 1789', *Wool Record*, LXXX, 1951.
'Isaac Holden and Sons Ltd., Bradford: Links with the Beginning of Machine Wool-Combing', *Wool Record*, LXXX, 1951.
'Traders in Wool for nearly Two Centuries', *Wool Record*, XXX, 1926, LXXIX, 1951.
Musson, A. E., and Robinson, E., 'The Early Growth of Steam Power', *E.H.R.*, VI, 1958.
Newmarch, W., 'An Attempt to Ascertain the Magnitude and Fluctuations of the Amount of Bills of Exchange', *Journal of the Statistical Society*, XIV, 1851.
Pankhurst, K. V., 'Investment in the West Riding Wool Textile Industry in the Nineteenth Century', *Y.B.E.S.R.*, VII, 1955.
Pollard, S., 'Investment, Consumption and the Industrial Revolution', *E.H.R.*, XI, 2, 1958.
'Capital Accounting in the Industrial Revolution', *Y.B.E.S.R.*, XV, 2, 1963.
'Fixed Capital in the Industrial Revolution in Britain', *J.E.H.*, XXIV, 3, 1964.
Postan, M. M., 'Recent Trends in the Accumulation of Capital', *E.H.R.*, VI, 1, 1935.
Priestley, J. H., 'Mills of the Ryburn Valley', *T.H.A.S.*, 1933; *T.H.A.S.*, 1934; *T.H.A.S.*, 1941.
Rimmer, W. G., 'Middleton Colliery, near Leeds, 1770–1830', *Y.B.E.S.R.*, VII, 1955.
Rostow, W. W., 'The Take-Off into Self-Sustained Growth', *E.J.*, LXVI, 261, 1956.

Saville, J., 'Primitive Accumulation and Early Industrialisation in Britain', *Socialist Register*, VI, 1969.

Schlumbohm, J., 'Productivity of Labour, Processes of Production and Relations of Production: Some Remarks on Stagnation and Progress in European Rural Industries', unpublished paper, 1979.

Sheppard, F., and Belcher, V., 'The Deeds Registries of Yorkshire and Middlesex', *Journal of the Society of Archivists*, VI, 5, 1980.

Sheppard, F., Belcher, V., and Cotterell, P., 'The Middlesex and Yorkshire Deeds, Registries and Study of Building Fluctuations', *London Journal*, V, 2, 1979.

Sigsworth, E. M., 'History of the Local Trade at Morley', *Journal of the Textile Institute*, XL, 10, 1949.

'William Greenwood and Robert Heaton', *Bradford Textile Society Journal*, 1951–2.

'The West Riding Wool Textile Industry and the Great Exhibition', *Y.B.E.S.R.*, IV, 1952.

'Leeds and Its Industrial Growth', no. 8, 'The Leeds Cloth Hall', *Leeds Journal*, XXV, 1954.

Solow, R. M., 'Technical Progress, Capital Formation and Economic Growth', *American Economic Review*, LII, 1, 1962.

Sombart, Werner, 'Die Hausindustrie in Deutschland', *Archiv Für soziale Gesetzgebung und Statistik*, IV, 1891.

Tate, W. E., 'The Five English District Statutory Registries of Deeds', *Bulletin of the Institute of Historical Research*, XX, 1943–5.

Taylor, A. J., 'Concentration and Specialisation in the Lancashire Cotton Industry, 1825–1850', *E.H.R.*, I, 1948–9.

Thirsk, J., 'Industries in the Countryside', in F. J. Fisher (ed.), *Essays in the Economic and Social History of Tudor and Stuart England* (Cambridge, 1961).

Vries, Jan de, 'Labour/Leisure Trade Off', *Peasant Studies*, I, 1972.

Ward, C. A. W., 'A Bibliography of the History of Industry in the West Riding of Yorkshire', *Proceedings of the Leeds Philosophical and Literary Society*, XIII, Part I, 1968.

Ward, J. T., 'West Riding Landowners and Mining in the Nineteenth Century', *Y.B.E.S.R.*, XV, 1963.

Weatherill, L., 'Capital and Credit in the Pottery Industry before 1770', *Business History*, XXIV, 3, 1982.

Wild, M. T., 'The Saddleworth Parish Registers', *T.H.*, I, 2, 1969.

Wilson, R. G., 'The Fortunes of a Leeds Merchant House, 1780–1820', *Business History*, IX, 1967.

Yamey, B. S., 'Scientific Book-keeping and the Rise of Capitalism', *E.H.R.*, I, 1949.

'Accounting and the Rise of Capitalism: Further Notes on a Theme by Sombart', *Journal of Accounting Research*, II, 2, 1964.

NAME AND PLACE INDEX

SUBJECT INDEX

acceptance houses, 121, 174
'acceptances', 170
accommodation bills, *see* bills of exchange
accounting practices, 21, 236–8, 268, 310 n7
agrarian environment: class structure, in transition to industrial capitalism (Brenner), 9, 282 n3; influence on company mills, 79–80; in proto-industrialisation, 55, 61–70
agriculture: by-employment in, 18, 19; finance from 18; and industry, 8, 9–12, 57–8; relation to textile industry, 85–104; zones of West Riding, 61–2, 289 n32
alpaca, 110, 134, 183, 297 n23
American War of Independence (1775–83), 110
apprenticeships, 31, 68, 150
artisan: capital, 16, 259, 260–1; landholding in West Riding, 18; resented transition to wage dependency, 84; *see also* family: economy; *Kaufsystem*
asset valuation, 237; *see also* depreciation of assets
attorneys, 19–20, 211–17, 266; borrowers from, 214; groups of, 213; loans from landowners, 93–4, 96, 212–15; London agents of, 213; relationship with banking, 214–17, 305 n30
auctions: of cloth in America, 171–3; duties, 176; of Australian wool (from late 1830s), 114, 119, 120–1, 129, 183

bank credit (1830–50), 121, 174–81, 192, 205; *see also* discount, bank
bankruptcy, 127–9, 203, 232–4; of private banks, 220
banks: competition between, 205, 306 n39; external credit and, 263; foreign, 175;

and industrial finance, 20, 218–23, 267, 269; industrial origins, 217–18; local links, 218, 306 n36; note issuing, 189; in West Riding, 50; *see also* joint stock banks; private banks
beaverettes, 26
bill brokers, 20, 170
bill-discounting, 20, 49, 108, 170, 186, 215–16, 224–5, 308 n80
bills of exchange, 108, 164, 170; at three months, 174, 179; against consignments, 169, 178; increasing use led to development of banks, 217; instruments of credit rather than of circulation, 188, 204–5
bills of lading, 121
billys, 33
blanket manufacture, 71, 110, 133; export, 242, 279
bond and warehouse system, 176
book-keeping, *see* accounting
'Bradford Principle', 168–71
brewing industry, 18

calimancoes, 26
camblets, 26, 68
canal companies, 149
capital: accumulation, 3–24; centralisation of, 35; expansion, 21–2; initial, 15–21; other than reinvestment, 252–4; sources of industrial, 14–24, 268–70, 284 n46; *see also* artisan capital; circulating capital; fixed capital; merchant capital
capital market: landowners and the, 93–6, 259; local and personal nature of Yorkshire, 19, 211–55, 265–7
carding, 29; mechanisation, 33, 42, 71; *see also* scribbling, carding and fulling mills

Printed in the United States
By Bookmasters